Public Policy and Social Issues

Public Policy and Social Issues

Jewish Sources and Perspectives

Edited by Marshall J. Breger

Westport, Connecticut
London

Library of Congress Cataloging-in-Publication Data

Public policy and social issues : Jewish sources and perspectives / edited by Marshall J. Breger.

   p. cm.

  Includes bibliographical references and index.

  ISBN 0–275–98165–7 (alk. paper)

  1. Jewish law—Moral and ethical aspects. 2. Jews—Politics and government. 3. Judaism and social problems. 4. Ethics, Jewish. I. Breger, Marshall J.
KBM524.I4.P83 2003
296.3'8—dc21   2003051765

British Library Cataloguing in Publication Data is available.

Library of Congress Catalog Card Number: 2003051765
ISBN: 0–275–98165–7

First published in 2003

Praeger Publishers, 88 Post Road West, Westport, CT 06881
An imprint of Greenwood Publishing Group, Inc.
www.praeger.com

Printed in the United States of America

The paper used in this book complies with the Permanent Paper Standard issued by the National Information Standards Organization (Z39.48–1984).

10 9 8 7 6 5 4 3 2 1

I dedicate this book to my wife, Jennifer. And also to our two daughters, Sarah Gavriella and Esther Meira, in the hope that they will always seek to be informed by Jewish law and tradition in all their endeavors.

Contents

Acknowledgments   ix

Introduction   1
   Marshall J. Breger

1. Personal Responsibility: The Foundation of Jewish Ethics   17
   Clifford E. Librach

2. *Tikkun Olam:* Perfecting God's World   35
   Jonathan Sacks

3. Sexual Responsibility and Jewish Law   49
   David Novak

4. Abortion and Jewish Law   65
   Barry Freundel

5. Euthanasia and Physician-Assisted Suicide in Jewish Law   79
   Steven H. Resnicoff

6. Environment in Jewish Law   109
   Manfred Gerstenfeld

7. Welfare Programs and Jewish Law   133
   Aaron Levine

8. The Ethics of the Free Market   165
   Meir Tamari

  9. Genetic Engineering in Jewish Law and Ethics   197
        Byron L. Sherwin

10. Jewish Family Values   217
        Joshua E. London

11. Judaism, International Relations, and American Foreign
        Policy   235
        Harvey Sicherman

Index   255

About the Editor and Contributors   277

Acknowledgments

This collection grew out of conversation with Ken Weinstein of the Hudson Institute, whom I wish to thank for his creative insights. It was materially aided by financial support from the Bradley Foundation of Milwaukee, Wisconsin, and the Carthage Foundation of Pittsburgh, Pennsylvania.

I want to thank as well Joshua London for his editorial assistance and my indefatigable assistant, Julie Kendrick, for her secretarial support.

At the Columbus School of Law, Catholic University of America, Interim Dean Robert Destro was a source of continual encouragement, as was former dean Bernard Dobranski (now dean of the Ave Maria Law School). I thank them both.

Introduction

Marshall J. Breger

Despite the old adage that "Jews live like Episcopalians but vote like Puerto Ricans," the normative Jewish tradition suggests something very different for a distinctly Jewish public policy. As we shall see below, forging public policy using normative Judaism as one's guide advances a politics that differs wildly from the American Jewish political experience. Indeed, this tradition propounds a profoundly conservative—though not, as we shall see, wholly "right wing"—politics. First, however, it is important to understand the normative context that informs and guides a distinctly Jewish public policy.

One of the most remarkable facts about the Jews is that they continue to exist as a people. They alone among the early nomadic tribal peoples have survived and persist intact, recognizable, definable, and connected to one another. Despite military defeats, dispersion, apostasy, assimilation, violent anti-Semitism, the Holocaust, and various other organized efforts to destroy them over the centuries, the Jewish people remain in small but vital, vibrant, and vigorous communities. Their history makes a mockery of reason and logic, according to which the Jewish people should have long since disappeared. Yet somehow the Jews continue to function and actively contribute to the world around them in a fashion and manner greatly disproportionate to their numbers.

After the rebellion against Rome was suppressed and the Holy Temple was destroyed, the Jewish theocratic commonwealth ended; no longer were there any sovereign actors or any coercive political authority. The dissolution of the state did not, however, bring an end to Jewish politics. The Jews of the Diaspora—from Babylonia, to Egypt, Syria, Rome, and eventually across all of Europe, North Africa, and the Americas—still organized communities; made public choices about the distribution of power and influence; developed community laws; collected taxes for security, welfare, and education; and maintained relations with their non-Jewish host authorities.

Although there is no definite, inarguable reason to account for such Jewish continuity, there is a distinct and approachable consistency and commonality to this survival. In every epoch since their exile, the Jews have shown a tenaciously vibrant involvement with their religious and communal tradition. In Judaism, the quest for spiritual meaning has never been primarily a personal confession for the lonely man of faith. Rather, as the Bible clearly demonstrates, the Judaic conception of a meaningful spiritual life is communal in orientation. The full Jewish covenant with God emerges by way of a collective drama of redemption in which the Israelites are liberated from Egyptian bondage by their unique relationship with God and are then collectively given the Torah at Sinai. This covenant is enacted on a daily basis through the ethical, religious, and political forms of community life. Consequently, the loss of Jewish sovereignty cannot stamp out this communal existence.

The development of these religious and political forms of community life is no great mystery. Normative, that is to say rabbinic, Judaism developed a way of life regulated and mediated by legal norms, comprehensive and precise in scope, that sustained the community. This communal orientation is all pervasive: The prayer liturgy is formulated in the plural and the most significant aspects of religious worship require a quorum of at least ten men. More substantially, the celebration of the Sabbath and the festivals were established such that they are both familial and communal. The individual quest for spiritual meaning and fulfillment finds both a location and structure only in the community.

Moreover, this Rabbinic development was propounded, enacted, and elucidated as the logical and necessary concomitant of the covenant and the revelation at Sinai. These communal laws and forms are, thus, principally independent of the political entities within each community; Rabbinic authority is not rooted in political power or in wealth, but in learning. The most substantial aspect of this tradition, the root and source of all this "learning," is the vast library of traditional, textual Judaic sources.

The development of communal laws, practices, and customs shares a distinct and more or less unified tradition of textual and intertextual citation, reference, and cross-reference. The didactic, deliberative process of legal construction takes place in a world of textual sources and is recorded such that each published attempt is considered a contribution and becomes an active part of the library of textual sources. Adding to this source literature are the attempts at codification and, of course, commentary. It is a radically text-centered tradition; it is from this life-sustaining tradition that Jewish public policy can be derived and devised.

CONSIDERATION OF JEWISH POLITICAL THOUGHT AND ACTION

Before jumping headlong into the Jewish normative sources, however, there are two important, and perhaps delicate, matters that should be addressed. The first is to understand on which side, if any, Jewish public policy is likely to fall in terms of the classic Left versus Right political divide. The second is to recognize and understand why a distinctly Jewish public policy is going to seem very different from what is generally thought of as American Jewish politics.

LEFT VERSUS RIGHT POLITICAL DIVIDE

The most interesting question of Jewish politics centers on how best to categorize a distinct Jewish public policy in terms of the traditional political spectrum. Is the political side of normative Judaism best characterized as left wing, or is it best characterized as right wing—as those labels are currently understood?

The question is a good one, but in many respects it is an unfair one, or rather, an imprecise one. Strictly speaking, since the Jews are the oldest extant polity in the Western world—the Catholic Church is at least 1,500 years younger—and their origins are to be found in the non-Western, or Oriental world, it is very difficult to assign Western, post-Enlightenment labels in a way that entirely captures or elucidates the core of this normative tradition. Unlike most of the Western liberal political tradition, for example, Judaism does not have a rights-based system of legal jurisprudence or political process. As it has been recently noted,

The Jewish tradition, is a duty-based legal system; rights are not the fundamental coin in the realm of Jewish law. While almost all rights can be expressed as duties, and the reverse, legal systems make statements about their core values when they express legal norms in one form or the other. In Jewish law, the core value is legal duty.[1]

That said, the question is easily, albeit imprecisely, answered: Normative Judaism can justly be said to fit more comfortably on the political Right than on the Left, or more Conservative than Liberal, particularly along the lines of traditionalists like Edmund Burke.[2] Of course, this answer might not entirely satisfy the question. For one thing, the current political divide has shifted such that Burke no longer sits so comfortably on the Right, or Conservative, side of the fence. In fact, as a more libertarian-minded economics has driven much of contemporary American politics, it is very hard to tell whether even Adam Smith, much less his personal friend Edmund Burke, still can be said to be comfortably within the Conservative camp.[3] Still, on the assumption that these labels do convey meaningful and recognizable distinctions, the Judaic normative tradition, both in terms of political outlook and general public policy, does have much affinity with a conservative thinker like Burke and others of his sort. As Professor Michael Wyschogrod once wrote in *Judaism* magazine (October 1983, 12):

Judaism has never been radical in the economic or political sense of that word. It has been a religion of law against anarchy, of reverence for the past and love for its traditions and heritage. It has always had a very realistic appraisal of what lurks in man and the necessity for social and political bounds within which responsible freedom is exercised.[4]

A rudimentary glance at the sources confirms Professor Wyschogrod's observation. The tradition has always put great stock in economic freedom and highly valued the creation of wealth. As Jonathan Sacks, the chief rabbi of the British Commonwealth, recently put it, "there is no doubt that, for the most part, Jews and Judaism itself found free competition and trade the system most congruent with their values." Indeed, as Rabbi Sacks continued, central to the Jewish view is the idea that God "seeks the free worship of free human beings, and two of the most powerful safeguards of freedom are private property and economic independence." Indeed, "for a ruler to abuse property rights is, for the Hebrew Bible, one of the great corruptions of power."[5] Thus, Marxism and other forms of socialism are entirely rejected by the tradition.[6]

Consistent with conservative thought, the Jewish tradition eschews the redistribution of wealth through taxation.[7] Instead, the community is expected to ensure that the poor have access to help when they need it, through charity and, more importantly, through job creation. So, with wealth comes responsibility, and successful businessmen are expected to set an example of philanthropy and assume positions of community leadership.[8] Wealth is deemed a divine blessing, and therefore, it carries with it an obligation that it be employed for the benefit of the whole community. Yet, even though the tradition allows for mild regulatory measures to protect communal interests, radical economic measures stand strictly outside of normative Jewish thought.[9]

Further, consistent with Burkean conservative thought, the Jewish tradition takes a negative, or at least highly somber, view of human nature: "The tendency of man's heart is toward evil from his youth" (Genesis 8:2). By recognizing that evil and selfishness are more natural to people than goodness and altruism, the Jewish tradition acknowledges that evil stems from the human heart, not from exogenous social factors. Nor is it assumed in the tradition that people are easily shamed or shaped into proper behavior through better social interaction, as the rabbis observed: "Ten people join together to steal a beam, and are not ashamed in each other's presence" (Babylonian Talmud, Kiddushin 80b). Or, more famously, consider the following debate between two rabbinic schools of learning found in the Talmud (Babylonian Talmud, Eruvin 13b):

> For two and a half years, the House of Shammai and the House of Hillel disputed. The House of Shammai argued that it would have been better for man had he not been created, and the House of Hillel argues that it was better for man to have been created.
>
> In the end, a vote was taken, and it was decided: "It would have been better for man not to have been created, but now that he has been created, let him examine his deeds." Others say, "Let him consider his future actions."

Whether taking account of one's soul or contemplating future activity, the emphasis throughout the source literature is on individual human responsibility: "A person is always liable for his actions, whether awake or asleep" (Babylonian Talmud, Bava Kama 3b). The Jewish tradition also places tremendous importance on maintaining social order against anarchy: "Pray for the welfare of the government, for were it not for the fear of it, people would swallow each other alive" (Pirkei Avot 3:2).[10]

Equally important is Burke's emphasis on communal tradition as the benchmark for social morality. One need not refer to Shalom Aleichem's Tevye and his classic number "Tradition" in the epochal musical *A Fiddler on the Roof* to understand the importance Judaism places on the *masorah*, the tradition. Thus, in Judaism the idiosyncratic customs of individual communities take on the attributes of law for members of that community. Visitors to a synagogue in another community are encouraged to follow the custom of the synagogue they are in, rather than that of their home place of worship.

This affinity between the political side of normative Judaism and Conservatism can be seen starkly in the convergence of their respective fundamental visions. Consider, for example, Russell Kirk's definition of a Conservative:

> The 20th century Conservative is concerned, first of all, for the regeneration of spirit and character—with the perennial problem of the inner order of the soul, the restoration of the ethical understanding, and the religious sanction upon which any life worth living is founded. This is conservatism at its highest.[11]

This, in many respects, comports very comfortably with aspects of the Jewish normative vision. As Rabbi Sacks writes in chapter 2, the Jewish normative vision presents:

[T]he voice of the individual in an age of collectivism, of the community in an era of radical individualism, of education in times of mass illiteracy, of the moral limits of power against totalitarian regimes, of the objective constraints of morality in an age of the 'sovereign self,' of responsibilities when society embraces a culture of rights . . . [and in this way our action] bears witness to the Divine presence . . . flooding this transitory life with momentary radiance and giving us as much of an intimation as we will see of a world where heaven and the human spirit touch. A fragment of perfection, no more, but it is enough to win a small victory for the hope that God will one day complete what we began. (pp. 44–47)

Indeed, the more one reads of conservative thought in the Burkean, or traditionalist, mode, the more one can find nuances and ideas that bear a striking similarity to concepts that are very tightly woven into the Jewish normative framework. Nor does this convergence rest solely on such wide notes. As much of this volume will bear out, these two approaches show some very definite convergence in the realm of praxis and policy.

There are, however, some definite points of divergence, particularly in Conservatism's more libertarian guise. Judaism is not, after all, merely a political or social philosophy, and the bulk of Jewish legal and ethical strictures are addressed as much to the community as a recognized moral and social unit as they are to the individual conscience. The Torah furnishes a blueprint for the perfection of the moral and social fabric of society as well as the individual soul. Although individual political and economic freedoms are deemed crucial in normative Judaism, they are not held sacrosanct. A libertarian along the lines of a Robert Nozick[12] or a Murray Rothbard[13] might well feel uncomfortable with the polity of normative Judaism. For there are specific times and places in normative Judaism where societal claims outweigh individual claims—of course, these instances are highly specified and delimited (see chapters 6, 7, and 8).

For libertarians, by contrast, individual claims are held sacrosanct, and although the state is given a highly specified and delimited sphere of operation, its actions and its functionaries are held suspect. As David Boaz put it, "Power always corrupts, and the power of government to tell people how to live their lives . . . is always a temptation to corruption."[14] More importantly, however, libertarianism approaches the conceptual framework of all politics with a centripetal self-orientation that necessarily pits the individual against the group and that vitiates and often denigrates communal and social bonds.[15] As Edward H. Crane, president of the CATO Institute, the premier libertarian public policy organization in Washington, DC, rather typically—though more levelheaded than most—put it: ". . . there are only two basic ways to organize society: coercively, through government dictates, or voluntarily, through the myriad interactions among individuals."[16] For libertarians, "the political society is of necessity based on coercion."[17] In this way, libertarianism stands in stark contrast to the flavor and substance of normative Jewish public policy.

One intriguing issue is the extent to which this Jewish focus on the community as a source for social and political norms translates today into a focus on the state. Thus, in traditional Jewish society, the community had significant welfare and education responsibilities. In some medieval communities, such as was common throughout Germany, Poland, and Spain, the Jewish community had taxing power and could enforce its edicts both criminally and civilly. During this period of time, of course, the Jewish community lacked political sovereignty. Thus, we do not know how *statist* Judaism is, only that local communities are "thick" with social responsibilities. How much the Catholic principle of "subsidiarity" applies to Jewish *political life* is unclear.

AMERICAN JEWISH POLITICS

In approaching the subject of Jewish public policy, it is important to recognize and understand why a distinctly Jewish public policy seems to diverge sharply from what is generally thought of as American Jewish politics.

A familiar figure throughout Jewish history is the *shtadlan* or "intercessor." The *shtadlan* was a high-level intermediary, often a businessman, who ran interference with kings and potentates on behalf of the Jewish community.[18] The *shtadlan*'s influence with European rulers was personal, and his focus was on individual cases and rarely on general rules of law.[19]

By the nineteenth century, defining the Jewish political agenda was rarely a problem for Jewish political activists. The central Jewish political issue was civil emancipation—the effort to eliminate political disabilities from Jews as a class. Issues included the right to vote, the right to hold public office and the right to own land. These status disabilities were more easily susceptible to collective remedies. In the last century, the impetus shifted to assistance to distressed communities abroad and the removal of social and economic discrimination at home.

Jewish interest groups continue to do a great deal of the *shtadlan*'s work, both in terms of individual case handling and facilitating individual grants and contracts. The servicing of grant and regulatory problems of yeshivas and Orthodox community organizations by Agudath Israel—a religious public policy organization—is a good modern-day example of *shtadlanut*.

These groups also focus on a form of post-emancipation Jewish politics "informed by the liberal politics of individual rights."[20] This approach concerns itself with the protection of the civil and political rights of individual Jews. Thus, Jewish political organizations have long supported the claims of individual Jews who sought to be free of discrimination in housing, employment, and in the provision of government services. The 1960s saw the disintegration of this approach "due to the impact of ethnic pluralism, whose two main features were the legitimation of claims upon American society in group terms and the use of public and militant ethnic assertiveness."[21]

Not surprisingly, then, recent years have seen the growth of a different kind of Jewish representation in the public square. Such an approach is less personal and less focused on individual requests and more attuned to general public policy issues, both those obviously of concern to the Jewish community and those less so.

One feature of Jews in American politics is the high premium placed on community unity in the political sphere. This obsession with unity has been very successful in the past. But this unity has not come about because of Jewish skill in political tactics or strategy. It has come about because of the existence of a real unity of purpose.

The politics of power requires internal discipline in agenda setting. In large measure, Jewish strength comes from Jewish unity. The member of Congress who believes that Jews everywhere will hate him forever if he votes against foreign aid exemplifies this. Rightly or wrongly, most non-Jewish congressmen expect that there exists a Jewish point of view.

Historians will differ on the actual extent of unity within the Jewish community. With the hindsight of nostalgia, stippled realities have turned into softer hues. Just as all Jews remember their ancestors in "the old country" as rabbis, so all immigrants inhabited Irving Howe's *World of Our Fathers*.[22] The recalibration of memory aside, the rite of passage for the Jewish immigrant generation was remarkably similar. As American Jews learned English, entered trades, and moved from the working to the middle class, their group interests were largely similar, and their politics were as well. By the time of the New Deal, American Jews were a basic part of the Roosevelt coalition. That a common experience should lead to a homogeneous political perspective ought not surprise us.

Although there has been recent talk of a greater diversity of political opinions within the Jewish community,[23] American Jews have been most tightly bound this past century with political Liberalism.[24] While the numbers today are not so commanding as in the past, it is clear that the bulk of American Jews still resonate and self-identify with the appellation "liberal."[25] Thus, it should be no surprise that the Jewish public square is largely a liberal square. Indeed, it would be odd if it were not. The Jewish community's closest ties are still with the liberal Democrats, whose congressmen often keep a spare yarmulke in their pocket just in case. The community's nascent relationship with the Republican right, whether based on support for Israel or other reasons, is still too young for the fruit it may bear to be appropriately graded.

Because American Jewish politics has followed along these lines instead of finding guidance and inspiration from a detailed exploration of the traditional sources, it displays very little direct relationship, or even re-semblance to, a distinctly Jewish public policy. It has been crafted, rather, with an eye toward politically partisan affiliation and gain, largely for reasons of perceived, practical and ideological expedience.

THE SOURCES

As a practical matter, the only area in which the statements of the rabbis carry religious authority is when they speak as interpreters of Halakhah, or Jewish law. Yet this does not much limit the scope of authority because Halakhah is not limited to matters of ritual and prayer. Indeed, Halakhah, like individual Jews themselves, has something to say about everything. Halakhah has a view on the warp and woof of life's details ranging from how you wash to the timing of sexual relationships. Its scope enables the Halakhic masters, the rabbis of superior learning, to give guidance and to give decisions on commercial matters and on social and political issues.

The ultimate source for Halakhah is God's revelation, the Torah. This includes more, however, than just the Five Books of Moses. At Sinai, God delivered the revelation in two forms: the Written Law, also known as the Mosaic Law, and the Oral Law. The Oral Law was given as an interpretive guide to the 613 commandments found in the Mosaic Law. The Oral Law is thus the source for all Jewish interpretation and implementation of God's law. For existential historical reasons, the Oral Law found its way into written form around 250 C.E. It was partially redacted in the Mishnah, which became the focal point of rabbinic learning. Roughly three centuries later, however, historical necessity again demanded further redaction of the Oral Law that resulted in the Gemara.

The Mishnah and Gemara together make up the Talmud. The Jerusalem Talmud was sealed in the fifth century, and the Babylonian Talmud was concluded a century later. Strictly speaking, the Talmud is not a codex but an expansive encyclopedia of oral traditions reaching back to Moses. The rabbis of the Talmud did not restrict themselves to the Jewish legal tra-dition but also to Aggadah, which constituted the rest of the oral tradition. Included in Aggadah are matters of theology, philosophy, ethics, history, and morality.

The rabbis included part of this literature in the Talmud, but much of it is represented by a parallel rabbinic literature in the form of homiletic works, translations, and commentaries on the Bible. This body of writings represents the conceptual framework that lies behind the Jewish legal rul-ings. The nature of this textual relationship is such that Halakhah cannot be properly understood without the background of Aggadah, and Ag-gadah cannot be understood without the Halakhah. As Rabbi Abraham Joshua Heschel put it:

Indeed, the surest way to forfeit *aggadah* is to abolish *halakhah*. Without *halakhah*, *aggadah* loses its substance, its character, its source of inspiration, its security against becoming secularized. By inwardness alone we do not come close to God. The purest intentions, the finest of devotion, the noblest spiritual aspirations are fatuous when not realized in action.[26]

The Talmud has remained the major subject of Jewish study in all generations, and not only for rabbis and judges but also for laymen. This has ensured that the Jewish law and its Aggadic dimensions formed an integral part of all strands of Jewish societies. Further, the commentaries and notes written by each generation and each center of learning have contributed to the tradition and become additions to the textual library. In this way, the Torah, both the oral and written traditions, has formed the conceptual framework for all aspects of normative Jewish life.

The textual library does not end there, however, as this framework required accepted and authoritative legal rulings compiled and written in the form of legal codes. These codes of Jewish law had the added benefit of widening the accessibility of the textual tradition to the non-Talmudic scholar for whom the sheer bulk of the Talmudic literature proved far too cumbersome and opaque. By presenting the accepted and authoritative legal rulings on practical subjects, the codes served as the general reference on the requirements and obligations of Jewish observance.

Chronologically, the first and most comprehensive of all the codes is the fourteen-volume *Mishneh Torah* written by the Rambam, or Maimonides (Rabbi Moses ben Maimon), the twelfth-century physician and scholar.[27] The most widely used and most widely studied codex is Rabbi Yosef Caro's (1488–1575) *Shulhan Arukh*, or Set Table.[28]

The other substantial component of this textual library, is the responsa literature. The term "responsa literature" refers to all written Halakhic rulings made by rabbis in response to questions submitted to them in writing, throughout the post-Talmudic period from the fifth or sixth century to the present day. This literature reflects the living interpretation and actual application of Jewish law in daily life. Professor Menachem Elon, in his book *Ha-mishpat ha-'ivri* (Jewish Law), describes the relationship between Halakhic literature and responsa literature:

The authors of collections of *halakhot* and *halakhic* decisions draw their conclusions by abstract study of the *halakhic* material available to them. . . . In responsa literature, by contrast, the reader is thrust into the midst of a living legal reality, listens to the facts and arguments that the litigants present, and accompanies the decisor (a rabbi who undertakes to issue a *halakhic* ruling) at each stage of his legal inquiry. The problem facing the student and researcher of responsa literature is that [this literature] plunges them into a world of creativity, the inner sanctum of the laboratory. They are partners in experiments, creation, and comprehensive and profound legal analysis. They hear the objective socioeconomic background description that is incorporated into the *halakhic* debate, and they are privy to the explicit or implicit allusions to the decisor's vacillations and efforts to arrive at an answer and a legal solution that both rest on precedent and meet the many needs of his contemporaries.[29]

There are, it has been estimated, over 300,000 responsa published in over 3,000 books by various authors.[30] Responsa literature is also important because both the rabbi making the decision and, to some extent, the questioner incidentally record history without bias, such that the historical facts they mention are reliable. The historical facts that surface in this literature deal with the political and legal status of Jews, the locations of various Jewish communities, Jews' attitudes toward non-Jews in economic and social matters and in questions of beliefs and views, community institutions, juridical and fiscal affairs, folklore, and the various decrees and persecutions the communities were subject to.[31]

Through this rich library of traditional sources, all aspects of Jewish legal, ethical, communal, political, and philosophical thought can be found and studied. These sources of normative Jewish thought and practice are openly available to all that choose to immerse themselves in its study. To some extent, the sources have taken on an additional importance in Jewish life. As Michael Walzer has written, "[the centrality of the sources] derives only in part from the centrality of revelation; it has a second source in the loss of every other center, the absence for so much of Jewish history of a land, a shrine, and a state. The key texts . . . function as a surrogate home."[32]

It is because of these sources that each individual Jewish community can sustain itself in a fashion and manner both true to its heritage and connected with and recognizable to every other Jewish community the world over. It is this normative tradition that has sustained the Jewish people as a people and, more importantly, as a religious people distinct from all other peoples and all other faiths.

JEWISH PUBLIC POLICY

This ability to adapt politically, and survive intact as a people suggests, at minimum, that the Jewish tradition can and, indeed, does speak to the modern world and can contribute to American political discourse. This collection of essays is an attempt to initiate this conversation.

The following chapters progress from the core principles of ethical behavior that govern individual human action to the national principles that govern relations between sovereign nations. Each chapter addresses an area of contemporary concern—ethics, social justice, sex, abortion, euthanasia, environmental conservation, welfare, economics, genetics, and foreign policy—and, in the manner and fashion of rabbinic Judaism, attempts to elucidate normative Jewish responses to public policy issues and propose distinctly Jewish public policy solutions.

Rabbi Librach argues that individual responsibility is the authentically Jewish, as well as the strongest, foundation for a relevant code of ethics; the concomitant context, of course, is the freedom to choose between right and wrong, good and evil. As Rabbi Librach's argument makes clear, freedom finds meaning only in social responsibility. Rabbi Sacks explores the true meaning, obligation, and role of the concept of "repairing the World," or *Tikkun Olam,* and demonstrates that, despite the more contemporary, liberal understanding, it is not a byword for modern welfare-state politics. One byproduct of this, despite popular rationalizations to the contrary, is that much of the practice of modern American Jewish political activity is out of synch with *Tikkun Olam* rightly understood.

Professor Novak, in the process of arguing in favor of protecting traditional marriage, delineates a larger political common ground between all moral peoples, Jews and Christians alike, and briefly develops a process for advancing Jewish public policy. Rabbi Novak also makes a case for practicing Jews to take more seriously, and articulate more clearly and more fully, those religious obligations that have a practical civic component. Rabbi Freundel analyzes the Jewish position toward the abortion debate, staking out a position that does not entirely line up with either the pro-choice or the pro-life position, while Professor Resnicoff grapples with euthanasia, suicide, and the Jewish way of coping with suffering.

Dr. Gerstenfeld develops the contribution Judaism can make to environmentalism, both in terms of policy and in academic study. As such he rejects radical "Green" movements as "neo-pagan," making clear that, in the Jewish tradition, "the earth," as Thomas Jefferson famously expressed it, "belongs in usufruct to the living." In matters of political economy, both Professors Levine and Tamari address the Jewish approach to economic justice; Levine deals specifically with welfare policy and the Jewish social obligation to the poor, while Tamari addresses economic policy and regulatory issues. In both essays, the primary concern is to broadly elucidate the policy implications of their desired claims of general obligation, rather than furnish a complete and comprehensive blueprint or white paper to fully direct current governmental policy.

Professor Sherwin's chapter on bioengineering demonstrates that the Jewish tradition is less concerned with "playing God" and more with human reason than is sometimes ascribed to people of faith in contemporary debate. In the course of doing so, Sherwin also delves into regulatory issues of medical funding and research and the larger philosophical concerns relating to our notions of human identity, morality, and medical propriety. Mr. London's chapter on family values reminds us that the vital core of the Jewish way of life—as a faith and as a polity—is the family and, as such, should be protected and supported. Finally, Professor

Sicherman considers foreign policy and international relations and develops a Jewish approach to diplomacy and war, and the ultimate ends of statehood. Given that peace is always and ever the primary desire, it is fitting and in keeping with Jewish tradition that Sicherman should develop his theme through recourse to the Messianic promise.

Each of these contributions should be understood to demonstrate *an*—but not necessarily *the*—authoritative statement of Jewish public policy. Each is an original and interpretive attempt to capture the body and soul of the sources as they apply to public policy, but as in all areas of the normative Jewish tradition, they are meant to be argued and grappled with so as to test the soundness of both the logic and conclusion of each essay. This volume, in other words, should not be seen to be the final word, but rather the first in what ought to be a lively and ongoing dialectic.

NOTES

1. Daniel Pollack, *Contrasts in American and Jewish Law*, ed. Daniel Pollack (Hoboken, NJ: Yeshiva University Press, 2001).

2. Irving Kristol, "On the Political Stupidity of the Jews," *Azure* No. 8, (Autumn 5760/1999): 47–63; see also Gertrude Himmelfarb, "A Dead White Male Comforts a 20ᵗʰ Century Jew," *The American Enterprise Magazine* (March/April 1997): 64–65.

3. Jerry Z. Muller, *Adam Smith in His Time and Ours: Designing the Decent Society* (New York: The Free Press, 1993).

4. Michael Wyschogrod, comments on Melvin Tumin, "Conservative Trends in American Jewish Life," *Judaism* Vol. 13, Nos. 1–4 (1964): 145.

5. Jonathan Sacks, "Markets and Morals," *First Things* No. 105 (August/September 2000): 23–28.

6. See Meir Tamari, chapter 8; also see Meir Tamari, *The Challenge of Wealth: A Jewish Perspective on Earning and Spending Money* (Northvale, NJ: Jason Aronson, 1995), 219–20.

7. See Aaron Levine, chapter 7.

8. See, generally, Meir Tamari, *The Challenge of Wealth*.

9. See Aaron Levine, chapter 7; also see Meir Tamari, *The Challenge of Wealth*, 219–20.

10. See also Babylonian Talmud, *Avodah Zarah* 4a: "As it is with the fishes of the sea, the one that is larger swallows the others, so it is with humankind. Were it not for the fear of the government, everyone greater than his fellow would 'swallow' him."

11. Russell Kirk, *The Conservative Mind: From Burke to Eliot*, 7th ed., rev. (Washington, DC: Regnery, 1995), 472.

12. Robert Nozick, *Anarchy, State, and Utopia* (New York: Basic Books, 1977).

13. Murray N. Rothbard, *For a New Liberty: The Libertarian Manifesto* (New York: Collier-Macmillan, 1978).

14. David Boaz, *Libertarianism: A Primer* (New York: Free Press, 1997), 13.

15. See Roger Scruton, *A Dictionary of Political Thought* (London: Macmillan,

1982), 271: "[libertarianism is] a radical form of the theory of *laissez-faire*, which believes that economic activity must be actively liberated from the bondage of needless political constraints in order to achieve true prosperity . . . [libertarians are prepared to] wage war on all institutions through which man's vision of the world is narrowed."

16. Cited in David Boaz, *Libertarianism: A Primer* (New York: Free Press, 1997), 15.

17. Ibid.

18. This section draws from earlier forays on this general topic by the author, including: "Jewish Activism in the Washington 'Square': An Analysis and Prognosis," in *Jews and the American Public Square: Debating Religion and Republic*, ed. Alan Mittleman, Robert Licht, and Jonathan D. Sarna (Lanham, MD: Rowman & Littlefield, 2002): 153–86; "For Ourselves and for Others: Defining Jewish Interests" in *The New Jewish Politics*, ed. Daniel Elazar (Lanham, MD: University Press of American and Jerusalem Center for Public Affairs, 1988), 57–64; "Political Interest vs. Moral Agenda," in Letty Cottin Pogrebin, Marshall J. Breger, and Steven Windmueller, *Shaping the American Jewish Agenda* (Los Angeles: Wilstein Institute, 1992), 12–23; "Responses by Marshall Breger," in *Who Speaks for American Judaism? Competing Approaches to Public Issues*, ed. Seymour N. Siegal (Washington, DC: Ethics and Public Policy Center, 1983), 5–9, 18–22.

19. See, generally, Selma Stern, *The Court Jew* (Philadelphia: Jewish Publication Society of America, 1950).

20. Peter Y. Medding, "The 'New Jewish Politics' in the United States: Historical Perspectives," in *The Quest for Utopia: Jewish Political Ideas and Institutions through the Ages*, ed. Zvi Gitelman (Armonk, NY: M.E. Sharpe, 1992), 125.

21. Peter Medding, "New Jewish Politics," 126.

22. Irving Howe, *World of Our Fathers* (New York: Harcourt Brace Jovanovich, 1976).

23. Murray Friedman, "Are American Jews Moving to the Right?" *Commentary* 109, 4 (April 2000): 50.

24. Michael Walzer incisively points out that liberalism, as we know it today, is among the Jews a product of emancipation or, more precisely, "emancipation in exile." Michael Walzer, "Liberalism and the Jews: Historical Affinities, Contemporary Necessities," in *Values, Interests and Identity: Jews and Politics in a Changing World*, ed. Peter Y. Medding (New York: Oxford University Press, 1995) (Studies in contemporary Jewry XI), 3.

25. A 2001 Zogby poll finds the number to be 48.5 percent (see James J. Zogby, *What Ethnic Americans Really Think*, Zogby Culture Polls 52 [Utica, NY: Zogby International, 2001]). In an earlier survey conducted by Steven Cohen, 32 percent of Jews classified themselves as liberal or very liberal (Steven M. Cohen, *The Dimensions of American Jewish Liberalism* [New York: American Jewish Committee, 1989], 39).

26. Abraham Joshua Heschel, *Between Man and God: An Interpretation of Judaism*, ed. Fritz A. Rothschild (New York: Harper & Bros., 1959), 177.

27. Less than fifty years after Rambam, Rabbi Yaakov ben Asher, later known as the Tur, compiled a codex known as the *Arba'ah Turim* (the Four Rows, which refers to the jewels in the breastplate of the high priest in Temple times). Virtually all of the later codes, legal commentaries, and rabbinic decisions adopted the Tur's

four-category arrangement: These are (1) the *Orah Hayyim*, or Way of Life, which deals primarily with the laws of Sabbath observance; the festivals; and the laws and liturgy of the daily, Sabbath, and festival prayers; the (2) *Yoreh De'ah*, Teaching of Knowledge, which principally deals with the laws of permitted and forbidden things—dietary laws, ritual purity, idolatry, usury, et cetera; (3) *Even ha-Ezer*, the Stone of Help, which is concerned with the laws of marriage, divorce, and other family matters; and (4) *Hoshen Mishpat*, the Breastplate of Judgment, which contains the bulk of Jewish civil and criminal law.

28. The *Shulhan Arukh* represents a synopsis of Caro's monumental earlier work, the *Bet Yosef*, which follows and comments on the Tur, and presents an analysis of Caro's own legal decisions and provides the exact sources for them. The *Shulhan Arukh*, particularly after substantial addition by Rabbi Moses Isserles (1520?–1572), became the most universally accepted to the whole Jewish world. Most of the additional codes and commentaries that followed, as well as contemporary efforts, are largely based on Caro's work.

29. Menachem Elon, *Ha-mishpat ha-'ivri* (Jerusalem: Magnes, 1973), part 3, 1215.

30. Ibid., part 3, 1221.

31. Ibid., part 3, 1223.

32. Michael Walzer, "Introduction: The Jewish Political Tradition," in *The Jewish Political Tradition*, vol. 1 of *Authority*, ed. Michael Walzer, Menachem Lorberbaum, and Noam J. Zohar (New Haven: Yale University Press, 2000), xxiv.

CHAPTER 1

Personal Responsibility: The Foundation of Jewish Ethics

Clifford E. Librach

Ethics is the foundation stone of human community. It is the basis for such concepts as fairness, decency, dignity, and compassion. Manners and etiquette are its most obvious outward manifestations. These are normative behaviors that make the strange and foreign at once neutral and accessible. The great and meek, the pauper and aristocrat, the scholar and illiterate meet on the plane of manners. But the principle on which such self-regulation of civilization stands is ethics: the philosophy of human responsibility.

The disciplines of philosophy, both ancient and modern, have delivered to us numerous schemes and intellectual formulations for the realization of ethics. Perhaps the most compelling nonreligious justification was expressed by Immanuel Kant, who posited ethics as a necessary correlative to mutuality. The basic principle of Kantian ethics is respect for the dignity of every human being. In the very human-ness of the other is contained Kant's imperative of human respect and affirmation.

Such an idea, extraordinary in its scope and power, stands nevertheless as an inadequate justification for ethics in (1) its deliberate avoidance and omission of acknowledgment of its religious source, and (2) the concomitant description of the moral universe as occupied only by humanity and not by God as well.[1] Jewish neo-Kantian formulations, the most prominent among them advanced by Ahad Ha'am and Hermann Cohen, may modify Kant's purely "objective" value of justice, but these derivative philosophies fail to embrace and demonstrate the unique role that religion, here rabbinic Judaism, has in justifying ethics against the threatening abyss of moral chaos.

This is so for it was religion—Judaism—that first presented the abstract principle of love as the basis of ethics. Such has been the overarching thrust of rabbinic exegesis of the Torah's classic formulation: "Love your neighbor as yourself."[2] For Rabbi Akiva, this was "the great maxim of the Torah."[3] His rabbinic interlocutor, Ben Azzai, demurred,[4] preferring instead Genesis 5:1, containing the central rule: "This is the book of the generations of man; in the image of God created He him." In Ben Azzai's reading, we not only see humanity's essential unity as a basis for ethics but, pace Kant and his intellectual disciples, that this unity is determined by nothing so much as the identification and definition of each one of us as a being bearing a soul, in the image of Almighty God. "If you put a man to shame," Rabbi Tanhuma is reported to have said, "know that you are putting to shame the image of Almighty God."[5] Ethics has no finer explanation.

I contend that love, even as extended and abstracted as the rabbinic tradition has surely accomplished, is a necessary but insufficient standard for ethics; that beyond love is honor, *kavod* in Hebrew, which is owed to the other and is beyond not only affection but mirror-image identification as well. And, finally, that a third elemental force, that of human responsibility for the decisions we make and fail to make, is essential to ethics, as imparted to the world by Judaism.

ON LOVING YOUR NEIGHBOR

Translation is interpretation. The words of Torah, presented in the sacred scroll without vowels, punctuation, or emphasis, have yielded a veritable tradition of varied meaning by virtue of pressing meaning from words and even letters. So, the standard reading of "Love thy neighbor as yourself" (Leviticus 19:18) is not without or above challenge.

Rabbi Akiva's elevation of these words to the marquee principle of all of Torah[6] is surely a justified and colorable claim. Thus, though Ben Azzai may have been correct in his analysis of foundation,[7] Akiva was correct in his focus on human behavior and its proper attributes. Love, an attachment of abiding human loyalty that is only initiated by affection or attraction, begins with the self, which, in turn, becomes the logical, necessary, and natural starting ground for its expansion to the other—the desired, the acknowledged, the stranger, even the despised.

Hillel's famous Aramaic formulation; "[w]hat is hateful to you, do not do to another,"[8] erroneously deemed inferior to its positive rendition in the Christian Bible,[9] is clearly classic in its scope and simple majesty. What is hateful to you—the one to whom your love is routine, expected, natural, and expanding—do not do to any other, not just within the circle of yourself, your family, and your progeny, but beyond, to concentric circles distant and further still. Of course, this is not outside of the reality of human territoriality and priority. Judaism knows enmity and proffers the enemy no surrender, no gratuity, no "other cheek."[10] Priority is anticipated and even celebrated.

After all, inasmuch as Jewish ethics is founded on the concept that all human beings are created *b'tzelem elohim*, in the image of God, such must necessarily include one's own self. Self-denial, or the subordination of one's self in preference to the needs of the other, however noble, stoic, and worthy it may seem as a Western cultural model or basis for service, is not elevated as an ethical virtue in Judaism. The simple reason for this is that the self is no less worthy, no less deserving, no less entitled to love and is thus the first order of care and charity.

So, as the aphorism would have it, "charity begins at home." Rabbinic Judaism is without hesitation on this score: In the distribution of scarce resources, relatives take precedence over strangers and the inhabitants of one's city take precedence over the needy of other localities.[11]

Why? For the simple reason that self-denial can lead to excessive generosity, which can lead to nothing less than poverty and suffering.[12] Deuteronomy 15:4 ("[t]hough there should be no poor in your midst") is read to mean that generosity should not supersede the legitimate needs of the self, causing one to become destitute and a public charge.[13] But the very sage who declared this moral rubric, Rab Judah, hastens to note that "he who strictly observes this standard, will eventually be brought to it."[14] The meaning here is clear: As a corrective to the apparently justified haughty disregard of the needy, the one who always puts himself and the preservation of his wealth first—in order to avoid penury—will eventually himself be brought to poverty. As amplified by Rashi, self-interest legitimately takes precedence according to Jewish law, but Jewish law is the beginning and not the end of ethical obligation, which should take one beyond the law[15] for the sake of piety, charity, and justice.[16]

A contradiction? No. Self-interest has justified precedence when the "playing field is level," when the stakes between the self and the other are equal, in other words. But in cases where one is better able to sustain loss without pain or penalty or one's comparable risk of the same is clearly a fraction of that of the other, Rab Judah's admonition assumes normative control. It follows and mitigates a mishnah which (again, assuming equal risk), renders the recovery of one's own property a priority over that of one's father or teacher and the property of one's teacher over that of one's father.[17]

The vectors of justified self-interest, or self-love, are set out in a pair of famous Talmudic tales. In one,[18] the hypothetical ethical crisis is proposed: two men, wandering in the desert and dying of thirst, one having discovered a jug of water sufficient to sustain life for one but not both. The debate once more invokes the storied Rabbi Akiva, here opposed by his contemporary, Ben Peturah. The latter insists, on this fact pattern, that they should share the insufficient water and die together in a tragic celebration of mutual love and self-sacrifice. Akiva stands against this superficially seductive and uncritical reading, looking to Leviticus 25:36 ("thy brother shall live *with thee*")[19] as scriptural support, here justifying consumption of the water by the finder of the jug. Simple equity would appear to side with Ben Peturah. Shared risk should require, it would seem, shared access to a lifeline (even though discovered by only one). But the moral oddity of requiring that two should die rather than one because sympathy trumps selfishness is itself absurd: Akiva's counterintuitive resolution is thus presented as later, superior, and normative in Judaism. The man who found the jug can save only one life—and it should be his own.

The opposite boundary is no less stark. The great Babylonian Amora named Rabbah was confronted by one with the following classic moral dilemma:[20] the governor of my town has ordered me: "Go and murder so-and-so; if not, I will kill you." Rabbah's epigrammatic answer is an essay on the limits of self-love: "Let him rather slay you than that you should commit murder; who knows that your blood is redder than his? Perhaps his blood is redder." As self-love is legitimate and even primary, it has its necessary moral limits. One life cannot be sacrificed for another;[21] the life of every individual is of equal value.

A more nuanced reading of Leviticus 19:18 is thus indeed plausible. The text may not read "Love your neighbor [or the other] as yourself; I am the Lord." But rather this: "Love your neighbor! Like you [with unlimited opportunity to ignore the needs of the other], I am the Lord [Whose love of you should be reflected and emulated in your love of the other, your neighbor, your stranger, as yourself]."[22] And this love—however sophisticated, unromantic, and unrequited—is a necessary but insufficient basis for ethics. It is insufficient only in the usual confusing and tentative emotional basis of its initiation. Without human love there is no ethics; with only love, ethics teeters on an often subjective matrix.

HONOR IN ETHICS

"If love depends upon one selfish end, when that one end ceases, so will the love. But if it does not depend upon one selfish end—such [honor] will never die."[23] The insufficiency of love as the ultimate ground of ethics is resolved by the additional acknowledgement of honor, in Hebrew *kavod*—literally "weighty"—as an identically significant justification for ethics. The significance of honor is that it is not determined by a volatile emotion (love) that begins with the self and follows—pursuant to Torah instruction—with outreach to the person of the other. Honor is a less emotional and more abstract, intellectual concept: It signals the absolute and eternal value of every single human being, which arises from the idea, founded on religion, of each human being's having been created in the

image of Almighty God. Standing alone, love can be confusing and awkward, a misrepresentation of passion or fascination, an unstable and sometimes egotistical excursion. Honor, in Judaism, may be seen as love's
ballast, signifying the manifestation of one of religion's great ideas: the
absolute worth of every person. Accordingly, rabbinic ethics unites love
and honor in an intertwined conceptual unity, insisting that both be the
hallmark of our human mutuality and together the foundation of ethics.

"Let the honor of your fellow be as precious to you as your own."[24]
This, the words attributed to Rabbi Eleazar, is a Rabbinic standard that is
superimposed on the biblical injunction of love. The Bible's "failure" to
enjoin the honor of one's fellow human being is thus corrected by the
rabbinic tradition.[25]

The standard of expected behavior is often established by reference to
the negative consequence of our failure to sustain it—a standard, as it
were, of unacceptable conduct.

"A *tanna* [one who has committed the Mishnah to memory] said before
Rab Nachman bar Isaac: One who publicly pales the face of his fellows is
as though he shed blood! And he [Rab Nachman] responded: You put it
well, as indeed have I seen this—the redness going out and the paleness
coming in. Abaye asked Rab Dimi: What do [the Jews of] Palestine avoid
most? He replied: Making faces white. . . . It would be far better for a man
to throw himself into a fiery furnace than to publicly shame his fellow."[26]

"If with regard to the stones [of the Temple altar] that have no concept
of good and evil, the Holy One, Blessed be He, insists that they not be
treated with disdain or disrespect; surely then with regard to your fellow
human being, created in the image of the One whose speech created the
world, the requirement is that such a one as this shall never be treated
with contempt or degradation."[27] And the same point is made regarding
the ministering angels, who are not burdened with the evil impulse. If
they grant honor and praise to each other, how much the more so should
human beings—in whom the evil impulse exists—behave similarly.[28]

The *yetzer harah*—the evil impulse—is said to be the source of rank
egotism and self-absorption. To the extent that this controls our relationships or inhibits our outreach or ability to honor our fellow human creatures, we are charged with the responsibility to subdue and overcome it.[29]

"Great is the dignity of a human being"—a Talmudic principle applied
by Rabbi Yochanan ben Zakkai to a common thief[30]—is an ethical rubric
that, when applied, imposes the duty to treat inferiors as equal, equals as
superior, and superiors as worthy of esteem.[31]

"A favorite saying of the Rabbis of Yavneh [in Palestine] was: 'I am
God's creature and the ignoramus is also God's creature. My work is
urban and his is rural. I wake early for my livelihood and he wakes early
for his livelihood. Indeed, he does not presume to have my skill nor
should I presume to have his.' How can one say, 'I do a lot in support of

Torah values and he does nothing'? Here's what we have been taught: One may do much or one may do little—it is all the same, provided each is motivated by [service to God in] heaven. . . .

"We should always strive to be on the best of terms with our brethren, with all our relatives and with everybody—even with the heathen in the street; in order that we may be beloved [in heaven] above and well-liked [on earth] below and be acceptable to our fellow beings. It was said of [no one less than] Yochanan ben Zakkai that no man ever greeted him first, not even a heathen in the street."[32]

Love and honor thus unite to form the matrix of ethics, the source of which is our creation at the hands of Almighty God. Love, which begins with the self and expands outward, is due from each of us to the other inasmuch as (a) God loves us, and (b) we exist as a reflection of that Divine image. The love is bolstered—amplified, really—by the attribute of honor, which is more abstract and cognitive than love, often emotional and insecure. In the face of either or both, we are instructed and compelled to treat another as we ourselves would be treated. The attribution of our creation to God, and no other, requires that we see the other in our midst as—at some level—an equal. On this rock stands the ethical obligation.

EXPLORING PERSONAL RESPONSIBILITIES

Love and honor justify ethics. But the antecedent and primary rationale for them lies in the definition of a human being, which yields a theology of human responsibility. Ethics, or the duty to the other, depends on a being endowed with the ability to choose, reject, and accept. Rabbinic Judaism celebrates no idealized human attribute so much as the capacity to choose, for which responsibility is the elementary by-product. In choosing, one acts toward good or evil, and the responsibility is neither surrendered to elements of nature nor attributable to forces of external manipulation. There is, therefore, no ethics and no Judaism without human responsibility. It is to the Torah and its exegesis that we turn for the amplification of this ethos.

Adam and Eve

Modern critics apply modern values. There is perhaps no biblical language more prone to harsh rebuke by modernity than the so-called "curse of Eve"—said to be a hopelessly antique embrace of misogyny. The familiar scene is a cultural icon. Adam and Eve (primordial humanity) have been warned by the Almighty to refrain from eating of the tree of knowledge of good and evil.[33] Despite God's warning,[34] the primal woman Eve yields to the suggestion of the biblical serpent,[35] and of the tree of knowledge of good and evil "she took of its fruit and did eat, and gave also to her husband with her, and he did eat."[36]

Centuries of Christian commentary have imparted to civilization the reading of this moment as a Primal Fall, an Original Sin that humanity has, from its accomplishment until our own day, struggled to overcome and defeat.[37] Indeed, it is the standard theological representation of normative Christianity[38] that the crucifixion of Lord Jesus was the necessary compensating redemption for this Original Sin—the sacrifice to end all sacrifices.[39]

In the punishment meted by the Almighty to serpent, woman, and man,[40] we find that the serpent is condemned to mobility without legs,[41] that the man is condemned to agriculture—the procurement of livelihood by the sweat of his brow,[42] and the woman condemned to pain in childbirth[43] and, most offensive to modern sensibility, subservience to her male mate ("[y]our desire [or lust] will be for your husband, so that he will dominate you").[44]

Against this regnant reading and interpretation stands the far less celebrated reading of the rabbinic tradition, which sees in the Bible's account of the Garden not a snapshot of history and a Fall, but a philosophic treatise on life and death, human sexuality, and a passion to achieve.[45] God's admonition not to eat of the fruit of the tree is a warning that knowledge, "in the biblical sense" (so the modern sarcastic usage) or sexual energy will introduce the vectors of procreation and death—the latter a necessity to prevent the Malthusian catastrophe and to promote the force of civilization itself: the urgency to create, sustain, organize, and bequeath. Innocence and eternal life or sexuality and death—this was the choice; and the embrace of the second option is our inherited condition.

What, then, of the so-called curse of Eve and its superficial offense to modern sensibilities? Just this: It is no curse but a metaphoric description of vulnerability and dependence. The once-heralded "maternal instinct"—now again in vogue—stands unsatisfied without at least the seed of a man. "Your desire will be for your husband so that he will dominate you."[46] In short, following psychology's *principle of least interest*, in a two-person relationship, the one who has the least to gain—or feels that he has less at stake—is in the dominant position.[47] Men in their middle years may become wistful for progeny and legacy,[48] but young men are historically notorious for avoiding the "burden of matrimony." Their power in a sexual or romantic partnership may be in inverse relation to their investment in its success.

Accordingly, it is the eternal predicament of women that their sense of fulfillment through the conception, carrying, bearing, and rearing of children compels their dependence on a male, if for no other reason than sheer biological necessity. Men can, and do, maraud and sport, prepared to impregnate and abandon responsibility to the point of cultural crisis.[49]

Women, needing a man to complete their destiny, are, by this condition, vulnerable to subjugation and abuse. The Torah, here, says nothing else.

This reading might be merely fanciful and tendentious were it not confirmed by a parallel text only a few verses away. Once the "expulsion" from the Garden is effective, history and time have begun, and we are introduced to the beginning of human experience in the tale of Cain, Abel, and fratricide. To Eve, God speaks of the man in her life, saying, "Your desire [or lust] will be for your husband";[50] to Cain, He speaks of Demon Sin, the temptation to evil, the urge to wrong, to violate, to abuse, to mistreat and be wicked.[51] "His desire will be for you"—sin is itself not an independent force but dependent on you, inanimate without your assent. It [Demon Sin] is crouched in subservient repose, awaiting Cain's [and all humanity's] signal. But the Torah does not say that it waits to strike at your every foible, to penetrate every microscopic fissure of your moral shield, poised in aggressive anticipation of power, mastery, and Mephistophelean success. Rather does it say in language directly parallel to the malediction pronounced on Eve that it crouches like a doleful and obedient hound at the gate, awaiting his master's permissive gesture or voice—"His [Demon Sin's] desire will be for you; yet you may dominate him."[52]

This is the point, the major premise, to which the prior wordplay (the "curse of Eve") was the minor and penultimate clause. We do not commit sin because of the devil, or our genetic predisposition, our flawed and error-prone parentage, or the deprivation of our economic or social circumstance. We commit sin because we open the door to its allurement, we permit it workplace and station, soil and nutrients in our soul, personality and ultimate behavior. It is in our hands to master sin, to "dominate him," and the will to do so is ours and ours alone.

Human sin is thus projected as within the control of human responsibility. It [sin] needs the human invitation to abode and success. You, Cain—humanity—may dominate it and prevent its authority and manifestation in your life. You must open the door behind which it crouches to let it in.[53] Temptation is eternal, but human evil and immorality are voluntative. We act or fail to act; and we are responsible.

Tamar and Judah

Yet another Genesis excursion into personal responsibility is the enigmatic and apparently incongruous[54] story of Judah, Leah's fourth son, and Tamar, his daughter-in-law (Genesis 38). The outline of the tale is familiar: Jacob has learned of the evident death of Joseph, his son by Rachel, and is in bitter mourning for him, though we learn that, in fact, Joseph has been at that very time sold as a slave by his Midianite captors to Potiphar, courtier of Egypt's pharaoh.[55]

Judah is introduced to us in this short chapter as a man of virile prowess and a sire of sons: He married a Canaanite woman who bore him Er, Onan, and Shelah. The oldest of these, Er, married Tamar. Er's death meant that brother Onan had the classic obligation to sire a son who would be credited to the dead Er, but his refusal so "displeased God" that Onan also died, leaving Tamar (and the deceased legacy of Er) childless. Shelah was too young to wed, so Judah (evidently oblivious to the horrors of losing two sons in succession) instructed Tamar to wait for him to mature and fulfill his legal obligation, at last giving child and legacy to Tamar and her dead husband.

What follows is a stark and dramatic tumble of plot and character that culminates in the Bible's most celebrated act of ethical heroism.

After "a long time," Judah's wife dies—said "long time" during which young Tamar has been presumably waiting patiently per Judah's instruction. Tamar is said by the text to know that Shelah (the youngest and now only surviving son of Judah) is now of age but that no arrangement for their union has been completed. She waits for the end of Judah's formal period of mourning for his wife, and then acts out a bold and daring scheme: Disguising herself as a harlot, she attracts none other than Judah, father of her dead husband, who leaves as a surety for her fee, the ancient equivalent of today's credit card wallet: his seal, cord, and staff.

From this liaison Tamar conceives, but she returns to her widowhood in behavior and dress. Judah finds nothing but frustration as he inquires and searches about for the prostitute to pay so that he may redeem his worthy seal, cord, and staff. His anger unappeased, he is further informed that his daughter-in-law Tamar has not only turned to harlotry but that she is pregnant. His reaction is predictable: She should be burned as a shame to the family.

Tamar then protests as if at law. She asks that Judah be shown the seal, cord, and staff and advises: The man whose possessions are these, such is the one who has sired my child. "Please recognize [haker-na] to whom do these belong. . . . [and] Judah recognized [vayaker] them."[56]

Here are comingled elements of male domination and rank misogyny, of treachery and the opportunity to avoid shame by silencing, exile, or murder. This is a moment of unequaled balance between father and child, man and woman, wealth and poverty, power and subservience. How will Judah (who will, for this reason, become the ancestor of King David and his line) respond to such a frontal challenge? His answer is a monument to ethics, to human dignity and personal responsibility: She is, he says, more correct than am I.[57]

How classic a moment is this in all of literature, and how powerful a demonstration of righteousness, decency, and justified ethical responsibility. No excuse, no explanation, no power play, no legalese or obfuscation: She is more right than am I. Rightness and not shame is his standard.

Impulsive like his brothers, with whom he joined in abandoning young Joseph to the pit,[58] Judah here emerges as a man thoughtful, mature, responsible, and, accordingly, ethical.

Joseph

Now the virtue of accountability and Judah's role as its principal biblical model assumes its clarity. Genesis 38 is no longer a discrete fable of neo-feminist guile, but a vivid foreshadowing of the sublime ethical character of Judah, which will justify his ultimate status as the progenitor of Jewish royalty and the namesake of its people.[59]

As well, or perhaps more importantly, Judah establishes the ethical ballast to reconcile his fractured family, uniting his brothers, the sons of Leah, with Jacob, their self-absorbed and deeply flawed father, and they, in turn, with their seriously compromised half-brother Joseph.

Who is Joseph? He is the son of Jacob and Rachel, Jacob's favored wife, an apparently indulged dandy,[60] whose half brothers (all sons of the less-preferred Leah) despise his familial status[61] and proffered clairvoyance.[62] They so scorn his conceit and paternally designated rank that they scheme to abandon him[63] and present his blood-stained tunic to father Jacob, who will indeed conclude that their concoction of a fatal attack by a wild beast[64] explains his loss. Joseph, assumed dead by his father for years, in fact survives in Egyptian captivity where he emerges as shrewd, perceptive,[65] and morally disciplined.[66] This is a matter of considerable irony. As Robert Alter brilliantly notes, "[w]hen we return from Judah to the Joseph story (Genesis 39), we move in pointed contrast from a tale of exposure through sexual incontinence to a tale of seeming defeat and ultimate triumph through sexual continence—Joseph and Potiphar's wife."[67] Joseph emerges to be a figure of national significance, fully assimilating into Egyptian society[68] and rising to the position of Pharaoh's viceroy, or prime minister.[69] The sons of Leah, now led by fourth-born Judah, encounter Joseph as they descend to Egypt in desperate search of food during a famine. There, in the face of Joseph—now unidentified and unidentifiable—they confess their perfidy.[70] And Joseph's suppressed anger compels him to manipulate the circumstances in order to see evidence of his maternal ancestry, namely his full brother Benjamin, whom the sons of Leah had left behind with their father.[71]

The drama reaches its dual climax in the final reunion of them all—first the brothers[72] and then Joseph with Jacob[73]—as the now-eloquent Judah[74] waters the soil of family reconciliation with a paradigmatic display of personal responsibility and ethical rectitude.

The pith of this narrative is the virtue of personal responsibility as the antecedent key to justice and love. And Judah, not Jacob or Joseph, is the hero.

The dramatic and psychological problem is not so much that the brothers despise Joseph as it is that they are deeply offended by their father, Jacob, whose preference for Joseph and his mother Rachel is an understatement. How painful it must be for Judah to represent his father to Joseph as one who speaks only of "two children from one wife."[75] Jacob is in fact the father of thirteen children from two wives. Yet this is indeed Jacob's nearsighted self-image. His prior behavior has established not only his preference for Rachel and her children, but his immoral collapse as a responsible father. When Shimon and Levi violently defend the honor of their defiled sister Dinah,[76] they and their brothers are no doubt shocked at father Jacob's apparently tepid reaction to the crime (he says absolutely nothing) and his awkward anger at their emotional revenge (he accuses them of spoiling his reputation by taking vengeance on their sister's rapists).[77] "Shall he [they mean their own father] then treat our sister [Jacob's daughter!] as a harlot?"[78]

It is thus Jacob who is the counterexample to human responsibility. Even concerning his beloved and favored Rachel, the Bible's brilliant wordplay demonstrates the patriarch's obtuseness. At one point, Jacob, in flight from Lavan with Jacob's two wives (Lavan's daughters), Leah and Rachel, is ignorant of and impervious to Rachel's vulnerability. She, who has stolen her father Lavan's teraphim and hidden them in her camel saddle, Genesis 31:34, feigns menstruation as a foil to his manual search for the statuettes (verse 35). Jacob is insulted for himself—"how dare you suspect my thievery"—clueless of Rachel's danger. "I have taken responsibility for your sheep [in Hebrew, *rachel-echah*]," he protests to Lavan,[79] implying (the wordplay on Rachel *echah*) his greater concern for livestock than loved ones.[80]

Joseph, in Egypt, is at this point bereft of ethical compass—he has yet to inquire of his father in Canaan during this seventeen-year hiatus—with his Egyptian (thus foreign and symbolically alien) language, name, dress, and exalted station. Father Jacob is also deeply flawed, hopelessly insensitive to the emotional plight of his children. So it is Judah, who, as we have seen, understands only too well what an assurance (*ervon*)[81] can mean, having survived his shame at the hand of Tamar, who now presents *himself* as responsible assurance (*eh'eirvenu*—from the same Hebrew root) for his half brother.[82] Having learned the abiding power of human accountability, he offers himself in the stead of any possible surety, "[I] have taken responsibility for the lad to [return him unharmed to] my father."[83]

And it is thus Judah's sense of personal responsibility that advances and justifies this narrative as a morality tale. In the face of such honor, the assimilated Joseph loses his composure and control[84] and exclaims, "I am Joseph!"[85] (speaking more to himself than to his familial entourage). Joseph's Jewish roots are reattached and the family members (representing the nascent Jewish people) are reconciled because responsibility (exemplified by Judah) has trumped myopia, presumption, and denial (exemplified by Jacob and Joseph).

THEOLOGICAL IMPLICATIONS

What remains to be addressed, finally, are the theological implications of the ethic of responsibility. What is the role of God in directing our behavior, the element of choice, the will to do good over evil, right over wrong, less damage over more?

These questions have no more powerful a modern context than the Shoah, the inferno of 1933–45 during which German civilization sought and largely achieved the annihilation of the European Jewish community. Who, in the final and universal analysis, is responsible? Is it the Nazis and the supportive or, at best, passive European dominion? Or does responsibility for such unspeakable horrors rest with God, insofar as God was apparently indifferent and chose not to intervene and protect those whose annihilation He had promised to prevent?[86] Or does responsibility, in fact, rest on the shoulders of *am yisrael*, the Jewish people, whose very exercise of choice—the condition precedent to the ethics of responsibility—resulted in such continuous, gratuitous, and arrogant sin as to merit, by God's righteous judgment, the national punishment that now is evil's synonym?[87]

The noted rabbinic scholar and Holocaust survivor David Weiss Halivni has recently and directly addressed this matter to inspired conclusion.[88] After acknowledging the taunt of simplistic theism, suggesting that the sins of Jews brought compensating disaster to themselves[89] by the divinely directed hands of the Nazis and their European codependents, Weiss Halivni asserts an unqualified condemnation of such an idea or suggestion. He supports his rejection by reference to the Torah, Prophets, Writings, and sages—"The Shoah was not the consequence of sin."[90]

From the Torah, Weiss Halivni cites Leviticus 26:44 ("And yet for all that, when they are in the land of their enemies, I will not cast them away, nor will I loathe them, to destroy them utterly, and to break my covenant with them"). Exile, perhaps,[91] but not annihilation can be attributed to God's punishment. So speaks the Torah.

Jeremiah is the evidence from the Prophets. His prayer in 10:24 is primary: "Chastise me, O Lord, *but in measure,*[92] not according to your anger, lest you reduce me to nothing." This, when combined with God's promise—the affirmative answer by God to Jeremiah's prayer—is identified by Weiss Halivni in 30:11 and 46:28: "For I am with you to deliver you, declares the Lord. I will make an end of all the nations among which I have dispersed you. But I will not make an end of you. I will not leave you unpunished, but I will chastise you in measure." "In measure," that is such that "our corporate life will continue even after your chastisement."[93]

Within the Writings, Weiss Halivni points to Nehemiah 9, the sacred author's expansive historical survey from the time of creation[94] to his own day.[95] God's punishment for Israel's insolent and obstinate behavior is assayed but acknowledged as a precursor to her appeal to heaven—an appeal heard ("you heard them from heaven and rescued them out of your great compassion"[96]) by God over and over again. God spared Israel then, out of His mercy, love, and grace; so, too, He saved Israel in our day from the threshold of total erasure.[97] From the rabbinic sages, Weiss Halivni brings clear evidence of their judgment that divine rebuke and punishment—the suffering of Israel—shall nevertheless not mean its near extinction.[98] And in no case is there a sin or transgression that merits a punishment like the Shoah in its enormity,[99] its cruelty, hatred, racism, and unprecedented lack of rebellion by, or means of escape for, the victims.

Weiss Halivni then pronounces "sympathy" with the proposition "that in order for a person to achieve responsibility for his actions, he must be fully free, without any obstacles, any external influences."[100]

To be sure, the knowledge of good and evil itself influences a person to choose the good; but when he chooses evil, he must, in order to merit punishment, have committed evil fully out of free choice, without any external intervention. Any kind of intervention, even from God, reduces a person's responsibility for his actions. It is possible, therefore, that God will remain aloof. In order not to diminish a person's freedom to act—and thereby diminish his responsibility—God may stand apart, facing utter evil without intervening and without responding. Something like this happened in the time of the Shoah. God did not intervene and did not respond, but stood apart.

In order, then, for good and the opportunity so to choose to exist, evil must also exist and be *equally available* as an option. This is the theological framework that permits—even exalts—human ethical choice and responsibility. Further, the well-known Kabbalistic doctrine of Isaac Luria[101]— that of *tzimtzum*, the theory of divine contraction—applies with special force here. God's withdrawal from total control was necessary at Creation's threshold in order to accommodate human freedom and autonomy. Such contraction (*tzimtzum*) itself needs adjustment and even periodic regeneration. It is a cosmic act of correction to adjust the moral vacuum, sometimes finding God acting in history and sometimes finding Him in painful willed corresponding paralysis ("Lest the divine presence devour the *tzimtzum* all together, and vitiate free will"[102]). When such an act of regeneration—having no parallel in history—occurs (as it did), "humanity [is] brought to the summit of its moral freedom, to be exercised for good or for evil."[103] The responsibility for the Holocaust lies with its perpetrators, who were not mere puppets of the Almighty force, but free moral agents—whose ethical options and whose very humanity mirror our own.

In order for us—any of us—to be capable of ethical behavior (showing love and honor to our fellow human being), we must know that our single human endowment is the capacity to choose and to accept on ourselves and impose on others responsibility therefor. When we do, we permit ethics—civilization by means of personal responsibility—to flourish. When we do not, we limit and abuse human freedom and advance a worldview that reduces human beings to creatures without duty, known only by their impulse without restraint and their passion without honor.[104]

NOTES

1. In this and many other insights within, I am grateful for the seminal and instructive essay by Chaim W. Reines, Israel's Treasure, *Tradition* vol. 2, pp. 282–292 (No. 2, Summer 1960).

2. Leviticus 19:18.

3. *Sifra, Kedoshim.*

4. Ibid.

5. *Genesis Rabbah* XXIV:7.

6. Supra n. 3.

7. Supra note 4 and accompanying text.

8. Babylonian Talmud, *Shabbat* 31a.

9. Matthew 7:12 ("Do unto others as you would have them do unto you."); cf., Luke 6:31. See Samuel Sandmel, *A Jewish Understanding of the New Testament* (Cincinnati: HUC-JIR Press, 1956), 151; Francine Klagsbrun, *Voices of Wisdom: Jewish Ideals and Ethics for Everyday Living* (New York: Pantheon Books, 1980), 37.

10. Cf. Matthew 5:39.

11. Babylonian Talmud, *Bava Metsia* 71a.

12. The compulsion to share or to prevent hunger does not imply a correlative obligation to suffer for the sake of another or for others in general.

13. Babylonian Talmud, *Bava Metsia* 30b, 33a.

14. Ibid.

15. *Lifnim mshurat ha din.* Cf., Babylonian Talmud, *Bava Metsia* 30b.

16. Rashi to Babylonian Talmud, *Metsia* 33a, s.v. *ha m'kayem b'atzmo kach.*

17. Babylonian Talmud, *Bava Metsia* 33b.

18. Babylonian Talmud, *Bava Metsia* 62a.

19. Emphasis added. The reading clearly implies priority of the self.

20. Babylonian Talmud, *Sanhedrin* 74a.

21. Mishnah *Ohalot* 7:6. This is the standard rabbinic text in support of the mandated abortion of a fetus that is threatening the life of the mother.

22. Cf., Judah Goldin, trans., *The Fathers According to Rabbi Nathan* (New Haven: Yale University Press, 1955), 86 [hereinafter *The Fathers*].

23. Mishnah *Avot* 5:16.

24. *The Fathers*, 78.

25. The need for "correction" of the Torah text is not its inadequacy, but its density. The Rabbinic attention to honor as an obligation is an amplification and necessarily implied expansion of the Torah's concept of human love.

26. Babylonian Talmud, *Bava Metsia* 58b–59a.

27. *Mekhilta, Yitro,* Saul Horowitz, ed., 245.

28. *The Fathers,* 101.

29. Babylonian Talmud, *Bava Metsia* 32b.

30. Babylonian Talmud, *Bava Kama* 79b.

31. Cf. *The Fathers,* 86.

32. *Berakhot* 17a.

33. Genesis 2:17.

34. Ibid.

35. Genesis 3:1–6.

36. Genesis 3:6.

37. Trude Weiss-Rosmarin, *Judaism and Christianity: The Differences* (Middle Village, NY: Jonathan David, 1943), 45; *Catechism of the Catholic Church* (Washington: United States Catholic Conference, 1994) §§ 390, 397, 416.

38. Ibid.

39. Ibid.

40. In that order. Genesis 3:14–19.

41. Genesis 3:14.

42. Genesis 3:19.

43. Genesis 3:16.

44. Genesis 3:16. The usual and customary translation of the second clause, "And he shall rule over you," King James Version; New International Version is firmly based on the traditional reading made famous by St. Augustine and the medieval Christian exegetes. Followed by premodern popular commentary, this passage has been exaggerated in two separate eras for two separate purposes and to two separate and erroneous conclusions. In the former, the Western culture of male domination, female subjugation, and chauvinism used this clause as a biblical warrant, a permissive proof text, for male economic cultural and psychological authority and power. In the latter, modern feminism strangely affirmed this out-of-context misreading in insisting that such a clause justified qualifying the biblical canon as hopelessly sexist and at sharp variance with our own modern (and . . . thus) superior attitudes and values regarding equality of the sexes and the need for women to be free from male domination and dependence. We argue here, infra, that both are wrong. The biblical text does not say what it is accused of saying, namely that women shall be subservient to men. And what it says (that a woman will live with the frustrating truth that a man is necessary to her sense of fulfillment in child bearing) is but a minor clause in a wordplay leading to a major clause, Genesis 4:7, which addresses the reality of sin and our responsibility therefor.

45. The within analysis is drawn largely from the outstanding treatment of these Genesis passages in Herbert Chanan Brichto, *The Names of God* New York: Oxford University Press, 1998), 79–99.

46. Ibid., 98. The translation is Brichto's.

47. Ibid., 98–99.

48. It was most revealing in this regard that a famous gay American poet of the mid-twentieth century, Allen Ginsburg, spoke longingly of his desire for children as he reached middle age.

49. What, then, of the institution of marriage and the Western cultural convention of attaching the father's name to that of the children he sires? Is not marriage the use of law to impose a quid pro quo on the male animal? In exchange for

sexual access, he must bear financial and social responsibility for its issue—children. Said children bear the name of their father, presumably to ensure such assignment of responsibility when the alternative is that they become a public charge.

50. Brichto, op. cit., 98. The translation of Genesis 4:7 is Brichto's. See Rashi to Genesis 4:7, s.v. *v'ata timshal bo;* Malbim to Genesis 4:7, s.v. *v'ata timshal bo.*

51. Ibid.

52. Genesis 4:7. Brichto, op. cit., 98.

53. Ibid., 99. The same point is made in the rabbinic interpretation of Deuteronomy 11:26 ("Behold I have set before you this blessing and a curse.") Rav Eleazar said that simultaneous to this pronouncement on Sinai, "out of the mouth of the Almighty *did not* go forth good and evil" (Lamentations 3:38) but rather did human responsibility begin its reign as the foundation of human behavior and ethical conduct. Evil comes to those who do evil; good comes to those who do good. Rab Haggai affirmed this, quoting God: "Not only did I set before you two paths [i.e., good and evil] but I have gone *lifnim mishurat hadin* [beyond the limit of mere regulation] in that I have said clearly to you 'Therefore choose life'" (Deuteronomy 30:19). God's is the explanation, opportunity, and invitation. The choice and consequence are ours alone. See *Deuteronomy Rabbah* IV:3 (*Re'eh*).

54. See E.A. Speiser, trans., "Genesis," in *The Anchor Bible* (Garden City, NY: Doubleday, 1962), 299.

55. Genesis 37:36.

56. Robert Alter, *The Art of Biblical Narrative* (New York: Basic Books, 1981), 9–10. Alter's brilliant analysis, on which this reading is dependent, is a demonstration of modern criticism redeeming the genius of traditional rabbinic exegesis. "In many cases a literary student of the Bible has more to learn from the traditional commentaries than from modern scholarship." Ibid. at 11.

57. Genesis 38:26. Cf., Rashi to Genesis 38:26, s.v. *kee al kayn lo n'tateeha;* Malbim to Genesis 38:24–26, s.v. *zonta Tamar kalatecha;* Sforno to Genesis 38:26, s.v. *tzadekah meemeinee.* The traditional rabbinic reading affirms Alter's astute observation, supra note 58.

58. Genesis 37:25–28.

59. Cf. Genesis 49:8–12; The English word "Jew" is clearly derivative of the Hebrew "Yehudah."

60. Cf. Genesis 37:3.

61. Genesis 37:4.

62. Genesis 37:5.

63. Genesis 37:19–20.

64. Genesis 37:31.

65. Genesis 39:2–4.

66. Genesis 39:10.

67. Robert Alter, op. cit., 10.

68. In extraordinary contradistinction to the well-known midrash relating the integrity of the Israelites during their Egyptian captivity, *Bemidbar Rabbah* XIII:20; *Shir ha Shirim Rabbah* IV: 12 § 1, Joseph changed his language, Genesis 42:23; his name, Genesis 41:45; and his style of clothes, Genesis 41:42.

69. Genesis 41:41.

70. Genesis 42:21.

71. Genesis 42:19–20.

72. Genesis 43:29, 44:18–45:9.

73. Genesis 46:28–31.

74. Genesis 44:18–34 is one of the most magnificently articulated pleas in the entire biblical canon.

75. Genesis 44:27.

76. Genesis 34:25.

77. Genesis 34:30.

78. Genesis 34:31.

79. Genesis 31:38.

80. Hear Jacob plead with his father-in-law: "*Anochi achateinah, mi'yadee t'vaksheinah*" (I accept the blame for any [destroyed livestock]; you demanded [and received compensation] from my hand) (Genesis 31:39). This passage is heard in echo when Judah pleads with Jacob, years later, to let little Benjamin proceed to Egypt with the sons of Leah (Genesis 43:9) so as to permit the family to survive famine: "*Anochi eh'eirveinu; mi'yadee tevakshenu*" (I will take responsibility for him; you will [be able to] demand him from my hand.)

81. Genesis 38:18—the signet ring, cord, and staff that he left as a guarantee of his payment to the presumed prostitute.

82. Genesis 43:9.

83. Ibid.

84. Genesis 45:1.

85. Genesis 45:3.

86. Leviticus 26:44; Jeremiah 30:11, 46:28. See infra.

87. This is precisely the position articulated in September 2000 by Rabbi Ovadia Yosef, spiritual leader of SHAS in Israel, as recalled by David Weiss Halivni: "Rabbi Yosef spoke of the connection between sin and suffering and declared that the Holocaust was the result of sin and that the many religious people who were killed in the Holocaust had been sinners in a previous life." Peter Ochs, "Introduction to David Weiss Halivni's 'Prayer In The Shoah,'" *Judaism* 50, 199 (Summer 2001): 259.

88. David Weiss Halivni, "Prayer in the Shoah," *Judaism* 50, 199 (Summer 2001): 259. Inspired yes, definitive no. "If the Shoah were not the result of sin, then it would be difficult to explain why God was apparently indifferent in our days and chose not to intervene. Why, for example, did God intervene with the Egyptians (bringing them plagues, against the laws of nature); but not in Auschwitz? Why in Auschwitz did He lend human evil unlimited authority to destroy and be destroyed? Did God's promise to Jeremiah not obligate Him, as it were, to intervene every time Israel was in danger of annihilation and to prevent it? Why did He not prevent the worst annihilation in human history? There is no answer. . . . [Again], I certainly have no answer to this question and must be instructed by Isaiah's words, when he rebuked King Hezekiah and said, according to Talmudic tradition: 'Why do you concern yourself with the secrets of the Merciful One?' (*b'hadi kivshi d'rachmana lamah lakh?*)' "(Babylonian Talmud, *Berakhot* 10a)."

89. See note 89 supra.

90. 50 *Judaism* 3:268, Summer (2001): 269.

91. Leviticus 8:28 and 20:22 ("Do not defile yourselves in any of these ways . . . [lest] the land . . . vomit you out the way it vomited out the nation that came

before you"; And the fourth blessing of the *Rosh Hodesh Musaf Amidah: mipnei chatoteinu galinu me'artzenu*—"On account of our sins we were exiled from our land").

92. Emphasis added.

93. 50 *Judaism* 3:268, Summer (2001): 272.

94. 9:6: "You made the heavens, the highest heavens, the earth and everything that is on it."

95. 9:36: "Here we are today."

96. 9:28.

97. 50 *Judaism* 3:268, Summer (2001): 275.

98. Ibid., at 276.

99. Ibid., at 279. ("It is estimated that, in one week in Auschwitz, more Jews died through a terrible variety of deaths, than in all the previous persecutions put together. The quantitative difference is so great that the difference in quantity itself, becomes a difference in quality. We read in Lamentations, 'Little children begged for bread,' (4:4); in Auschwitz, Maidanek, and the other death camps, there were no little children. They were gassed immediately.")

100. Ibid., 283.

101. Ibid., 284.

102. Ibid., 285.

103. Ibid.

104. Moral freedom is obviously not a guarantee of political freedom. The Shoah may have occurred in the midst of some cosmic divine self-imposed incapacity, which did not ensure that human freedom would be used for good. The failure of civilization to resist Nazism in its earlier stages was due to the failure of civilization's moral and political will. In the late twentieth century, victory over Communism was an achievement of moral, not merely political, significance. Domestic social welfare policy is no less subject to this critical analysis. Human beings are not simply needy and dependent creatures, but agents in a moral universe whose freedom is necessary for ethics to be a possibility.

CHAPTER 2

Tikkun Olam: Perfecting God's World

Jonathan Sacks

The concept of *Tikkun Olam*—perfecting or repairing a fractured world[1]—poses the question of what role we are called on to play as Jews in the wider society of which we are a part. Central to an understanding of Jewish identity, the question is in some ways the most fascinating facing Jewish life today. To answer it, however, we must first set it in conceptual and historical context.

I begin with a fundamental distinction. There are questions in Jewish life to which the answer lies in a book: one of the great codes of Jewish law such as the *Shulhan Arukh,* or the responsa literature (rabbinic questions and answers, a genre that dates back to the early Middle Ages). Many issues in Jewish life—what is permitted and what is forbidden—undergo little change over the centuries. When we ask whether a certain kind of food is kosher, or whether it is permitted to perform a particular act on Shabbat, the answer will be the same whether the question was posed in 1897, 1997, or 2097. This is Judaism in its aspect of timelessness. I call it, using an ancient name, *Torat Kohanim* (the "priestly law")[2] because the priest in biblical times was the role model in Jewish history of the enduring nature of *kedushah,* sanctity, as a structure of eternity in the midst of time. The Talmudic sages themselves called Torah *chayei olam,* "eternal life," as opposed to worldly concerns (in which they even included intercessionary prayer) which they called *chayei sha'ah,* "temporal life." It is often this dimension we have in mind when we speak of Torah in the life of the Jew.

However, there is another kind of Torah, which has been somewhat in eclipse for two thousand years but which occupies no less significant a place in biblical sensibility. I call this (using a locution of Rabbi Zvi Hirsch Chajes[3]) *Torat Nevi'im*, "prophetic Torah." While the priest represents eternity, the prophet inhabits history. The prophets were the first human beings to see God in history, and to view time itself as having the shape of a narrative—a story with a beginning, middle, and end, or a journey with a starting point and a destination. Priests—and following them, the great masters of Halakhah, Jewish law—were charged with protecting the elements of Judaism that do not change. The prophets were attuned to a different wavelength, alert to the aspects of Jewish life that do change—in which today's challenge is not the same as yesterday's or tomorrow's. Because the religious life—the life of the covenantal people as it responds to circumstance—is an extended journey, the destination does not change, but we do. We move. Where we are today is not where we were yesterday. Each year, generation, and era poses a distinct challenge. Identifying this is the task of *Torat Nevi'im* and it needs a special kind of sensibility.

If one looks for guidance on *Tikkun Olam* in the Halakhic codes and responsa, one finds that it occupies a surprisingly limited space. One might infer that the idea is marginal to Jewish life. That would be an error. The explanation is rather to be found in the fact that it properly belongs not to *Torat Kohanim* but to *Torat Nevi'im*. One ought to look less in the literature of Halakhah and eternity, more in the literature of the Aggadah, part of whose function is to continue the prophetic vocation of seeing history through the eyes of faith. *Tikkun Olam* is a subject we will understand only if we use a historical sensibility. What is it to see the present as part of the Jewish journey through time?

To begin with Genesis, the book of our "beginnings"—what are its themes? Two predominate. The first is the promise of a land. The first words to Abraham from God are "Go away from your land, your birthplace and your father's house to the land that I will show you."[4] Time and again through Genesis the subject returns as a leitmotiv in the lives of Abraham, Isaac, and Jacob and their wives: the promise of the land, a journey to the land, exile from and return to the land. Simple though it sounds, it is fraught with unexpected obstacles. Abraham has to bargain to buy a burial place for Sarah.[5] Isaac has to contend with the Philistines over wells he has dug.[6] Jacob, seeking a small plot on which to pitch his tent, has to buy it for an inflated price.[7] Four books and several centuries later, Deuteronomy draws to a close with the Israelites still not having crossed the Jordan and taken possession of the land of promise. It ends with a poignant scene of Moses seeing the land from afar, having been told that he will not be permitted to set foot in it.[8] There is a Promised Land, but there is a distance between promise and land.

There is a second theme: the promise of children—again deferred, difficult, beset with problems and disappointed hopes. God tells Abraham,

"I will make you a great nation." Later He adds, "I will make your children as numerous as the dust of the earth." On a third occasion, He takes Abraham outside and tells him to look at the stars. "Can you count them? If you can, so will your children be numbered."[9] Yet the years pass, and no child comes. Sarah is infertile. So is Rebecca. So is Rachel. The patriarchs and matriarchs undergo a prolonged agony of waiting before their prayers are answered. Towards the end of his life, Moses says to the Israelites, "Not because you are many did God choose you, for you are the smallest of all people."[10] There is the promise of children, but this, too, is difficult, delayed. These are Genesis's overarching themes: God's gift of a land and children, set out at the beginning of Jewish time.

Turning now from the ancient to the immediate past: What have been the predominant themes of Jewish life in the past hundred years? The year 1997 was the 100th anniversary of the first Zionist Congress and the 50th anniversary of the birth of the State of Israel. The first Zionist Congress in Basel, Switzerland, was a remarkable occasion, the first time Jews had convened politically from all parts of Europe to attempt something widely believed by Jews and non-Jews alike to be impossible. That a nation that had suffered exile for 2,000 years would return home, that a people powerless for two millennia should regain political power—such things had never been done before. Most believed it could not be done. Theodore Herzl, determined to prove them wrong, said, "If you will it, it is no dream."

For a hundred generations, Jews prayed more in hope than in expectation for the ingathering of exiles. In the past century it has happened: Jews from 103 countries, speaking 82 languages, have come back to our ancestral home. Our ancestors prayed "Restore our judges as at first," meaning, let there be somewhere in the world where Jews are not ruled by others but rule themselves. Since 1948, that, too, has occurred. They prayed that God and His people would one day "return to Your city, Jerusalem," and since 1967 Jerusalem has been rebuilt and reunited. The sages said that even the simplest Jew saw at the Red Sea what the greatest of later prophets were not privileged to see. That, I believe, has been the good fortune—the *zekhut*—of those who lived through the first half century of the State of Israel. The first theme has been the land.

The second drama has been the demographic fate of the Diaspora. Having lost a third of our people in the Holocaust, we discovered—most powerfully in the 1990 National Jewish Population Survey—that we were losing our children under conditions of freedom, through outmarriage, assimilation, late marriage, low birthrates, and other forms of attrition. These tendencies evoke an ancient memory. According to the book of Exodus, when the Israelites left Egypt, *vachamushim alu bnei Yisrael me'eretz Mitzrayim.*'[11] The phrase is normally translated as "the Israelites left Egypt armed." Rashi, however, interprets *chamushim* to mean a fifth: "Only a fifth of the Israelites left Egypt."[12] The other 80 percent disappeared through assimilation; in some parts of the world it is happening again today.

Once again we find ourselves praying the Jewish prayer first uttered by Rachel: "Give me children, or else I die."[13] Only now are we in a position to appreciate the courage and foresight of that remarkable handful of Jewish leaders—figures like the late Lubavitcher Rebbe, Rabbi Joseph Soloveitchik, Rabbi Yaacov Kaminetsky, and Rabbi Aaron Kotler—who came to the United States and built Jewish day schools and yeshivot, knowing that to defend a country you need an army, but to defend a faith, you need schools. Just as the Zionist movement rebuilt the State of Israel, so these individuals rebuilt *Torat Yisrael*, the other "homeland"[14] of the Jewish people.

That, at the simplest level, is what it is to read history prophetically, covenantally—meaning, as part of the continuing drama between God and the Jewish people, a drama defined by certain key terms and recurring themes. Contemporary Jewish history marks a return to the great preoccupations of the patriarchal era: children and a land, Jewish continuity and Jewish sovereignty. These were not the overriding concerns for Jews during the eighteen centuries between the collapse of the Bar Kochba rebellion (135 C.E.) and the early twentieth century. One way (to be sure, not the only way), therefore, of understanding the present is that it has placed us back in the narrative of *Bereishit*, of our beginnings as a people. Following through the logic of this interpretation, the obvious question is: Were these all, or was there *another* theme in Genesis, a third promise?

There was. It is stated no less than five times in Genesis.[15] Its first occurrence comes in God's opening call: *venivrechu b'cha kol mishpechot ha'adamah,* "Through you all the families of the earth shall be blessed."[16] This phrase calls for serious theological reflection. The Torah, as any reader will testify, is a *particularistic* document. It is about the fate of one family, which becomes a tribe, then a collection of tribes, and then a nation. It is commanded to live differently from its neighbors, not adopting their culture, their customs, or their faith. Yet it is clear from the third promise that Israel's fate as a nation under the sovereignty of God is of more than Jewish concern and consequence. The covenantal family, so the Torah promises, will have an effect on others. Those who bless it will be blessed. Those who curse it will be cursed. "Through you shall all the families of the earth be blessed."

Thus, when Sarah dies and Abraham comes to the Hittites to buy land for her grave, they call him "a prince of God in our midst."[17] He is not one of them. His faith is not theirs. Yet they recognize something unmistakably spiritual in his bearing. His *kedushah*, as it were, is neither private nor unintelligible to his neighbors. Similarly, at the end of his life, Moses urges the Israelites to be careful in keeping Torah law "since this is your wisdom and understanding in the eyes of the nations. They will hear all these rules [*chukkim*] and say, 'This nation is surely a wise and understanding people.'"[18] Israel's message, Moses implies, is not for Israel alone.

These are intimations of what it might be—in the language of the second paragraph of the *Aleinu* prayer, *letakken olam bemalkhut Shaddai*, "to perfect the world under the sovereignty of God." The people of the covenant, despite the fact that they are called on to live apart ("not reckoned among the nations"), are nonetheless charged with being the people of whom it is said "all the nations of the world will realize that God's name is associated with you."[19] By transforming ourselves, we help to transform the world.

What theology might lie behind this idea? One of the most striking features of *Bereishit* is that, though its theme is the story of one people, it does not begin with that people. It begins instead with Adam and Eve, Cain and Abel, Noah and the Flood, Babel and its builders—archetypal narratives of humanity as a whole. On the face of it, this is a digression from the core narrative. As Rashi reminds us,[20] at least one of Judaism's ancient sages wondered why the Torah began with creation at all, since its purpose is not cosmology but axiology, not "How did the universe come into being?" but "How then shall we live?" The question is fundamental.

Broadly speaking, the pre-Abrahamic narratives divide into two: the period from the first humans to Noah, and the period from Noah to Abraham. Both begin with an affirmation that the human person is "in the image of God":

God created man in His image; in the image of God He created him; male and female He created them. (Genesis 1:26)

He who sheds the blood of man shall by man have his blood shed, for God made man in His own image. (Genesis 9:6)

The similarity between these two verses is obvious. So, too, is the difference. The first is *ontological*, the second *covenantal*. The first tells us what we are, the second what we are called on to do and not to do. Both are universal. They have nothing to do with the particular covenant with Abraham and his descendants. They are about mankind as such, and their presence as part of the prologue to the history of Israel is of immense significance. *To be a Jew is to participate in the universal project of mankind* as well as in the particular covenants of our history.

Equally significant is the fact that the two narratives, from Adam to Noah and from Noah to Babel, are *stories of failure*. The first is a set of variations on the theme of nemesis. Adam and Eve sin, Cain murders, and by the time of Noah the world is "filled with violence." Man has become less than man. That is the first way we can fail to live "in the image of God."

The second is a story of hubris. Thanks to archeology and ancient history, we know in considerable detail what was at stake in what Eric Voegelin[21] calls the "cosmological" civilizations symbolized by Babel. The first city-states of Mesopotamia were culturally mythological and socially hierarchical. The birth of agriculture in the fertile river valleys of the ancient world meant that, for the first time, the production of economic surpluses allowed some to accumulate great power over others. There was a division of society into rulers and ruled. Not only was this an empirical fact, but it was seen as a metaphysical destiny. The hierarchy on earth mirrored the hierarchy in the heavens. That is one of the basic functions of myth (Plato offered his own version in *The Republic*—people were divided into men of gold, silver, and bronze), and it justified Karl Marx's famous critique of religion as the canonization of social inequality and the neutralization of discontent, the "opium of the people." The sin of Babel was born when men decided to make the gods in their image instead of allowing God to remake us in His. The Torah puts it simply. The builders on the plain of Shinar sought to reach heaven, disregarding that "the heavens are the heavens of the Lord; the earth He gave to the children of mankind." Babel is what happens when man aspires to be more than man, forgetting that we are "the image" of God, not God Himself.

Judaism—beginning with the call to Abraham—is born in the aftermath of failure. What is the significance of this fact? The most compelling interpretation is this: There are two ways of teaching morality. The first is by universal rules. The second is by particular examples. These are very different enterprises. It is one thing to learn a series of general imperatives—"Thou shalt not murder," "Thou shalt endeavor to create justice," and so on. It is something else to adopt a role model and see how he or she lives. The first is more general, but the second is more vivid, existential, compelling. A role model inspires, teaches, guides; above all, he or she shows us how to translate the universal into the particularities of time and place. Since the dawn of civilization, people have told stories, but it took Tolstoy in *War and Peace* to show us how to capture the interactions between individuals and the fate of nations in the form of a novel. All cultures make music, but it took Beethoven, in the string quartets he wrote at the end of his life, to show us how music might reach to the very depths of spirituality. Without living examples, general rules are mere abstractions. They do not show us enacted possibilities.

That is what happens in the fateful move from Babel to Abraham. The covenant with Noah (the universal set of rules) remains in place, but now there will be a person, a family, ultimately a nation, who will serve as a living example of what it is to act, form relationships, and ultimately create a society, in the conscious, constant presence of God. The children of Israel would be called on to be the particular exemplifications of a universal truth—that we are God's image on earth, the one species in whom He has vested His highest hope, that in and through our humanity we might find a way back to His divinity. "You are My witnesses,"[22] says God to Israel through Isaiah. You are the people whom I have called on to live in such a way that, through your individual lives and collective history, people will see the presence of God and know that I exist, not only in the echoing infinities of space but in the human heart and in what R. Aharon Lichtenstein memorably called "societal beatitude."

The covenant with Noah is not enough. Babel proved that, as have tyrannical empires ever since. Humanity needs role models. That is what God asked of Abraham's children when He gathered them together at the foot of Mount Sinai and asked them to become "a kingdom of priests and a holy nation."[23] Every religion has priests; Judaism was the first to make the radical demand that every person should consider him- or herself a priest (i.e., one in unmediated relationship with the Divine). Every religion has holy individuals, places, and times; Judaism was the first to insist that every individual, place, and time is to be sanctified, made holy. Judaism is the particular embodiment of universal truths, the living witness to God whose breath we breathe, whose image we are.

If so, we can say something fundamental about the Jewish vocation. We were the people who were born in slavery to teach humanity the meaning of freedom. We were the people who suffered homelessness to teach mankind the need for a people to have a home. Our ancestors were the quintessential strangers to teach the world that "Thou shall not oppress the stranger."[24] Jews were the people who walked through the valley of the shadow of death to teach humanity the sanctity of life. They became the people who were always small but yet survived to teach that a nation endures "not by might nor by strength but by My spirit, says God."[25] Most significantly, we were the people who were always different, to teach humanity the dignity of difference.

Paul Johnson, a Catholic, has written one of the great histories of the Jews and Judaism. In it, he wrote, "One way of summing up four thousand years of Jewish history is to ask ourselves what would have happened to the human race" had no Jewish people come into being. "Certainly, the world without the Jews would have been a radically different place. Humanity might have eventually stumbled upon all the great Jewish insights. But we cannot be sure. All the great conceptual discoveries of the intellect seem obvious and inescapable once they are revealed, but it requires a special genius to formulate them for the first time. The Jews had this gift. To them we owe the idea of equality before the law, both divine and human; of the sanctity of life and the dignity of the human person; of the individual conscience and so of personal redemption; of the collective conscience and so of social responsibility; of peace as an abstract ideal, and love as the foundation of justice, and many other items that constitute the basic moral furniture of the human mind. Without the Jews it might have been a much emptier place."[26] I find that both moving and profound. Sometimes non-Jews understand us better than we understand ourselves. Our task is *letakken olam bemalkhut Shaddai*, "to perfect the world under the sovereignty of God," by the lives we lead, the acts we do, the role models we become.

Why, then, does the Halakhic literature say so little about this? The answer is straightforward. For 2,000 years, it had no practical relevance. Jews were dispersed, scattered, exiled, disempowered. Max Weber called them a "pariah people." Christians spoke of the wandering Jew, the "old" Israel, displaced, superseded, and rejected by God. Islam treated Jews as *dhimmis*, second-class citizens, the people who had falsified scripture by writing Isaac in place of Ishmael. "Ought," say the philosophers, "implies Can." Or, as Halakhah puts it, *Anus Rachmana patrei*, God exempts those who are powerless to act. The idea that Jews might contribute to the human project was rejected a priori by those among whom they lived. Jews were to be treated as means, not ends; useful but without dignity or civil rights. *Tikkun olam*, under these circumstances, was more theoretical than real, an aspiration, not an obligation that could be acted on.

Yet one fact shines through this otherwise depressing history. Jews never abandoned the idea. *Tikkun olam* survived in a real if residual sense. In the mystical literature, for example, we find cosmologies in which, through keeping the mitzvot, we mysteriously mend a fractured world.[27] In the second paragraph of the *Aleinu* prayer, it becomes the hope that God will do what we cannot. In the Talmud, *tikkun olam* is translated into the limited task of sustaining social order.[28] Each of these represents a determination to keep the concept alive under the highly circumscribed room for action available to Jews under conditions of exile and displacement.

The greatest trauma occurred in the nineteenth century. European Enlightenment and emancipation held out an extraordinary promise to Jews: civil equality in the new secular nation-state. That offer, however, came with a tacit condition: that Jews ceased to be different, distinctive; that, in effect, they ceased to be Jews. This was an appalling dilemma, and we should be generous in our understanding of those Jews who believed that it was possible to square the circle, to be universalists without being particularists, to be Jewish while at the same time editing out of Judaism the very beliefs, laws, and prayers that made Jews what they were. It was then that phrases like "the Jewish mission," "a light to the nations," and later *tikkun olam*, itself, became code words for the abandonment of everything that set Jews apart and gave them their paradigmatic character.

In Michael Wyschogrod's pointed words, "ethics" became "the Judaism of the assimilated."[29] The result was that *tikkun olam* and its cognate concepts became anathema to those committed to Halakhah. That was, and still is, a tragedy. Understandable and justified in its time, that attitude has now become dysfunctional.

Today, for the first time in two thousand years, we have in the State of Israel the opportunity to construct a macrosociety on the basis of Judaic principle. In the pluralistic liberal democracies of the West, we have both a vote and a voice. When we speak, we are heard. When we teach, we are heeded. We are able to fulfill the great command of *Kiddush Ha-Shem* not by dying, but by living, for the sake of God. To turn our back on these challenges would be a massive failure of *Torat Nevi'im*, the prophetic imagination.

Having spoken about examples, let me give some. I think, in this context, of the late Professor David Baum, a deeply religious Jew and Britain's leading pediatrician. Having developed a number of inventions to reduce infant mortality, he became president of the Royal College of Pediatrics and Child Health, and then went to Brazil, Thailand, and Ethiopia to help them develop their child-care facilities. He did the same in Moscow and became a close friend of Mikhail Gorbachev's. His final project—having visited the Balkans and seen the casualties of war—was to build a pediatric center in Kosovo. It was while raising money for this on a sponsored bicycle ride that he suffered the heart attack from which he died at the young age of fifty-nine. David was a religious Zionist, and though he lived in Bristol, he was buried, at his request, in Rosh Pinah. The last project he was able to complete was a child-care center in Gaza. His Zionism, he said, meant ensuring that Palestinian children had access to the same level of medical care that Israeli children did. His life was a *Kiddush Ha-Shem*.

Lord (Robert) Winston, Britain's leading fertility specialist, is another role model. A committed Orthodox Jew, he has built a state-of-the-art facility for genetic and stem cell research in the Hammersmith Hospital, London. On the shelves of his office, between the learned journals on genetic engineering, are volumes of Torah commentary. As well as being a pioneer in the field, he is Britain's best-known television doctor, having produced many widely seen and award-winning documentaries on human biology. In one of these programs, on the brain, he ended by turning to the camera and saying, "Until now I have spoken as a scientist. But there is one thing I cannot explain as a scientist, namely consciousness. For this I need an older word. I call it the soul." At that point, the scene shifts to a scene of Robert Winston wearing a yarmulke and reading from a Torah scroll. That footage, seen by tens of millions of people around the world, was an act of great courage. It is not easy, in the current environment, for a scientist to make a public declaration of religious faith, and to do so as a Jew. That, too, was a *Kiddush ha-Shem*.

The late Sue Burns suffered from a rare spinal condition, which meant that she was bedridden for life, unable even to sit up in a wheelchair. As her disability deepened, it would have been easy for her to retreat into self-pity or despair. Instead, she decided to use her suffering to help others. She had phones and a computer installed by her bedside and set up a helpline for others similarly handicapped. She became their support and companion. She was the one they turned to for advice of all kinds. When she was honored by the queen, she became the first person to be carried into Buckingham Palace on a hospital bed to receive her award. Typically, she said that it was not for her; she was merely receiving the honor on behalf of all handicapped people. Despite her almost total disability, I never saw her without a smile, even when she told me she knew she was about to die. She, too, was a *Kiddush ha-Shem*.

One could multiply examples almost indefinitely, but I hope the general point is clear. Whether the operative rubric is *darkhei shalom,* or *gemillat chassadim,* or *vehalakhta biderachav,* or *Kiddush ha-Shem* or *tikkun olam,* the principle remains what it was in the first words spoken by God to Abraham: "through you shall all the families of the earth be blessed."

Three points remain to be emphasized. The first is that I am proposing a paradigm shift in our understanding of particularism and universalism. The belief that these constituted a dichotomy, an either/or, was one of the most disastrous errors of the nineteenth century. *Either* one is a universalist, in which case you abandon kashruth, Shabbat, *teharat ha'mishpachah* (family purity), and the entire code of *kedushah* (the classic expression was the 1885 Pittsburgh Platform: "We hold that all such Mosaic and rabbinical laws as regulate diet, priestly purity, and dress, originated in ages and under the influence of ideas altogether foreign to our present mental and spiritual state"), *or* one is a particularist and keeps to a minimum all contacts with the outside world.

Assimilation or segregation—that was the choice as then framed; and it was an error from beginning to end. *Particularism is the Jewish form of universalism*—that has been my argument. It is only by being different that we have something different to contribute to society. It is when we are true to our heritage, and ourselves, that we become a blessing to others. *By being what we uniquely are, we give what only we can give.* To quote Paul Johnson again:

The Jews were not just innovators. They were also exemplars and epitomizers of the human condition. They seemed to present all of the inescapable dilemmas of man in a heightened and clarified form. They were the quintessential "strangers and sojourners." But are we not all such on this planet, of which we each possess a mere leasehold of threescore and ten? The Jews were the emblem of homeless and vulnerable humanity. But is not the whole earth no more than a temporary transit-camp? . . . It seems to be the role of the Jews to focus and dramatize these common experiences of mankind, and to turn their particular fate into a universal moral.[30]

We become universal by being faithful to our particularity. Only if we preserve the sanctity of the family can we speak authoritatively about the family. Only if we keep Shabbat do we have something original to say about work, rest, and the limits of human striving. Only by studying Torah do we become role models of intellectual growth and education as the key to human dignity (I lose count of the number of times I have been asked by non-Jews to address educational conferences and think tanks). The idea that we might have something to contribute to society by becoming the same as everyone else—going with the flow, swimming with the tide, embracing every politically correct fashion as if it were the latest version of iconoclasm instead of the slavish conformism it actually is—is an error to which Jews are peculiarly prone, but it is an error unworthy of reflective minds. Reread Tom Wolfe's classic essay, "Radical Chic," to be cured of it forever.

Second, there is no Halakhah of *tikkun olam*, and it is a mistake to look for one. Halakhah is about aspects of life that do not change. The challenge of *tikkun olam*—of knowing which issues to address, which strategic interventions to make—calls for a prophetic sensibility, meaning, the ability to hear, within God's word for all time, the particular resonance for *this* time. At best, one can articulate general principles. (The classic example is the opening two chapters of Rambam's *Hilkhot De'ot*. Seeking to give structure to the unsystematic body of Jewish ethics, the Rambam does something remarkable. He imports into Judaism a virtue-ethic, something not hitherto found in the literature—see *Teshuvot R. Avraham ben ha-Rambam*, 63. By this means he is able to lay the foundation for a generalized Jewish account of ethical character as opposed to a set of proverbs and maxims.) Developing a prophetic sensibility is the command of the hour for Jewish thinkers and Jewish thought.

Third, and this I cannot emphasize sufficiently, a Jewish involvement in the public square is not a politics of *Jewish interests;* it is a politics of *Judaic principle*. Jews have always defended Jewish interests. That was the basis of *shtadlanut* politics in the Middle Ages, and remains the work of Jewish organizations today—fighting anti-Semitism, defending the cause of Israel, promoting Jewish rights, and so on. This is right, proper, and necessary, but certainly not distinctive. Every ethnic and religious group does likewise and would be ill advised not to. I have been talking about something else: about *Judaism as the sustained countervoice in the conversation of mankind;* the voice of the individual in an age of collectivism, of the community in an era of radical individualism, of education in times of mass illiteracy, of the moral limits of power against totalitarian regimes, of the objective constraints of morality in an age of the "sovereign self," of responsibilities when society embraces a culture of rights, of free will against genetic determinism, altruism against the "selfish gene," the irreplaceability of the human person against the temptations of reproductive cloning, and so on through a list whose items cannot be predicted, merely recognized when they appear.

Will this make a difference? Will we win the argument? Will we "perfect the world"? The short answer is: We have no way of knowing. Faith, *emunah*, is not certainty. It is the courage to live with uncertainty, the courage of which Jeremiah spoke when he said, "I remember the devotion of your youth, how as a bride you loved Me and followed me through the desert, through an unsown land."[31] For me, the principle of *aron nosei et nos'av* is sufficient: "the ark carried its carriers."[32] Lifting others, we lift ourselves. The challenges are real, immediate, and demanding. Not for two thousand years have we had the chance to shape a society under conditions of sovereignty. Rarely before have we had the chance to stand as free and equal citizens and be listened to, if not with uncritical acceptance, then at least with a genuinely attentive ear. In the years in which, as Chief Rabbi, I have been involved in public life, I have come to two conclusions: *non-Jews respect Jews who respect Judaism. Non-Jews are embarrassed by Jews who are embarrassed by Judaism.* Let us carry the dignity of difference with pride.

It is fair to say that Jewish leadership in our time has not yet risen adequately to the challenge. Either it has turned inward, focusing on strengthening Jewish identity, or it has been relatively vacuous, embracing an amorphous "social justice" with little Judaic content and still less intellectual rigor. Here and there, there have been exceptions; may their number increase. But how will history judge us if, like Jonah asked to carry a message to Nineveh, we turn and run away, preferring the security of disengagement and the quiet life of separatism, spared of all ethical challenges because, in our heart of hearts, we doubt our capacity to meet them?

When Rabbi Tarfon said, "It is not for you to complete the work,"[33] he meant, I think, that the concept of *tikkun olam* is like navigating a ship by the stars. A sailor does not aim to reach them; he has his thoughts on an earthbound destination. But turning his eyes heavenward allows him to chart a route. So it is with "perfecting the world." This side of messianic time, we will not get there. There is a limit to how straight we can make the "crooked timber of humanity." But it remains a navigational aid, the template of our ideals. The greatness of Judaism is that, knowing all we do of suffering, persecution, violence, injustice, and the almost limitless capacity of human beings to commit evil in the name of high ideals, we never gave up hope; never gave up trying to make the world more just, less arbitrary and cruel, one act at a time, one day at a time, knowing that we will not complete the work but neither are we free to abdicate from it.

Tikkun olam, that vast and majestic aspiration, in the end comes down to this: that each of us, by the integrity with which we conduct our business or professional lives, the grace and gentleness we bring to our relationships, the beauty that radiates from our homes, the way we use words to heal, not harm, bears witness to the Divine presence, the *shekhinah*, that exists wherever we make space for it, flooding this transitory life with momentary radiance and giving us as much of an intimation as we will see of a world where heaven and the human spirit touch. A fragment of perfection, no more, but it is enough to win a small victory for the hope that God will one day complete what we began.

NOTES

1. This chapter was first delivered as an address to the Orthodox Union West Coast Convention, Los Angeles, December 1997/Kislev 5758. It has been extensively rewritten for publication, June 2002/Tammuz 5762.

2. This was the original rabbinic name for the book of Leviticus.

3. Rabbi Zvi Hirsch Chajes, *"Torat Nevi'im,"* in *Kol Sifre Maharatz Chajes* (Jerusalem: Divrei Hachamim, 1958), 1:1–136.

4. Genesis 12:2.

5. Genesis 23.

6. Genesis 26.

7. Genesis 33:19.

8. Deuteronomy 32:49–51.

9. Genesis 12:2, 13:16, 15:5.

10. Deuteronomy 7:7.

11. Exodus 13:8.

12. Rashi ad loc.

13. Genesis 30:1.

14. The metaphor—"the Torah is the portable homeland of the Jew"—was coined by Heinrich Heine.

15. Genesis 12:3, 18:18, 22:18, 26:4, 28:14.

16. Genesis 12:3.

17. Genesis 23:6.

18. Deuteronomy 4:6.

19. Deuteronomy 28:10.

20. Commentary to Genesis 1:1.

21. Eric Voegelin, *Order and History,* vol. 1, *Israel and Revelation* (Columbia, MO: University of Missouri Press, 1956).

22. Isaiah 43:10, 12.

23. Exodus 19:6.

24. Exodus 22:20, 23:9.

25. Zechariah 4:6.

26. Paul Johnson, *A History of the Jews* (London: Weidenfeld and Nicolson, 1987), 585.

27. See Gershom Scholem, *Major Trends in Jewish Mysticism* (London: Thames and Hudson, 1955), 244–86, for an introduction to the concept of *Tikkun* in the mystic school of R. Isaac Luria.

28. Babylonian Talmud, *Gittin*, 32 et seq.

29. Michael Wyschogrod, *The Body of Faith* (Minneapolis: Seabury Press, 1983), 181.

30. *A History of the Jews*, 586.

31. Jeremiah 2:2.

32. Tosefta, *Sotah* 8:6.

33. Mishnah, *Avot* 2:21.

CHAPTER 3

Sexual Responsibility and Jewish Law

David Novak

JEWS, JUDAISM, AND PUBLIC POLICY

Before advocating what a Jewish public policy stand should be on any specific issue, one should have some clear understanding of why there should be a Jewish public policy stand at all in a non-Jewish, secular society like the United States or Canada. By "public policy," I mean what a particular group, like the Jews, itself proposes or endorses for the larger secular society in which it is a full and active participant. By a "secular society," I mean a society that does not look to any singular revelation of God in history to be its founding event, thus allowing members of any or no religious tradition to be equal participants in its human founding. Without serious consideration of this question, a "Jewish" stand on any public policy issue in this secular society is likely to be ineffective insofar as its justification has not been rationally argued in public discourse. Without such a general rational justification, the initial reaction of the society at large, to whom such a Jewish public stand on any specific issue, like sexual responsibility, is being addressed, is very likely to be: "Who are the Jews to be telling *us* what *they* think *we* should do?" Indeed, lack of such clear understanding, or at least clear explication, of this prior, political question has prevented some Christian groups (who have far more experience than the Jews in taking such stands on public policy issues) from being as politically persuasive as they might have been. We Jews, who are relative newcomers to the business of advocating a stand on public policy issues in a secular society, should take appropriate heed.

A Jewish public policy stand should be formulated according to three criteria: (1) ethical, (2) philosophical, and (3) political. It is also important that this be the order of the process of formulation. Yet, unfortunately, too much Jewish public policy advocacy in the United States and Canada is formulated in the reverse order; that is, political tactics are first proposed, then some sort of philosophical argument is thought up as a rationalization for these tactics, and some sort of allusion to the Jewish normative tradition—Jewish ethics—is added on finally, if at all. However, it is important that the Jewish ethical argument come first.

We Jews should be sure that what we plan to propose is either specifically mandated by the Jewish normative tradition (Halakhah) or is, at least, not in violation of it and, also, guided by some of the more general principles (what some like to call "values") that inform and inspire Jewish law (Torah in the broadest sense). In other words, we should know why what we could propose for society at large is minimally what we should propose to ourselves—even if we could not propose this to society at large because it would not be interested in what we had to say to it on a specific issue or any issue at all. (Fortunately today, because of greater cultural pluralism, society at large does seem to be interested in what Jews can propose to it and for it.[1]) Second, we Jews should develop a philosophical argument as the rational ground for what we are proposing to the human beings who comprise this society or any society, that is, by criteria that could be universal. At this level, the argument is more intellectual than strictly political. Third, we Jews should develop a political strategy for implementing what we think is a moral stand for society in general and our society in particular. As we shall see later, such a political strategy is never a full implementation of the larger philosophical/moral argument. That is, we can say more to ourselves ethically than we can say to the larger culture philosophically, and we can say more philosophically to the culture than we can say to the larger society politically or legally. Also, the political argument should be conducted internally on the basis of what is good for the Jews; externally on the basis of what is good for our society at large. I shall try to show why these two political criteria, the one internal (Jewish) and the other external (secular) should always be consistent with each other.

The specific public policy I would like to address here is one that is facing our society, politically, legally, culturally, and ethically/religiously. The issue is same-sex marriage. What should a Jewish public policy position be on this issue? How should this position be argued to ourselves? How should it be argued to others?

ETHICAL CRITERIA

I must stipulate at the outset that at this primary level of Jewish discourse I can only attempt to speak to and for those Jews who believe the

Torah to be God's normative revelation to the Jewish people at Mount Sinai and to be continually accepted by them thereafter. I call those Jews "traditional." To nontraditional Jews, be they religious or secular, I can only address the same type of philosophical arguments I would address to morally earnest gentiles in the larger multicultural context. Only the political argument I propose later in this chapter could be addressed to nontraditional Jews as Jews on the basis of Jewish self-interest.

Any permission of marriage between members of the same sex—two men or two women—presupposes that homoerotic acts are permitted by Judaism. The fact is, though, that they are prohibited without controversy in the normative Jewish tradition: very explicitly between men, less explicitly but ultimately just as definitively between women.[2] I say "homoerotic acts" rather than "homosexuality" because homoerotic acts are freely chosen by human persons whereas homosexuality might very well be a human affection that is not freely chosen by those who experience homosexual desire constantly and often exclusively. It would seem that those homosexuals whose affection interferes with their moral stance should feel free enough to seek out the type of psychotherapy that regards homosexuality to be an emotional disorder and that, maximally, attempts to redirect heretofore homosexual desire, or a type of psychotherapy that, minimally, attempts to enable homosexuals to refrain from acting on this desire and for them to maintain a fair amount of emotional equilibrium in the process. Without a commitment to therapeutic intervention by both patient and therapist, there is little chance that anyone having strong homosexual desire could resist engaging in homoerotic acts. Judaism can prohibit explicit acts; it can only recommend that problematic desires be treated.

Nevertheless, there is a movement today, being fostered by homosexual advocates, that wants to delegitimatize, professionally or even legally, those psychotherapies that attempt to curtail homoerotic behavior by reorienting homosexual desire. But any such movement denies the moral freedom of those persons who desire to change their personal habits that interfere with their overall intention of a moral way of life. Such therapies are immoral only when they practice deceit on their patients by exaggerating the probability of their success in achieving the desired result. Because psychotherapy is something that most Jews readily seek out for their emotional problems, and because a fair percentage of psychotherapists have always been Jews, it behooves the Jewish community to support the right of those psychotherapists committed to treating homosexuals who desire sexual reorientation to do so without fear of professional stigmatization. For Jewish homosexuals committed to sexual reorientation, and for Jewish psychotherapists committed to helping them, this whole enterprise can be argued politically on grounds of religious liberty.

Since all homoerotic acts are prohibited, Jewish tradition could certainly not in any way regard a union between two (or perhaps more) men or two (or perhaps more) women to be a marriage, the sacred covenant (*kiddushin*) that is restricted to a man and a woman, indeed a Jewish man and a Jewish woman, indeed certain Jewish men and certain Jewish women. This is what Judaism requires of Jews among ourselves. Indeed, the prohibition of practicing sexually immoral acts (homoerotic acts, along with incestuous, adulterous, and bestial acts) is so grave that it admits of no dispensations, even if one's life is at stake. In this gravity, it is joined by the prohibitions of murder and idolatry.[3] This prohibition, then, lies at the core of what it means to be commanded by God, on which all authentic Judaism stands or falls.

The first question any Jew should ask himself or herself is not "What does the Jewish religion say about *X*?" but, rather, "What does *our* holy Torah require *us* to do in situation *X*?" In other words, "What does *my* God and the God of *my* Jewish ancestors demand of *me* here and now?" The former question could be asked by anyone; the latter question, however, could only be asked by a Jew. There can be and there always have been disputes about just *what* is commanded in any specific situation, but there can be no dispute among traditional Jews *that* the Torah does require something to be done in any significant human situation; that is, there can be no dispute that God has indeed spoken to us forever in His commandments about everything.[4] Without that sense of divine commandment (mitzvah), I do not see how any public proposal can claim to be coherently—that is, traditionally—Jewish.

PHILOSOPHICAL CRITERIA

Unlike most of its other prohibitions, indeed most of its sexual prohibitions, the Jewish tradition presents the prohibition of homosexuality to be universal. This comes out in the rabbinic explication of the biblical verse that introduces us to human sexuality in the story of the first man and the first woman (Adam and Eve): "A man shall leave his father and his mother and he shall cleave to his wife so that they become one flesh" (Genesis 2:24). The Talmud explicates this verse to be the natural sexual claims human persons ought to rightfully make on each other.

Rabbi Akiva says that "his father" means *his father's wife;* "his mother" means *his mother literally;* "he shall cleave" means *but not with a male;* "to his wife" means *but not with someone else's wife;* "so that they shall become one flesh" means *with whom one can become one flesh,* thus excluding various kinds of animals with which one cannot "become one flesh."[5]

The use of the male "he" and "his" does not limit these prohibitions to men. They just as much apply to women. Accordingly, we can extend these prohibitions to a woman having sex with *her mother's husband*, and to a woman having sex with *another woman*, and a woman having sex *with an animal*.[6] Finally, since sex with these persons is prohibited, and since sex is a necessary part of marriage (thus in many legal systems, nonconsummation of a marriage is grounds for annulment), it stands to reason that this confines marriage to nonincestuous, nonadulterous, male-female unions.[7] In rabbinic jurisprudence, this overall prohibition (*gillui arayot*) is one of the *seven Noahide laws* that are seen to be binding on all humankind.[8] The Noahide commandment to every society to adjudicate disputes involving these universal laws (like the prohibitions of murder and robbery) would require society to proscribe as best it can sexually immoral acts. Nevertheless, whereas it is often impossible for society to control illicit, private liaisons, it is surely possible for society to refrain from giving any kind of public approval to such illicit unions. That means, minimally, not recognizing them as marriages and not extending to them the benefits society does accord to legitimate marriages.

The moral prohibition of homoerotic acts cannot be understood unless it is seen together with its interrelated prohibitions of incest, adultery, and bestiality. Taken together, all of these prohibitions seem to presuppose the positive injunction to "be fruitful and multiply" (Genesis 9:1), namely, that humans ought to live in families and confine their sexual activity to prescribed roles in that domestic context.[9] This is considered to be of such import to essential human life in the world that all sexual acts are to be conducted for the sake of the survival and flourishing of the family. Sexual acts that are unjustified by familial claims are considered to be so contrary to human well-being that they are proscribed. Thus, bestiality seems to be proscribed because it violates the distinctly human limits on the family (even though many higher animals themselves live in some sort of family-like groups). Thus, adultery seems to be proscribed because it violates the integrity of the marriage bond, which is the very foundation of the family. Thus, incest seems to be proscribed because it violates the distinct roles of parents and children and siblings. And, thus, homosexuality seems to be proscribed because it violates the differentiation of sexual roles within the family and, especially, because it denies the fundamental purpose of sexuality, which is procreation and the continuing bond between the female parent/mother and the male parent/father thereafter.[10]

Furthermore, human sexual drives are so powerful, so violent, that they become dangerous to human well-being unless structured by the family, whose identity is rooted in procreation. It seems that anyone who regards sexuality to be so inherently benign that it can simply structure itself may not have experienced, or may have suppressed, both the intense pleasure and the intense pain of human sexuality in all its uncanniness.[11] That is why there is a fundamental human need for sexual responsibility, which for Judaism and many other traditions, means being *responsive* to the family's moral claim to be the exclusive domain for licit sexual acts, and only for those sexual relationships that enhance familial integrity.[12]

This is an abstract, as it were, of the much larger rational argument that needs be made in order to more fully understand the rationale behind the prohibition of homoerotic acts, which is a prohibition many other cultures besides Judaism (and Christianity) have regarded as *natural* and *rational* in that *nature* is the rationally known structure of existence, and *reason* is the way this structure shows itself to humans (as *Homo sapiens*) and makes claims on them.[13] Only a much larger argument could deal with the many counterexamples and logical problems the advocates of the morality of homoerotic acts have often raised in public discourse.[14] Nevertheless, since the argument is hardly new or parochial, one can assume that it can be made with at least a predictable plausibility.

The question now is to what extent and to what effect traditional Jews and other advocates of what some like to call "family values" can make a public argument against the moral acceptability of homoerotic acts and the moral acceptability of "gayness," which is the public advocacy of homosexuality as an ideology. So, the question as regards the Noahide prohibition of sexual immorality, homosexuality more specifically, is to what extent and to what effect traditional Jews can advocate legal restraints on its practice in our present-day society.

POLITICAL CRITERIA

If the consumption of alcoholic beverages proved to be ineffective during national Prohibition in the United States (1920–33), primarily because most people regarded such a prohibition to be an unwarranted invasion of their privacy, then one can see why the legal prohibition of sexual acts between consenting adults, who are the only cogent subjects of privacy, is bound to fail, even where it still survives de jure. (Most people find sex, whatever their preference, more necessary for their well-being than drinking. And, most people engage in sex more privately than they drink or use narcotics.) The best example of this is the growing tendency of North American jurisdictions to ignore the legal prohibition and penalization of prostitution. (In my city, Toronto, so-called Escort Services openly advertise, including advertisement of exactly what "services" the consenting "escorts" are offering their consenting "clients.")

Some moralists and jurists can cogently argue whether there is a "right to privacy" in principle that is anything more than a conditional public entitlement. After all, even consenting adults have to originally solicit the consent of other consenting adults in public. In other words, the realm of privacy presupposes the public realm in a way that the public realm certainly does not presuppose the realm of privacy.[15] The social and cultural fact, however, is that the vast majority of citizens in democracies are convinced that the right to privacy is original and, hence, irrevocable. Most citizens think of the privacy of their bodies, particularly their genitals, as being the primary locus of this original, unconditional, right to privacy. Indeed, the mistake of many political conservatives in our society is to assume that people's desire for other things is greater than their desire for other bodies; that is, they underestimate lust and overestimate greed. In other words, people are more concerned about governmental interference with what goes on in their beds than they are concerned with what goes on in their businesses. Hence, based on both moral principle and political prudence, I think it is folly for traditional Jews or traditional Christians or traditional whatever to argue for the legal penalization of homoerotic acts.

Because of the unambiguous stance of the Jewish tradition against the practice of homoerotic acts by anyone, and because this stance can be presented in a rational argument, it is clear that Jews have the resources, both ethical (or theological) and philosophical, to argue against homosexuality as an ideology based on public criteria of the common good. Now, this does not mean that traditional Jews need initiate debates with ideological homosexuals—gays—or their heterosexual supporters. As discourse, such debates are too frequently hollow and inevitably descend to the level of personal insult and demonization of opponents by one side or the other or both (epithets like "faggot" or "dyke" or "homophobe" often come to be uttered or strongly implied). They are best avoided whenever possible.[16] Nevertheless, the latest project of the gay movement has been to petition for the right of same-sex couples to marry under civil law. That is not only asking society not to penalize—that is, to permit—homoerotic acts in private, but it is asking society to give its official approval by designating as a *marriage* the union of persons who have made homoerotic acts the foundation of their relationship. By this designation, society would be conferring on same-sex couples the privileges it confers on heterosexual couples who choose to officially marry. But both society in general and the Jewish community in particular have an important stake in what is now called "traditional" marriage.

By traditional Jewish criteria, the official, public sanction of same-sex/homoerotic unions is far worse than simply ignoring homoerotic acts done in private by consenting adults. An example of this greater disapproval, if not often active opposition, is found in the Talmud. Despite the almost unanimous rabbinic disapproval of the moral standards of the Roman rulers of Palestine in the first centuries of the Common Era, the following begrudging approval of one official Roman policy was made by Ulla, a Palestinian sage who lived in Babylonia: "They do not write a marriage contract (*ketubah*) for males."[17] (Lest it be thought lesbianism is exempt, a conceptually parallel rabbinic text criticizes the society destroyed by the Flood in the time of Noah because "they wrote marriage documents—

gomasiyot—for males and for females."[18]) Nevertheless, the question is: How does a traditional Jew argue against same-sex marriage in a society like that of the United States or Canada, where, unlike ancient Rome, same-sex marriage has a real chance of becoming the norm?

At this point one must distinguish between a moral argument and a political argument in the contemporary situation. Thus, a moral argument against same-sex marriage would argue that homosexuality is an immoral way of life that, maximally, the state should outlaw and, minimally, not privilege by permitting homosexual couples to officially marry. However, as we have already seen, there is not enough of a moral consensus about the immorality of homoerotic acts per se so that one could launch an argument for their legal prohibition. The premise of any such argument is so evenly disputed, though, that any such argument would not be able to move effectively to any publicly acceptable, practical conclusion. It would be a rhetorical dead end. That type of moral argument stands a better chance of some success, or at least not certain defeat, when conducted in more secluded intellectual or religious enclaves. Nevertheless, a political argument against same-sex marriage does not need any agreement on the immorality of homoerotic acts to be its premise. That is because a political argument need not pose its essential question to be about homosexuality as a way of life; instead, its essential question is: What is the primary interest of the secular state in officially sanctioning the institution of marriage at all? Heretofore the state has shown an interest in marriage as a public institution limited to opposite-sex unions. Could that interest be extended coherently to marriage as an institution that included same-sex unions? That requires a better understanding of what the public interest in marriage altogether truly is. That also requires a better understanding of whether marriage is an institution created by the state or one that the state has inherited from sources prior to its founding.

It would seem that the only cogent interest the state can have in the institution of marriage is its interest in the welfare of children, who are to become the future citizens of the state. Since children are best raised by their natural parents, the state has an interest in privileging marriage between a man and a woman, which is the union through which most children are brought into the world and raised into adulthood. (And, indeed, we have seen much social pathology in those ethnic groups in our society where a large number, even the vast majority, of children are born to unwed parents and raised by only one of them.) Since the vast majority of male-female marriages result in children, the state generally extends the privileges of marriage to any heterosexual couple physically capable of conducting a marriage, even though some marriages do not result in children, either by design or by accident. (By the principle *de minimis non curat lex*, that is, the law does not concern itself with exceptional cases, we do not require proof of fertility or procreative intention in order for a man and a woman to marry each other, since most women and men who marry are fertile, and most of them intend to have children together.[19])

Despite the well-known fact that some gay men do permit their semen to be used to inseminate women to whom they are not married or with whom they have not been sexually intimate, and despite the well-known fact that some lesbian women are inseminated with the semen of men to whom they are not married or with whom they have not been sexually intimate, it is even more well-known that homosexual unions themselves do not produce these children. That is no less the case even if a homosexual couple raises a child whom one of them has either sired or borne. In fact, based on the moral sensibilities the Jewish tradition nurtured in me and other Jews (and that other family-centered traditions have nurtured in their adherents), it is offensive that a man in our society may sire a child with the impunity of not being required to assume fatherly responsibility for *his* child, or that a woman in our society may bear a child with the impunity of not being required to assume motherly responsibility for *her* child. That is because I think the Jewish tradition teaches that *all* children have a right to know who sired them and who bore them, and *all* children have a claim on those who sired them and who bore them—even if for whatever reason the natural parents permitted their own child to be adopted by others.[20]

The fact is that most heterosexual unions do intend on having children and raising them, and that most of these unions do indeed result in children. (But the dangerous social fact of the high rate of divorce in our society, leaving what used to be called "broken homes," diminishes the significance of the institution of marriage even for those who do not divorce.) The fact also is that only a small minority of homosexual unions, whether between two women or between two men, either intend to raise children or to facilitate one of the partners in becoming a natural parent. Because of this, by the criterion of generalizability in legislation, the state has no reason to be interested in same-sex unions at all. If the state recognizes a right to privacy, then same-sex unions should have the same status as friendships between private parties in our society, which is to have no official status at all. It would be an unwarranted intrusion of the power of the state to require friendships between two or more persons to be officially registered in order to receive certain political privileges. It is true that the state has an interest in friendship since friends make better citizens than enemies.[21] Nevertheless, the best way the state can encourage friendship is to ignore it by leaving citizens alone to cultivate *their* friends without any official license.

It seems to me that homosexual unions should have the status of private friendships in our society, which some people will pursue because they find these unions morally attractive and others will avoid because they find them morally repulsive. If any of these private friendships needs some official structuring, as, for example, designating a friend rather than a family member to have custodial authority over a person or to inherit his or her property, this can be stipulated through a private contract. In other words, homosexuals who are involved in long-term relationships and who are often alienated from their natural families have a legitimate concern that their partners, who are most concerned with their welfare, should have custodial authority over them in case of physical or mental disability, and they should also be able to inherit their property in case of death. Nevertheless, this concern can be met without redefining civil marriage into ultimate incoherence. It can be met in the same way all other nonfamilial relationships are structured when need be: by private contract. In other words, the state can adequately meet these legitimate needs of homosexual friends without, however, officially sanctioning and privileging the sexual component of these relationships by designating these relationships themselves to be marriages.

We also need to know just how many homosexual couples actually want the institution of marriage at all. I have heard some homosexuals decry marriage as a *cultural* institution so thoroughly "heterosexist" that they are better off staying away from it altogether. Could it be that only a vocal minority of "marriage minded" homosexuals have taken it on themselves to claim marital rights for all homosexuals?[22] Could it be that only they want the approval of heterosexist society, whereas the majority of homosexuals neither needs that approval nor wants it? Furthermore, even wanting the right of marriage for those homosexuals who want to exercise that right, some homosexuals, who themselves do not want to exercise that right, are prescient enough to know that social pressures on them to exercise that right will quickly turn it into a duty. These pressures could easily come from both the majority heterosexist culture and from the minority homosexual culture. The heterosexist culture could say to all homosexuals: "We will only tolerate your unions at all when you *submit* them to the *control* of the state, the majority of whose citizens *we* are." The homosexual culture could say to all homosexuals: "All of us *must* marry in order to ensure the *recognition* of our way of life, with all its political benefits, by *them*: the majority heterosexist culture."

CONTRACTS AND COVENANTS

The question of contract, when discussed in connection with the question of marriage, further enlightens us about the character of marriage in our society: first, its political meaning; second, its historical meaning.

It is a mistake to treat marriage as being essentially a contract. If it were a contract, there is no reason why it should be restricted to two persons only, a restriction that, as far as I know, homosexual advocates are still willing to accept despite their demands that the institution of marriage be radically redefined. But, if it is essentially a contract, why should it be limited to two persons? What about a ménage à trois? Furthermore, as far as I know, homosexual advocates are still willing to accept that a sexual relationship is integral to a *marital* union of persons. But, if it is essentially a contract, why deny intentionally nonsexual relationships the right, perhaps even the duty, to be called *marriages*? The political meaning of marriage is inadequately understood when marriage is reduced to the more simple level of a contract.[23]

These are powerful objections to those liberals, whether homosexual or heterosexual, who are unable to distinguish between familial relationships based on status and commercial-like relationships based on contract. Whereas commercial-like relationships are created de novo and wherein individuals are the primary units, familial relationships are based on communal *tradition* wherein the family is the primary unit. Since the first purpose of the family is the procreation and nurture of the next generation, it stands to reason why the family is founded in the union of a man and a woman, why the dissolution of marriage should require considerable responsibility on the part of the man and/or woman who is breaking up a family unit, and why parents and children remain responsible for each other forever. The fact that there are commercial aspects involved in marriage, mostly involving responsibility for property either brought into the marriage or resulting from the marriage, does not mean that marriage itself is, in essence, a contract. The historical meaning of marriage is that it is an intergenerational reality (diachronic), which could not be captured by the bilateral (synchronic) character of a contract.[24]

Even civil marriage is more like a covenant in the biblical sense (*brit*), which is a relationship initiated by a free agreement (its *terminus a quo*) but having no stipulated conclusion (its *terminus ad quem*).[25] And, even though at times a divorce is either permitted or mandated, this is to be regarded as an unintended accident *to* the marriage, not to be a necessary result *from* the marriage.[26] Furthermore, when there are children in a marriage, even the dissolution of the marriage by divorce does not relieve the former husband and wife of their *joint* parental responsibilities, that is, until "death do us part." All of this should show why the extension of official marital recognition to same-sex unions will distort its essential meaning to such an extent that there will be no inherent reason to limit it in any way at all. But without essential limitation, marriage itself would be generalized out of existence. (In logic, this is called the "fallacy of generalization.") What freely initiated human relationship could not be considered a marriage when marriage is nothing more than a private agreement?

POLITICAL STRATEGIES

Since Jews, even by the admission of many friends and many enemies, have as strong and as coherent a tradition as can be found anywhere—especially as it pertains to family matters—it would seem that Jews, who are unambivalently committed to that tradition, ought to recognize the dangers to the whole social order posed by the radical innovation of same-sex marriage. This is a moral (if not literally Halakhic) and political requirement for Jews to assume sexual responsibility in the larger secular society in which we live and where we are, happily, fully enfranchised with all the rest of our fellow citizens as political equals. I want to suggest here that the actively political aspect of our overall sexual responsibility to be taken by Jews could employ two different strategies.

The first strategy is to make common cause with other traditionalists in our society who are opposed to this radical innovation precisely because they positively affirm the vital role of families in the life of our society. It is certainly not an issue about which Jews could possibly sustain a public argument by ourselves alone. Moreover, this strategy has judicial and legislative aspects to it. Judicially, it means participating in attempts to defeat lawsuits that challenge the historical definition of marriage in the courts. However, that leaves the question in the hands of judges, who are mostly unelected, and who are thus not answerable to civil society for any decision they make one way or the other. Considering the fact that more and more judges today, in both the United States and Canada, are products of a legal education that has become less and less respectful of tradition, even legal victories on this front might very well be ephemeral. So, with that possibility, even probability, in mind, one should look to a legislative defense of traditional marriage and family. That, of course, assumes that the legislators better reflect the more socially conservative attitudes of the people who elected them and to whom they are very much answerable. If that is true, then I suggest we traditional Jews support legislative efforts, like the Defense of Marriage Act in the United States, to eliminate the radical challenge same-sex marriage poses to the institution of marriage we are committed to for all people. Optimally, this should be an amendment to the United States Constitution so that it cannot be overturned by any future Supreme Court.

Nevertheless, social conservatives like traditional Jews must also contemplate the possibility that the people, the American or Canadian electorate, are as radicalized as are the media and the universities, which along with religious communities are the main culture-forming institutions in our society, and both of which in general not only tolerate but promote homosexuality as a valuable way of life. If so, and the people do not politically oppose, or do not politically oppose sufficiently, the innovation of same-sex marriage to stop it, neither judicially nor legislatively, because they no longer have any reason to do so, then I suggest something more radical is called for.[27] I think social conservatives like traditional Jews should be prepared, in the event that the courts permit same-sex couples to marry (as they almost have done in Vermont already), to avoid civil marriage altogether. After all, traditional Jews now only allow the state to confirm their marriage, whose essence is a religious covenant, not a secular contract.

Since there is no civil obligation to marry civilly and certainly no religious one, and since civil marriage would now be contrary to what we believe *any* marriage to be, the moral integrity of our own covenantal marriages would be better served if we avoided a public institution we believe promotes a moral wrong.[28] Furthermore, from 30 to 40 percent of heterosexual couples in North America who are engaged in "long-term relationships" (i.e., who live together regularly and do not just "sleep together" irregularly) are doing so without benefit of marriage, civil or religious. Since numerous legal accommodations have already been made for such couples, what social or economic harm would there be if social conservatives like traditional Jews became, in effect, like conscientious objectors—in this case to civil marriage, like Mennonites conscientiously avoid military service? Finally, since of all the heterosexual couples in North America, the vast majority of traditional (almost always formally religious) couples have opted for civil marriage as well, whereas the majority of unwed couples are not traditionalists, it would seem that any large-scale traditional/religious departure from civil marriage would make more and more people wonder what purpose civil marriage serves if the majority of heterosexual couples will have turned their backs to it.

In other words, traditional/religious folks might have to call for a far more radical reappraisal of marriage than gay advocates are now calling for. This would mean, in effect, the most radical renegotiation of the social contract possible because nothing is more basic to human identity than one's definition of family. Indeed, I think such a suggestion would cause gay advocates to pause inasmuch as the very attraction of civil marriage (or religious marriage in those liberal religious communities where same-sex marriage has a chance of being accepted) might well be that the small homosexual minority thinks it can be accepted by the large heterosexual majority on the question of family (as opposed to the question of privacy, on which most heterosexuals are willing to let homosexual consenting adults do what they please by themselves). If civil marriage becomes a largely homosexual cause, might not its attraction be severely curtailed? Without wide-scale communal approval, marriage loses its public significance. These are all matters that traditional Jews who are serious about their participation in civil society need to consider. I offer them as philosophical suggestions, certainly not as ethical/Halakhic mandates, although on some more specific questions these suggestions could possibly lead to such mandates.

JEWISH SELF-INTEREST

Traditional family life, founded in a heterosexual marriage, is very good for the Jews. Judaism begins at home and must regularly return there. No matter how public Judaism becomes, it must always remain domestic. Yet, Jews, even Jews in the State of Israel, are very much influenced by the larger cultural world we find ourselves in. Indeed, in an age of increasing globalization, which is itself a Western phenomenon, even the most pious Jews are less isolated from wider cultural influences than they were in the past, whether they like it or not, and whether they admit it or not. The increasing loss of prestige for the traditional family in our own day has led to more defections from traditional Jewish life than the efforts of all foreign missionaries combined. Among other things, it had led to a dangerously low Jewish birthrate. Jews do not need a society that promotes the specifically Jewish way of life. Jews can do that by themselves with God's help. But Jews do need a society that is supportive of our general moral commitments, like our commitment to the family, which actually precedes the specific emergence of Judaism in the world. (Abraham and Sarah were already married before God chose them, and they remained married after God chose them.) Even when we lived under Christian or Muslim rule, we were able to live as Jews, even thrive as Jews, and this was at least partially due to the fact that neither Christianity nor Islam was promoting moral standards that were in essential conflict with our own.[29] In fact, their moral standards were remarkably similar to our own, and due to our overlapping histories, that moral similarity is no accident.[30] This is especially so as regards sexual/familial morality. Nevertheless, our problems with their political, social, and economic discrimination against us, and their frequent attempts to pressure us into conversion to their religions, made our moral commonality an insufficient reason to want to remain under their rule. For that reason, almost all Jews have been great proponents of a secular civil society and government wherever we have lived. The task is to support the secular society without being seduced into secularism, which always becomes anti-Judaic, even when not anti-Semitic. By "secularism," I mean the ideology that denies even the possibility that participants in a secular society can make a valid commitment and contribution to that society based on a religious foundation.[31]

The success of such political alliances depends on these Christians' being able to convince Jews that the promotion of our moral commonality—that is, the Judeo-Christian ethic—is not a ruse for proselytizing Jews, or for the re-establishment of an officially Christian society, that is, a return to "Christendom." There is, of course, such a risk in making these new alliances, but I think the effort is worth it now, barring sufficient evidence to the contrary in the future.

In summary, then, support for traditional marriage is in the best interest of the world, in the best interest of the Torah, and in the best interest of the Jews. Such support is very much a way Jews can exercise sexual responsibility in the secular political order in which we now live.

NOTES

1. See David Novak, "The Jewish Ethical Tradition in the Modern University," *Journal of Education* 180 (1998): 21–39; *Jewish Social Ethics* (New York: Oxford University, 1992), 225–43.

2. See David Novak, "Religious Communities, Secular Society, and Sexuality: One Jewish Opinion," in *Sexual Orientation and Human Rights in American Society*, ed. Martha C. Nussbaum and Saul M. Olyan (New York: Oxford University Press, 1998), 11–28; also, *Jewish Social Ethics*, 84–117; *Covenantal Rights* (Princeton, NJ: Princeton University Press, 2000), 166–86.

3. Babylonian Talmud [hereafter "B."]: *Sanhedrin* 74a.

4. See Mishnah, *Avot* 5.22; *Avot de-Rabbi Nathan* 18.2; *Tosefta, Sotah* 7.7; B. *Hagigah* 3b re Ecclesiastes 12:11.

5. B. *Sanhedrin* 58a.

6. See B. *Yevamot* 76a and *Tosafot*, s.v. *"mesolelot"*; Maimonides, *Mishneh Torah, Hilkhot Issurei Biah* 21.8 re Leviticus 18:3.

7. For the indispensability of sex in Jewish marriage, see, e.g., B. *Kiddushin* 19b and *Rashi*, s.v. *"be-davar she-be-mammon"*; B. *Ketubot* 63a-b; B. *Nedarim* 90b and Rabbenu Nissim (*Ran*), s.v. *"ha-shamayim."*

8. *Tosefta, Avodah Zarah* 8.4; B. *Sanhedrin* 56a–57a; also, David Novak, *The Image of the Non-Jew in Judaism* (New York and Toronto: Edwin Mellen Press, 1983), 198–222.

9. See B. *Yevamot* 63b; *Genesis Rabbah* 34.14. Cf., B. *Sanhedrin* 59b re Deuteronomy 5:27 and *Tosafot*, s.v. *"ve-ha."*

10. These prohibitions are described in the Talmud (B. *Yoma* 67b re Leviticus 18:3) as being norms, which "even if they had not been written in Scripture, they would have been written anyway." That is, they are discoverable by ordinary human reason and their general proscription does not require a particular revelation to Israel. Thus, they are not initiated at Sinai but, rather, are included in the Sinaitic revelation and thereby further specified and deepened in their ultimate covenantal meaning. See David Novak, *Natural Law in Judaism* (Cambridge, United Kingdom: Cambridge University Press, 1998), 82–89. In this chapter, my concern is more with the more immediate, rational meaning of these norms than with their more ultimate, covenantal meaning. Hence, their theological significance is largely bracketed, although never denied or explained away. See Ibid., 12–26.

11. See Song of Songs 8:6–7; B. *Kiddushin* 30b.

12. Thus the purpose of marital sex can be seen to be both procreation and the overall duration of the union between the two parents (or would-be parents), keeping them together as a woman and a man for the sake of the overall unity of the family, which is the place children are not only conceived and born but, just

as importantly, raised to adulthood. And, even when adults, our children need their parents' intact union as a guide for their own marriages. Thus, the biological and social meanings of marriage are essentially intertwined. See B. *Ketubot* 47b re Exodus 21:11.

13. See Novak, *Natural Law in Judaism*, 122–28.

14. See Novak, "Religious Communities, Secular Society, and Sexuality."

15. It should be remembered that our word "privacy" comes from the Latin *privare*, as in "de-prived" in English, that is, deprived of primary communal interaction. Hence privacy is an abstraction from the public realm; the public realm is not projected out of privacy. See Hannah Arendt, *The Human Condition* (Chicago: University of Chicago Press, 1958), 53–65.

16. See B. *Yevamot* 65b re Proverbs 9:8.

17. B. *Hullin* 92b.

18. *Leviticus Rabbah* 23.9.

19. For the recognition of the criterion of generality in human law, see *B*. Eruvin 63b and parallels. See Maimonides, *Guide of the Perplexed*, 3.34; Novak, *Covenantal Rights*, 157–65.

20. Regarding adoption in Jewish law, see David Novak, *Law and Theology in Judaism* (New York: KTAV, 1976), 2:60–63; "The Legal Question of the Investigation of Converts," in *Jewish Law Association Studies* (Atlanta: Scholars Press, 1987), 3:170–72.

21. See Aristotle, *Nicomachean Ethics*, 8.1/1155a23–24.

22. See Andrew Sullivan, "Here Comes the Groom: A (Conservative) Case for Gay Marriage," *New Republic* 201 (August 28, 1989): 22.

23. Thus, in Jewish law, the essential obligations of husband and wife to each other are stipulated by public decree. Only supplementary matters may be stipulated as a private matter between husband and wife. See *Mishnah, Ketubot* 4.7–12. Cf., Maimonides, *Mishneh Torah, Hilkhot Ishut* 16.1 and Vidal of Tolosa, *Magid Mishneh* thereon.

24. See esp. Maimonides, *Mishneh Torah, Hilkhot Ishut* 1:1.

25. See David Novak, *Law and Theology in Judaism* (New York: KTAV, 1974), 1:1–14. Also, see John Witte, Jr., *From Sacrament to Contract* (Louisville, KY: Westminster John Knox Press, 1997).

26. For rabbinic embarrassment over intentionally temporary marriages, see B. *Yoma* 18b. Cf., B. *Gittin* 90b re Malachi 2:14.

27. For a critique of Jewish attempts to link Jewish religious marriage to civil marriage, see David Novak, "Jewish Marriage and Civil Law: A Two Way Street?" *George Washington Law Review* 68 (July/September 2000): 1059–78.

28. For the prohibition of complicity in wrongdoing, see B. *Avodah Zarah* 55b.

29. For premodern Jewish-Christian moral agreement, see Yair Hayyim Bachrach, *Responsa: Havot Yair* (Lemberg, 1896), no. 31, p. 20d. For the rabbinic principle that Jews must adhere to general moral consensuses in society with non-Jews, see B. *Bava Kama* 113a–b. Cf., Jacob Emden, *Responsa: She'elat Yavets* 2 (Altona, 1739), no. 15, p. 9a.

30. For the recognition of the gentile adoption of some important aspects of biblical morality, see *Tosefta, Sotah* 8.5 and B. *Sotah* 35b re Deuteronomy 27:8.

31. See Stephen Carter, *The Culture of Disbelief* (New York: Anchor Books, 1994).

CHAPTER 4

Abortion and Jewish Law

Barry Freundel

Few issues are as divisive in modern Western society as the issue of abortion.[1] Frequent debate, large rallies, even tragic violence and murder are all part of the pro-choice/pro-life contretemps. As time has gone on, the issue has come to symbolize many things other than abortion for secular society. These include feminism, women's roles, the source of morality, sexual freedom, and the meaning of responsibility. For Judaism, however, none of these issues are central to the abortion discussion.[2]

Two factors help make that statement a reality. First, the language of pro-choice/pro-life is a language of rights and the question of proper application of rights is a basic pursuit of Western society and its legal and cultural institutions.[3] For Judaism, the language of rights is rarely central, is often a poor fit, and can even be inappropriate if one is seeking to understand Judaism in its own terms. The Torah presents us with 613 commandments or responsibilities. We never speak of the number of rights it presents us with. "Right to choose," "right to life," and "right to one's body" are the slogans of the abortion debate, and they are, at least, uncomfortable concepts for Judaism. Substituting "responsible choices," "responsible to one's life," and "responsible to one's body" would bring to bear a language much more familiar and comfortable to Jewish tradition. Responsibility is the touchstone of Judaism, not rights.

Second, from our earliest sources on the subject, Judaism had never taken what one might describe as either a pro-choice or pro-life position. Our sources simply do not allow us to do so. As a religious matter, I think that we become inauthentic when we take positions that are inconsistent with our tradition and we should always speak as Jews from within the wisdom of our tradition.

Jewish law derives its position from real cases. Before getting to what the Talmud says about abortion, however, it is important to point out that the Talmud simply presents the law. It does not present rationales. Further, the law it presents is in reality an intuitive and sophisticated response.

If one takes away the political issues, if one takes away any religious teachings that we may have, intuitively I believe every one of us would, if we look at the question objectively, recognize that a fetus is not the same thing as an ingrown toenail. If you leave a fetus alone it will become, at the very least, a singular, unique, and infinitely valuable human being of which there will never be another that is its like. Here lies the basis for common ground between Christians and Jews. We would all agree to this description of what a fetus will be at least in a few months. One can debate about what status the fetus has presently, but we all agree about what it will become. On the other hand, at least for many people, the fetus does not intuitively rise to the same status as the mother or to that of any other independent human life. Perhaps because of its dependency, perhaps because we're not sure about its viability, or maybe simply because it is in the womb and it is not walking around in our world, a fetus doesn't seem to many people to be the same as the mother. It is from this starting point that Judaism begins its discussion of the issue.

Virtually all authorities that discuss this issue from a Jewish perspective begin with this Mishnah that appears in *Ohalot*.

If a woman is in hard travail, one cuts up the child in her womb and brings it forth member by member, because her life comes before that of [the child]. But if the greater part has proceeded forth, one may not touch it, for one may not set aside one person's life for that of another. (Mishnah, *Ohalot* 7:6)

This Mishnah is obviously not "pro-life," at least in the radical iteration of that position, as Halakhah[4] here allows and even requires[5] an abortion when a mother's life, and perhaps her health, are in danger.

This Mishnah is also clearly not pro-choice. It does not allow abortions under any and all circumstances, only when the mother is in considerable distress. By inference, abortion is prohibited in situations not involving a serious threat to the fundamental well-being of the pregnant mother. That the Mishnah makes a point of stipulating, "because her life comes before that of [the child]," indicates that in the absence of this consideration, abortion cannot be sanctioned.[6] While the question of "How much distress is enough?" is a critical consideration that will occupy much of the rest of our discussion, clearly inconvenience, or unhappiness with the gender of the fetus, would be insufficient grounds for abortion. Indeed, the flavor of the Jewish tradition's view of abortion in general—even though it finds occasion for allowing the practice in certain strictly delimited particulars—finds suitable expression in the fundamental rabbinic work on Jewish mysticism, the *Zohar:*

There are three [persons] who drive away the Divine presence from the world, making it impossible for the Holy One, blessed be He, to fix His abode in the universe and causing prayer to be unanswered. . . . [The third is] he who causes the fetus to be destroyed in the womb, for he destroys the artifice of the Holy One, blessed be He, and His workmanship. . . . For these abominations the Spirit of the Holiness weeps. . . . (*Zohar,* Shemot 3b)

This Mishnaic "requirement" to have an abortion, it is worth noting, played a small role in recent American legislative history. The United States Supreme Court in 1990, in a case known as *Employment Division v. Smith,*[7] seems to have removed many constitutional protections from people practicing their religion. An attempt was made to restore those freedoms through a bill known as the Religious Freedom Restoration Act, or RFRA.[8] Some in the Christian community were concerned that people might use this act to claim that they had a religious right to an abortion under American law as their religion mandated that they have one in some circumstances. On researching the question of which religious groups might have a tradition requiring an abortion, only one such group was found—traditional Jews.

Returning to the Mishnah, our medieval commentators and codifiers take up the question of abortion and appear to be of two minds in understanding the law. The crux between the two positions is the status of the fetus, though this issue is handled in an entirely different fashion than in the Christian understanding.

Maimonides[9] takes the position that abortion is mandated in this case because the woman in difficult labor is effectively being pursued by the fetus.[10]

This too is a negative commandment: not to have compassion on the life of the pursuer. Therefore the sages ruled that when a woman has difficulty in labor one may dismember the embryo within her, either with drugs or surgery, because he is like a pursuer seeking to kill her. (*Mishneh Torah, Hilkhot Rotzeah Ushmirat Hanefesh* 1:9)

The law pertaining to a *pursuer* in Jewish law is well established: If *A* threatens to kill *B,* then *C* is permitted to kill *A* in order to save *B.*[11] So, just as one may injure and even kill—if no other option is available—someone chasing another individual and trying to kill him, so, too, the fetus is endangering the mother's life and is thus considered a functional pursuer who may be terminated as a last resort.[12]

Maimonides' formulation of "fetus as pursuer" should seem to grant the fetus significant status,[13] perhaps even full human status.[14] A nonfetal pursuer is a human being. The only reason he can be terminated is because he is engaged in actions that are a direct threat to the pursued and no other means of protection is available. Maimonides seems to be equating "human being as pursuer" and "fetus as pursuer."[15] Granted human status, however, a fetus commands a presumption that it must be protected. Overcoming that presumption is a heavy burden that presumably can be met only by either a direct threat to the life of the mother or perhaps by something almost as serious. Thus, it would seem, outside of these few cases, that abortion is forbidden.

Supporting this view is Maimonides' acceptance and codification of a position that abortion for a gentile is a capital crime.[16] His position is taken from a discussion in the Talmud:

It is stated on the authority of R. Yishmael "[that a gentile may be condemned to death] even for killing a fetus." What is the reason of R. Ishmael? It is the verse "he who sheds the blood of man, in man shall his blood be shed" (Gen. 9:6). What is the meaning of "man in man"? This can be said to refer to a fetus in its mother's womb. (Babylonian Talmud, *Sanhedrin* 57b)[17]

Maimonides' ruling, that abortion outside of the type of specific case presented in the Mishnah is forbidden, finds similar support in Tosefot's Talmudic commentary in this context:

concerning the fetus for whose killing a gentile is liable and a Jew is exempt: Even though he is exempted from punishment, it [i.e., the killing of a fetus] is not permitted. (*Sanhedrin* 59a, s.v. *Lekah*)[18]

So, although Jewish law does not designate a punishment for abortion, it is a forbidden activity. Similarly, there are those, like Rabbi Isser Yehuda Unterman (1886–1976), the former Ashkenazi Chief Rabbi of Israel (from 1964 to 1972), who confer humanlike status to the fetus and consider abortion as something on the order of homicide. This idea finds support from a statement in the Gemara (Babylonian Talmud, *Arachin* 7b):

Said R. Nachman in the name of Samuel: "when a woman dies on the Sabbath while she is on the birthstool, one brings a knife to cut her abdomen and remove the fetus . . . even if one must carry the knife by way of the public domain."

Permitting the violation of the Sabbath laws against carrying from a public domain to a private domain in order to save the fetus must imply, says Rabbi Unterman, that the fetus represents human life, for it is only to save human life that the Sabbath can be violated.[19]

It seems clear, at the very least, that the fetus is granted some form of humanity and, thus, some form of protected status. As such, abortion should occur, by Maimonides' formulation, only under very restrictive circumstances.[20]

Others, among them Rashi,[21] take a very different view. For them, abortion is performed for the "mother in difficulty" because the fetus is not a full-fledged human life until it emerges from its mother.[22] As Rashi comments:

". . . removing it limb by limb." This is because as long as it has not emerged into the world it is not a human being, and therefore it can be killed in order to save its mother. (Rashi on Sanhedrin 72b, s.v. *Yatzah Rosho*)

Since the mother's human status is obviously complete and intact, she will come first whenever her significant interests and those of the fetus are at cross-purposes.[23] Lending support to this approach are a number of Talmudic sources[24] and one biblical passage:

And if men strive together and hurt a woman with child, so that her fruit depart, and yet no harm follow, he shall surely be fined, according as the woman's husband shall lay upon him; and he shall pay as the judges determine. But if any harm follow, then thou shalt give life for life, eye for eye, tooth for tooth, hand for hand, foot for foot, burn for burn, wound for wound, bruise for bruise. (Exodus 21:22–23)[25]

Were the fetus a full human being, and its death, therefore, negligent homicide, monetary compensation would not be the expected punishment—indeed, such payments are specifically prohibited in the Bible. As the Torah states, "You shall take no ransom [Hebrew: *kofer*] for the life of a murderer" (Numbers 35:31). Negligent homicide, by biblical law, requires the perpetrator to leave his home and undergo a period of exile[26] in one of forty-eight designated refuge cities.[27] No monetary compensation is allowed in such a circumstance.[28] This would seem to indicate that causing a miscarriage is not negligent homicide, and, therefore, that the fetus is not fully a human being.[29] As Nachmanides succinctly explained, "Apparently, the fetus is not regarded as a living person, as is evident from the fact that in the Bible feticide is treated as a monetary matter" (Ramban, *Niddah* 44a, s.v. *Tinok*).

There is some explicit Talmudic support for this position. Consider, for example, the following Mishnah and its discussion in the Gemara:

Mishnah: The execution of a pregnant woman who is condemned to death is not postponed until after she gives birth. But once she is on the birthstool, the execution is postponed until after she gives birth.

Gemara: Said R. Judah in the name of Samuel: "Before such a woman is executed she is struck across her abdomen, so that the fetus will die prior to the execution, to prevent her dishonor at the time of execution." (*Arachin* 7a)[30]

This source would seem to grant no more than minimal status to a fetus. And so we find, for example, the lenient opinion of Rabbi Joseph Trani (1568–1639), known as Maharit. Rabbi Trani denied abortion any dimension of homicide, arguing, instead, that abortion is prohibited only because it is included under the general prohibition against the wounding of one's body.[31] This prohibition is based on the biblical verse "surely your blood of your lives will I require" (Genesis 9:5); is discussed in the Gemara (*Bava Kama* 90b); and, according to Maimonides,[32] derives from the fact that Halakhah considers the body to belong to God, not the individual. So Maharit can explain the dispensation for abortion provided by the above Gemara by arguing that since the woman is about to die, the prohibition against wounding one's body obviously does not significantly factor in. As for the prohibition on abortion, once the condemned woman begins to give birth, Maharit explains that at the point of birth the fetus acquires independent status as a human, as indicated in the Gemara (cited earlier), which allows the violation of the Sabbath to protect the fetus. After all, this Talmudic dispensation to violate the Sabbath on the fetus's behalf applies only after the mother has died while in labor. Once the mother has died, the fetus cannot be regarded as a "man in man" (as in Genesis 9:6), but rather as an independent life whose path is being blocked; thus, it is considered as if it were already born. It is only at that point, Maharit argues, that the fetus has sufficient status as a human for the Sabbath to be violated on its behalf. Before that point, the fetus is not human, and the dispensation to violate the Sabbath does not apply.

Within this more lenient approach, there is greater room to expand what constitutes a "threat" to the mother. The most permissive ruling in this regard, one that later authorities have taken strong exception to, is that of Rabbi Jacob Emden (1697–1776), who permits abortion not only when the mother's health is compromised but also in cases of "grave necessity," such as when continuation of the pregnancy would subject the mother to great pain.[33] Such abortions are sanctioned by Rabbi Emden if performed before the onset of labor, at which time the fetus has "torn itself loose" from the uterine wall.

A view similar to that of Rabbi Emden is voiced by Rabbi Ben Zion Uziel (1880–1953, first Sephardic Chief Rabbi of Israel).[34] The case brought to his attention concerned a woman threatened with approaching deafness if her pregnancy were allowed to run its normal course. Following the line of reasoning advanced by Rabbi Jacob Emden, Rabbi Uziel allows abortion when any consideration of merit is demonstrated, as long as labor has not yet begun:

It is clear that abortion is not permitted without reason . . . but for a reason, even if a weak reason [Hebrew: *ta'am kalush*], such as to prevent her public shame, we have precedent and authority to permit it.

Both Rabbi Emden and, more obviously, Rabbi Uziel rely on the above Gemara (*Arachin* 7a). Thus, we see that this approach generally, and this source specifically, would permit abortion in a far broader range of situations than reliance on Maimonides' formulation would lead us to accept.[35]

Consistent throughout these sources, however, is the understanding that once the mother has begun to give birth, the fetus is considered more fully human and an abortion at that stage would be strictly forbidden by all authorities. The first Mishnah we cited informed us that during labor itself, abortion is a possibility only if it is absolutely necessary to save the life of the mother, but forbidden entirely once the fetus has emerged. So, too, we saw that the Gemara will not allow a scheduled execution to proceed once the woman is in labor, specifically so as to save the fetus. Further, once labor has begun, the Gemara permits the violation of the Sabbath in order to try and save the fetus. Clearly, during labor the fetus attains a more fully human status. While not necessarily as fully human as the mother, the fetus has, nonetheless, substantial claim to life and to protection. Thus Jewish law according to all authorities prohibits "partial birth abortion."[36]

Mentioning labor brings, however, the question of stages in pregnancy and their effect on the abortion question to the fore. Emergence is mentioned in the first Mishnah cited above. This point in the pregnancy process is described in some sources as "the emergence of the head of the fetus,"[37] and in others as, "emergence of the majority of the fetus from the mother."[38] As we have seen, the beginning of labor also is an important moment.[39] Furthermore, some, more modern commentators understand the subservient nature of fetal life to maternal life as reflecting fetal dependence on the mother.[40] Therefore, when the fetus reaches independent viability, such viability may itself represent an Halakhically significant change in its status.[41]

So, too, the very beginning of pregnancy may be different. The Mishnah in *Niddah* 30a informs us that a miscarriage that occurs prior to the fetus's attaining the forty-day period does not engender the spiritual impurity, or *tumah*, of childbirth ordained by the Bible (Leviticus 12:2–5). Another source for this ruling on the first forty-day period of pregnancy is found in the Talmud:

Mishnah: The daughter of a priest who has relations with an Israelite continues to eat terumah; if she becomes pregnant she does not eat terumah.

Gemara: Rav Chisda said: "She should immerse herself and then eat terumah until the fortieth day after conception . . . for if she is pregnant, it is considered to be mere water until the fortieth day (Yevamot 69b).

These sources appear to teach that fetal development within the initial forty days of gestation is insufficient to warrant independent standing in Halakhah—"mere water." Similarly, according to Rabbi Yehuda Rosanes, author of *Mishneh le-Melekh,* the spiritual impurity associated with a dead body is not attendant on an embryo expelled during the first forty days of gestation.[42] And, furthermore, many hold the opinion that a fetus cannot acquire property prior to the fortieth day of development.[43]

Indeed, many authorities are more lenient in allowing abortion during these forty days than they would be subsequent to this moment in the fetus's development.[44] Consider, for example, Rabbi Yechiel Ya'akov Weinberg, who is of the opinion that prior to forty days of pregnancy there is no prohibition at all. After forty days, he permits abortions for the sake of the mother's health, but with significantly greater hesitation.[45]

Please note that the count is from the moment of conception, not from the date of the last period as contemporary doctors calculate it. The Halakhic count adds about two weeks to the number, thus putting this transition point toward the end of the second month of pregnancy. It is also worth noting that in Halakhah, unlike the Catholic tradition, the question of ensoulment is entirely irrelevant to abortion. The question of ensoulment is dealt with in the Talmud. In *Sanhedrin* (91b), there is a discussion that yields the conclusion that ensoulment takes place at the moment of conception. In another passage (*Sanhedrin* 110b), the issue of the time at which the immortal soul enters the body is raised and various views are recorded. These range from the moment of conception to the moment at which the child begins to respond to blessings. None of these discussions, however, are ever referred to in any Halakhic treatment of abortion.

A contemporary discussion that incorporates and illustrates many of the elements highlighted above is the debate between Rabbi Eliezer Waldenberg and Rabbi Moshe Feinstein on aborting a fetus that tested positive for Tay-Sachs disease. Tay-Sachs is a Jewish genetic disease afflicting primarily people of Eastern European ancestry; it manifests itself early in a child's life in the form of both physical and mental retardation. If both parents carry the Tay-Sachs gene, they can produce (statistically in one out of four cases) a baby that has two Tay-Sachs genes in its genetic makeup. Tragically, that baby will contract the disease and will die, probably by age three or four, though certainly not much later.[46]

Bearing such a child and watching it wither and die is certainly emotionally difficult for the parents. But is that sufficient to allow abortion?

Rabbi Waldenberg allows such an abortion until the seventh month of pregnancy; Rabbi Feinstein does not. Rabbi Waldenberg explains his opinion thus:

It is clear that in Jewish law an Israelite is not liable to capital punishment for feticide. . . . An Israelite woman was permitted to undergo a therapeutic abortion, even though her life was not at stake. . . . This permissive ruling applies even when there is no direct threat to the life of the mother, but merely a need to save her from great pain, which falls within the rubric of "great need." Now, is it possible to imagine a case in which there is more need, pain, and distress than the present one, in which the mother is confronted by [the prospects of] a suffering child whose certain death is only a few years away and nothing can be done to save it? One might also take into account the pain and suffering of the child afflicted with this disease. Consequently, if there is going to be a case in which the halakhah would permit abortion for a great need and in order to alleviate pain and distress, this would appear to be a classic one. (*Responsa Tzitz Eliezer* 13:102)

Rabbi Feinstein responded to Rabbi Waldenberg's lenient decision in the following terms:

I have therefore ruled that even where the doctors claim that the mother's life is in danger unless an abortion is performed, and even though the Sabbath and other commandments must be broken in such circumstances . . . abortion is forbidden until the doctors are absolutely certain that the mother will die. This is because the basis for therapeutic abortion is the pursuer principle, and in order to be considered a pursuer the danger must be established beyond all doubt. It is also quite obvious that the medical condition of the fetus is irrelevant, so that even those fetuses that will not develop into viable children, e.g., victims of Tay-Sachs disease, may not be aborted. The reason for this is that there is no actual danger to the mother's life and the fetus is not, therefore, a pursuer. It is irrelevant that great suffering may be caused to both parents as a result of the pregnancy running to term.[47]

It is here that the extent of the range of options on abortion can be seen. Neither Rabbi Waldenberg nor Rabbi Feinstein would prohibit abortion if the mother's life were in danger. Neither would permit abortion if the baby was healthy and the couple wanted to delay having children for a few years. Indeed, even the most lenient scholar would see abortion as a serious violation if performed when Halakhically unjustified.[48] Where the debate is joined is on the relative value of fetal life versus parental emotional distress. Rabbi Feinstein seems to follow Maimonides' view, while Rabbi Waldenberg appears to be a disciple of Rashi's. In other words, although Rashi's approach would lead to many more circumstances where abortion might be deemed permissible than would Maimonides' approach, both approaches clearly restrict abortions such that the modern political context does not really have application. Also, both approaches would result in far fewer abortions than what is currently permitted in the United States.

The breadth of the debate may, however, lead us to "choice" in one very unfortunate circumstance, although that choice may be deemed very humane. Imagine a woman who is pregnant but who also, unfortunately, has cancer. If she takes chemotherapy for the cancer the fetus will die, but this may be her only chance to survive. If she doesn't take chemotherapy, she may well die but the baby will have a chance. Analyzing the situation Halakhically, Maimonides would seem to forbid the use of chemotherapy. The fetus is not the pursuer, the cancer is. There should be no license to kill an innocent bystander to save the mother.

Rashi, on the other hand, who sees the fetus as subservient to the mother, should require chemotherapy. As stated above, the mother's survival interests come before those of the fetus.

At least one contemporary responsum allows the mother's choice in such a case to be the determining factor.[49] Her choice to take the chemotherapy can find support in Rashi's position, thus allowing her to save her own life, or we can support her decision not to take medicine from Maimonides' words and allow her child to provide a legacy for her. As long as the choice is made with full disclosure of all necessary and relevant information, her choice can be respected and accepted.

Finally, this author is saddened by the many Jewish groups that have aligned themselves with either the pro-choice movement (and this is by far the largest group) or (more rarely) the pro-life movement. Those that have aligned themselves with the pro-life position are very careful in their writings to explain the differences between themselves and those who identify themselves as pro-life, but I am not sure the public perceives the differences. In my view, the differences are critically important, particularly if we are to succeed here. As we have seen, Judaism accepts neither position. It would seem to be far more authentic and appropriate to stand for . . . what we stand for. From lenient to restrictive, we are still within a paradigm that allows for much restriction and, perhaps, legislation to prevent most of what goes on in this country's abortion clinics, but we would not favor banning abortion entirely.

Particularly as most polls show that the majority of Americans do not want unrestricted abortions but do want abortion available under serious circumstances, there seems to be a responsive audience for what we have to say. If such a position were taken as public policy in this country, the vast majority of abortions performed in this country each year would be illegal, but abortion could be used, for example, to save the life of the mother. We do not need the polls to validate our position, but we can serve a valuable societal role in supporting the popular morality on this issue simply by being true to our tradition. In that way we may also be able to prevent many abortions that even the most learned interpreters of our tradition would find to be illegal, immoral, and close to, if not over, the line of actual murder.

It is my view that the debate about abortion in this society is not really about abortion any longer. Instead it has become a symbol of a whole series of other issues that have somehow become embodied in this issue. Therefore, any compromise one way or the other on this issue makes people think that they have given in on the much larger debate. The larger conflict to which I refer can be described in several ways: secularism versus religionism, liberalism versus conservatism, or autonomy versus authority. The common question is, do I locate the source of moral authority within me, or do I see it in some outside, objective set of standards that come from God or from some other objective source? You can see the abortion debate as the hallmark of the warriors of the sexual revolution as opposed by those who see traditional morality as the proper way to function. Further, you can see it as the symbol of the radical feminist movement against those who oppose their agenda. Unfortunately, all of those things get caught up in the abortion debate. This makes it difficult to stay focused on the abortion issue. It also makes it more difficult to find common ground.

Yet, there is common ground. In whatever way we finally determine the status of the fetus, we can agree on the unreproducible uniqueness of that entity. It is in this agreement that, it seems to me, there is a lot of room for us to work together, to try to advance the cause of allowing many potentially infinitely valuable human beings to come into this world and to make their contribution to society and to the service of God.

NOTES

1. See Eva R. Rubin, *The Abortion Controversy: A Documentary History* (Westport, CT: Praeger, 1994).

2. Some of the articles on this subject from a Torah perspective are, A. Lichtenstein, "Abortion; A Halakhik Perspective," *Tradition* 25, 4 (1991): 3–12; J. David Bleich, "Abortion and Jewish Law," in *New Perspectives on Human Abortion*, ed. Thomas W. Hilgers, Dennis J. Horan, and David Mall (Frederick, MD: University Publications of America, 1981), 405–19; Idem, "Abortion in Halakhik Literature," *Tradition* 10, 2 (1968): 72–120; Fred Rosner, "The Jewish Attitude Toward Abortion," *Tradition*, op. cit., 48–71.

3. In the United States, the language of the Declaration of Independence and the Constitution makes the pursuit and protection of rights the center of the American enterprise.

4. The Hebrew term for the system of Jewish law.

5. See, however, R. Shlomoh ha-Kohen of Vilna, who was of the opinion that although abortion to save the mother's life is permitted, it is by no means obligatory. He held the view that the obligation to save a life is suspended when such

a life could only be preserved at the cost of another's life—even though such action involves no overt transgression. These views are found in a responsum addressed to R. Moshe Horwitz and incorporated by the latter in his *Yedei Mosheh* 4:8.

6. See R. Yair Hayyim Bachrach (1638–1702, German Rabbinic scholar), *Responsa Havot Yair* 31.

7. 494 U.S. 872 (1990).

8. Pub. L. No. 103-141, 107 Stat. 1488 (1993) (codified as amended at 42 U.S.C. § 2000bb-2000bb-4 (1994)) (held unconstitutional by *City of Boerne v. Flores*, 521 U.S. 507 (1997)).

9. R. Moses ben Maimon (Maimonides or Rambam, 1138–1204, Spain, North Africa, and Egypt, perhaps our most important post-Talmudic sage).

10. Although some challenge this understanding of Maimonides' position on the subject. See R. Yair Hayyim Bachrach, *Responsa Havot Yair* 31; R. Yehiel Yaakov Weinberg (1885–1966, German Talmudic scholar), *Responsa Seridei Aish* 3:127, particularly in light of Maimonides' use of the term *rodef* or "pursuer" in *Mishneh Torah, Hilkhot Nizkei Mamon* 14:15.

11. Babylonian Talmud, *Sanhedrin* 57a, 72 aff.

12. *Seridei Aish,* loc. cit.

13. See *Seridei Aish,* loc. cit., citing R. Yehezkel ben Judah Landau (1713–1793, Chief Rabbi of Bohemia), *Noda Biyehuda, Mahadurah Tinyanah, Hoshen Mishpat* 59.

14. See *Sehdei Aish,* loc. cit., citing R. Haim Ozer Grodzinsky (1863–1940, Vilna), *Responsa Ahiezer* 3:72:3.

15. See R. Joseph ben Moses Babad (1800–1874/5, Polish Rabbi and author) *Minchat Chinuch* 296.

16. *Mishneh Torah, Hilkhot Melakhim* 9:4.

17. This is the source of Talmudic and post-Talmudic debate. See R. Eliezer Waldenberg (b. 1917, member of Israel's supreme rabbinical court and prolific writer of responsa) *Responsa Tzitz Eliezer* 9:15:3.

18. According to R. Moses Feinstein (1895–1986, leading Halakhic authority of American Jewry), *Responsa Iggrot Moshe, Hoshen Mishpat* 2:69.

19. See Rabbi Unterman's *Noam* 6, 1–11; also his earlier *Responsa Shevet mi-Yehudah,* vol. 1, pp. 29ff.

20. See *Responsa Iggrot Moshe* cited in n. 14 and *Noda Biyehuda, Mahadurah Tinyanah, Hoshen Mishpat* 59.

21. R. Solomon b. Isaac (1040–1105) Franco-Germany, Judaism's leading commentator on the Bible and Talmud.

22. See also *Minhat Hinukh,* loc. cit., and the commentary of *Hazon Ish* to *Mishneh Torah, Hilkhot Rotzeah Ushmirat Hanefesh* 1:9.

23. See Joseph ben Moses Di Trani (1568–1639, Safed, Jerusalem, and Turkey), *Responsa Maharit* 1:99; R.M. Feinstein, loc. cit., denies the validity of this responsa while others accept it (see *Tzitz Eliezer* 7:48). See also *Responsa Tzitz Eliezer* 9:51 citing *Responsa Torat Hesed* and *Responsa Yavets* 1:43.

24. Along with the source from Babylonian Talmud, *Arachin* cited below, see also Babylonian Talmud, *Shabbat* 151b, *Sanhedrin* 80a–b, 84b, *Gittin* 23b, *Nazir* 51a.

25. Babylonian Talmud (*Bava Kama* 84a) makes clear that the phrase "eye for eye" is not to be taken literally, but instead refers to the payment of monetary compensation. Maimonides states that the payment of compensation was always

the tradition and has been the practice since the time of Moses (*Mishneh Torah, Hovel u-Mazik* 1:1–6).

26. Exodus 21:13, Numbers 35, Joshua 20.

27. Maimonides *Mishneh Torah, Hilkhot Rotzeah Ushmirat Hanefesh* 8:9 based on Numbers 35:6–7.

28. Numbers 35:32.

29. *Responsa Maharit,* loc. cit., and *Tzitz Eliezer* 9:51:3.

30. For different understandings of exactly what this means, compare Rashi's, ad loc., comments to the Mishnah on the page with *Tosafot* Talmudic commentary known for its use of parallel sources and sharp questioning written primarily by Rashi's grandsons and their associates, ad loc., s.v. *Yashvah al hamashber.*

31. *Responsa Maharit* 97, 99. These two responsa should be read together. Also, see note 22 above.

32. *Mishneh Torah, Hilkhot Rotzeah Ushmirat Hanefesh* 1:4.

33. *She'elat Yavets* 43; see also *Torat Chesed, Even Ha-Ezer* 42:32.

34. *Responsa Mishpetei Uziel, Hoshen Mishpat* 3:46.

35. See general discussion in the responsa from *Seridei Aish* and *Tzitz Eliezer* cited here.

36. See Matthew Berke, "Jews Choosing Life," *First Things* 90 (February 1999): 34–36, and see *Responsa Tzitz Eliezer* 9:51:3.

37. Babylonian Talmud, *Sanhedrin* 72b, *Tosefta Yevamot* 9:9.

38. This is the reading of the Mishnah from *Ohalot* cited above; see also Jerusalem Talmud *Shabbat* 77a (14d). Interestingly, Jerusalem Talmud *Sanhedrin* 44a–b (26c) reads, "if the *head and the majority of the body* emerged."

39. The section from *Arachin* cited above mentions this point in time as significant.

40. R. Israel ben Gedaliah Lipschutz (1782–1860, German Rabbinic scholar), *Tiferet Yisroel, Boaz to Ohalot* 7:6.

41. This appears to be the source of *Tzitz Eliezer*'s limiting permission for abortion in the case of Tay-Sachs to no longer than the seventh month. See Rabbenu Nissim of Gerona (1310–1375?), (also known as Nissim ben Reuben Gerondi (the RAN), an important Spanish Talmudist) and Rabbenu Asher ben Jehiel (1250–1327, Asheri or Rosh, German Talmudist and legal scholar) to *Yoma* 82b who pave the way for this position in their discussion of circumstances where a fetus in utero can become a "child with a door locked in front of it."

42. *Mishneh le-Melekh, Hilkhot Tumat Met* 2:1.

43. *Shakh, Hoshen Mishpat* 210:2; *Zofnat Pa'aneach* 59.

44. See *Responsa Havot Yair,* loc. cit., *Tzitz Eliezer* 7:48.

45. *Seridei Aish,* 3:127.

46. From the National Institute of Neurological Disorders and Stroke (NINDS) Tay-Sachs Information Page, http://www.ninds.nih.gov/health_and_medical/disorders/taysachs_doc.htm.

47. Loc. cit., and "Testing to Determine the Health of a Fetus and the Prohibition of Abortion for Tay-Sachs Disease," in *Halakhah Urefuah* 1:304–6.

48. See *Responsa Tzitz Eliezer* 7:48

49. *Responsa Tzitz Eliezer* 9:51:3 and see also *Responsa Seridei Aish,* loc. cit.

CHAPTER 5

Euthanasia and Physician-Assisted Suicide in Jewish Law

Steven H. Resnicoff

In recent years, secular and religious commentators have debated with a growing sense of urgency the propriety of various end-of-life decisions such as suicide, the refusal of life-preserving medical treatment, and physician-assisted dying. Moreover, these questions seem increasingly to have captured the attention of judicial, legislative, and executive authorities throughout the United States and elsewhere. This chapter briefly reviews some of these developments and then attempts to examine these issues from a Jewish perspective.

Because subtle ethical considerations turn on precisely what these terms mean, we begin by clarifying how they are used in this chapter. "Suicide" means any voluntary act, such as the ingestion of poison, intended to cause one's death. The "refusal of life-preserving medical treatment" refers both to initial rejection of such treatment as well as to the termination of treatment already begun. "Medical treatment" applies not only to curative or palliative care, but also to the provision of hydration and nutrition. "Physician-assisted dying" is used to include both "physician-assisted suicide," where physicians provide legally competent patients the means with which to commit suicide, and "voluntary physician euthanasia," where, at the request of legally competent patients, physicians directly end their patients' lives, such as by administering lethal injections. Thus, we will not address either the definition of death[1] or the appropriateness of substituted judgment whereby others might make decisions for legally incompetent patients. Rather, we will limit our discussion to scenarios involving legally competent individuals who are clearly alive.

SECULAR LEGAL DEVELOPMENTS

While a number of secular societies, including England, have at times criminally punished suicide or attempted suicide,[2] this has not been the prevailing rule in the United States.[3] Nevertheless, many states, by common law or statute, forbid assisting a suicide,[4] and these laws have been applied to physicians who enable patients to obtain the means with which to end their lives. In 1997, the United States Supreme Court, upholding New York and Washington laws, unanimously ruled that a patient has no federal constitutional right to physician-assisted suicide.[5]

State constitutions, however, may provide their citizens or residents with rights beyond those conferred by the federal Constitution. As a result, it is theoretically possible that a state ban against physician-assisted suicide could be invalid as violative of a state constitutional right. However, the highest court of no state has reached this conclusion. In fact, several state supreme courts have expressly upheld statutes outlawing assisted suicide against challenges based on state constitutional provisions. On September 21, 2001, for instance, a panel of justices of the Supreme Court of Alaska unanimously held that the Alaska Constitution does not provide a mentally competent, terminally ill individual the right to obtain prescribed medication to hasten his death.[6] In 1997, the Florida Supreme Court held that its law against assisted suicide did not violate the state constitutional right to privacy.[7]

On the other hand, nothing in the federal Constitution or, apparently, in the constitutions of the various states seems to preclude a state from enacting legislation permitting physicians to assist legally competent patients to commit suicide. Efforts to enact such laws have been unsuccessful in over twenty states,[8] including California, Illinois, Iowa, Massachusetts, Michigan, Nebraska, New Mexico, New York,[9] Rhode Island, and Washington.[10] In November 2000, a referendum to legalize physician-assisted suicide was narrowly defeated in Maine, and a bill to allow physician-assisted suicide failed in the Hawaii Senate on May 2, 2002.[11] Legislative initiatives, pro and con, continue to be debated in various state legislatures.[12]

The only state to have enacted such legislation is Oregon, which passed its Death with Dignity Act in 1994.[13] Under this law, a "qualified patient" can receive physician assistance in obtaining drugs to end his life. A "qualified patient" is one who: (1) is terminally ill and expected to live no more than six months; (2) makes at least two oral requests and one written request for the physician's assistance in dying; (3) convinces two physicians that he is sincere and that the requests are made voluntarily and deliberatively; (4) is not influenced by depression; and (5) is informed of "the feasible alternatives, including, but not limited to, comfort care, hospice care and pain control." After a qualified patient has waited for fifteen days, the law permits physicians to prescribe a barbiturate sufficient to cause the patient's death. Even the Oregon law does not allow doctors to engage in voluntary physician euthanasia. Throughout the United States, physician euthanasia seems to constitute murder, as a Michigan court concluded when it upheld the second-degree murder conviction of Dr. Jack Kevorkian.[14]

Even when a state, such as Oregon, enacts a statute favoring some sort of physician-assisted dying, federal government action may be able to restrict the practical impact of such legislation. Attorney General John Ashcroft, for instance, has taken the position that any physician who prescribes federally controlled substances for the purpose of hastening a patient's death violates the federal Controlled Substances Act of 1970. On November 6, 2001, he directed federal agents to enforce this law against physicians acting under Oregon's Death with Dignity statute. On November 20, 2001, a United States federal district court judge issued a temporary restraining order against compliance with Ashcroft's directive,[15] and a permanent injunction was entered on April 17, 2002.[16] At the time this chapter was written, Attorney General Ashcroft had announced his intention to appeal this decision. Of course, it is also possible that new federal legislation might be enacted to further attenuate the effect of any current or future state law leniencies.[17]

In the absence of a specific statute like Oregon's, the extent to which controlled substances may be used to alleviate pain is somewhat unclear, because these substances may cause a patient's death. The United States Supreme Court has stated that prescribing such drugs would not violate state laws against assisted suicide provided that the physician's purpose was to palliate the patient's pain and not to cause his death.[18] As a practical matter, this makes it difficult to criminally convict offenders, because the prosecution bears the heavy burden of establishing the physician's improper intent beyond a reasonable doubt. The Supreme Court has not yet ruled as to the extent to which the federal Constitution allows federal law to prohibit physician-assisted suicide even if a state should purport to allow it or to criminalize a physician's negligent prescription of palliative drugs leading to a patient's unintended death. In the past few years, Congress has considered, but not enacted, just such legislation, under the somewhat misleading title, the Pain Relief Promotion Act.[19]

Several foreign countries, including Canada and South Africa, explicitly criminalize assisted suicide.[20] Australia's Northern Territory passed a law allowing active euthanasia in 1995, but the Australian Senate overruled this statute on March 25, 1997, by a vote of 38 to 33.[21] Although the legislatures of several nations are considering laws authorizing certain forms of physician-assisted dying, and courts in a few others, such as Colombia[22] and Japan, have expressed approval of physician-assisted suicide under certain conditions,[23] the Netherlands and Belgium are the only countries that have formally enacted laws permitting physician-assisted dying. The Netherlands' law—effective as of April 1, 2002—actually allows physicians to practice euthanasia if: (1) the patient is suffering greatly, (2) there is no other way to reasonably palliate the patient's suffering, (3) the patient voluntarily requests euthanasia, (4) the physician and patient have a long-term relationship, (5) the physician consults at least one other independent doctor, and (6) the procedure is performed in a medically appropriate manner.[24] The Belgian law was passed on May 16, 2002, and is in several ways more restrictive.[25]

In contrast to the raging secular debate in the United States regarding physician-assisted dying, state and federal law fairly firmly establishes a legally competent patient's right to refuse potentially life-preserving medical treatment. Thus, as the United States Supreme Court stated in a 1997 decision involving the constitutionality of New York's law against assisted suicide, "In New York, as in most States, it is a crime to aid another to commit or attempt suicide, but patients may refuse even lifesaving medical treatment."[26] Treating someone against his wishes usually constitutes an illegal battery[27] and, according to the United States Supreme Court, violates his constitutional right to privacy.[28]

This secular right to refuse treatment is not entirely unlimited and may be trumped by important state interests.[29] Nevertheless, most courts seem inclined to vindicate the patient's decision unless it appears to be irrational, especially if the patient suffers from a terminal illness.[30]

JEWISH LAW PERSPECTIVE

Most secular arguments favoring the right to commit suicide, to obtain physician assistance to do so, and to refuse life-preserving treatment seem to be substantially based on one or more of three assumptions, each of which is rejected by Jewish law. Because these secular concepts are so familiar and fundamental, they provide a useful structure within which to contrast Jewish and secular perspectives.

Secular Assumptions

One common secular assumption is that there is no afterlife, no "World to Come." As a result, secularists ignore the positive effects that life in this world may ultimately have for a person when he enters the World to Come. Some of the arguments in support of lenient rules for allowing a patient to end his life under particular circumstances are based on qualitative judgments regarding the value of the patient's life. Even if this type of qualitative assessment were appropriate, a position that Jewish law rejects, such secularists, by ignoring the afterlife, would be woefully underestimating life's benefits.

Another important secular assumption is that each person is an independent being endowed with natural rights but bearing little or no affirmative obligations to others, certainly having no duty to suffer a burdensome existence for the benefit of others. Accordingly, if a person had to morally justify the decisions he makes as to his body, he would generally not need to consider the consequences of such actions to others.

Finally, many secularists axiomatically assume that a person's body and life are his own, and that he has some fundamental entitlement, often referred to as the right to "personal autonomy," to decide what to do with them, so long as his choice does not involve action that directly harms others.[31] According to this argument, it is morally right that a person be allowed to make such decisions, irrespective of whether the decisions themselves, according to any objective criteria, are morally good. In fact, the purported primacy of the entitlement to choose for oneself may be predicated on the assumption that there are no criteria with which to evaluate the morality of the choices themselves.

THE WORLD TO COME

Belief in an afterlife is one of the essential principles of Jewish law. Rabbi Maurice Lamm aptly emphasizes this principle's importance:

The conception of an after-life is fundamental to the Jewish religion. . . . The denial of the after-life constitutes a denial of the cornerstone of the faith. . . . Indeed, the Mishnah (Sanhedrin X, 1) expressly excludes from the reward of the "world beyond" he who holds that the resurrection of the dead is without biblical warrant. Maimonides considers this belief one of the 13 basic truths which every Jew is commanded to hold. . . .

Philosophers, such as Hasdai Crescas in the fourteenth century, changed the formulation of the basic truths, but still kept immortality [of the soul] as a fundamental principle without which Jewish religion is inconceivable. Simon Ben Zemach Duran, in the early fifteenth century, reduced the fundamentals to three, but resurrection was included. Joseph Albo, in the same era, revised the structure of dogmas, and still immortality remained a universally binding belief. No matter how the basic principles were reduced or revised, immortality remained a major tenet of Judaism.[32]

Indeed, conviction in an afterlife is inextricably linked to the equally fundamental Jewish principle of divinely administered reward and punishment. The Mishnah was compiled by Rabbi Yehuda Hanasi, circa 175 C.E. Rabbi Yehuda relied heavily on the teachings of Rabbi Meir. In-

deed, the Talmud states that any anonymous Mishnah is really the position of R. Meir according to the teaching of Rabbi Akiva.[33] One of R. Meir's
principal teachers was an outstanding scholar named Rabbi Elisha b.
Abuya. Nevertheless, at some point, R. Elisha lost his faith in Judaism,
and the Talmud refers to him as "*Aher*," "a different person." The Talmud
suggests that it was Aher's failure to believe in an afterlife that led him
to abandon his faith:

R. Yaakov said, "There is not a single commandment in the Torah whose reward
is [explicitly stated] at its side [i.e., in immediate proximity to the commandment
itself] which is not dependent on [belief in] the resurrection of the dead. For example, with respect to [the commandment of] honoring parents, it is written, 'that
your days may be prolonged, and that it may go well with you.' In reference to
[the commandment of] sending away [a mother bird from] the nest [before taking
the bird's young that are in the nest], it is written, 'that it may be well with you,
and that you may prolong your days.' Now, if a person's father says to him, 'Go
up to the loft and bring me some young birds,' and he ascends to the loft, sends
away the mother bird and takes its young, and on his return falls from the loft
and is killed—where is this person's happiness and where is this person's pro-
longing of days? But 'in order that it may be well with you' means on the day
that is wholly good [i.e., in the afterlife]; and 'in order that your days may be long,'
means on the day that is wholly long [i.e., in the afterlife]." . . . R. Yoseph said:
"Had *Aher* interpreted this verse as did R. Yaakov, his daughter's son, he [*Aher*]
would not have sinned." Now, what happened with *Aher?* Some say, he saw an
event of this nature. Others say that he saw the tongue of Huzpit the Interpreter
dragged along by a swine [after Huzpit was executed by the Romans]. "The mouth
that uttered pearls [of Torah knowledge] licks the dust!" he exclaimed. He [then]
went out and sinned.[34]

Although Jewish authorities disagree as to the precise nature of the
afterlife,[35] there is agreement that the reward for fulfillment of the commandments is so great that most of it, at least, must be dispensed in the
afterlife and not in this world of ephemeral existence.[36] Because *Aher* dis-
believed in an afterlife, he thought that any reward could only be given
in this world. As a result, he wrongfully believed that the incidents he
observed disproved Judaism.

Secularists who disbelieve in the afterlife fail to appreciate the purpose
of life in this world or the significant benefits that can be achieved in each
of its moments. As a result, from a Jewish perspective, they sorely mis-
calculate life's value and mistakenly justify a person's decision to terminate it.

MAN'S INDEPENDENCE OR INTERDEPENDENCE

Judaism rebuffs the concept of man as an essentially independent actor.
Instead, it posits the existence of a network of interrelationships between

and among Jews, non-Jews, and God. The deeds of one Jew, whether good or evil, affect all Jews.[37] Not only are the Jewish people judged together, but their actions influence the moral climate within which they make moral decisions. Therefore, Jews need to be concerned with how their actions affect others, as well as with how others act and affect them.

The rhetorical question, "Am I my brother's keeper?"[38] reflects the attitude of the world's first murderer; it is a sentiment that Judaism rejects. Rather, as Jewish authorities explain, just as "the world was built with kindness,"[39] the world was built for men to do kindnesses toward each other.[40] The commandment to "love your fellow as yourself"[41] is a basic Jewish precept,[42] and it prevents man from ignoring the consequences his decisions have for others.

PERSONAL AUTONOMY AND OBJECTIVE MORAL VALUES

Judaism believes that, in many instances, there is a criterion that determines whether a particular course of conduct is morally correct. The criterion is whether Jewish law requires or favors the conduct, on the one hand, or proscribes or discourages it, on the other.

In contrast to historical polytheism's belief in a plurality of morally flawed gods, Judaism accepts God as morally perfect and His commandments as prescribing proper conduct. As Walter Wurzburger explains, the recognition of universally applicable ethical principles was one of the principal innovations of Jewish religious thought:

Jewish monotheism represents a radically different approach to religion. Its novelty consisted not primarily in the substitution of the belief in one God for the plurality of gods worshiped in polytheism. What was even more revolutionary in the Jewish conception of monotheism was, as against the pagan emphasis upon divine power, the attribution of moral perfection to God. ... Worship of God involves commitment to abide by His will and the ethical norms He demands.[43]

Thus, if God's law requires or encourages a particular act, the act is righteous, and if it forbids or discourages the act, the act is wrongful.

While Judaism believes that each person has "free will," the belief in free will should not be confused with the secular argument in favor of personal autonomy. According to Jewish belief, free will is the *power* to choose between good and evil and to act on that choice. Thus, a person has the power to contravene God's will by choosing to do evil. Of course, Judaism does not maintain that a person has the "right" to do so. On the contrary, a person is commanded to utilize his free will to do good, and he faces divine retribution should he choose evil. Consequently, in ascertaining whether a particular choice is morally appropriate, a Jew must ascertain what, if anything, Jewish law has to say about it.

As I have explained elsewhere, Jewish law is not a straitjacket.[44] In critical ways, it provides considerable flexibility for personal choice among various permitted options. Nevertheless, as to the many cases in which Jewish law speaks clearly, a person is obligated to comply with the morally correct guidance it provides. Now that we have examined Judaism's position as to these three secular assumptions, we can consider each of the end-of-life decisions in detail.

SUICIDE

Jewish law clearly and emphatically rejects the assumption that a person's body and life are his to do with as he pleases. They belong to God, who declares that "The souls are Mine,"[45] and man merely serves as His bailee.[46] Judaism posits that God, who is omniscient, omnipotent, and benevolent, created everything that exists pursuant to a divine plan. Although not all of His purposes are revealed, one of them is for man to experience spiritual growth and to be "holy."[47] Part, although not all, of this process involves the manner in which man copes with the challenges life presents. Consequently, Jewish law not only forbids a Jew to kill himself,[48] but it forbids him to wound himself.[49] Indeed, Jewish law requires that a Jew take affirmative steps to protect and preserve his life.[50] If necessary, a Jew is directed to commit many types of acts that would otherwise be capital offenses, such as the violation of the Sabbath laws, in order to save his life or the life of another.[51]

Judaism regards suicide as an especially opprobrious transgression. A person who commits suicide is called a murderer, punishable at the hands of heaven.[52] Although virtually all Jews, even sinners, are promised a place in the World to Come,[53] suicides are excluded.[54] In addition, Jewish law provides that suicides are to be buried in a separate, distant place in the cemetery and to be denied certain rites of mourning.[55] As a practical matter, however, because rabbinic authorities cannot usually be certain whether a person was legally competent when he killed himself, they rarely treat a death as a suicide.

By committing suicide, a person demonstrates gross ingratitude for life and the opportunities it presents. On one level, life in this world provides an opportunity for earning reward in the afterlife. On a somewhat deeper level, Jewish philosophy believes that by performing God's commandments, a person can increase his spirituality and intensify his relationship to God.[56] These accomplishments are intrinsically, and not merely instrumentally, important. Nevertheless, by enhancing his spiritual sensitivity, a person also transforms himself into someone who can better appreciate and utilize the opportunities available in the World to Come. Perhaps this is the meaning underlying Rabbi Akiva's Mishnaic statement, "This world is like a corridor leading to the World to Come. Prepare yourself in the

corridor so that you can enter the banquet hall."[57] One must prepare himself in this world so that he is better suited to participate in the World to
Come. A person who commits suicide belittles and discards this
opportunity.

By ending his life, a person also deprives himself of the chance to repent
for past sins, because repentance is only possible during life.[58] In fact,
although a person's death itself usually effectuates, or helps effectuate,
atonement for many of his misdeeds, suicide brings no expiation. Instead,
the act of suicide adds yet another, serious transgression to a person's
account.[59]

In addition to denying his obligations to God, a person committing
suicide often reflects callousness to his duties to his dependents and to
the possibly deleterious effects his suicide may have on others. Some commentators think that by killing himself, a person diminishes the image of
God, for man is made in that image.[60] By reflecting a cheapened image of
human life, suicide may lead to less respectful and tolerant interaction
among people.

More fundamentally, perhaps, the act of suicide denies God's authority
as to matters of life and death. Consider the Talmudic discussion of the
following biblical passage:

In those days [King] Hezekiah was sick unto death and the prophet, Isaiah the
son of Amoz, came to him and said unto him, "Thus said the Lord: Command
your house, for you shall die and not live."[61]

The phrase "for you shall die and not live" seems redundant. The Talmud, however, explains that it means "you shall die in this world and not
live in the World to Come." Hezekiah asked why he warranted such a
harsh sentence. Isaiah responded by saying it was because Hezekiah had
not engaged in procreation. To this, Hezekiah replied, "I saw by means of
the holy spirit that wicked children would descend from me." Isaiah re-
torted, "What have you to do with the plans of the All-Merciful? You
should do what you are commanded to do and let the Holy One, blessed
be He, do that which is pleasing to Him."[62]

This Talmudic passage seems difficult to understand, because the obligation to procreate is an affirmative commandment,[63] and loss of one's
place in the World to Come is not the prescribed punishment for failure
to perform an affirmative commandment. The late Rabbi Haim Shmuelevitz, a twentieth-century scholar, explains that Hezekiah's punishment
was so severe because of the reason he failed to perform the commandment. Hezekiah's conduct was driven by his concern over the consequences that would flow from fulfillment of the commandment. In a sense,
this behavior reflected a lack of trust in God and His divine plan. Moreover, says R. Shmuelevitz, Hezekiah's conduct was regarded as a form of

rebellion against the Creator's authority.[64] An implicit rejection of God's dominion regarding end-of-life decisions seems to be at least as blameworthy.

Some secularists contend that a person should be permitted to commit suicide—and should be entitled to physician-assisted suicide—when the "quality" of his life is unacceptable, such as when he suffers from intractable emotional or physical pain. Normative Jewish law, reflecting the views of a majority of Jewish law authorities, rejects this contention.[65] As at least one authority explicitly argues, if suicide were allowed on such grounds, the exception would swallow the rule, because it is just such pain that drives most people to contemplate suicide.[66] Man is charged with sanctifying himself by contending with life's challenges and fulfilling God's commandments.

To demonstrate that pain does not justify suicide, many cite, among other sources, the Talmudic description of the execution of R. Hanina b. Teradion:

[The Romans] found R. Hanina b. Teradion sitting and occupying himself with the Torah, publicly gathering assemblies, and keeping a scroll of the Law in his bosom. Straightaway they took hold of him, wrapped him in the Scroll of the Law, placed bundles of branches round him and set them on fire. They then brought tufts of wool, which they had soaked in water, and placed them over his heart, so that he should not expire quickly. His daughter exclaimed, "Father, that I should see you in this state!" He replied, "If it were I alone being burnt it would have been a thing hard to bear; but now that I am burning together with the Scroll of the Law, He who will have regard for the plight of the Torah will also have regard for my plight." His disciples called out, "Rabbi, what do you see?" He answered them, "The parchments are being burnt but the letters are soaring on high." [His disciples said] "Open your mouth so that the fire enter into you [and kill you quickly]." He replied, "Let Him who gave me [my soul] take it away; no one should injure oneself."[67]

Thus, even though R. Hanina b. Teradion was suffering agonizing pain, he did not take any affirmative action to end his life.

Of course, as the Talmud itself testifies, compassion is a particularly distinctive Jewish trait.[68] How is the concern for compassion reconciled with the law forbidding suicide? First, Jewish belief assumes that, because God is omniscient, omnipotent, and benevolent, whatever He does is for the best, even if His purposes are not fully comprehended.[69] Thus, Jewish law assumes that suffering is designed for a person's own best interests as well, perhaps, as for the best interests of others.

Even if, in a particular case, the specific benefit that suffering is supposed to accomplish is unknown, there are many possibilities. The Talmud explains, for instance, that suffering may atone for a person's sins, allowing him to avoid considerably harsher punishment in the World to

Come.[70] Similarly, suffering sometimes serves as a reminder to someone to repent and, thereby, obtain atonement for his sins. Consequently, the Talmud counsels that a person who confronts what he considers to be misfortune should examine the righteousness of his deeds.[71]

Although a person may not be guilty of actual sin, he may nonetheless have allowed his relationship to God to become attenuated, and suffering may help to reawaken and reinvigorate this awareness of God. The Talmud states that if two people, A and B, have the same needs and A prays for B's need to be fulfilled, A's need is answered first.[72] While it seems appropriate that A, who has demonstrated sincere concern about his fellow's needs, should receive divine assistance, the question arises as to why A should receive such assistance first. One possible answer to this question is that the reason why A lacks something is to cause him to remember God and to pray to Him. If A is already praying to God for B's benefit, there is no longer any reason for A to lack anything.[73]

Dealing successfully with suffering may also enable a person to develop his inner holiness, while, at the same time, permitting him to earn reward in the World to Come. Similarly, by steadfastly bearing his pain, a person may reinforce the faith of others, helping them and earning divine reward. Jewish authorities suggest other reasons as well.[74]

Second, some Jewish authorities suggest that life with pain, even excruciating pain, is better than death. They cite, for instance, the case of a *Soteh*, a woman accused of adultery under certain specific circumstances, who was required, in the times of the Temple, to drink a certain potion.[75] If guilty, the *Soteh* would die—but not always immediately. The Talmud explains that if, unrelated to the adultery, the woman had other merits, the potion would cause a degenerative, lingering death. Although this condition would presumably involve physical and emotional pain, it was nonetheless considered a reward in contrast to immediate death.[76]

Third, however, Jewish law does not prevent a person from taking steps to avoid or eliminate his suffering. For example, a person may seek psychological or physical treatment to alleviate emotional or physical afflictions. Some medical literature indicates that antidepressant therapy can in many cases eliminate a patient's suicidal desires,[77] but many physicians are insufficiently trained to recognize and treat depression. Similarly, studies show that there are potent palliative medications for most physical pains, but there is an inadequate awareness of them.[78]

Nevertheless, Jewish law rejects the doctrine of "double effect" and would not permit treatment that would obviously hasten the patient's death, even if the patient and the doctor honestly declared that their subjective intent was to ease the pain and not to hasten the patient's death.[79] Their foreknowledge of the death would be sufficient to make the action wrongful. The position of the United States Supreme Court is less clear.

Jewish law permits a person to cope with pain by praying to God and asking to be released from his suffering, even if the release be through death.[80] Requesting such relief from God reaffirms, rather than repudiates, God's sovereignty in these matters. By contrast, a person who commits suicide because of his suffering wrongfully denies God's ability to answer his prayers.

An extreme modern-day case of duress tested these teachings. Rabbi Ephraim Oshry, an authority in the Kovno Ghetto in 1941, reports that German soldiers would sadistically murder children in front of parents and wives in front of husbands before finally killing the husbands.[81] On October 27, 1941, two days before 10,000 members of the Kovno Ghetto— men, women, and children—were taken away to be killed, a respected member of the ghetto tearfully approached Rabbi Oshry and said that he simply would not be able to endure watching his loved ones suffer. For this reason,[82] he asked whether it would be permissible for him to kill himself. Although Rabbi Oshry noted the view of *Besamim Rosh,* he ruled that, notwithstanding the extenuating circumstances, it was not a priori permissible for the man to commit suicide.[83]

Although the overwhelming number of Jewish law authorities rule that suicide is prohibited for the purpose of avoiding pain, there is considerable support for the notion that suicide may be permitted in order to sanctify God's Name (*Kiddush Ha-shem*) or to avoid desecration of God's Name (*Hillul Ha-shem*). Some authorities argue that a person sanctifies God's Name by killing himself rather than allowing himself to be forced to commit sexual immorality or idolatry. These scholars find evidence for this Halakhic view in a story found in the Talmudic tractate Gittin.[84] The Romans were transporting by boat 400 Jewish boys and girls to be used for illicit sexual purposes. Rather than be forced to participate in their captors' plans, these captives—whom the Talmud extols—plunged into the ocean, preferring to be drowned. Indeed, Rav Yaakov ben Meir (*Rebbenu Tam*), an outstanding twelfth-century scholar, cites this episode as proof that, "[w]here people fear that idol-worshipers will force them to sin through torture that they will be unable to withstand, it is a 'mitzva'[85] for them to smite themselves."[86] Similarly, some authorities explain that King Saul, when helplessly wounded on the battlefield, sought to commit suicide because he feared he would be captured and coerced, through torture, to commit idolatry, thereby desecrating God's Name.[87] This view of Jewish law seems to have been relied on by thousands of Jews throughout our history who, when faced with the prospect of forced conversion, committed suicide.[88] Nonetheless, not all authorities agree that suicide is permitted even for these important purposes.[89]

PHYSICIAN-ASSISTED DYING

As stated at the outset, by "physician-assisted dying," we mean both voluntary physician euthanasia and physician-assisted suicide. Jewish law regards any affirmative act of euthanasia as murder, even if the patient's death is only hastened by a few moments.[90] In this respect, Jewish law agrees with secular law throughout the United States, and disagrees with the law of the Netherlands and Belgium. But one might ask, "How do Jewish authorities know that this prohibition applies even when a person 'compassionately' terminates a suffering patient's life at the patient's own request?"[91] Rabbi Jacob Zevi Mecklenburg, a nineteenth-century scholar, derives this rule from the following biblical passage:

The blood of your lives will I require; from the hand of every beast will I require it, and from the hand of man, from the hand of a person's brother, will I require the life of man. If one spills the blood of a man, one's [own] blood will be spilled by man.[92]

R. Mecklenburg asks what lesson is learned from the phrase, "from the hand of a person's brother, will I require the life of man."[93] A proscription against fratricide seems to follow logically from the prohibition against ordinary homicide. Indeed, fratricide may even appear more abhorrent than simple murder of a stranger. According to Jewish law's oral tradition, if a rule can be logically derived, there is no need for it to be explicitly stated in the Torah. Consequently, this biblical passage must communicate some additional message. R. Mecklenburg argues that the apparent surplusage is necessary to outlaw an act of killing even when the act is motivated by "brotherly love," that is, by a misguided desire to mercifully end the life of a person suffering from excruciating pain.[94]

What about physician-assisted suicide, where the physician does not directly kill the patient but, instead, "merely" furnishes the patient with the means with which he can kill himself? Jewish law's fundamental view is that where the patient is not allowed to commit suicide, the physician should not provide the patient with the means of committing suicide. Thus, Jewish law disagrees with Oregon's Death with Dignity statute to the extent that the latter allows physicians to assist suicides that, according to Jewish law, should not be taking place.

The precise nature of the Jewish law proscription on the provision of assistance varies depending on the circumstances of each case. For example, if the patient actually needs the physician's help in order to end his life, the physician is biblically forbidden to provide it.[95] If a Jewish patient has alternative sources of assistance, then a physician who aids him may only be guilty of violating a rabbinic prohibition.[96]

As already mentioned, Jewish law recognizes the Jewish people as a unique community in which each member has a special relationship with, and correspondent duties to, each other member. As a result, if the patient and physician are both Jewish, Jewish law not only forbids the physician from assisting the suicide, but affirmatively obligates him to take appropriate steps to dissuade the patient from taking his life. Thus, Jewish law requires the physician to try to "rescue" the patient from his suicidal intentions. The physician might not only have to arrange for the patient to have psychological and medical therapy but, if necessary, might have to spend his own money to do so.[97] Similarly, suppose that, under Jewish law, the patient would be forbidden to refuse a particular therapy; yet, nonetheless, the patient refuses. Theoretically, the Jewish law duty to rescue might require the physician to treat the patient against his wishes.[98] For a number of practical reasons, coercive treatment is not likely to be often obligatory in the United States. First, in some situations, Jewish law does not demand that patients submit to certain treatments.[99] Second, secular law generally forbids nonconsensual treatment. As a result, other persons—such as nurses or administrators—might effectively prevent a physician from providing coercive treatment. They might accomplish this either by refusing to provide necessary assistance or by directly interfering with his efforts. Third, Jewish law places limits on the extent of monetary and nonmonetary loss a person must incur to fulfill his duty to rescue.[100] In many cases, physicians in the United States would not be required to run the risks arising from treating patients against their will.

REFUSAL OF LIFE-PRESERVING MEDICAL TREATMENT

Jewish law and U.S. law differ considerably regarding the refusal of life-preserving medical treatment. Unlike secular law, Jewish law substantially limits a patient's right to refuse such treatment. As already mentioned, Jewish law not only prohibits a person from ending his life, but it also requires that he take affirmative steps to preserve his life for as long as possible.[101] Even if a patient suffers from pain that cannot be adequately palliated, he is generally required not only to accept but to affirmatively seek life-preserving treatment. Moreover, in a society governed by Jewish law, a patient who refuses such treatment can be treated without his consent.[102]

Despite this general rule, there may be some exceptions. We will consider only the principal one, which involves what Jewish law calls a *goses*. On the one hand, the *goses* is alive just as any healthy person, and anyone who hastens his death is guilty of murder.[103] On the other hand, a *goses* is someone who is already in the midst of the metaphysical act of dying. He is expected to expire imminently. Jewish law assumes that a *goses* experiences extreme pain. Even if the *goses* is comatose and, according to his physician, does not suffer, R. Moshe Feinstein, a leading twentieth-century authority, states that we assume that the *goses* experiences metaphysical pain. It is only that the doctor's equipment is not designed to detect it.[104]

Jewish law authorities express three basic positions as to the "treatment" of a *goses*.[105] First, virtually all authorities agree that one may remove anything that is impeding the soul's departure. Rabbi Moshe Isserles (Rema), a leading sixteenth-century authority, for instance, states that if someone nearby is chopping wood and the noise he is making prevents the *goses* from expiring, one should stop him from chopping.[106] Nevertheless, many of these authorities contend that medical treatment that preserves the *goses*'s life is not to be regarded as an "impediment" and that it should be provided even if doing so requires violation of the Sabbath laws.[107]

A second view acknowledges the distinction between impediments to death and medical treatment, but asserts that there is no *obligation* to provide medical treatment to a *goses*.[108] Medical treatment can be provided on the Sabbath only when doing so is an effort to fulfill the commandment of saving life. Consequently, according to this view, it would not even be permissible to provide such treatment to a *goses* on the Sabbath.

The third view fails to distinguish between an impediment to death and medical treatment. Each is improper and is to be removed. Indeed, this view prohibits any action, including the provision of medication, designed to prolong the life of a *goses*.[109] Even according to this view, however, any affirmative action, such as movement of the *goses*, that may directly hasten the *goses*'s death, is strictly forbidden.

According to all three of these perspectives, a *goses* has the right to refuse anything that would fall into the category of an "impediment." According to the second and third views, but not according to the first, a *goses* seems to have the right to refuse medical treatments. As a practical matter, however, a variety of factors makes reliance on any of these lenient positions extremely difficult. In any actual case, it would be necessary to consult with an expert Jewish law authority for guidance.

The major practical complication arises from the fact that a patient who wrongfully refuses life-preserving treatment violates the obligation to preserve his health, a duty arising directly from the Torah, which was communicated directly from God,[110] rather than a duty arising from a rabbinic rule. Jewish law is especially strict as to Torah law and not only forbids action (or inaction) that definitely violates the law, but even forbids such conduct where there is some doubt as to whether it violates the law. Consequently, if conduct would constitute a violation of Torah law under any of the three views regarding a *goses*, Jewish law would prohibit that conduct. The fact that one or two of the other views would rule leniently merely raises a doubt as to whether the conduct is a violation, and Jewish law rules stringently, as to a matter involving Torah law, even in the face of such doubt.

Even relying on a leniency as to which all three views agree—the removal of impediments to the dying process—is not so simple. For instance, while some authorities might regard a ventilator as an impediment that prolongs a patient's death, others would characterize it as medical treatment that extends the patient's life.[111] According to this latter characterization, the first of the three views regarding a *goses* would clearly forbid removal of the ventilator.

Another problem is that there is considerable debate as to criteria that determine whether a person is a *goses*, and according to most authorities any special leniency applies only to a *goses*. The *Rema* does not define a *goses* as any person whose physical condition is known by expert doctors to be imminent. Instead, he describes a *goses* as a person with a specific symptom, that is, a person who "brings up secretion in his throat on account of the narrowing of his chest."[112] Most Jewish law authorities held that it was impossible for a *goses* to live for more than a very short time, such as seventy-two hours,[113] even with whatever forms of medical intervention were available. Consequently, it is not clear whether someone falls into the category of a *goses* if either: (1) he lacks the precise symptom mentioned by the *Rema*, or (2) modern medical intervention could maintain his life for longer than seventy-two hours. Although some contemporary authorities sharply limit the category of *goses*,[114] some others apply a much more inclusive test.[115]

Whenever an affected person fails to fall within the narrow definition of *goses*, there would be a possibility that the person is not a *goses* and that no leniency would apply. Consequently, so long as a possible violation of Torah law were at stake, Jewish law would seem to rule stringently and proscribe reliance on any leniency.

Despite this general analysis, however, there is considerable debate as to whether a person may refuse life-preserving treatment if one or more of the following factors is present: (1) The patient is terminally ill and the treatment will only prolong the patient's temporary, extremely painful condition, and (2) the treatment is not well established, is painful, is risky, and/or is not likely to succeed.[116]

Some authorities think that the degree of pain someone experiences will only in truly exceptional cases excuse someone from the duty to prolong her life.[117] Others seem less reluctant to rule that terminally ill patients in great pain can refuse treatment that will only prolong their agonizing existence. Of course, as a practical matter, this debate is only relevant in those instances in which the pain is medically uncontrollable. Where it is controllable, it should be controlled.

Those who are more lenient as to the refusal of medical care often rely on the Talmudic discussion of the final illness of Rabbi Yehuda HaNasi, known as *Rabbi*, the compiler of the Mishnah. *Rabbi* was suffering greatly.[118] Both the rabbis and *Rabbi*'s devoted female servant, well known for her devotion and intelligence, prayed around the clock for *Rabbi*'s complete recovery.[119] As time passed, however, *Rabbi*'s servant saw that the prayers were not to be fulfilled. Although *Rabbi* remained alive, he suffered excruciating pain. Finally, she concluded that it would be better for *Rabbi* if he were to die, and she prayed for that.[120] But she soon saw that her prayer would not be accepted so long as the rabbis continued their unabated prayers for *Rabbi*'s recovery. She therefore threw an urn from the roof of the academy to the ground, smashing it and startling the rabbis, causing a brief halt in their prayers. At that moment, *Rabbi* died.[121]

Many commentators cite the conduct of *Rabbi*'s servant as evidence that someone who sees that another is greatly afflicted and that there is no meaningful prospect for alleviating or curing the person's pain should pray for that person's death.[122] Not all commentators, however, agree that one should pray for another's death even under these circumstances.[123] In addition, at least one authority, Rabbi Haim Palaggi, states that persons who might have an improper bias, such as those responsible to care for the patient, should certainly not pray for the patient's death.[124]

Rabbi Moshe Feinstein, a foremost twentieth-century authority, however, states that this Talmudic episode not only justifies praying for a person's death but also calls for the rejection of life-sustaining medical treatment for terminally ill patients who can live no longer than a few weeks or so and who are experiencing excruciating pain. If the treatment can only temporarily prolong their life of agony, Rabbi Feinstein argues that nontreatment is appropriate, while repeating that, of course, no affirmative act to terminate the patient's life is permissible.[125] Rabbi Shlomo Zalman Auerbach, another leading twentieth-century scholar, similarly considers a patient's pain and suffering in ruling that it is permissible for a person to refuse surgery that, even if successful at saving her life, would cause her to remain paralyzed for life.[126]

There seem to be two principal ways of perceiving the conceptual framework for the Feinstein-Auerbach approach. One possibility is that it generalizes the *Rema*'s rule for removing obstacles preventing a *goses* from dying.[127] Feinstein, for instance, believes that there is metaphysical pain associated with the process of being a *goses*. Consequently, a terminally ill person who has little time to live and who is experiencing unmanageable pain may seem quite similar to a *goses*.[128]

There are a number of problems with the analogy to a *goses*. First, of course, the Feinstein-Auerbach approach is squarely at odds with the many authorities who believe that medical intervention is required even to save the life of a *goses*. Second, the approach fails to provide meaningful guidance as to the degree of pain a terminal patient must experience to be compared to a *goses*. Third, the Feinstein-Auerbach view fails to specify how short a period of time to live a terminally ill patient must have to be compared to a *goses*. Finally, their position does not explain how one can effectively quantify a person's pain or predict when she will expire.

Moreover, is it really persuasive to argue that the fact one can pray for death means that one can refuse treatment? Those who disagree with the Feinstein-Auerbach position, for instance, argue that while one is alive, one has the duty to perform commandments, including the commandment to prolong one's life. Praying for death is not inconsistent with fulfillment of this duty. A person can always ask the Master of the Universe to release her from her duty. Meanwhile, however, the duty must be done.[129]

Rabbi J. David Bleich, a contemporary American scholar, suggests a different way to understand the Feinstein-Auerbach approach, based on the inherent limits on what a person is required to endure rather than transgress a Torah prohibition. The general rule is that one must give up all of one's wealth rather than do something that violates such a proscription.[130] On the other hand, compliance is excused if it will cause a person a loss that is greater than the loss of all of his wealth. Thus, when asked whether it was permitted to take an organ from a cadaver to effectuate a life-saving transplant against the wishes of the deceased's surviving relatives, Feinstein replied in the negative. He stated that a person is not required to give up more than all of his wealth to save another's life. He then cited a Talmudic passage as proof that such treatment of the corpse would presumably cause the surviving relatives to suffer more emotional distress than would the loss of their entire fortunes.[131] Because this loss was more than what was required of these surviving relatives, the organs could not be involuntarily taken.[132] Similarly, Bleich contends, Feinstein[133] may be justifying a person's right to refuse medical treatment in cases involving excruciating pain on the assumption that the patients would be willing to give up their entire fortunes rather than suffer for a more prolonged period.[134] If so, however, Bleich questions how often this assumption would be correct, particularly in light of improved palliation procedures.[135]

Some of the authorities who disagree with the Feinstein-Auerbach approach of permitting terminally ill patients to refuse treatment because of their pain may nonetheless rule that such refusal is justified in individual cases based on the nature of the treatments involved. Thus, a person is not generally obligated to submit to "unproven" experimental treatments.[136] Indeed, a person may not even be allowed to take some medications because of the attendant risks.[137]

Similarly, in determining whether someone who is ill should, or must, take treatment on the Sabbath or use unkosher substances even during the week, commentators consider: (1) whether the effect of the treatment is physiological or metaphysical; and (2) whether the goal is to ameliorate the patient's painful or dangerous symptoms or merely to prolong the patient's present condition.[138]

Furthermore, even according to the view that permits the refusal of treatment in certain situations, many, but not all, authorities believe that the patient may not refuse any procedure that satisfies his basic needs, such as nutrition, hydration, and oxygen, or that beneficially deals with complications of his condition, such as antibiotics for pneumonia, that "any other patient would willingly accept."[139] Indeed, under strict Jewish law, physicians would be required to perform such procedures even against the patient's objection.

CONCLUSION

Jewish law's approach to the degree of discretion afforded a competent patient as to end-of-life decisions is based on its fundamental conception of man's role, and God's role, in the world. Judaism believes that life is immensely important, that it provides man with the opportunity to perfect his character and become holy, to draw close to God, to prepare himself for eternal life in the World to Come and to influence his fellows to do the same. Man can accomplish this by fulfilling God's law, for it is assumed to be morally correct. In all situations, that law forbids man from engaging in suicide or physician-assisted suicide and requires him to accept life-preserving treatment.

NOTES

1. There is considerable controversy among Jewish law authorities as to whether the so-called brain-stem death or whole-brain death criteria establish death under Jewish law. See, for example, Abraham S. Abraham, *The Comprehensive Guide to Medical Halachah* (New York: Feldheim Publishers, 1996), 173. This debate is irrelevant to this chapter, however, because this chapter addresses issues involving patients who are conscious and legally competent.

2. The European Court of Human Rights upheld Britain's law against assisted suicide in *Pretty v. The United Kingdom*, No. 2346/02, European Court of Human Rights, 4/29/02. See, for example, Clare Dyer, "Dying Woman Loses Her Battle for Assisted Suicide," *British Medical Journal* 324, 7345 (May 4, 2002), reported at 2002 wL 12634321.

3. See, generally, *Washington v. Glucksberg*, 521 U.S. 702 (1997). See also Wayne R. LaFave and Austin W. Scott, Jr., *Substantive Criminal Law*, volume 2, § 7.8 (St. Paul, MN: West Publication Co., 1986), ("In some states attempted suicide, which was a common law misdemeanor, was at one time a crime, but the prevailing view has long been otherwise") (footnotes omitted).

4. Id., especially notes 28–31 (describing and citing specific state statutes).

5. See *Washington v. Glucksberg*, supra n. 3 and *Vacco v. Quill*, 521 U.S. 793 (1997). Several earlier state courts had similarly rejected federal constitutional challenges to laws against assisted suicide. See, for example, *Sanderson v. People*, 2000 C.J.C.A.R. 3169, 12 P.3d 851 (Colo. 2000) (Colorado law did not violate the federal right to free exercise of religion); *Krischer v. McIver*, 22 Fla. Weekly S443, 697 So.2d 97 (Fla. 1997) (Florida law did not violate the federal constitution's equal protection clause).

6. See *Sampson et al. v. State of Alaska,* No. S-9338 (Alaska, Sept. 21, 2001) (upholding manslaughter law as it applies to physicians who would assist patient suicides by prescribing medications to hasten their deaths). See also "Alaska High Court Rejects Plea to Legalize Assisted Suicide," *Andrews Nursing Home Litigation Reporter* 4, 5 (Nov. 16, 2001), ANNHLTGR 12.

7. *Krischer v. McIver,* 22 Fla. Weekly S443, 697 So.2d 97 (Fla. 1997).

8. Faye Girsch, "Equalize the Right to Die," *National Law Journal* (March 29, 1999), A22, col. 1.

9. See *Washington v. Glucksberg,* supra n. 3 (discussing results of New York State's Task Force on Life and the Law).

10. See Martin Gunderson and David J. Mayo, "Restricting Physician-Assisted Death to the Terminally Ill," *The Hastings Center Report* 30, 6 (November 1, 2000) (referring to the legislative efforts in Washington in 1991, California in 1992, and Michigan and California in 2000) WL 17342995; Rita L. Marker, "Kids and Euthanasia," *The Human Life Review* 26, 1 (January 1, 2000), 2000 WL 25872891 (1997 Illinois "Dignity in Dying Act," Illinois HB 691, never made it out of committee); Catherine Edwards, "Social Measures Do Well on Ballot," *Insight* magazine 16, 46 (December 11, 2000), 2000 WL 26643719. See also "Physician-Assisted Suicide: Court Activity, Recent U.S. Developments," http://www.religioustolerance.org/euth_us3.htm (reporting on California's February 2000 rejection of a proposed "Death with Dignity Act").

11. See, for example, "Gay Rights Advocates Mull Next Move," *Bangor Daily News* (11/29/2000), 2000 WL 28978321 (reporting results of referenda of November, 2000); "Hawaii Legislature Rejects Physician-Assisted Suicide Bill," Associated Press Newswires (5/2/02), APWIRES 22:02:00.

12. See Web pages sponsored by the Death with Dignity National Center, at http://www.deathwithdignity.org/legislative/legislativehome.htm.

13. *Or. Rev. Stat.* 127.800 et seq. (1995). This statute has withstood efforts to repeal it. See Rita L. Marker, supra n. 10.

14. *People v. Kevorkian,* 248 Mich. App. 373, 639 N.W.2d 291 (Mich. App. 2001), appeal denied, *People v. Kevorkian,* 642 N.W.2d 681 (April 9, 2002) (Table, No. 120561); Cert. denied, *Kevorkian v. Michigan,* 537 US 881 (2002).

15. *State of Oregon v. Ashcroft,* No. CV01–1647-JO. See, generally, Bill Hewitt et al., "Last Wish," *People* (November 26, 2001), 62.

16. *State of Oregon v. Ashcroft,* 192 F.Supp.2d 1077 (D.Or 2002).

17. As to the possibility of federal political action, see, for example, "Congress Determined to Overturn Oregon Law," *Compassion in Dying,* Issue 10 (August 1998), at http://www.thebody.com/cid/aug98/congress.html.

18. See, for example, *Vacco v. Quill,* supra n. 5.

19. See, generally, Robert Klinck, "Pain Relief Promotion Act," *Harvard Journal of Legislation* 38, 249 (2001); Christin A. Balt, "The Pain Relief Promotion Act of 1999 and Physician-Assisted Suicide: A Call for Congressional Self-Restraint," 38 *San Diego Law Review* 38, 297 (2001).

20. See http://www.religioustolerance.org/euth_wld.htm.

21. Ibid.

22. Faye Girsch, supra n. 7 (referring to 1997 decision of Colombia's Constitutional Court).

23. See http://www.religioustolerance.org/euth_wld.htm (referring to Colombia and Japan).

24. Raphael Cohen-Almagor, "An Outsider's View of Dutch Euthanasia Policy and Practice," *Issues in Law & Medicine* 17 (2001): 67,; M.D. Harmon, "Holland Legalizes Euthanasia, Opening Door That Should Stay Shut," *Portland Press Herald* (April 16, 2001), 2001 WL 6487855.

25. See the BBC Web site, http://news.bbc.co.uk/I/hiword/europe/1992018.stm (5/16/2002).

26. *Vacco v. Quill*, supra n. 5 (footnotes omitted).

27. See, for example, *Superintendent of Belchertown State School v. Saikewicz*, 373 Mass. 728, 370 N.E.2d 417 (1977); *Schloendorff v. Society of New York Hospital*, 211 N.Y. 125, 105 N.E. 92 (1914).

28. In *Cruzan v. Director, Missouri Department of Health*, 497 U.S. 261 (1990), the Supreme Court was asked whether a parent could authorize termination of treatment—including disconnection from a life-preserving ventilator—of a comatose, and therefore legally incompetent, adult daughter. The Court assumed that the child, if she were competent, would have the constitutional right to terminate the treatment. In *Washington v. Glucksberg*, supra n. 4, the Supreme Court stated that although a legally competent adult had a federal constitutional right to terminate treatment, he did not have the right to commit suicide through the ingestion of poison or to have someone provide him with such poison.

Although many lower federal and state court opinions also support this proposition, a few early decisions reached contrary results, especially where the treatment at question (such as a blood transfusion) involved little physical risk or pain and was expected to enable the patient to make essentially a complete recovery. See, generally, Kristine Cordier Karnezis, "Annotation: Patient's Right to Refuse Treatment Allegedly Necessary to Sustain Life," 93 *A.L.R.3d* 67 (1979).

Some of these cases examined whether the patient could refuse treatment based on his constitutional right to free exercise of religion.

29. *Cruzan v. Director, Missouri Department of Health*, supra n. 28.

30. See, for example, *Saikewicz*, supra n. 27, p. 426 n. 11.

31. Thus, even though, according to the personal autonomy assumption, a person's hands are his own, he has no entitlement to use them to strangle someone else.

32. Maurice Lamm, *The Jewish Way in Death and Dying* (New York: Jonathan David, 1969), 224–25.

33. Babylonian Talmud, *Sanhedrin* 86a.

34. Babylonian Talmud, *Kiddushin* 39b.

35. Maurice Lamm, supra n. 29, 25–26; Aryeh Kaplan, *Immortality, Resurrection, and the Age of the Universe: A Kabbalistic View* (Hoboken, NJ: KTAV, 1993), 29–44.

36. Babylonian Talmud, *Kiddushin* 39b, R. Shimon b. Zemah Duran (*Rashbatz;* fourteenth through fifteenth centuries), *Magen Avot, Pirkei Avot* 2:21.

37. R. Yehuda he-Hasid, *Sefer Hasidim* 93, 233, 601. See also R. Aryeh Kaplan, *Handbook of Jewish Thought* II, 136–37: When a single Jew sins, it is not he alone who suffers, but the entire Jewish people. In the Midrash, this is likened to passengers on a single huge ship. Though all the passengers may be very careful not to damage the hull, if one of them takes a drill and begins drilling holes under his own seat, the ship will sink, and all will drown. In the same manner, whenever any Jew does not keep the Torah, all others are affected spiritually. Such actions may even precipitate physical suffering for the Jewish people. [Citations omitted.]

38. Genesis 4:9.

39. Psalms 89:3.

40. *Rashbatz,* supra n. 36, 1:2.

41. Leviticus 19:18.

42. *Orkhot Tzaddikim, Sha'ar ha-Rahamim,* s.v. *ha-Rahamim Zot* (anonymous author; fifteenth century).

43. Walter Wurzburger, *Ethics of Responsibility* (Philadelphia: Jewish Publication Society, 1994), 4.

44. Steven H. Resnicoff, "Professional Ethics and Autonomy: A Theological Critique," in *Law and Religion: Current Legal Issues 2001,* ed. Richard O'Dair and Andrew Lewis (London: Oxford University Press, 2001): 329-48.

45. Ezekiel 18:4.

46. See, for example, R. Eliezer Waldenberg, *Tzitz Eliezer V, Ramat Rachel* 29(1); Abraham S. Abraham, "Euthanasia," in *Medicine and Jewish Law,* ed. Fred Rosner (Northvale, NJ: Jason Aronson, 1990), 123; J. David Bleich, "Life as an Intrinsic Rather Than Instrumental Good: The 'Spiritual' Case Against Euthanasia," *Issues of Law & Medicine* 9, 139 (1993): 144 ("[m]an's interest in his life and in his body are subservient to those of the Creator. . . . [I]t is the Creator who is the ultimate proprietor of human life. . . . ").

47. Leviticus 19:2 ("You shall be holy, for I, your Lord, your God, am holy").

48. Most authorities identify the verse, "The blood of your lives will I require" (Genesis 9:5), as a source of this law. See, for example, Maimonides; *Mishneh Torah, Hilkhot Rotzeah U'Shemirat Nefesh* 2:2, 3; Rabbi Nissim Gerondi (*Ran;* fourteenth century), Babylonian Talmud, *Shevuot* 28a (citing this verse as one of two sources). See, generally, Menachem Elon, ed., *Encyclopedia Judaica* (Jerusalem: Keter Publishing Group, 1972), s.v. "Suicide: In Jewish Law," by Haim Cohn. Interestingly, after identifying this verse as the source for the prohibition against suicide, Rabbi Yosef b. Babad states that, because this verse does not apply to non-Jews, non-Jews are not forbidden to commit suicide. See R. Yosef b. Babad (nineteenth century), *Minhat Hinukh,* Commandment 34.

49. Maimonides, supra n. 48, *Hilkhot Hovel U'Mazik* 5:1. See also Babylonian Talmud, *Bava Kama* 90b.

50. See, for example, Maimonides, supra n. 48, 11:4 (citing the verse, "Be careful, very careful for your lives" [Deuteronomy 4:9]); R. Moshe Sofer, *Hatam Sofer, Yoreh De'ah* 326 (citing Deuteronomy 4:9 and Leviticus 18:5, "and you shall live by [the commandments]"). See also R. Yehudah he-Hasid (1150–1217), *Sefer Hasidim* 675.

51. See, for example, Abraham, supra n. 1, 23–24; Weiner, R. Shlomo Zalman Auerbach (twentieth century), *Minhat Shlomo* 91.

52. Maimonides, supra n. 48, *Hilkhot Rozeah U'Shemirat Nefesh* 2:2; R. Yehiel Michoel Tukazinsky (twentieth century), *Gesher ha-Hayyim* I, 269 (arguing that because life belongs to God, there is basically no difference between killing oneself and killing someone else).

53. Mishnah, *Sanhedrin* 10:1.

54. Babylonian Talmud, *Sanhedrin* 90a. See also Rabbi Ephraim Oshry (twentieth century), *Shut Mi-Ma'amakim* I:6, pp. 46–47 (citing various authorities).

55. *Shulhan Arukh, Yoreh De'ah* 345; Maimonides, supra n. 48, *Hilkhot Avel* 1:11.

56. See, for example, Rabbi Yisroel Meir HaKohen, *Shemirat ha-Lashon,* part II,

ch.2; Aryeh Kaplan, *The Handbook of Jewish Thought* (New York: Moznaim Pub. Corp., 1979), 74.

57. Mishnah, *Avot* 4:21.

58. See, for example, Fred Rosner, "Suicide in Jewish Law," in *Jewish Bioethics,* ed. Fred Rosner and J. David Bleich (New York: Hebrew Pub. Co., 1979), 327; Irving M. Bunim, *Ethics From Sinai* (New York: Feldheim Publishing Co., 1966), 2:152. Many authorities assert that even if a person tries to repent from his act of suicide between the time of his action and the time he dies, his repentance will not be effective. See, for example, Rabbi Yaakov b. Asher, *Arba'ah Turim, Yoreh De'ah* 348.

59. Rosner, supra n. 8, 326; Maimonides, supra n. 48, *Hilkhot Teshuvah* 1:4, 2:1; R. Basil Herring (twentieth century), *Jewish Ethics and Halakhah for Our Time* (New York: KTAV and Yeshiva University Press, 1984), 74.

60. See R. Tukazinsky, supra n. 52.

61. Isaiah 38:1, as translated in Bleich, supra n. 46, 141.

62. Babylonian Talmud, *Berakhot* 10a.

63. *Sefer HaHinukh,* Commandment 1. Authorship of this work has historically been attributed to Rabbi Aharon b. Yosef ha-Levi (1235–1300), although scholars debate whether this attribution is correct.

64. Rabbi Haim Shmuelevitz (twentieth century), *Sihot Mussar* 35.

65. See, for example, Herring, supra n. 59, pp. 76–77 (citing views and arguing, in part, that Maimonides believed it was impermissible to commit suicide merely to avoid pain); Rabbi Zvi Hirsch Eisenstadt, *Pithei Teshuvah, Shulhan Arukh, Yoreh De'ah* 345:2 (citing authorities); Moshe Sofer, supra n. 50; Eliezer Waldenburg, supra n. 46; Rabbi Shlomo Luria, *Yam Shel Shlomo, Bava Kama* 8:59; Tukazinsky, supra n. 52, p. 273; R. Ephraim Oshry, *Responsa from the Holocaust* (New York: Judaica Press, 1989), 34:34–35. The author of *Besamim Rosh,* however, is quoted as saying that someone who kills him- or herself because of his or her sufferings is not considered an illegal suicide. See, for example, Tukazinsky, 273. Authorship of *Besamim Rosh* is disputed. Although it was initially attributed to Rabbenu Asher (Rosh), a leading fourteenth-century scholar, most Jewish law scholars seem to believe that it was written by a writer who was much more recent and far less authoritative. See, for example, Herring, p. 77, and Moshe Sofer, supra n. 50. Indeed, Sofer argues that a scholar such as Rosh could not possibly have disagreed with the clear lesson to be drawn from R. Hanina b. Teradion, discussed later in the text, and therefore brands the *Besamim* Rosh a forgery!

66. Tukazinsky, supra n. 52, 273.

67. With few exceptions, this translation is the same as that found in Babylonian Talmud, *Avodah Zarah* 18a (London: Soncino Press, 1960).

68. Babylonian Talmud, *Yevamot* 89a.

69. See, for example, Babylonian Talmud, *Berakhot* 60b ("Everything that the All-Merciful One does is for the best"); *Orkhot Tzaddikim* (Anonymous; fifteenth century), *Sha'ar ha-Simhah,* s.v. *Vi-khain Ki-She'yesh;* Rabbi Yehuda Halevi, *ha-Kuzari, Ma'amar* 3:11.

70. Babylonian Talmud, *Berakhot* 5a.

71. Ibid.

72. See, for example, Rabbi Shlomo Yitzchaki (*Rashi;* eleventh century), Genesis 21:1; Babylonian Talmud, *Bava Kama* 92a.

73. I believe I heard this explanation given by Rabbi Avigdor Miller (twentieth century) on one of his taped lectures.

74. See, for example, R. Yaakov Yisrael Baifus (contemporary), *Longing for Dawn*, trans. R. Nachman Bulman (Rechasim, Israel: Tashbar HaRav Publishers, 1995), 82–105.

75. Numbers 5:11–31.

76. See, for example, J. David Bleich, supra n. 46 (stating that this sentiment is also expressed in Psalm 18: "The Lord has indeed punished me, but He has not left me to die"). See also R. Auerbach, supra n. 51; Abraham S. Abraham, *Nishmat Avraham, Yoreh De'ah* 339:4. Of course, it may be that a particular person's suffering could exceed the pain involved in a *Soteh's* lingering death. If so, the case of the *Soteh* would not prove that continued life coupled with excessive pain would be a boon.

77. See, for example, Timothy E. Quill et al., "The Debate Over Physician-Assisted Suicide: Empirical Data and Convergent Views," *Annals of Internal Medicine* 128 (April 1, 1998): 552–58; *Washington v. Glucksberg*, supra n. 5.

78. See, for example, Gunderson, supra n. 10, 205–208.

79. R. Abraham, supra n. 1, 178 ("A person with severe pulmonary disease who requires morphine because of intense pain may be so treated, only if the dose is carefully titrated so as not to cause life-threatening respiratory depression, or if the treatment is accompanied by artificial respiration"). Of course, Jewish law does allow some degree of risk to be taken in order to palliate suffering medically. See, for example, Rabbi Jacob Emden (1697–1776), *Mor U'Ketzia, Orah Hayyim* 328.

80. See, for example, *Ran*, Babylonian Talmud, *Nedarim* 40a; R. Auerbach, supra n. 51; Shlomo Zalman Auerbach, *Minhat Shlomo* 91; Rabbi Moshe Feinstein, *Iggrot Moshe, Hoshen Mishpat* II:73; Rabbi Yehiel M. Epstein, *Arukh ha-Shulhan, Yoreh De'ah* 335:3; Bleich, "Treatment of the Terminally Ill," *Tradition* 30, 51 (1996): 79, n. 12; Abraham, supra n. 46 (citing authorities). Additional Talmudic examples apparently approve praying for the death of someone who is suffering uncontrollably. See, for example, Babylonian Talmud, *Bava Metsia* 84 (after Reish Lakish died, Rabbi Yochanan was greatly depressed, and the rabbis prayed for his death); Jerusalem Talmud, *Shabbat* 19:2 (Rabbi Ada bar Ahava accidentally mutilated his son during circumcision in such as way that the son would not be able to marry; to save his son from disgrace, he prayed that the boy die and his prayer was answered). The authorities seem to think that if one can pray for the death of another who is suffering, certainly the person who is suffering can pray for her own death. See also Babylonian Talmud, *Taanit* 23a (Honi the Circle-Drawer awoke from a seventy-year sleep, suffered severe emotional distress, and prayed for death); I Kings 19:4 (Eliyahu); Jonah 4:8 (Jonah).

81. Ephraim Oshry, *Responsa from the Holocaust* (1989), 34.

82. The man also believed that by killing himself in the ghetto he would be able to be buried in the Jewish cemetery rather than have his remains mistreated by the Germans. Ephraim Oshry, supra n. 81.

83. Rabbi Oshry originally published a two-volume Hebrew edition of his responsa, entitled *Shut MiMa'amakim* (1959), and he later published a condensed one-volume English version, *Responsa from the Holocaust* (1989). In the English version, his ruling is clear: "Although the man knew he would definitely be subjected to unbearable suffering by the abominable murderers, and so hoped to be buried

among Jews, he still was not allowed to commit suicide." Id., 34. Although I personally interpret the longer, Hebrew version of this responsum as reaching this same conclusion as to the a priori impermissibility of such a suicide, see Ephraim Oshry, *Shut MiMa'amakim* I:6 (1959), at least one commentator construed that responsum as ruling in agreement with *Besamim Rosh*. See Basil F. Herring, supra n. 59, 78. When I spoke by phone with Rabbi Oshry, who lives in Brooklyn's Lower East Side, to discuss the different interpretations of his responsum, he strongly emphasized that he had written that the suicide was forbidden.

84. Babylonian Talmud, *Gittin* 57b.

85. The word *Mitzva* literally means "commandment." Nonetheless, from the fact that Rabbenu Tam does not use the word *Hiyuv* (obligation), he does not appear to think that one is strictly required to kill oneself in such circumstances, but that one who does so acts commendably and is deemed to have fulfilled a commandment.

86. Tosafot, *Commentary on Babylonian Talmud, Avodah Zarah* 18a, s.v. *Vi'al*. See also Babylonian Talmud, *Bava Batra* 3b (A Hasmonean woman jumped to her death from a rooftop rather than allow herself to be wed by a slave). In tractate *Gittin* itself, the commentary of the Tosafists seems to cite two justifications for the captives' conduct. *See* Tosafot, *Commentary on Babylonian Talmud, Gittin,* 57b, s.v. *Kofzu.* The first is arguably ambiguous, but could be read as justifying suicide to avoid torture. If so, it might support the view of the *Besamim Rosh,* supra, n. 65, unless a distinction is made between suffering that arises naturally (and that does not justify suicide) and that which occurs as a result of another man's free will (which might justify suicide). In any event, the second justification seems to be the same as that given by Rabbenu Tam in tractate *Avodah Zarah.*

87. See, for example, R. Yosef Saul Nathanson, *Sho'el U-Meshiv* I, part 1, no. 172. For a discussion of various explanations of the case of King Saul, at I Samuel 31:1–6 and II Samuel 1:1–16, see Noam J. Zohar, *Alternatives in Jewish Bioethics* (Albany, NY: SUNY Press, 1977, 54-58); and Steven H. Resnicoff, "Jewish Law Perspectives on Suicide and Physician-Assisted Dying," *Journal of Law and Religion* 13, 289 (1998–99): 304–8.

88. See, for example, Basil F. Herring, *Jewish Ethics and Halakhah For Our Time* (1984), 76; Haim Shmuelevitz, *Sihot Mussar,* 36; Eugene Newman, *Life & Teachings of Isaiah Horowitz* (1972), 190 (citing historical examples). Sometimes before killing themselves, parents killed their children to prevent the children from being forcibly converted. This would be consistent with the position that killing oneself is a form of murder. See J. David Bleich, *Treatment of the Terminally Ill, Tradition* 30, 51 (1996): 79, n. 12 (citing this view). Accordingly, just as killing oneself might be permissible as an alternative to forced conversion, killing another might also be permissible. But see Yaakov Weiner, *Ye Shall Surely Heal: Medical Ethics from a Halachic Perspective* (1995), 7–8 (questioning this argument).

89. See, for example, Shlomo Luria, *Yam Shel Shlomo, Bava Kama* 8:59 (rules that such killings are prohibited). See, generally, Yaakov Weiner, *Ye Shall Surely Heal: Medical Ethics from a Halachic Perspective* (1995), 4–6; *Da'at Zekainim MiBa'alei HaTosafot, Commentary to Genesis 9:5;* Yosef Karo, *Beit Yosef on Shulhan Arukh, Yoreh De'ah* 157. For a more complete discussion of these exceptions, see Steven H. Resnicoff, "Jewish Law Perspectives on Suicide and Physician-Assisted Dying," *Journal of Law and Religion* 13, 289 (1998–99): 308–12.

90. See, for example, Immanuel Jakobovits, *Jewish Medical Ethics* (New York: Bloch, 1959), 123–35; J. David Bleich, *Judaism and Healing* (New York: KTAV, 1981); Fred Rosner, *Biomedical Ethics and Jewish Law* (New York: KTAV, 2001) (citing various authorities), 248, 251.

91. An alternative to the answer provided by R. Mecklenburg might be directly based on the fact that the prohibition against suicide applies even when a person is suffering. If the person who is afflicted is not permitted to end his own life, there is little reason to believe that someone else should be able to put him to death at his request.

92. Genesis 9:6.

93. Genesis 9:5, as translated by J. David Bleich, supra n. 46.

94. Jacob Zevi Mecklenburg, *ha-Ketav Ve-ha-Kabbalah* 20, 5th ed. (1946), cited by J. David Bleich, supra n. 46. See also R. Abraham, supra n. 1, 193 (citing sources).

95. Leviticus 19:14 ("Before the blind, do not place a stumbling block").

96. For a detailed discussion of these biblical and rabbinic prohibitions, see, generally, Steven H. Resnicoff, "Helping A Client Violate Jewish Law," in *Jewish Law Studies*, vol. 10, ed. Hannah Sprecher (Binghamton, NY: Global Publications, 2000).

97. See R. Moshe Feinstein, *Iggrot Moshe, Yoreh De'ah* IV:54(2) ("Even if through this rescue the doctor will become forced to spend a great sum of money to pay for the [medical] equipment and other medications, he is obligated to do so").

98. Some Jewish law authorities debate whether individual Jews have the right or duty to coerce other individuals to fulfill their Jewish law obligation. Contrast, for example, Rabbi Aryeh Leib, *Kitzot ha-Hoshen, Hoshen Mishpat* 3:1 (arguing that only Jewish courts may exercise such coercion) to Rabbi Yaakov, *Nitivot ha-Mishpat, Hoshen Mishpat* 3:1 (contending that individuals may coerce other individuals). In what seems to be clearly a minority view, one modern commentator, Rabbi Shilo Refael, is said to argue that only a religious court composed of judges with special authorization transmitted in a direct line from Moses would be permitted to use such coercion. See Haim Povarsky, "Is Euthanasia Permissible Under Jewish Law?" *Jewish Law Report* 23 (August 1994). Nevertheless, many Jewish law authorities who lived long after this special authorization ceased to be transmitted have ruled that coercion could be used to force people to take medical treatment. See, for example, Rabbi Avraham Abeli Gombiner, *Magen Avraham, Orah Hayyim* 328 (6) ("if the patient refuses to accept the prescribed treatment [because doing so would desecrate the Sabbath], we compel him to do so"); Abraham, supra n. 1, 53 (citing authorities).

99. For instance, because some treatments are risky or of questionable benefit, a patient may not be required to undergo them, even if his doctors recommend them.

100. See Resnicoff, supra n. 87, 317.

101. See, for example, authorities cited supra n. 50.

102. See supra n. 98.

103. See, for example, *Shulhan Arukh, Yoreh De'ah* 339:1 ("A goses is considered alive for all matters . . ."). See also Mishnah, *Semahot* 1:1; Maimonides, supra n. 55, *Hilkhot Avel* 4:5.

104. R. Feinstein, supra n. 80.

105. Some authorities actually differentiate between two stages—the beginning

of this death process and the final moment when the soul tries to escape the body—and contend that the special rules regarding impediments and treatment only apply at the second stage. See, for example, Waldenberg, *Tzitz Eliezer* VIII:89(14).

106. *Rema, Yoreh De'ah* 339:1.

107. See, for example, R. Yaakov Reischer (1670–1733), *Teshuvot Shevut Ya'akov* I:13; Rabbi Shlomo Eger, *Gilyon Maharsha, Shulhan Arukh, Yoreh De'ah* 339:1; Rabbi Eliezer Waldenberg, *Tzitz Eliezer* V, *Ramat Rachel* 28; R. Abraham, supra n. 76, *Orah Hayyim* 329:4(11) (citing sources), *Yoreh De'ah* 339:2 (stating "so long as it is not clear that the [*goses*] is definitely dead, he is called a live person for all purposes, and a doctor is obligated to treat him in every way that is possible and appropriate . . . even if there is only a small chance that the patient will remain alive and even if the patient may stay alive for only a short while"); R. Yisroel Meir HaKohen, *Mishnah Berurah, Bi'ur Halakhah* 329:4; Bleich, supra n. 80, 69–70.

108. See, for example, J. David Bleich, *Judaism and Healing* (New York: KTAV, 1981), 140 (mentioning this view).

109. See J. David Bleich, *Bioethical Dilemmas: A Jewish Perspective* (New York: KTAV, 1998), 81 (mentioning this view).

110. Jewish law is predicated upon the proposition that Torah law comprises two elements that were divinely communicated to Moses: a Written Law, as set forth in the Five Books of Moshe, and an Oral Law, which explains, interprets, and supplements the Written Law. See, generally, Maimonides, *Introduction to the Mishnah;* Menachem Elon, *Mishpat Ivri* 1:179; H. Chaim Schimmel, *The Oral Law,* 19–31; Barukh Epstein, *Torah Temimah,* on Deuteronomy 12:21.

111. See, for example, R. Hayyim David ha-Levi (twentieth century), "Nittuk Holeh she-Afsu Sikkuyav Lihyot mi-Mekhonat Melakhutit," 2 Tehumin 297 (1981), cited by Menachem Elon et al., *Jewish Law (Mishpat Ivri): Cases and Materials* (New York: Matthew Bender & Company, 1999), 649–50.

112. *Rema, Even ha-Ezer* 121:7, *Hoshen Mishpat* 211:2, as translated by J. David Bleich, supra n. 80, 77. See also Rabbi Fred Friedman, "The Chronic Vegetative Patient: A Torah Perspective," *J Halacha & Contemporary Soc'y* 26 (1993): 88–109 (stating that the "current pathophysiological explanation would be a person who is asphyxiating on his own secretions which accumulate in the airway").

113. See, for example, R. Feinstein, *Iggrot Moshe, Hoshen Mishpat* II:75 (argues that if someone who is thought to be a *goses* survives more than seventy-two hours, it is more likely that the person never was a *goses* than that the person was from the small minority of *gosesim* that survive more than seventy-two hours). But see Rabbenu Asher b. Yehiel (Rosh; 1250–1327), Babylonian Talmud, *Moed Katan* (*gesisah* lasts three or four days).

114. Rabbi J. David Bleich, for instance, states that the Rema's description is a "necessary criterion of gesisah [i.e., being a *goses*]." J. David Bleich, "Treatment of the Terminally Ill," *Tradition* 30, 51 (1996): 63. See also the following statement of Rabbi Ahron Soloveitchik, cited by Bleich: "The situation of a *goses* does not even have to be considered since today very few, if any, patients manifest the symptoms of a *goses*" (ibid., 58).

115. See, for example, Menachem Elon et al., supra n. 111, 648–654. Elon seems implicitly to suggest that certain lenient rulings authored by R. Moshe Feinstein, a leading twentieth-century authority, were based on an expansive definition of *goses*. I have discussed the difficulties with R. Feinstein's position elsewhere; see

Steven H. Resnicoff, "Physician-Assisted Suicide Under Jewish Law," *DePaul Journal of Health Care Law* 1, 589 (1997).

116. The ensuing text regarding the possible right to refuse life-preserving treatment is taken from Steven H. Resnicoff, "Jewish Law Perspectives on Suicide and Physician-Assisted Dying," *Journal of Law and Religion* 13, 289 (1998–99): 338–44.

117. See, for example, J. David Bleich, "Treatment of the Terminally Ill," *Tradition* 30, 3 (1996): 51 (arguing that such refusal would be justified only in a rare instance in which intractable pain were so great that the person affected would be willing to give up all of her wealth in order to escape it).

118. This episode is discussed in Babylonian Talmud, *Ketubot* 104a.

119. She prayed:

The immortals [i.e., angels] desire Rebbe [to join them] and the mortals [i.e., the Rabbis] desire Rebbe [to remain with them]; may it be the will [of God] that the mortals overpower the immortals.

See Moshe Tendler and Fred Rosner, "Quality and Sanctity of Life in the Talmud and the Midrash," *Tradition* 28, 1 (1993): 18, 22.

120. She changed her prayer to: "May it be the will [of God] that the immortals overpower the mortals." Id.

121. Babylonian Talmud, *Ketubot* 104a.

122. See text and citations of n. 80. See also Bleich, supra n. 80, 51, 56, and 59 (stating own view and quoting statement by Rabbi Ahron Soloveitchik).

123. See, for example, Eliezer Waldenberg, *Tzitz Eliezer V, Ramat Rachel* 5, and VII:49, *Kuntres Even Yaakov,* perek 13 (one should not pray for someone else's death).

124. Haim Palaggi, *Hikkekei Lev* I, *Yoreh De'ah* 50, discussed in J. David Bleich, "Treatment of the Terminally Ill," *Tradition* 30, 3 (1996): 51, 56–57.

125. See Moshe Feinstein, *Iggrot Moshe, Yoreh De'ah* II:174(3).

126. Shlomo Zalman Auerbach, *Minhat Shlomo* 91 (arguing, however, that it would be preferable for the patient to choose treatment). Ironically, Rabbi Auerbach begins by stating that we have no measuring stick with which to evaluate life and that we would repeatedly transgress the laws of Sabbath to save the life of someone who is suffering, is totally incompetent, and who could fulfill no commandments. Nevertheless, in rendering his ultimate ruling allowing the patient to refuse the prospective surgery, he counts as a relevant factor the negative qualitative features associated with the life of one who is paralyzed.

127. See, for example, Abraham S. Abraham, "Euthanasia," in *Medicine and Jewish Law,* ed. Fred Rosner (1990), 129 (appearing to implicitly make this argument): "Is Euthanasia Permissible Under Jewish Law?" *Jewish Law Report* (August 1994): 25; Fred Friedman, "The Chronic Vegetative Patient: A Torah Perspective," *Journal of Halacha and Contemporary Society* 26 (1993): 88, 100, n. 28

128. Interestingly, Rabbi Feinstein emphasizes that the justification for refusing life-preserving treatment is only because of pain and is not to be confused with an overall "quality of life" analysis. He explains that the life of a mentally incompetent or a person in a permanent vegetative state must be prolonged as much as possible so long as the person is not experiencing pain. See Moshe Feinstein, *Iggrot Moshe, Hoshen Mishpat* II:74(1); J. David Bleich, "Treatment of the Terminally Ill," *Tradition* 30, 3 (1996): 51, 71.

129. See, for example, J. David Bleich, "Treatment of the Terminally Ill," *Tradition* 30, 3 (1996): 51, 56, 59 (stating own view and quoting statement by Rabbi Ahron Soloveichik); Eliezer Waldenberg, *Tzitz Eliezer* XV:40.

130. See *Shulhan Arukh, Orah Hayyim* 656:1.

131. Moshe Feinstein, *Iggrot Moshe, Yoreh De'ah* II:174(4).

132. Rabbi Feinstein encouraged relatives in such a case to voluntarily permit the transplant. See Moshe Feinstein, *Iggrot Moshe, Yoreh De'ah* II:174(4).

133. Bleich uses this same analysis to explain responsa by certain other Halakhic authorities as well. See J. David Bleich, "Compelling Tissue Donations," *Tradition* 27, 3 (Spring 1993): 59–89, 82, n. 24.

134. Generally, a person does not have to endure as much of a loss to avoid performing an affirmative commandment as he does to avoid violating a negative commandment. See, for example, *Shulhan Arukh, Orah Hayyim* 656:1. See Steven H. Resnicoff, "Jewish Law Perspectives on Suicide and Physician-Assisted Dying," *Journal of Law and Religion* 13, 289 (1998–99): 298–301. Because the duty to safeguard one's life could be viewed as an affirmative commandment, why doesn't the lower standard apply? One reason is that the duty to safeguard one's life may refer to taking precautions to avoid danger, but the duty to save one's life may arise from the same commandment that requires one to save another's life, the commandment not to "stand idly by your fellow's blood." A person may be considered his own "fellow." There are also other ways of explaining why the "all one's wealth" standard applies.

If Bleich is correct and the Feinstein-Auerbach approach is using the "all your wealth" test, why are the patients only permitted passively to refuse treatment? Why shouldn't they also be permitted to violate the negative commandment against murder and commit suicide? The answer to this is that the "all your wealth" test does not apply to the rules against murder, idolatry, or illicit sexual affairs; one is simply not permitted to violate these prohibitions.

135. Id., 76.

136. See Jacob Emden, *Mor U'ketzia* 328; Alfred Cohen, "Whose Body? Living With Pain," *Journal of Halacha and Contemporary Society* 32 (1996): 39, 49. See, generally, J. David Bleich, *Contemporary Halakhic Problems*, vol. 4, 203–17.

137. As to what extent a person may risk her life by taking experimental treatment or to reduce pain, see, for example, Yaakov Weiner, *Ye Shall Surely Heal: Medical Ethics from a Halachic Perspective* (1995), 75–81; Moshe Feinstein, *Iggrot Moshe, Hoshen Mishpat* II: 73(9) (allowing surgical removal of patient's testicles in prostrate cancer in order to reduce pain; argues that reduction in pain would prolong patient's life); Abraham S. Abraham, *The Comprehensive Guide to Medical Halachah* (1996), 10:4, p. 53; Alfred Cohen, "Whose Body? Living With Pain," *Journal of Halacha and Contemporary Society* 32 (1996): 39, 49.

138. See, generally, Yaakov Weiner, *Ye Shall Surely Heal: Medical Ethics from a Halachic Perspective* (1995).

139. See Rabbi Zev Schostak, "Ethical Guidelines for Treatment of the Dying Elderly," *Journal of Halacha and Contemporary Society* 22 (1991): 62, 83 (citing this as the view of Rabbis Feinstein and Auerbach, while acknowledging dissenting views); Avraham Steinberg (twentieth century), 4 *Enziklopedyah Hilkhattit-Refu'it*, s.v., *Noteh la-mut*, 56–58, cited by Elon, supra n. 111.

CHAPTER 6

Environment in Jewish Law

Manfred Gerstenfeld

The specificity of the Jewish attitude toward issues we now call "environmental" derives largely from its normative character. According to Jewish
tradition, the Hebrew Bible contains 613 commandments.[1] A number of
these have environmental implications. These biblical laws should not be
confused with Jewish law as it is interpreted today in the orthodox tradition. From the time of Moses onward, oral laws that accompanied and
explained the written Torah were passed down from generation to generation and interpreted by them.

The written and oral law are one in Judaism. Rabbi Yehuda Hanasi
(known as *Rabbi*) wrote down the latter in the Mishnah early in the third
century C.E. Since then, Jewish law (Halakhah) has continued to develop
through rabbinical interpretation. Within this framework, environmental
regulations have also evolved. One may consider Maimonides' (1135–
1204) Laws of the Neighbors,[2] which group *inter alia* a large number of
regulations in the area of prevention of nuisance and pollution, as the first
Jewish environmental codex.

Biblical narratives and wisdom texts, as well as Jewish thought expressed in the midrash Aggadah (the non-Halakhic elements of rabbinical
interpretation of scripture), strengthen the concepts found in the normative literature. Little research has been done so far.[3] What has been studied
already, however, demonstrates that the environmental motifs in classical
Jewish texts are numerous.[4]

JEWISH ENVIRONMENTAL STUDIES

Despite the many points of interaction between Judaism and environmental issues, and widespread interest in the Western world in environ-

mentalism, the field of Jewish environmental studies is only at its beginning. The increasing interest in the interface of religion and environment, as demonstrated, inter alia, by conferences and the establishment of journals in the field, may act as a stimulus.

The United Nations has understood the need to mobilize organized religious communities for the environmental cause. In an individualistic, postmodern society, everybody determines what suits him or her in the environmental discourse. Religions, however, start from defined value positions: they have relatively consolidated worldviews and many followers. Mobilizing them for a better environment means mobilizing masses.[5] Judaism will have to find its place in this discourse.

The development of Jewish environmental studies as an academic field faces formidable handicaps, however. Few people have the basic knowledge in both Jewish and environmental studies to carry out in-depth research on Jewish attitudes toward the environment and environmentalism. Second, the collection of research material requires a concerted effort, as there is no systematic way of accessing it. Probably partly as a result of this, the necessary financial backing for developing the discipline is lacking.

TWO CATEGORIES OF APPROACH

Contemporary society is facing a multitude of environmental issues. Modern environmentalism refers to the world of thought and action of those currents and individuals who consider protection of the ecosystem or the environment a central goal for society. It is highly heterogeneous and continues to develop in a large variety of directions: philosophical, ideological and ethical, political and practical. More often than not, the relationship between these is confused or, at least, unclear.[6] Perceptions also vary greatly as to what environmentalism's concrete goals should be.

Contemporary Judaism is heterogeneous as well. Its interrelationship with environmentalism and the environment has many aspects. Current positions of Jews toward the environment divide into two main categories. The first is grounded in the systematic analysis of traditional Jewish sources, combined with the people's experience over the centuries. Consolidated Jewish viewpoints on key environmental issues and ideology are developed from these. Writers in this category identify with an orthodoxy-oriented approach, even if this is not necessarily their own mode of practice.

The second category consists of those who offer personal environmental views, often using selected Jewish sources to substantiate their statements. The Jewish tradition has been centered on text for thousands of years. It is only from the first category that a coherent Jewish position toward environmental issues and the environment in general can be developed.

In order to provide a somewhat representative picture of Jewish environmental policies, one can analyze what classical Judaism has to say about several of the main contemporary environmental concerns. These include the protection of nature, animal welfare, limiting the use of natural resources, the prevention of pollution and nuisance, and land policies. Many of the "environmental" regulations in Jewish law refer to more than one of these elements.

In order to broaden the reader's perspective, the Jewish attitude toward three other important aspects of the contemporary environmental discourse also will be discussed: the meeting between environmental and economic interests, the attitude toward key elements of the sustainability issue, and the challenge of society's renewed interest in paganism that has environmental aspects.

RELATIONSHIP TO NATURE

Specific commandments concerning the normative relation of Judaism toward nature include the prohibitions of wanton destruction (*bal tashkhit*) and the mixing of species (*kilayim*). The former is the Halakhic principle most often mentioned in modern Jewish writings referring to environmental issues.

This law derives from the Bible:

When in your war against a city you have to besiege it a long time in order to capture it, you must not destroy its trees, wielding the ax against them. You may eat of them, but you must not cut them down. Are trees of the field human to withdraw before you into the besieged city? Only trees that you know do not yield food may be destroyed. You may cut them down for constructing siege works against the city that is waging war on you, until it has been reduced.[7]

One of the oldest collections of rabbinical traditions, the *Sifre*, written around 300 c.e., extended the law of wanton destruction to prohibit diverting waterways:

From where do we know that one may not divert the arm of a river (which supplies water to a city)? Because it is said "You shall not destroy (the city's) trees in any way." It is said "by swinging an axe against them." This would seem to prohibit only the use of iron tools. From where do we know then not to divert the flow of water? Since it is said "You shall not destroy its trees"; this includes all modes of destruction.[8]

Over the centuries, the prohibition of wanton destruction has been further extended by rabbinical authorities. It now covers the prohibition of destruction without purpose of anything, including one's own possessions.

DIFFERENT DEFINITIONS

Jewish regulations concerning the environment should be seen within the hierarchical order of a theocentric worldview. Modern man's definition of wanton destruction is not necessarily identical to that of the Jewish tradition. When elements of nature become objects of idolatry, that is, in pagan cults, the Bible tells the Israelites to demolish them: "You must destroy all the sites at which the nations you are to dispossess worshipped their gods, whether on lofty mountains and on hills or under any luxuriant tree. Tear down their altars, mash their pillars, put their Asherahs to the fire, and cut down the images of their gods, obliterating their name from that site."[9]

A far-reaching interpretation of the prohibition of wanton destruction is found in a rabbi's dissenting opinion mentioned in the Talmud. Rabbi Hisda says, "Whoever can eat bread made from barley and eats bread from wheat, transgresses the prohibition of *bal tashkhit*."[10] Rabbi Papa says, "Whoever can drink beer and drinks wine, transgresses the prohibition of *bal tashkhit*."[11] The Talmud indicates, however, that these opinions are not accepted, as one should not eat inferior food, but rather care more for one's body than for money.

In the Talmud, another minority opinion indicates that one is not allowed to use fuel uneconomically. Rabbi Zutra says, "Whoever covers an oil lamp [when it is burning] and leaves a nafta lamp open [when it is burning] transgresses the prohibition against wanton destruction."[12]

MAIMONIDES'S APPROACH

Among the prohibitions that Maimonides explicitly lists in his codex under the prohibition of wanton destruction are the breaking of utensils, the tearing of clothes, the destruction of buildings, the blocking of wells, and the destruction of food.[13] He writes that they are valid not only in times of war, but at all times.[14]

Maimonides also applies the principle to what one places in the grave. He states that it is preferable to give clothes to the poor than "to throw them to the worms [in the grave]. Whoever puts too many clothes on the dead transgresses the prohibition of *bal tashkhit*."[15]

The medieval *Sefer HaHinukh* refers to the ethical aspects of this prohibition: "And this is the way the pious and the people of good actions behave: they like peace, are happy in the well-being of others, bring them closer to the Torah, and will not destroy even a mustard seed from the world."[16]

Although, at first sight, the destruction of surplus food could be considered wanton destruction, it is permitted in the interests of guaranteeing supplies. The Talmud relates that, every Friday, Rabbi Huna would send a messenger to the market to buy all the surplus vegetables remaining in the market. These would be thrown in the river. He did not give them to the poor, as they would then count on it and this, in turn, would affect market prices. He did not feed them to animals, because one should not give them human food. Rabbi Huna's reason for destroying the produce was that, if he did not, the people left with their wares would no longer bring vegetables to the market.

The nineteenth-century scholar Rabbi Samson Raphael Hirsch, a leader of the German ultra-orthodox community, interprets the law against wanton destruction as "the most wide-ranging warning to man not to abuse the position he has been given in the world for moody, passionate or mindless destruction of things on earth. Only for the wise use has God put the earth at his feet, when He said: 'Master it; rule over it.'"[17]

Avoiding waste is a recurrent motif with Hirsch. Rashi, the main medieval biblical and Talmudic commentator, explains why Jacob, who first brings his family and possessions over the Yabok River on his return to Canaan, then crosses back again and remains alone on the far bank. He comments briefly that Jacob crossed back over the river because he wanted to check that he had forgotten nothing.[18] Hirsch elaborates: "The just man also sees as sacred the smallest value of honestly-acquired possessions that he may neither waste nor heedlessly allow to decrease, and for whose use he must be accountable."[19]

CONTEMPORARY JEWISH LAW

Contemporary Halakhah addresses a limited number of environmental aspects. Several discussions of wanton destruction can be found. One contemporary authority, Rabbi Yitschak Silberstein, reviews issues such as the permissibility of disposing of old bread and of food leftovers from wedding halls.[20] He says that pious people do not throw away old bread and educate their children not to be so spoiled as to only eat fresh bread.

People who have not reached this degree of piety can be taught not to actively throw the bread away in the garbage, but to lay it on the side of a road or on hedges, without wantonly destroying it. Rabbi Silberstein underlines that there is no sin in not eating it.

With regard to the owners of halls: a better solution than throwing away the surplus food requires more time. In Rabbi Silberstein's opinion, the destruction of time is no better an approach than the destruction of food, especially as the poor who come begging are not satisfied with bread. Nobody will collect and eat it, so there is no transgression of the prohibition of wanton destruction. He adds that it may be a good thing that the owners of halls do care about their time in this case, while they usually do not throw away better food.[21]

Rabbi Ovadia Yosef, the former Sephardi Chief Rabbi of Israel, addresses the issue of laying flowers on a coffin.[22] To avoid transgressing the prohibition of wanton destruction, he recommends that the communities that practice this custom—such as Egyptian Jews—use inexpensive wreaths only.

ANIMAL PROTECTION

With regard to animal protection, the main Halakhic principle is to prevent suffering to living creatures (za'ar ba'alei hayim). A very important example of this is the prohibition of eating a limb of a living animal (ever min hahai). This commandment is related to a biblical text: "But make sure you do not partake of the blood; for the blood is the life, and you must not consume the life with the flesh."[23]

Most biblical commandments are relevant only for Jews. The latter, however, is one of the seven Noahide laws that, according to Judaism, all humanity should obey. The Talmud says, "The rabbis learned: 'Seven laws were imposed upon the Noahides. Establishing laws, and [the prohibition of] blasphemy, idolatry, incest, murder, robbery, and [the use of] a limb of a living animal.' Rabbi Hananya ben Gamaliel says 'also the blood of a living animal [is forbidden].' Rabbi Hidka says 'also their castration.'"[24]

In both versions of the Decalogue, reference is made to animal protection. In Exodus, it says concisely, "Six days you shall do your work, but on the seventh day you shall cease from labor, in order that your ox and your ass may rest."[25] In Deuteronomy, the text reads: "the seventh day is a Sabbath of the Lord your God, your ox or your ass, or any of your cattle may rest as you do."[26]

Yet another biblical example of animal protection is the prohibition, "You shall not plow with an ox and an ass together."[27] This would obviously be unfair to the weaker animal. A further commandment says, "You shall not muzzle an ox while it is threshing."[28]

Other biblical texts call for a limit to animal suffering. One of these reads, "no animal from the herd or from the flock shall be slaughtered on the same day with its young."[29] Yet another commandment stresses sending a mother bird away from her nest (shiluah haken) if one wishes to take her young: "If, along the road, you chance upon a bird's nest, in any tree or on the ground, with fledglings or eggs and the mother sitting over the fledglings or on the eggs, do not take the mother together with her young. Let the mother go, and take only the young, in order that you may fare well and have a long life."[30]

THE TALMUD AND LATER TEXTS

The Talmud tells us, furthermore, that it is forbidden for man to eat before feeding his animals. This is related, in the Jewish tradition, to another biblical text: "I will also provide grass in the fields for your cattle—and thus you shall eat your fill."[31]

Rabbinical authorities have frequently spoken out against hunting. A leading eighteenth-century rabbinical scholar, Rabbi Yehezkel Landau, better known as the Noda Biyehuda, says in a responsum, "The only hunters mentioned in the Torah are Nimrod and Esau. Hunting is not a sport for the children of Abraham, Yitzchak and Ya'akov. . . . How can a Jew go to kill a living creature only with the purpose of hunting for pleasure?"[32]

Hunting also has an element of wanton destruction. When an animal is killed in this manner, it is usually unfit for kosher consumption. The Jewish dietary laws require slaughter in a specific way by a qualified expert.

FUR COATS, ANIMAL EXPERIMENTATION, AND BULLFIGHTS

Various contemporary responsa refer to the protection of animals. A few years ago, the wearing of fur coats led a concerned Israeli to put a question to Rabbi Chayim David Halevi, at that time the Sephardi Chief Rabbi of Tel Aviv. In his decision, he analyzes the Bible's attitude toward animals. Rabbi Halevi sees this as an issue of ideological and moral significance because God created both man and animals. Furthermore, rabbinical decisions permit hunting for food but forbid the practice of hunting for sport. Even those rabbis who allow hunting for furs do so only if the animal is killed quickly and without suffering.

Rabbi Halevi writes that an expert in the field confirmed that animals are usually caught with methods that cause great pain. He adds that, even if the animal is needed for medical purposes, one may only do so if as little pain as possible is caused. In light of these considerations, Rabbi Halevi concludes that killing animals "in a painful way in order to beautify and warm oneself with their skins" is forbidden.[33]

Animal experimentation has been discussed specifically by various modern rabbinical authorities.[34] The late Rabbi Yechiel Ya'akov Weinberg,[35] a prominent twentieth-century authority, permits this. He considers the elimination of human pain and suffering to be more important than the prevention of pain in animals. Rabbi Eliezer Waldenberg,[36] another leading rabbi, also considers medical experimentation permissible, yet he stresses that efforts must be made to minimize the animals' pain.

In one of his responsa, Rabbi Ovadia Yosef condemns bullfights: "The bullfight is in total contradiction to the spirit of our holy Torah. It is an expression of the culture of sinners and cruel people which Jews should not be."[37] He underscores that the prevention of unnecessary cruelty to animals is a major Torah prohibition, adding: "Whoever goes to the stadium to watch bullfighting and pays an entrance fee is an associate of destructive people and helps those who transgress."[38]

A responsum from Rabbi Benzion Meir Uziel, the first Sephardi Chief Rabbi of Israel, refers to the suggested application of electric shocks to animals before they are slaughtered. He forbids this, one of the reasons he gives being that strictly applied Jewish ritual slaughter ensures a minimum of animal suffering.[39]

RESOURCE POLICIES

The main biblical commandment concerning natural resources is the law of the sabbatical year (*shemita*): "Six years you shall sow your land and gather in its yield; but in the seventh you shall let it rest and lie fallow. Let the needy among your people eat of it, and what they leave let the wild beasts eat. You shall do the same with your vineyards and your olive groves."[40] The same prohibitions regarding the working of the land apply to the jubilee year. In addition, "the land must not be sold beyond reclaim, for the land is Mine; you are but strangers resident with Me."[41]

In the sabbatical and jubilee years, the Jew was allowed neither to plow land nor to sow seeds. Whatever grew by itself served as food for the poor and for animals. From a modern environmental point of view, one might say that the sabbatical year serves to prevent exhaustion of the land.

The laws of the sabbatical and jubilee years apply only to the Land of Israel. They gave rise to a Halakhic debate when the first Zionist settlements were established in the late nineteenth century. Today, adherence in Israel to the sabbatical year is almost total, even if it has mainly a symbolic character. The predominant practice throughout the country is an arrangement for fictitiously selling land to Gentiles. In recent years, the orthodox have increasingly adhered strictly to these laws, not eating produce from land owned by Jews.

The concept that God, not man, owns the land is also expressed in the early biblical story of Cain and its interpretation in the Jewish tradition. From the context of the text, it is understood that his offering is not prime produce: "In the course of time, Cain brought an offering to the Lord from the fruit of the soil; and Abel, for his part, brought the choicest of the firstlings of his flock. The Lord paid heed to Abel and his offering, but to Cain and his offering He paid no heed."[42]

Cain's sacrifice is rejected because he fails to recognize God's ownership and brings a defective offering. The Midrash interprets his offering as "refuse,"[43] saying that Cain resembles a bad serf who eats the first fruits and honors the king with the last ones.[44]

EMERGENCY POLICIES

The commandments *bal tashkhit* and *shiluah haken*, both mentioned earlier, express resource policies as well. In the Talmud, a number of cases are also mentioned that explain how one has to treat resources in various emergency situations. An example is the distribution of drinking water.

One discussion concerns the case of two people walking on the road, one of whom holds a canteen of water. "If they both drink from it, both of them will die [as there is not enough to keep both of them alive]; and if one of them drinks all of it, [only] he will reach an inhabited area. Says Ben Peturah: 'It is better that the two of them drink and they both die, than one see the death of the other.' Until Rabbi Akiva came and taught 'Your brother shall live with you. Your life precedes that of your brother.'"[45]

Another case is mentioned in the Tosefta. Two people walk in the desert, one with a barrel of water, the other with a barrel of honey. If the water barrel cracks, then the owner of the barrel of honey has to pour out the honey and save the water of the other by pouring the water into the barrel that had formerly held the honey. The reasoning behind this is that water keeps people alive in the desert and honey doesn't.[46] When they reach an inhabited area, the owner of the water barrel has to repay the owner of the honey barrel for the value of the honey lost.[47]

Another discussion in the Talmud deals with the priorities of water use in a city well that is insufficient for all needs. "[If the choice is] between their life and that of others, their life takes precedence over that of others; [between] their cattle and others' cattle, their cattle take precedence; [between] their laundry and the laundry of others, their laundry takes precedence; [between] the lives of others and their laundry, the lives of others takes precedence over their laundry. Rabbi Yossi says [in a minority opinion]: 'Their laundry takes precedence over the lives of others.'"[48]

The biblical narrative also illustrates resource policies. It indicates specifically that man may use natural resources for his benefit. The Israelites are told that when they come into their land, they will mine copper from its hills.[49] When Joseph's descendants complain to Joshua on entering Canaan that they have not been given enough land for their numbers, he tells them to clear forest land in the hill country.[50]

Consumption based on normal use of the earth's resources is encouraged. For example, those who have planted a vineyard without harvesting it are exempt from mobilization in times of war.[51]

PREVENTION OF POLLUTION AND NUISANCE

There are many references to the prevention of pollution and nuisance in Jewish law. One biblical commandment refers to the burial of excrement even in times of war: "there shall be an area for you outside the camp, where you may relieve yourself. With your gear you shall have a spike, and when you have squatted you shall dig a hole with it and cover up your excrement."[52] Another refers to a priest who has dealt with certain offerings in the Tabernacle: He "shall then take off his vestments and put on other vestments, and carry the ashes outside the camp to a clean place."[53]

Commenting on this, Maimonides says that the remains should be protected in these places "from being dispersed by wind and pigs."[54] Meiri, another medieval commentator, says that they should be kept "from being washed away by floods."[55]

Although Jewish graves in biblical times may have been situated near individual houses, Jewish cemeteries in later periods had to be placed outside residential areas as pollution-causing hindrances. The Mishnah says, "One removes the place where dead animal bodies were gathered; the graves and the tanneries, for 50 cubits from the town. One only puts a tannery on the east side of town."[56] One explanation of this last regulation is that the hot east wind tends to blow slowly, and thus does not bring bad odors to the town. Another is that east winds are infrequent in the Land of Israel.

Another type of hindrance concerns darkening the light of somebody's window. The Mishnah states that it is forbidden to construct a wall within four ells of a neighbor's window.[57] The Talmud explains that one should not block out the light coming in at his window.[58]

A community can prevent a citizen from letting water from his roof be conducted into the public domain.[59] Another ruling forbids a person to cause nuisance indirectly by working with blood or meat: shrieking birds are attracted by the waste produced; these, in turn, cause filth with their bloody feet, which may upset sensitive or sick neighbors.[60]

Some public policy issues we would not consider strictly environmental today are nonetheless closely related to it. For example, it is clearly specified which citizens are supposed to pay in the event of the breakdown of a collective water system.[61] Similarly, regulations for privacy are established; for instance, the ruling that one should not be in a position to look into one's neighbor's house.[62]

THE SPECIAL CASE OF JERUSALEM

There were special regulations for Jerusalem. It is written in the Talmud, "One should not erect a dung-heap there. One should not build a kiln there, one should not establish vegetable and fruit gardens, with the exception of the rose garden which has been there since the time of the first prophets. One should not raise chickens there. One should not leave a corpse there overnight."[63]

This brings with it an economic price. Due to the prohibition against kilns in Jerusalem, all earthenware had to be brought in from elsewhere. The Talmud tells us that earthenware was brought from Modi'in.[64]

Another important issue in the contemporary environmental discourse is the "precautionary principle." We find in the Bible a precursor of the concept that one should lay out funds in order to prevent possible future risks: "When you build a new house, you shall make a parapet for your roof, so that you do not bring bloodguilt on your house if anyone should fall from it."[65]

LAND POLICIES

The regulations mentioned earlier on the sabbatical and jubilee years are one aspect of land policies. Another important commandment concerns the allocation of space. The Bible mentions forty-eight cities that, with their surrounding land, were allocated for the use of the Levites. They lived off the tithes from this land, which enabled them to devote their lives to the service of God.

These cities were spread over the territories of the other tribes: "Instruct the Israelite people to assign, out of the holdings apportioned to them, towns for the Levites to dwell in; you shall also assign to the Levites pasture land around their towns. The towns shall be theirs to dwell in, and the pasture shall be for the cattle they own and all their other beasts. The town pasture that you are to assign to the Levites shall extend a thousand cubits outside the town wall all around. You shall measure off two thousand cubits outside the town on the east side, two thousand cubits outside the town on the south side, two thousand cubits outside the town on the west side, and two thousand cubits outside the town on the north side, with the town in the center. That shall be pasture for their towns."[66]

The regulations for the Levite cities were applied for all cities.

ENVIRONMENTAL VERSUS ECONOMIC INTERESTS

The conflict between economic and environmental interests is a central issue in the development of contemporary environmental policies. Each normative system has to make hierarchical decisions, attributing priorities between alternatives. The Halakhic discussion on such issues frequently refers to what we now would call an environmental-economic conflict in a preindustrial society. As we are dealing with "core" controversies, the decisions may be relevant for approaches to less transparent contemporary issues.

With the development over the centuries of the prohibition of wanton destruction, clear economic benefits were required in order to allow, for instance, the removal of fruit trees. One case concerning wanton destruction is mentioned in the Talmud that from a contemporary reader's viewpoint assesses the hierarchy between economic and environmental considerations: "Rav says that one is not allowed to cut down a date palm which carries a kav [of fruits]. The objection was made: 'How much [fruit] should an olive tree carry so that it is prohibited to cut it down?' Rabina said: 'When it has a significant value [as wood] this is permitted.'"[67]

Another case is mentioned in which the norm is also determined on the basis of economic values: "Once the tenant of Shmuel brought him dates, and when he ate them, he discerned a taste of wine. He then asked him [the tenant] why it was so. He replied: 'They stand between vines.' So he said to him: 'They take away too much of the strength of the vine. Bring me their roots tomorrow [as proof that he had indeed taken them out].' Rabbi Hisda once noticed palm trees between his vines. Then he spoke to his tenant and said: 'Take their roots away: for [the price] of vines one can buy palm trees; for that of palm trees, one cannot buy vines.'"[68]

In the responsa literature, the theme of wanton destruction and its meaning is also mentioned. For example, Hatam Sofer,[69] the leading Ashkenazi authority in his time, is asked whether one can fell grapevines in order to build houses on the land, thereby yielding a profit to the owner. The rabbi considers this a more complex issue than is immediately apparent. He replies that if the land is needed, then the prohibition of *bal tashkhit* need not apply. Where possible, he stresses, however, the vines should be pulled out together with their roots and some soil, so that they may be planted elsewhere. He also points out the importance of making careful financial calculations before uprooting the vines: If this process does not yield profits, the act is prohibited.[70]

Several other issues of environmental-economic interaction are discussed in the Talmud. One rabbinical enactment in the public interest established that one is not permitted to raise goats and sheep in the Land of Israel because of the economic damage these animals cause to the vegetation.[71] Modern rabbinical authorities disagree to what extent this enactment is still valid in our time.

NUISANCE AND STENCH

In recent years, Western society has increasingly come to consider noise both a major nuisance and an issue of health protection. Over the centuries, several responsa have prohibited various types of such pollution. On the other hand, sometimes economic or other considerations are such that people have to put up with noise hindrance.

The Mishnah states that neighbors can prevent the opening of a store in a common courtyard by claiming that they cannot sleep due to the noise of customers' entering and exiting; however, they cannot object to the noise of a hammer or a grinding mill in a craftsman's home; nor can they object to the noise children make if one of the courtyard's residents is a religious school teacher. Once again we find here a calibration between environmental and economic interests.[72]

Two Tannaitic sources conflict on an issue of stench. The Mishnah says, "Whoever brings out into the public domain straw or chaff in order to turn it into fertilizer, and causes harm, is liable for compensation. Whoever wants to, may take it. When somebody brings cattle dung out into the public domain, and somebody is harmed, he is liable for compensation."[73] In contemporary terminology, we might say that the anonymous sages of this Mishnah give preference to the environmental considerations.

The Talmud brings another Tannaitic source that takes a different position. One might define it as giving preference to economic interests: "Rabbi Yehuda says 'In the season of bringing out of dung, man is allowed to bring out his dung into the public domain and heap it up there, so that it will be trodden under the feet of man and animals.'"[74] The Talmud tries to harmonize the two sources.

INTERNALIZING EXTERNALITIES

Zvi Ilani has analyzed the attitude in Halakhic literature toward environmental nuisance, and compares this with modern economic theories. He concludes that classical Halakhah occasionally internalizes externalities. He offers the example of somebody suffering from nuisance caused by his neighbor, for instance, air pollution. He is allowed to sell his neighbor the right to maintain the nuisance.[75]

Ilani adds that one consideration that determines policies on specific environmental hindrances is whether there is a reasonable alternative for the person who is causing the nuisance. In situations in which one's livelihood is dependent on it, and there is no possibility of working elsewhere, neighbors will have to live with it; for instance, in the case of the owner of a mill or a blacksmith who hits with his hammer and causes noise pollution.[76] On the other hand, there is nuisance for which no right can be given or sold to maintain it; for instance, nuisance that damages health or harms society.[77]

The Talmud also mentions a precursor case of what we would now call "potentially hazardous materials." The rabbis' precautionary policies lead to a serious reduction in the value of goods. For instance, there are a number of discussions about what happens if wine, oil, or water have been left standing open, as there is some suspicion that a snake may have got in and poisoned the substance. The regulation that is then applied says, "water which has stood open may not be poured onto the street. One may not [mix] it with plaster ... nor give it to one's own beasts or anyone else's beasts to drink."[78] However, another text says that one can give it to cats, because they eat snakes and so are not susceptible to snake poison.[79]

Yet another risk discussed is that one may not sell wild animals, because they present a danger to the public. This includes bears and lions.[80]

SUSTAINABILITY POLICIES

Whereas the attitude of Judaism toward most of the previous issues is largely determined by specific commandments and regulations, this is much less the case with regard to maintaining sustainability. This derives partly from the vague nature of the concept of sustainable development.

The two English terms "sustainability" and "sustainable development," often used interchangeably, have become key elements of the environmental discourse in the last decade, although they also refer to many other fields. The most commonly used definition of sustainable development is that of the United Nations Brundtland Commission: "Sustainable development meets the needs of the present without compromising the ability of future generations to meet their own needs."[81]

Economics Nobel Prize winner Robert M. Solow has pointed out how imprecise this concept is: "If you define sustainability as an obligation to leave the world as we found it in detail, I think that's glib but essentially unfeasible. It is, when you think about it, not even desirable The best thing I could think of is to say that it is an obligation to conduct ourselves so that we leave to the future the option or the capacity to be as well off as we are. It is not clear to me that one can be more precise than that."[82]

LEGAL ASPECTS

The way in which Judaism views this discourse's key elements can be analyzed only briefly here.[83] On the normative side, the prohibition of wanton destruction, the commandments of the sabbatical and jubilee years, and the laws of the Levite cities are some of the Jewish laws that favor sustainability.

An important element of the discourse on global sustainability is the need to guarantee the dignity and survival of all people. This includes ensuring sufficient food for the world's population. The discussion on individual sustenance, that is, what is currently called "meeting basic needs," is simultaneously part of the human rights discourse.

In ancient Israelite society, various laws supported the physical sustenance of the disadvantaged, in order to prevent malnutrition. Many of these laws are first encountered in the Bible: "When you reap the harvest of your land, you shall not reap all the way to the edges of your field, or gather the gleanings of your harvest. You shall not pick your vineyard bare, or gather the fallen fruit of your vineyard; you shall leave them for the poor and the stranger. . . ."[84]

MAN EXPELLED FROM HIS ECOSYSTEM

Many biblical narratives deepen our insight into the Jewish perception of human life and humanity's desirable behavior. Central in this worldview is that the sustainability of human life, and particularly that of the Israelite people, depends on obeying God's commandments and behaving according to His wishes.

This concept appears many times in the Hebrew Bible. Its earliest expression is found in the story of Paradise. Although Adam and Eve are forbidden to eat the fruit of the Tree of Knowledge, they disobey; this leads to their expulsion from the first sustainable society. From then on, they are forced to toil for their sustenance: "Because you did as your wife said and ate of the tree about which I commanded you, 'You shall not eat of it,' cursed be the ground because of you; by toil shall you eat of it all the days of your life "[85]

Cain's murder of Abel also radically changes his sustenance: He will never be able to live permanently in any ecosystem: "If you till the soil, it shall no longer yield its strength to you. You shall become a ceaseless wanderer on earth."[86]

Even more dramatically, immoral behavior leads directly to the Flood, which destroys almost all humanity: "All existence on earth was blotted out—man, cattle, creeping things, and birds of the sky; they were blotted out from the earth. Only Noah was left, and those with him in the ark."[87]

RELIGIOUS SUSTAINABILITY

The motif of cutting off man from his ecosystem because of actions that God disapproves of also appears in the story of the builders of the tower of Babel.[88] The same theme returns as well in the story of the destruction of Sodom and Gomorrah: "the Lord rained upon Sodom and Gomorrah sulfurous fire from the Lord out of heaven. He annihilated those cities and the entire Plain, and all the inhabitants of the cities and the vegetation of the ground."[89]

These examples indicate that the Bible sees sustainability primarily as a religious issue. This becomes even clearer in the figure of Lot. Abram—later Abraham—and Lot have so many flocks, herds, and tents that they put stress on the land's carrying capacity: "the land could not support their staying together, for their possessions were so great that they could not remain together."[90]

Abram leaves the choice of direction to Lot, who bases his decision on environmental and economic considerations, rather than religious ones. Lot chooses grazing grounds on the Jordanian plain, prime land with abundant water: "like the garden of the Lord, like the land of Egypt."[91] He pitches his tents near Sodom, however, and even in the city.

While the natural environment is attractive, the spiritual one is unsustainable, which will determine his future. Lot has to leave behind everything in his house; he becomes a fugitive, and his wife dies. He and his daughters are then forced to live in a cave, believing that they are the only people left in the world.[92]

FURTHER DEVELOPMENT

Many aspects of religious sustainability are developed further in the Hebrew Bible. The rainbow is the symbol of a covenant that guarantees partial sustenance—God promises that no further floods will destroy all living beings: "When I bring clouds over the earth, and the bow appears in the clouds, I will remember My covenant between Me and you and every living creature among all flesh, so that the waters shall never again become a flood to destroy all flesh."[93]

Isaiah prophesies that, even if major geological movements take place, this covenant will remain valid: "'For this to Me is like the waters of Noah: as I swore that the waters of Noah nevermore would flood the earth, so I swear that I will not be angry with you or rebuke you. For the mountains may move and the hills be shaken, but my loyalty shall never move from you, nor My covenant of friendship be shaken'—said the Lord, who takes you back in love."[94]

Whereas environmentalists' declared aim is to prevent the rapid deterioration of the ecosystem, in Isaiah's vision, improvement of the cosmic ecological system is even possible: "No longer shall you need the sun for light by day, nor the shining of the moon for radiance [by night]; for the Lord shall be your light everlasting, your God shall be your glory."[95]

MAINTAINING BIODIVERSITY

Another important element of the modern sustainability discourse is maintaining biodiversity. The Brundtland Report discusses the motives for this: "The diversity of species is necessary for the normal functioning of eco-systems and the biosphere as a whole. But utility aside, there are also moral, ethical, cultural, aesthetic, and purely scientific reasons for conserving wild beings."[96] In a secular world, one can take notice of this or not, and act accordingly or not. As long as one does not transgress the applicable laws of one's country, there is no convincing argument for the individual to protect species, unless it is useful to him specifically.

Besides the law of *kilayim* (which fosters constancy of species), key biblical narratives also indicate the importance of constancy of species. Such a concern seems to be indicated by God's relegating the naming of all animals to Adam in Paradise.[97] Through this "due diligence" action of taking an inventory of all creatures and naming them, their identity and specificity are recognized.

The Paradise narrative shows that animals were not threatened by the first humans, who were vegetarian.[98] The account of Noah who, on Divine instruction, gathers specimens of all animal species into the Ark, is a further paradigm of biodiversity.[99] Seven pairs of certain species of animals survive the Flood; only one breeding pair of other species are saved. In this way, God chooses to maintain biodiversity in the global catastrophe.

A sustainable Utopia is also prophesied in the Latter Days: "The wolf shall dwell with the lamb, the leopard lie down with the kid; the calf, the beast of prey, and the fatling together, with a little boy to herd them."[100] Similarly, Isaiah predicts, "The cow and the bear shall graze, their young shall lie down together, and the lion, like the ox, shall eat straw."[101]

The theme of the maintenance of species recurs both in the Talmud and in the Midrash literature. All creatures in God's world have a function, although they may not benefit humanity. One passage in the Talmud states: "Rabbi Judah says in the name of Rav, 'Of all that was created, nothing was created unnecessarily.'"[102] The reason is then given for the creation of the snail, fly, mosquito, snake, and spider.

VARIOUS OTHER MOTIFS

Judaism often speaks out against excessive consumption. One Talmud text says, "The rabbis said that a sage who holds lengthy meals everywhere, his end will be that he destroys his house, turns his wife into a widow, makes his children orphans, forgets his studies, and quarrels abound around him. His words remain unheard, he desecrates the names of Heaven, his teacher and his father, and he leaves a bad name behind him for his children and his grandchildren until the end of all generations."[103]

As for geochemical cycling, the idea that man is dust is frequently repeated in the Bible. Already in the third chapter of Genesis, God says to man, "By the sweat of your brow shall you get bread to eat, until you return to the ground—for from it you were taken. For dust you are, and to dust you shall return."[104] And Ecclesiastes expresses the same general idea about man and animals: "Both go to the same dust, both came from dust and both return to dust."[105]

Jewish sources also address other key elements in the sustainability discourse, for example, durability, recycling, and intergenerational equity. Jewish approaches to these issues are firmly placed within the framework of a theocentric worldview in which the environment is not the prime concern, but one important issue among several to be taken into account.

DEMATERIALIZATION

Dematerialization is another central motif in the sustainability discourse. If we look at this from the Jewish viewpoint, we see that the invisible God of Abraham was a radically new departure in the religious context of his society. Not only is this God nonmaterial, but it is also strictly forbidden to give Him a material shape. Judaism is generally against destruction, but idols must be destroyed; for this reason, the golden calf is ground down and thrown into a brook.[106]

For only 3 commandments among the 613, Jews must give their life rather than transgress. Not worshiping idols is one of them. From medieval times onward, many Jews died for *Kiddush Ha-Shem*, the sanctity of God's name, rather than being forced to convert to Christianity. A key issue here was the refusal to recognize the existence of a material divinity: God's son.

In the nineteenth century, when the Reform movement abandoned most of the key normative characteristics of Judaism, such as the dietary and Shabbat laws, there was only one thing it could not tolerate in liberal Christianity: the concept of the son of God. A nonmaterial God is fundamental to Judaism. Today, Jews for Jesus is the one group whose members call themselves Jews that is clearly outside the Jewish community.

THE "SPOLIATION OF NATURE" DEBATE

Within the fledgling Jewish environmental discourse, paganism in various forms is an important issue. This discourse initially developed as a reaction to the general "spoliation of nature" debate, which touched on both paganism and Judaism.

Referring to the Jewish roots of Christian attitudes toward nature, American historian Lynn White Jr. stated in a famous article in 1967 that Genesis 1:28 expresses the dualism of man and nature, and God's intention that man exploit nature for his benefit: "'Be fertile and increase, fill the earth and master it; and rule the fish of the sea, the birds of the sky, and all the living things that creep on earth.'"

While White did not specifically analyze the attitude of Judaism toward the environment, he did make one clear accusation: "Christianity inherited from Judaism not only a concept of time as nonrepetitive and linear but also a striking story of creation . . . God planned all of this explicitly for man's benefit and rule: no item in the physical creation had any purpose save to serve man's purposes."[107]

This debate is often linked to the current widespread revaluation of paganism. In the opinions of several prominent writers, paganism scores higher in the environmental context than monotheism. Lynn White wrote, "In antiquity every tree, every spring, every stream, every hill had its own genius loci, its guardian spirit. These spirits were accessible to men, but were very unlike men; centaurs, fauns, and mermaids show their ambivalence. Before one cut a tree, mined a mountain, or dammed a brook, it was important to placate the spirit in charge of that particular situation, and to keep it placated. By destroying pagan animism, Christianity made it possible to exploit nature in a mood of indifference to the feelings of natural objects."[108]

White's article generated many responses from various quarters, including a few from Jews. His accusations continue to be quoted in the "spoliation of nature" debate until the present day.

CLASSICAL PAGANISM

There is much evidence, however, that various pagan civilizations destroyed their environment. Furthermore, from an ideological view, paganism was far less friendly toward nature than White indicates. One Jewish author who has pointed this out is David Shapiro: "That pagan man has produced some of the greatest destroyers of nature is apparently ignored. Pagan man worshipped all forces of nature, the good and the bad. There was no more divinity attached to beneficence than to destructiveness. Aphrodite-Venus is a goddess and Ares-Mars is a god. Krishna, the beneficent, and Shiva, the destroyer are both gods. Why should paganism be more concerned with the preservation of nature than the Bible? Everything . . . points in the opposite direction."[109]

Among the Jewish authors who have identified pagan traits in environmentalist currents is Michael Gillis, who writes that the "pagan view can give rise to worship of animals, the sea, the soil or whatever. People are subject to these divinities and can only seek harmony with them. Such a view is manifestly ecological. . . . Ecologism is thus secular paganism."[110] Michael Wyschogrod unequivocally equates some elements of environmentalism with paganism. He states that, "upper ecology is 'nature religion,' primarily a religious attitude toward nature. . . . In relationship to the divine, upper ecology usually expresses itself as polytheism, the theological view that there are many gods. These gods dwell within the forces of nature and are symbols of these forces."[111]

NEOPAGANISM

Several neopagan sects see the world of Jewish (and Christian) thought as their enemy because there is no place in Judaism for either the divinity of nature or a "sacred earth." While many present forms of nature veneration are un-Jewish, some neopagan reconstructionists are anti-Jewish.

By the early 1990s, the Anti-Defamation League had identified one pagan camp, Odinism, with neo-Nazism.[112] A revival of "national" (*völkische*) neopagan groups is taking place in Germany today. This nationalism is characterized by the claim that the Northern race is different from other races. Peter Kratz, who focuses on New Age paganism, writes: "The opposition to Judaism and Christianity as supposed anti-nature religions is found in the same way in the Fascist ideology as in New Age. For both of them, the ideological starting-point is the identical criticism of Judaism and Christianity as supposedly being responsible for the destruction of Divine nature."[113]

Similarly, today, neo-Nazi groups continue to propagate environmental hypotheses. There are also striking similarities between their love of animals and nature as compared to their hatred of specific human communities, and the similar approaches of some marginal environmentalist groups.

THE NAZIS AND THE GREENS

The historian Walter Laqueur also identified certain affinities between the Nazis and the Greens: "'Blind industrialization,' 'materialist consumerism,' soulless modern society and generally speaking the excesses of modern technology were strongly opposed by the Nazi party, which always stressed the need to return to nature, to a simpler and healthier life."[114]

Wyschogrod defines the relationship between environmentalism and Nazism even more strongly, pointing out how deeply Hitler was influenced by concepts of evolution: "The stronger kills the weaker, and it is through this process that nature moves ahead. Hitler, of course, did not invent this theory. It has deep roots in Nietzsche."[115] The partial ideological affinity between Nazism and extreme environmentalism is a recurring theme for several contemporary authors.[116]

CONCLUSION

From the above, it can be seen that there are many touching points between Judaism and current environmentalism. They relate to a multitude of issues of which only a limited number have been touched on before. There are two main avenues for development through asking new questions: one is in the religious sphere, through queries on specific issues to rabbinical authorities. In this way, Jewish environmental law can gradually evolve. A good example of such a process is the rapid expansion of medical Halakhah over the past two decades.

The second is the development of Jewish environmental studies as an academic discipline. This will ensure an analysis of Judaism's many environmental aspects and their relevance to current issues and will demonstrate how rich the Jewish environmental tradition is.

A combination of the two will enable a better clarification of Jewish environmental policies. In view of the increasing attention being paid to the interrelationship between religion and environment in general society, this is also likely to find interest beyond the Jewish community.

NOTES

1. Biblical quotations are taken from the Jewish Publication Society's translation of the Bible.

2. Mishneh Torah, *Hilkhot Shekhenim.*

3. Manfred Gerstenfeld, "Jewish Environmental Studies: A New Field," *Jewish Political Studies Review* 13, 1 & 2 (Spring 2001).

4. For more details, see Manfred Gerstenfeld, *Judaism, Environmentalism and the Environment* (Jerusalem: The Jerusalem Institute for Israel Studies/Rubin Mass, 1998).

5. See Libby Bassett, ed., *Earth and Faith: A Book of Reflection for Action* (New York: Interfaith Partnership for the Environment/United Nations Environment Programme [UNEP], 2000), which also includes a very superficial section on Judaism and the environment.

6. See Manfred Gerstenfeld, *Environment and Confusion: Introduction to a Messy Subject* (Jerusalem: Academon, 1994).

7. Deuteronomy 20:19–20.

8. *Sifre* 203 (Finkelstein edition) on Deuteronomy 20:19.

9. Deuteronomy 12:2–3.

10. Babylonian Talmud, *Shabbat* 140b.

11. Ibid.

12. Babylonian Talmud, *Shabbat* 67b.

13. Maimonides, Mishneh Torah, *Hilkhot Melakhi* 6:10.

14. Ibid., Chapter 6:8–10.

15. Maimonides, Mishneh Torah, *Hilkhot Avel* 14:24.

16. *Sefer HaHinukh*, commandment 529. This work is often attributed to Rabbi Aaron Halevi from Barcelona around 1300. *Sefer HaHinukh* (Jerusalem: Eshkol, 1946).

17. Samson Raphael Hirsch, *Commentary on Deuteronomy 20:20* (Frankfurt am Main: Kauffmann, 1920). [German]

18. Rashi, Commentary on Genesis 32:25.

19. Hirsch, op. cit., Commentary on Genesis 32:25.

20. Rabbi Yitschak Silberstein, *He'arot be'inyan bal tashkhit. Tsohar, Kovets Torani* (1998), 48–75. [Hebrew]

21. Ibid., 50–52.

22. Responsa *Yabia Omer* Part 3, section 24.

23. Deuteronomy 12:23.

24. Babylonian Talmud, *Sanhedrin* 56a & b.

25. Exodus 23:12.

26. Deuteronomy 5:14.

27. Deuteronomy 22:10.

28. Deuteronomy 25:4.

29. Leviticus 22:28.

30. Deuteronomy 22:6–7.

31. Deuteronomy 11:15.

32. *Teshuvot* Noda Biyehuda, *Yoreh De'ah,* No. 10. [Hebrew]

33. Responsa *Mayim Hayim,* Tome Two, Tel Aviv, 1995, 50. [Hebrew]

34. Rabbi J. David Bleich, *Contemporary Halakhic Problems* (New York: Ktav, 1989), 3:237–50.

35. Responsa *Seridei Aish* 3:7.

36. Responsa *Tzitz Eliezer* 14:68.

37. Responsa *Yechave Da'at* I Part 3, section 66.

38. Ibid. He also quotes the Babylonian Talmud (*Avodah Zarah* 18b) where Rabbi Simon ben Pazzi comments that the verse "happy is the man who has not . . . taken the path of the sinners" (Psalms 1:1) refers to those who do not go to contests between wild beasts or between wild beasts and men.

39. Responsa *Piske Uziel Besheelot Hazman* 24.

40. Exodus 23:10–11.

41. Leviticus 25:23.

42. Genesis 4:3–4.

43. Bereishit *Rabbah* 22 (Theodor Albeck edition).

44. See also Yalkut Shimoni *Bereishit* 35.

45. Babylonian Talmud, *Bava Metsia* 62a.

46. There are other rulings which indicate the priorities of what should be saved in case of an emergency. For instance, if a container of honey breaks, the owner of a container holding wine must pour out the wine to save the honey; later, the owner of the honey must pay for the wine lost. See Babylonian Talmud, *Bava Kama* 81b.

47. Tosefta *Bava Kama* 10:28 (Lieberman edition).

48. Babylonian Talmud, *Nedarim* 80b. The same case is discussed in Tosefta *Bava Metsia* 11:33–36 (Lieberman edition).

49. Deuteronomy 8:9.

50. Joshua 17:15–18.

51. Deuteronomy 20:6.

52. Deuteronomy 23:13–14.

53. Leviticus 6:4.

54. Maimonides, Mishneh Torah, *Hilkhot Temidin Musafin,* Chapter 2:15.

55. Meiri, *Pesahim* 27. Menahem Meiri was a Talmud commentator who lived in Perpignan, 1249–1306.

56. Mishnah *Bava Batra* 2:9.

57. Mishnah *Bava Batra* 2:4.

58. Babylonian Talmud, *Bava Batra* 22b.

59. Emanuel Quint, *A Restatement of Rabbinic Civil Law* (Northvale, NJ: Jason Aronson, 1994), 5:105.

60. Ibid., 144. See also Babylonian Talmud, *Bava Batra* 22b/23a.

61. Babylonian Talmud, *Bava Metsia* 108a.

62. Babylonian Talmud, *Bava Batra* 2b.

63. Babylonian Talmud, *Bava Kama* 82b.

64. Babylonian Talmud, *Bava Hagigah* 26a.

65. Deuteronomy 22:8.

66. Numbers 35:2–5.

67. Babylonian Talmud, *Bava Kama* 91b.

68. Babylonian Talmud, *Bava Kama* 92a.

69. Rabbi Moses Sofer was born in Frankfurt am Main in 1762 and died in Bratislava in 1839.

70. Responsa *Hatam Sofer* 2:102.

71. See Nachum Rakover, *Eihut haSvivah* (Jerusalem: haMishpat haIvri, 1993), 42ff. [Hebrew]

72. Mishnah *Bava Batra* 2:3.

73. Mishna *Bava Kama* 3:3.

74. Babylonian Talmud, *Bava Kama* 30a.

75. Zvi Ilani, *Shikulei Ye' ilut beTipul beMitradim Ekologi'im beSifrut heHalakha beHashva'a im Te'oriot Kalkaliot Moderniot*. Shenaton Ha-mishpat Haivri Yearbook, vol. 16–17, (1990–91) 42.

76. Ibid., 61.

77. Ibid., 78–81.

78. See Babylonian Talmud, *Bava Kama* 115b; See also Mishnah *Terumot* 8:4.

79. Babylonian Talmud, *Shabbat* 128b.

80. Babylonian Talmud, *Avodah Zarah* 16a.

81. In 1983, the World Commission on Environment and Development was established, chaired by Gro Harlem Brundtland, then the Prime Minister of Norway. Its brief was to reexamine critical environmental and developmental problems, and to formulate realistic solutions for them. This was to be done while aiming for the continuation of human progress through development, and the continued availability of adequate resources for future generations. World Commission on Environment and Development, Our Common Future. (Oxford: OUP, 1987), 43.

82. Robert M. Solow, "Sustainability: An Economist's Perspective," in *Economics of the Environment: Selected readings*, 4th ed., ed. Robert N. Stavins (New York: Norton, 2000), 132.

83. See also Manfred Gerstenfeld, *The Jewish Environmental Tradition: A Sustainable World* (Jerusalem: The Jerusalem Institute of Israel Studies, forthcoming). [Hebrew]

84. Leviticus 19:9–10.

85. Genesis 3:17.

86. Genesis 4:12.

87. Genesis 7:23.

88. Genesis 11:5–6, 8.

89. Genesis 19:24–25.

90. Genesis 13:6.

91. Genesis 13:10.

92. Genesis 19:30–31.

93. Genesis 9:14–15.

94. Isaiah 54:9–10.

95. Isaiah 60:19.

96. The World Commission on Environment and Development, op. cit., 13.

97. Genesis 2:19–20.

98. Genesis 2:15–16.

99. Genesis 6, 7.

100. Isaiah 11:6.

101. Isaiah 11:7.

102. Babylonian Talmud, *Shabbat* 77b.

103. Babylonian Talmud, *Pesahim* 49a.

104. Genesis 3:19.

105. Ecclesiastes 3:20.

106. Deuteronomy 9:21.

107. Lynn White Jr., "The Historical Roots of Our Ecologic Crisis," *Science* 155 (March 10, 1967): 1203–7.

108. Ibid.

109. David S. Shapiro, "God, Man and Creation," *Tradition* 15, 1–2 (Spring-Summer 1975): 42.

110. Michael Gillis, "Ecologism: A Jewish critique," *L'Eylah* No. 34 (September 1992): 6–8.

111. Michael Wyschogrod, "Judaism and the Sanctification of Nature," *Melton Journal* 3 (Spring 1992): 6–7.

112. Letter from Alan M. Schwartz, Director of the ADL Research and Evaluation Department, to Jeffrey Kaplan, 4 December 1992, as quoted in: Jeffrey Kaplan, *Radical Religion in America: Millenarian Movements from the Far Right to the Children of Noah* (Syracuse, NY: Syracuse University Press, 1995), 161.

113. Peter Kratz, *Die Götter des New Age: Im Schnittpunkt von "Neuem Denken", Faschismus und Romantik* (Berlin: Elefanten Press, 1994), 17. [German]

114. Walter Laqueur, *Germany Today: A Personal Report* (London: Weidenfeld and Nicolson, 1985), 58.

115. Wyschogrod, op. cit.

116. See also Gerstenfeld, *Judaism, Environmentalism and the Environment*, op. cit.

CHAPTER 7

Welfare Programs and Jewish Law

Aaron Levine

Despite its status as an integral component of contemporary public policy, the welfare state finds its historical beginnings only as recently as the end of the nineteenth century. Its salient feature is that voluntarism alone is not relied on to alleviate the plight of the poor and disadvantaged. Instead, the government augments private efforts and legislates programs to protect individuals against specified contingencies and also steps in to guarantee people a minimum standard of living.

But in Judaism, these notions can be traced back hundreds, even thousands, of years. Society's duty to the poor is referred to in the Hebrew language as *tzedakah*. *Tzedakah* is defined as "justice" and implies a compulsory giving rather than a "charity" or free-will offering.[1] In this vein, the notion that the community should use coercion to ensure that the needs of the poor are attended to goes back to Talmudic times (300 B.C.E.– 500 C.E.).[2] Investigation of Jewish welfare law can therefore be very productive in formulating an agenda for the modern welfare state. Once we define poverty, we will identify Jewish Law's (Halakhah's) antipoverty goals. We will then proceed to demonstrate that Halakhah calls for a dual antipoverty system, consisting of both private and public components. Next, we investigate Halakhah's attitude toward income redistribution. In the end, we will see that Halakhah proves to be a useful tool for examining current public welfare policy and can even be used to evaluate and choose among competing antipoverty programs.

DEFINING POVERTY

Scholars have debated whether poverty should be defined in absolute or relative terms. Since the early 1960s, the U.S. government has adopted an absolute standard for poverty. Accordingly, the poverty line calculation begins by noting the cost of the bundle of food the Department of Agriculture deems as a nutritionally sound *minimum* food diet. Because poor families tend to spend about one-third of their incomes on food, the cost of the minimum diet is then multiplied by three to arrive at the poverty line income. In 1998, the Department of Agriculture estimated that the minimum bundle of food would cost about $5,553 for a family of four for a year. Multiplying this figure by three makes an income of $16,660 the poverty line for a family of four.[3] To put this figure in perspective, we need only note that the median[4] family income in the United States in 1998 was $46,750. By official definition, 12.75 percent of all Americans remained in poverty in 1998.[5]

However, many experts find defining poverty in absolute terms unsatisfactory. Consider that the notion of a subsistence budget includes subjective questions of taste and social convention. Housing that today is considered substandard often includes household appliances and plumbing that were unavailable to the millionaires of an earlier age.

Because of the shortcomings in the current definition, a panel of experts of the National Academy of Sciences recommended in 1995 that the definition of poverty be changed to reflect relative income status. The panel recommended that a family be considered poor if its consumption is less than 50 percent of the median family's consumption of food, clothing, and housing. Poverty in the relative income sense would decline when inequality decreased; poverty would be unchanged if the economy prospered with no change in the distribution of income and consumption.[6]

As discussed below, Judaism subscribes to a dual antipoverty system consisting of public and private components. The definition of poverty is therefore relevant to eligibility for both public and private assistance. We offer the proposition that Halakhah adopts an absolute standard for poverty, defined in terms of inability to achieve a subsistence standard of living. The subsistence standard of living will, however, include certain amenities, such as standard housing, that were not even available to the rich of many generations ago. Later, we shall see that the eligibility standard is somewhat liberalized when it comes to private assistance. We begin with the eligibility standard for public assistance.

ELIGIBILITY FOR PUBLIC ASSISTANCE

Halakhah's adoption of an absolute standard for poverty can be seen by the criterion the Mishnah prescribes for eligibility to receive agricultural gifts[7] in ancient Israel. In this regard, a household is classified as poor if its net worth falls below 200 *zuz* [Roman denarius]. When net worth consists of capital invested in business transactions, the minimum net worth shrank to 50 *zuz*.[8] The underlying rationale behind these figures, according to R. Ovadia b. Avraham Bartinoro (Italy, ca. 1456–ca. 1516), is that capital sums of these amounts generate subsistence for a year.[9]

What it takes in terms of net worth to generate subsistence is a function of both how inclusive the subsistence basket of goods and services is defined and also on the cost of obtaining that basket. In Talmudic times, poverty was defined in terms of having a net worth of less than 200 *zuz*. Today, in the United Sates, poverty would be defined in terms of a net worth that falls short of acquiring subsistence.[10]

But how is subsistence, itself, defined? Should subsistence be defined narrowly in terms of physiological survival? If so, anyone who can manage on his own to survive should not be eligible for assistance. But, perhaps, the eligibility for assistance should cover more than those who are on the very bottom of the economic scale. Let's also entertain the possibility that anyone who fails to achieve the *common standard of living* on his own should be regarded as poor and eligible for assistance. While we offer no precise benchmark, let's examine a number of definitions of poverty that Halakhah would reject.

One possibility is to conceptualize poverty as destitution. In the thinking of Sidney and Beatrice Webb, early twentieth-century social commentators, poverty and destitution were two distinct conditions:

Poverty is a relative term. Any person is poor who has less spending power than is common in the circle in which he lives By destitution we mean the condition of being without one or other of the necessities of life, in such a way that health and strength is so impaired as to eventually imperil life itself.[11]

From the perspective of Halakhah, destitution is far too narrow a definition of poverty. This is so because there is a duty more fundamental than *tzedakah* that demands us to rescue someone from a situation of destitution. This is the biblical duty of "Do not stand idly by the blood of your neighbor" (Leviticus 19:16).[12] This interventionist duty applies even when the would-be victim faces only a life-threatening danger rather than certain death.[13] Given the duty to extricate someone from life-threatening circumstances proceeding from Leviticus 19:16, the *tzedakah* duty spelled out separately at Leviticus 25:35 and at Deuteronomy 15:7–8, 10 must speak of deprivation that is less desperate than destitution.

Once it is recognized that every member of society is entitled to be extricated from life-threatening conditions, a relative element in the definition of poverty enters through the back door.

Consider that the housing of well-off nineteenth-century Americans was primitive by modern standards. Baths, for example, were rare even in the cities. No homes had electricity and few had gas. Fewer still had running water, and not even 2 percent had indoor toilets and cold running water.[14] Does that mean that the financial ability to acquire these amenities should not be factored into the index for poverty today? No. Living on a permanent basis without electricity, hot running water, or indoor toilets seriously jeopardizes one's health, especially the health of young children. The calculation of subsistence must therefore factor in the family's ability to acquire standard housing. If the family cannot manage this on their own, the family should be eligible for public assistance.

Let's now move to the other end of the continuum. Halakhah would also reject stretching the notion of poverty to include anyone who is below the common standard of living. This proposition proceeds from a number of considerations.

One proof is an examination of how a family's liquidity affected the 200-*zuz* criterion for eligibility for agricultural gifts in ancient Israel. Usually, claims for assistance on the basis of inadequate cash flow were denied when net worth exceeded the poverty line. Instead of relying on the public purse, the household was expected to liquidate its assets to increase cash flow to an adequate level.[15] There were, however, several exceptions to the general liquidity rule. One of these exceptions has direct relevance to the issue at hand. To be eligible for public assistance, an individual was not expected to sell his apparel, home, or any essential household article in order to obtain cash for basic subsistence, unless those items were made of gold and silver. In the case of gold and silver utensils, an indigent was required to sell the articles and replace them with less costly ones. Net worth was then recalculated, excluding the new and cheaper household items from total assets.[16] Now, if poverty is defined in terms of failing to achieve the common standard of living, the common standard of living of the neighborhood of the would-be supplicant should be taken into account. Specifically, if replacing the household articles effectively sets back the would-be supplicant's standard of living below the neighborhood common standard of living, the liquidation requirement should be waived.

Another proof that Halakhah does not define poverty as failure to achieve the common standard of living can be derived from the eligibility requirement to take funds from the *kuppah* (public charity chest). In Talmudic times, part of the public sector charity program consisted of weekly disbursements of money. In order to qualify to take from the *kuppah*, a person had to be unable to provide himself with fourteen meals. Funds for two meals per day for one week disqualified the individual from becoming a public charge for that week.[17] The Talmud refused to liberalize the eligibility requirement to fifteen meals in order to accommodate the religious obligation of eating three meals on the Sabbath. Instead, it observed Rabbi Akiva's maxim, "Treat your Sabbath like a weekday rather than be dependent on your fellow-beings."[18] Commenting on this passage, R. Solomon b. Isaac (*Rashi*, France, 1040–1105) explains that a person may not "impose on others the honor of his Sabbaths."[19] Since three meals on the Sabbath was a religious duty, having three meals on the Sabbath was certainly an aspect of the common standard of living. Denying an individual public charity funds to afford him the opportunity to fulfill the three-meal Sabbath requirement is, hence, tantamount to denying that person the use of public funds to achieve the common standard of living. So, the fourteen-meal criterion becomes understandable only if poverty is defined in terms of falling below a liberally defined subsistence level, but below the common standard of living.

It could be argued that this conception of subsistence is too narrow and should be expanded further to include amenities designed to safeguard the mental and emotional stability of the family. On these grounds one could argue that subsistence should include the ability to go on a vacation, enjoy a certain number of restaurant meals over the year, and have access to various forms of entertainment. These amenities relieve the drudgery of everyday life and therefore contribute to the emotional and mental heath of the family.

However, stretching the concept of subsistence beyond food, shelter, and clothing to include other commonly enjoyed amenities is very problematic. Recall that public assistance is denied to allow an individual to fulfill the three-meal Sabbath requirement. If assistance were denied to achieve the mitzvah (religious duty) of eating three meals on the Sabbath, it certainly would be denied to subsidize restaurant meals and vacations. What proceeds from the fourteen-meals standard is a subsistence notion that cannot be expanded beyond food, shelter, and clothing to include commonly enjoyed amenities.

The upshot of the above analysis is that eligibility for assistance is defined as a net worth level that does not afford a subsistence standard of living. Included in the calculations are only the cost of food, shelter, and clothing. In respect to these items, culturally determined factors should be taken into account because one's well-being is seriously threatened without certain modern upgrades. A case in point is standard housing facilities.

ELIGIBILITY FOR PRIVATE ASSISTANCE

The discussion thus far has dealt only with the standard to receive public assistance. What about eligibility to receive private funds? If the standard to receive private assistance were the same as the standard to receive public assistance, society's obligation to the eligible supplicant would be no more than to bring that person up to subsistence. But, this is not so. Once someone qualifies for assistance, society's duty toward that person is set forth at Deuteronomy 15:7–8: "Grant him *enough for his lack, which is lacking for him*" (*dei mahsoro asher yahsar lo*, henceforth *dei mahsoro*). To be sure, we are not required to make the poor wealthy,[20] but Halakhah understands *dei mahsoro* —"*which is lacking for him*"—as not just support for physiological survival. Evidencing this is the communal practice of conducting a special charity drive before the Passover season to enable the poor to purchase *mazah* for the holiday (*maot hittin*).[21] Note also that the community is obligated to finance the religious education of the children of indigent families.[22] Still another responsibility of the community is to help find an indigent a suitable mate and set up a household for the couple.[23] Finally, society must provide the needy supplicant with free health care.[24] The broad sweep of *dei mahsoro* leads to the proposition that once a person qualifies for assistance, our duty is to lift that person up to the common standard of living. Public funds are not expended on anyone who has achieved subsistence on his own. Nonetheless, anyone falling below the common standard of living qualifies for private assistance. Expending money on that person to bring him up to the common standard of living amounts to a legitimate use of *tzedakah* funds.

As far as private giving is concerned, expenditures beyond bringing someone up to the common standard of living, under certain conditions, qualify as *tzedakah, the conditions of which are as follows.*

Recall that claims for assistance on the basis of inadequate cash flow are denied when net worth exceeds the poverty line. In the case of gold and silver utensils, an indigent is required to sell the articles and replace them with less costly ones. Net worth is then recalculated, excluding the new and cheaper household items from total assets. But, this stringency pertains only to determine eligibility for public assistance. Eligibility for private assistance does not depend on such a sale.[25]

The difference in treatment of the liquidity problem between the public and the private sectors can be explained on the basis of the principle that selling off one's household articles and apparel in order to maintain subsistence is degradation. While one cannot expect to be supported by public funds to avoid this humiliation, the expenditure of private funds for this purpose is a legitimate use of charity funds.

Support for the notion that private charity funds may be used to prevent a supplicant from experiencing humiliation can be drawn from the law of *dei mahsoro* as it applies to luxuries:

"Grant him enough for his lack which is lacking for him."(Deuteronomy 15:7–8, 10) Even if he is lacking a horse to ride upon and a servant to run before him, you must provide these things for him They said about Hillel the Elder that he once took for a pauper from an aristocratic family—horse to ride upon and a servant to run before him. On one occasion [Hillel] could not find a servant to run before [the pauper], —so [Hillel] himself ran before him for three *milin*.[26] (Babylonian Talmud, *Ketubot* 67b)

Halakhah places a number of caveats on the charity duty of "a horse to ride upon." One caveat is that the duty applies only to a person who had been wealthy previously and as part of his lifestyle had become accustomed to ride on a horse and to have a servant run before him. We'll refer to this type of indigent as an "aristocratic pauper." If this person falls into poverty, *tzedakah* funds should be expended to maintain for him the standard of living he was accustomed to in better times. However, in respect to paupers who were never accustomed to the trappings of wealth in better times, the charity fund should not provide them with these luxuries now in their state of poverty.[27]

The Gaonim (the Rabbinic authorities in Babylonia during the ninth and tenth centuries) offer another caveat. In their thinking, supplying luxuries to an aristocratic pauper applies only *before* his plight is a matter of public knowledge. To prevent the aristocratic pauper's indigent status from becoming public knowledge, we even create for him the façade that he continues to enjoy his previous status of affluence. Such treatment protects the aristocratic pauper from the degradation that would inevitably accompany revelation of his indigent status. Once the aristocratic pauper's indigent status becomes public knowledge, we are no longer obligated to maintain his affluent façade. At this stage, accordingly, *dei mahsoro* no longer requires us to provide the aristocratic pauper with luxuries, notwithstanding that he enjoyed the amenities when he was wealthy.[28]

This Gaonic caveat for the *tzedakah* duty of "a horse to ride upon" makes the provision of luxuries to an aristocratic pauper solely a private sector matter. This is so because as soon as the aristocratic pauper applies for public relief, his poverty status becomes public knowledge, and at that point, society's duty to maintain a façade of affluence for him no longer applies. As far as a private person is concerned, so long as the aristocratic pauper's indigent status remains a secret, providing him with the luxuries he was accustomed to in better times is a legitimate use of *tzedakah* funds.

The Gaonim's caveat with respect to the aristocratic pauper finds support in the differential treatment Halakhah calls for between the public and private sectors in respect to the liquidity issue discussed above.

The eligibility standard for private funds, according to R. Shlomo Zalman Auerbach (Israel, 1910–1995), a leading contemporary authority, is far more liberal than the criterion we depicted above. In his view, an unemployed person whose total income, including income from capital and transfer payments from the government, does not afford him a "reasonable" standard of living qualifies for *private* assistance. What is "reasonable" will depend on the neighborhood in which he resides and the level of wealth to which he was formerly accustomed.[29]

R. Auerbach's income "inadequacy criterion" apparently finds precedence in the manner R. Yizhak of Corbeil translated the 200 *zuz* criterion for thirteenth-century France. Instead of understanding the 200-*zuz* criterion as subsistence in terms of capital adequacy, as his colleagues understood it, R. Yizhak rejected this notion. In his view, formulating the

200-*zuz* sum as an "income inadequacy" criterion applied only to former times, when agricultural gifts as well as institutionalized public welfare in the form of the charity chest (*kuppah*) and the charity plate (*tamhui*) were regularly available to people whose net worth dropped to the poverty line. Within a society of such institutional arrangements, a person could sell his assets today with the assurance that the community would provide for him tomorrow. However, in a world in which such gifts are less certain, the standard shifts from capital inadequacy (based on net worth) to income inadequacy. So long as a person's income (from all sources) for a given period remains below *subsistence* level, he is eligible for private assistance. R. Yosef Caro (1488–1575) records R. Yitzhak of Corbeil's view approvingly.[30]

In thirteenth-century France, the government did nothing to secure an indigent's future. In our times, however, because the poor can rely on government contributions in the way Talmudic indigents could depend on the various agricultural gifts, the 200-*zuz* standard should once again be formulated as subsistence in terms of capital adequacy. R. Auerbach's ruling should therefore not find precedence in R. Yizhak of Corbeil.

Defining poverty in terms of income inadequacy, as R. Auerbach does, leads to a work disincentive for those who have a small amount of capital but cannot survive on the income of that capital. Following an income inadequacy standard, such indigents receive private assistance and thus have little incentive to work. Under the capital inadequacy standard, however, these paupers become eligible for assistance only after depleting their capital. Faced with the choice of losing their savings, many might choose to earn a living instead.

HALAKHAH'S DUAL SYSTEM OF PUBLIC AND PRIVATE ANTIPOVERTY MEASURES

In Talmudic times, the public sector, as discussed earlier, was responsible to carry out various charity drives for the poor. Yet, no one can be compelled to contribute to the various charity drives until they have lived in the town for a minimum period of time.[31]

Widespread poverty forced many Jewish communities in the Rishonic period (mid-eleventh to mid-fifteenth centuries) to abandon most of the above elements of public philanthropy in favor of private philanthropy.[32]

The prominence given by the Talmud in describing public charity levies does not imply that the public sector has sole responsibility in the antipoverty area. Jewish social welfare, posits R. Samson Raphael Hirsch (Germany, 1808–1888), historically consisted of both public and private components. Public social welfare never displaced private philanthropy even when the various communal levies were operative; thus, we have the Talmudic dictum (*Nedarim 65b*) that anyone who becomes needy does not immediately apply for public relief. Rather, his relatives and friends first attend to his needs, and only then is the community required to make up the deficiency.[33]

An application of the above dictum is the ruling that public charity funds may not be used to support an indigent individual when the would-be public charge has a father of means. Instead, the father is forced to support the son. Coercion applies even when the father is not otherwise legally obligated to support his son, that is, the son is not a minor.[34] Similarly, public charity funds may not be used to support an indigent individual who is known to have wealthy relatives in the local area. Since the wealthy relatives are expected to support their indigent kin out of their own resources, public funds may not be used for this purpose, even though the wealthy relatives made contributions to the public charity chest.[35]

R. Hayyim Soloveitchik (Russia, 1853–1918) provides further clarification of the dual nature of the *tzedakah* obligation in Jewish law. Preliminarily, let's note that the *tzedakah* obligation is set out twice in the Pentateuch, once in Leviticus and again in Deuteronomy:

If your brother near you becomes poor and cannot support himself, you shall maintain him; he shall live with you, even when he is a resident alien. (Leviticus 25:35)

If one of your brothers is in need in any community of yours within your country which the Lord your God is giving you, you must not harden your heart nor close your hand against your needy brother. Rather, opening, you shall open your hand to him, and grant, you shall grant him enough for his lack which is lacking for him. Giving, you shall give him, and let your heart not feel bad when you give him, for because of this matter, Hashem, your God will bless you in all your deeds and in your every undertaking. (Deuteronomy 15:7–8, 10)

The repetition of the *tzedakah* obligation is taken by R. Hayyim Soloveitchik to convey that this duty has a dual aspect to it. In R. Soloveitchik's view, the Deuteronomy passage is directed to the individual, while the Leviticus passage is directed to society as a collective. Within the dual system, coercion has a limited role. Note that in connection with the Deuteronomy passage, the Pentateuch ties a reward to the performance of charity works. The rule is that whenever a reward is mentioned in connection with a biblical positive precept, the Jewish court will not force compliance but will rely on voluntarism instead. But, no reward is mentioned in connection with the Leviticus passage that speaks to society as a collective. Coercion should therefore apply.

The purpose of coercion, in R. Soloveitchik's view, is not to ensure that the members of the community in their capacity as individuals discharge their *zedakah* obligation, but rather to allow the public sector to carry out its own distinctive social welfare responsibility.[36]

Given the public-private nature of the *tzedakah* obligation, what is the proper division of responsibility between the two sectors? In attempting to answer this question, it is necessary to delineate Halakhah's antipoverty agenda. Setting out this program will equip us to address the issue of the proper division and balance between voluntarism and the public sector's role in the antipoverty program.

HALAKHAH'S ANTIPOVERTY PROGRAM *DEI MAHSORO*

Once an individual is deemed eligible for assistance, society's obligation, as discussed earlier, is to lift that person to the commonly enjoyed standard of living. An individual is, however, not qualified for public assistance unless he is in a deprived state. A deprived state translates into a net worth that does not generate subsistence, however broadly defined. Anyone who is below the common standard of living but who does not qualify for public assistance qualifies for private assistance to bring that person up to the common standard of living.

One final point: No individual is expected to shoulder alone the responsibility of providing *dei mahsoro*. This is so because *dei mahsoro* is a collective, rather than an individual, responsibility.[37]

DEI MAHSORO AND FISCAL RESPONSIBILITY

Recall earlier the dictum that anyone who becomes needy does not immediately apply for public relief. Rather, his relatives and friends first attend to his needs, and only then is the community required to make up the deficiency.

In respect to the coercive charity levy, the responsibility to relieve poverty, according to R. Solomon b. Abraham Adret (Spain, ca. 1235–ca. 1310), is not an equal per capita obligation, but rather is a responsibility proportional to wealth.[38]

In modern times, it is widely recognized that the ability of taxpayers to conceal such assets as cash and jewelry makes the wealth or net worth tax an impractical tax. If we assume that the rationale behind R. Adret's call for a wealth tax is the ability-to-pay principle, the use of a progressive income tax would serve as a good substitute equity guidepost for the charity levy in modern times.

PRESERVING THE DIGNITY OF THE POOR

Preserving the dignity of the poor is a central objective of Jewish charity law. The anonymous benefactor is praised highly in Halakhah: Maimonides ranks the anonymous gift to an anonymous recipient second in his list of eight types of charitable donations.[39] The lowest category of charity involves the person who gives ungraciously.[40]

EMPATHETIC AND PERSONAL INVOLVEMENT

Tzedakah requires more than financial outlay; it compels an emotional contribution. In this regard, in the Talmud, R. Isaac stated that "he who gives a small coin to a poor man obtains six blessings, and he who addresses to him words of comfort obtains eleven blessings." While the financial aspect of *tzedakah* is subject to a 20 percent upper limit,[41] there is no limit on one's obligation to devote time to the performance of good deeds.[42] Sharing the companionship of the poor and affording them social equality represent a high level of *tzedakah* and merit special blessing.[43]

R. Isadore Twersky (United States, contemporary) pointed out that according to the Jewish theory of philanthropy, personal contact with, and exposure to, the needy is essential. Twersky observed "the individual can never really isolate himself from the needy, *especially* in times of euphoria, pleasure and indulgence. The very nature of rejoicing and festivity includes sharing with others."[44] In accordance with this thought, Maimonides formulates the biblical command to rejoice with others during the festivals:

While one eats and drinks by himself, it is his duty to feed the stranger, the orphan, the widow, along with other despondent poor people. But he who locks the doors to his courtyard and eats and drinks with his wife and family, without giving anything to eat and drink to the poor and the bitter of soul—his meal is not a rejoicing in a divine commandment, but a rejoicing in his own stomach. Rejoicing of this kind is a disgrace to those who indulge in it.[45]

In addition, Halakhah prohibits a Jew from taking action that would dull his sensitivities to the suffering of his fellow man. This prohibition is derived not only by relating the biblical phrase "thou shalt not harden thy heart nor shut thy hand" (Deuteronomy 15:7) to hardening one's heart consciously and suppressing the inclination toward kindness, but also failing to perform affirmative acts of kindness.[46]

TYING CONTINUING SUPPORT OF THE POOR TO AN INVESTIGATION AGAINST FRAUD

Notwithstanding Judaism's sensitivity to the indignity of the poor, self-declaration of eligibility does not alone suffice to qualify a person for aid. An investigation of those requesting public assistance is also required. The need to monitor requests was a matter of Amoraic dispute:[47]

Applicants for food are examined but not applicants for clothes. This rule can be based, if you like, on Scripture, or if you prefer, on common sense. "It can be based if you like on common sense," because [the one with no clothing] is exposed to contempt, but not the other. Rav Judah, however, said that the applicants for clothes are to be examined but not applicants for food. This rule can be based, if you like, on common sense, or if you prefer on Scripture. "If you like on common sense," because [the one without food] is actually suffering but not the other.[48]

The Halakhah follows Rav Judah's view.[49] Therefore, a supplicant will be denied a subsistence income, other than a food allowance, pending the outcome of an investigation. Moreover, application of Rav Judah's reasoning compels us only to acquiesce to the supplicant's *initial* food request. Putting the supplicant on notice that further food aid will depend on the outcome of an investigation does not impose any suffering on an honest supplicant and is therefore consistent with Rav Judah's view. In this regard, R. Moshe Isserles (Poland, 1525 or 1530–1572) rules that charity wardens must probe the honesty of the supplicants' requests.[50] Accordingly, conducting an investigation to determine whether the food aid should continue is required.

SELF-HELP AND *DEI MAHSORO*

Judaism favors a social welfare program that discourages idleness and encourages work effort. The disdain for loafing is evident in the teaching that idleness leads to immorality.[51]

Discouragement of idleness follows also from the Halakhic disapproval of the "welfare mentality," as enunciated in Rav's advice to R. Kahana: "Flay carcasses in the marketplace and earn wages and do not say I am a priest and a great man and it is beneath my dignity."[52]

The *dei mahsoro* imperative, according to R. Ephraim Solomon b. Aaron of Lenczycza (d. 1619), becomes operative only after the supplicant has exhausted his efforts to generate subsistence for himself and his family by means of gainful employment. This limitation of *dei mahsoro* may be derived from the biblical duty to come to the aid of a neighbor who requests assistance to help him unburden his animal that is faltering under the weight of the load it is carrying: "If you see the donkey of a man who hates you lying helpless under its load, you must refrain from deserting him; you must be sure to help him unburden the animal." (Exodus 23:5)

Exegetical interpretation of the phrase "to help him" (*immo*) understands the obligation of the passerby to consist of *assisting* the owner in the unloading operation. Demanding that the passerby unload the animal himself constitutes, however, an unreasonable request on the part of the owner, and consequently need not be heeded. Under the assumption that the *immo* caveat applies to the charity obligation generally, R. Ephraim derives the principle that before a supplicant qualifies for public assistance, he must be willing to do his part, that is, exhaust his efforts to secure gainful employment.[53]

The issue of whether the caveat is confined to the unloading case or applies generally to the charity obligation, points out R. Aaron Lichtenstein (Israel, contemporary), was raised earlier by R. Menahem b. Solomon Meiri (Perpignan, ca. 1249–1306). Meiri reached no definite conclusion in regard to this issue. Notwithstanding Meiri's uncertainty and Rishonic silence on this matter, R. Ephraim's position apparently finds support in Maimonides' treatment of welfare fraud:

Whoever is in no need of alms but deceives the public and does accept them, will not die of old age until he indeed becomes dependent upon other people. He is included among those of whom Scripture says: "cursed is the man that trusteth in man (Jeremiah 17:5)."[54]

Now, if the deception Maimonides speaks of refers to outright fraud, that is, becoming a public charge when one's net worth is above the poverty line, why is the conduct described only as accursed behavior? More appropriately, such conduct should be characterized as constituting outright theft! Maimonides' failure to characterize the deceptive conduct as outright theft indicates that the deception he speaks of refers to the circumstance where the relief claimant is employable. Though he is technically qualified for relief on the basis of his poverty line status, becoming a public charge before exhausting all possibilities of securing employment constitutes accursed behavior.[55]

POVERTY PREVENTION AHEAD OF POVERTY RELIEF

Judaism teaches that *tzedakah* in its most noble form consists of preventing a faltering individual from falling into the throes of poverty. The position of such a person must be stabilized and his dignity preserved whether by making him a gift, extending him a loan, entering into a partnership with him, or creating a job for him.[56] Poverty prevention ranks as a higher priority than poverty relief.

Antipoverty—the Public-Private Division of Responsibilities: The most fundamental issue the public-private welfare system raises is the operational significance today of the Talmudic principle that the role of public welfare is only to fill in the deficiency that cannot be met by the relatives of the needy person.

Imposing the duty to support an indigent on his relatives and turning to public charity funds only if there is a deficiency is most appropriate in a poor society that is characterized by tremendous inequality in income and wealth. In this type of society, a household (*A*) whose income is above subsistence, but below the common standard of living, is in a peculiar position. *A* does not qualify for public assistance. Moreover, because *A* is above the poverty line as far as qualification for public assistance is concerned, nothing stops the public sector from taxing A to support public charity cases. But there is a great irony here. Anyone who supports A to bring him up to the common standard of living can use his charity-designated funds for this purpose. Given these circumstances, it would be unconscionable on the part of the public sector to require A to join in the support of B's relative when B is capable of meeting the relative's needs entirely himself.

Let's now change the scenario to a wealthy society where there are very few households below subsistence, but there are a large number whose incomes are above the common standard of living. Putting the *entire* brunt of support for those falling below subsistence on the relatives of these indigents is grossly unfair. This is so because *dei mahsoro*, as mentioned earlier, is a collective rather than an individual responsibility. To be sure, the relatives of the indigent are wealthy people. But, if charity funds are raised by means of a progressive income tax, the wealthy relatives will end up paying their fair share, and the rest of the population will also share in this burden in a manner roughly proportional to ability to pay.

What the above analysis points to is the proposition that as society's per capita incomes rises, the Talmudic notion that the role of public welfare is only to fill in the deficiency that cannot be met by the relatives of the needy is fully satisfied by setting up a public welfare system and financing it by means of a progressive income tax.

The next issue Judaism's public-private welfare system raises is how should we determine the appropriate division of responsibility in discharging Halakhah's antipoverty goals. In this regard, we propose the following: Because the public sector involvement entails coercion, the government should discharge Halakhah's antipoverty goals only when voluntarism would be less effective than governmental intervention. In what follows, we will subject the various antipoverty goals to this criterion.

INCOME REDISTRIBUTION AND JEWISH LAW

In some circles, as mentioned earlier, poverty is conceptualized in terms of the proportionality criterion. This approach defines poverty in relative terms. Regardless of their absolute income, this school asserts, families located in the lowest tenth (or fifteenth or twentieth) percentile of the national income distribution will feel psychologically alienated from society and believe they are victims of deprivation. Subscription to this criterion leads to the contention that there is no solution for the poverty problem short of something close to absolute equality of income and wealth.

But redistribution of income in order to effect greater equality in the distribution of income and wealth is not one of Halakhah's antipoverty goals. This proposition follows from a number of considerations, some of which have been discussed above.

One point against redistribution of income as an antipoverty goal is that Halakhah defines poverty for the purpose of qualification for public assistance in terms of physiological deprivation. This definition is, however, broad enough to afford the poor standard housing and free health care and to guarantee some of their religious needs such as the religious education of the young and the provision of matzo for Passover. Another point against the notion of income redistribution as an antipoverty measure is the dictum that our obligation to the poor consists of providing for their needs but there is no obligation to make the poor rich.

But the strongest evidence that Halakhah's antipoverty goals do not include a secret agenda to redistribute income comes from an examination of the minimum rate Halakhah sets for charity giving.

Talmudic sources differ as to whether the 10 percent charity obligation imposed by the Torah on agricultural produce[57] applies to income as well. Opinions in the matter range from an income tithe requirement arising from biblical law to one established by rabbinical edict. In his survey of the responsa literature, R. Ezra Basri (Israel, contemporary) concludes that the majority opinion regards the 10 percent level as a definite obligation, albeit by dint of rabbinical decree. In any case, devoting less than 10 percent of one's income to charity is considered by the rabbis to reflect an ungenerous nature.[58]

Because Jewish law requires a person to donate only 10 percent of his net income to charity, any additional contribution is considered *lifnim meshurat ha-din*, that is, beyond the letter of the law. Jewish law prohibits the community from coercing a person to act *lifnim meshurat ha-din*.[59] Consequently, a Jewish community may not enact a general charity levy-compelling donation of more than 10 percent. This protection of property rights prevents the community from accomplishing an income redistribution plan through the charity laws.

ECONOMIC MALAISE

If the economy is hit with a severe economic dislocation in the form of a depression, an escalating inflationary spiral, or a stagflation, private relief efforts will prove pathetically inadequate to turn the economy around. This is so because under voluntarism, we can hope for no more than a redistribution of income from the rich to the poor. In a severe economic dislocation, much more than this is required. Pulling the economy out of a depression, for example, requires an increase in aggregate demand, not just a redistribution of income from the rich to the poor. In a severe economic dislocation, what is needed is the restoration of a favorable economic environment. To accomplish this, confidence in the economy must be restored and appropriate incentives put into place. Success here requires government to implement an appropriate mix of monetary and fiscal policy.

PREVENTING POVERTY

Left to his own devices, the private citizen may be confronted with precious few opportunities to give charity at the level of preventing someone from falling into poverty. The combination of risk aversion and limited resources may work to limit private loan initiatives to finance vocational and professional education as business ventures. Moreover, unless an individual owns his own business, he will not be in a position to offer a needy person a job or partnership.

Government taxation accomplishes the pooling of some part of society's resources already destined for *tzedakah*. This fund could be used to extend interest-free loans to finance various job-oriented activities such as vocational training, professional education, and job training. Repayment of these loans could be geared to the level of the beneficiaries' future earnings.

Preventing poverty makes it a religious duty for the government to adopt the optimal mix of monetary and fiscal policies that would prevent the economy from falling into a recession. Another aspect of the government's responsibility to prevent poverty is a duty to implement any measures currently regarded as necessary to promote a depression-free economy. Mandatory insurance on bank deposits and margin requirements on the purchase of financial assets are examples of these measures.

FERRETING OUT FRAUD, UPLIFTING DIGNITY, ENCOURAGING SELF-HELP, AND BEFRIENDING THE POOR

On its own, the private sector would prove inadequate in fostering the value of self-help. Consider that *dei mahsoro* is a collective, rather than an individual, responsibility. This makes it unlikely that any one individual would end up being the sole support for a particular indigent. Far more likely is that a particular indigent would draw his support from many sources. What leverage would any single supporter therefore have in encouraging self-support, to say nothing of tying his support to efforts of self-help?

Moreover, within a system of voluntarism there is potential for explosive tension between the goal of promoting self-help and the value of befriending the poor. If *A* encourages *B* to engage in self-help, *B* might take *A*'s gesture as reflective of a begrudging attitude to support him and a callous disregard for his difficult plight. Consider also that the above strain is exacerbated if the private sector is burdened with investigating whether continued assistance is warranted.

If needy individuals must rely on private philanthropy to relieve their plight, the potential for exposing them to indignities is likely to proliferate. Within a system of voluntarism, it can be expected that some needy people will take initiative to organize support for themselves, suffering many indignities along the way. Other needy people will opt to suffer silently rather than come forward. To be sure, within a system of voluntarism there would be efforts to seek out and discover the poor who do not come forward. But, within this system, many of the poor will suffer significant indignities or remain unidentified.

By contrast, public sector involvement minimizes the number of embarrassing interactions the would-be recipient would have to otherwise put up with in arranging the support he needs. It simplifies the process, making the donor, in essence, faceless. Instead of approaching friends, relatives, and strangers, the individual seeking aid need only approach a government clerk and fill out an application. Within the framework of the public sector program, the source of any individual's stipend would also be derived from the entire tax base on a prorated basis. From the perspective of the recipient, the source of his stipend is hence anonymous.

Another advantage of public sector involvement is that it fosters an attitude of self-help. By setting limits on how long it will support a welfare recipient, the government effectively compels these people to find gainful employment. Cutting people off the welfare rolls after a limited time is not insensitive if the government concurrently offers job training programs, job search services, and a guarantee of a public sector job as a last resort.

Public sector involvement in welfare minimizes the potential for explosive conflict between the duty to encourage the poor to engage in self-help and the obligation to befriend them. Within this framework, the role of the private sector is to befriend the poor and practice social equality with them. Carrying out this role enhances the living standards of the poor both materially and emotionally.

HUMANISTIC CLIMATE

Tzedakah, as discussed above, requires more than just a financial outlay to the poor. Sharing the companionship of the poor and affording them social equality is also part of this duty.

Reliance on public funding carries with it the danger of creating the misperception that the total needs of the disadvantaged, both material and emotional, are being attended to by "others." The more society relies on public assistance to combat poverty, the less aware independent citizens will be of individual poverty cases. While anonymity preserves the dignity of the disadvantaged, it also isolates them and desensitizes the public to their plight. In a state reliant completely on government assistance for the poor, citizens will begin to concentrate their *gemilat hasadim* (acts of kindness) only on their inner circle of friends, creating social stratification.

Of course, there are merits to government programs. Certain problems of the disadvantaged are beyond the capacity of any single individual to handle. Since *dei mahsoro* implies a collective as well as an individual responsibility, institutions with professional staffs should handle individuals requiring constant and/or professional expertise, such as the handicapped.

There is, however, another side to this coin. While practicing social equality with the poor is an individual responsibility, voluntarism alone will not do the job. Government involvement is necessary to foster the humanistic impulse in society.

Paradoxically, as the commitment to alleviate misery and deprivation intensifies in the form of the creation and growth of institutions specifically designed to deal with these problems, society's humane impulse may very well weaken. This occurs when professionals are hired to attend to every aspect of the operation of these institutions and the public's involvement does not extend beyond making financial contributions toward their maintenance. Within this framework, an encounter with another human being's suffering may very well produce a muted reaction. Personal involvement or intervention on any level, the passerby might argue, is not necessary, as the welfare institutions he himself created will surely spring into action to aid the victim.

Yet, government can do much to encourage a humane spirit in society. It can, for instance, mandate educational institutions to require students to spend a certain number of hours each week providing companionship to the aged, shut-ins, and the infirm. Moreover, by dint of both their own personal examples and recruitment efforts, government officials can make voluntarism a status activity in society.

BASIC RESEARCH IN THE MEDICAL FIELD

Basic *dei mahsoro* needs of the poor are to be cured of sickness and to be relieved of the physical and mental suffering that accompany it. Halakhah gives expenditures for this purpose the highest ranking in charity giving.[60]

Consider that basic research is the building block in developing cures and treatments for devastating diseases. A steady and adequate expenditure in this direction, coupled with guarantees for free access for the poor, works to significantly improve the quality of life of the poor over time.

It is unlikely that the private sector alone, driven by the profit motive, will foster basic research in new drugs. Consider that basic research takes on the character of a pure public good. A pure public good is a good that is a preferred item in people's budgets but that, paradoxically, will not be produced because of the absence of the profit motive. This is the case in the issue at hand. Basic research is by its very nature an unfocused, general foray into the unknown, with no immediate practical objective in mind. Moreover, society will not optimally benefit from this activity unless findings of the research are shared. Yet, an adequate and ongoing financial commitment to basic research in the health-related field will likely produce discoveries that will enhance the quality of life for everyone. Investment in basic research in the health-related area is hence a preferred item in everyone's budget, but, paradoxically, it will never get off the ground because of the absence of the profit motive.

To be sure, relieving the suffering of the poor is a *tzedakah* obligation of high priority. But the voluntarism of the private sector alone will not spur basic research, even in the health-related fields. First, without guarantees that the poor will be given free access to the fruits of basic research in the health-related area, society will not treat this expenditure as part of its *tzedakah* obligation. Second, even if people would regard basic research in the health-related area as a welfare obligation, the expenditure would rate only a low-priority status. This is so because relieving misery *here and now* takes precedence over expenditures on basic research that works only to relieve the misery of the poor in future time periods. Another reason for neglect is that expenditures on basic research offer the prospect of producing useful findings only when the activity is conducted on a steady and large-scale basis. This may make people reluctant to contribute unless they are assured of widespread participation. Finally, reliance on voluntarism here would undoubtedly shortchange research on diseases that affect only a tiny percentage of the population.

The solution to the pure public good case is government taxation. In the case at hand, it will take no less than government taxation to assure that society's preferred expenditures on basic research in the health-related area would actually take place. No coercion is involved here, as the role of government is merely to actualize a demand for a preferred item in everyone's budget.

The pure public good phenomenon finds Halakhic recognition in the power it gives to the Jewish community to tax its residents to construct a town wall.[61] In respect to this levy, even majority opposition cannot legally block the project.[62]

The rationale behind the town wall levy is the presumption that all the permanent residents of the town regard security measures as a preferred item in their budgets. What the tax does, therefore, is merely eliminate the "free rider" motive in respect to an undertaking everyone desires.[63]

Given the pure public good character of basic research in the health-related area, taxation to ensure viability of this endeavor is, from the perspective of Halakhah, a legitimate function of government.

Commitment to relieving the misery of the poor over time hence requires the public sector to act *here and now* as a proxy for future time periods. It does so by taxing society for basic research in the health-related area to assure a steady and adequate expenditure for this purpose.

By ensuring a steady and adequate flow of research and development, government taxation effectively shifts the risk associated with the expenditure from private industry to society at large. Under this arrangement, private industry enters the drug-development field only when profit considerations motivate it to do so.

Public funding of basic research carries with it a regulatory responsibility. One aspect of this responsibility relates to the government's role in the area of welfare. It consists of a responsibility to ensure that the poor would be guaranteed free access to the drugs.

Another area of responsibility is the regulation of the pricing of pharmaceuticals. Elsewhere,[64] I have dealt with this issue.

RELIGIOUS EDUCATION OF THE YOUNG

Another area where a *dei mahsoro* need falls through the cracks in the private sector is the religious education of poor children. A high priority in Jewish charity giving, support for the religious education of poor children takes precedence over the support for the Torah study of older children.[65] Recall that in Talmudic times the community imposed a levy to finance the religious education of poor children. Why the religious educational needs of these children were not left to voluntarism can be explained by the concern that without a coercive levy this item would be neglected. Support for this cause must cede to higher priorities such as alleviating sickness of the poor and meeting the material needs of the desperately poor. Moreover, in the face of so many other charitable requests, including the demands of Jewish higher education and philanthropic institutions of all sorts here and in Israel, what's left of the family's resources to pursue *excellence* in the area of religious education of the young? What's left for the poor in this category? Almost nothing.

Assigning government the task of imposing a tax to finance the religious educational needs of poor children reflects Halakhah's attitude that without a coercive levy there would be little chance that sufficient resources and attention would be devoted to this cause. If this assessment is correct, it behooves the public sector to get the most mileage out of the resources it taxes for the religious educational needs of poor children. Toward this end, the government must consider alternative means of subsidizing the religious education of poor children and implement its subsidy by means of the least-cost method.

Perhaps the most efficient means of implementing a subsidy for basic Jewish education is through a voucher system. Provided minimal educational standards were met, recipients could use the vouchers at the school of their choice. The voucher could be designed to increase in value for the family if the parents get involved in the education of their children. For example, they could participate in parent-children study groups. Accountability is promoted because underperforming schools must then deal with dissatisfied parents withdrawing their children from the rolls and/or disqualification as a voucher school.

Finally, a performance component should be added for participating voucher schools. This adds to the accountability element and gives monetary incentives for high-performance schools to prosper and hence dominate the educational landscape.

Also, consider that one of the religious duties a father has toward his son is to teach him a craft.[66] Perhaps this duty can serve as a building block in making a case for government or, at least, private support of secular education, vocational and professional training for the poor.[67]

TEMPORARY AID TO NEEDY FAMILIES (TANF)

Now we turn to examining Halakhah's antipoverty ideology and program in terms of the recent changes in welfare law and the issue of choosing between competing antipoverty programs.

In 1996, the U.S. Congress passed the Temporary Aid to Needy Families Act. This act represents the latest thinking on public antipoverty policy.

Since 1935, the major welfare program in the Unites States was Aid to Families with Dependent Children (AFDC). Under AFDC, the federal government financed a share of AFDC benefits by matching grants to the states.

AFDC provided direct cash grants to families that had children but no breadwinner. Under this program, once monthly earnings exceeded a few hundred dollars, welfare payments were reduced by one dollar for each one dollar that the family earned as wages. Thus, if a member of the family got a job, the family was subjected to a 100 percent marginal tax rate.[68]

In 1996, the U.S. Congress passed the Temporary Assistance for Needy Families (TANF) Act. This legislation "reformed welfare as we know it." Instead of providing matching grants to the states, TANF provided a block grant to each state in a fixed amount. The block grant to each state was based on federal grants paid during the years between 1992 and 1995.

Instead of keeping AFDC intact and reducing the marginal tax rate, the new legislation effectively compelled welfare families to work. It did so by subjecting a family on welfare to a lifetime limit of sixty months of benefits. Adults in the program must engage in work activities after two years of benefits.

States may exempt up to 20 percent of their caseloads from the sixty-month time limit and may also use their own funds to provide assistance after sixty months. To take into account individual circumstances, many states have adopted policies to exempt families from the time limit during periods when they are not expected to work, such as when they are caring for a young child or dealing with personal or family crises. Similarly, some states allow for extensions to the time limit if a family has complied with program requirements but is unable to find employment.[69]

In the design of their TANF programs, many states have sought to guarantee that families who are working are better off than those who remain on assistance. They have done this by allowing employed families to keep a portion of their cash assistance grant and by providing assistance to reduce the cost of working, most commonly by subsidizing the cost of child care and by paying for initial expenses such as special work clothing or licensing fees and for transportation costs for a specified period of time.[70]

In implementing the work requirement provision, the states could opt to either encourage recipients to participate in education or training programs to increase their earnings potential or encourage them to enter the labor market as quickly as possible. TANF has been implemented almost entirely using a work-first model. Although states have the discretion under TANF to place some welfare money in education or training programs, few states have taken full advantage of this discretion.[71]

The salient feature of the new trend in welfare legislation is that the work-incentive problem is tackled by using the stick rather than the carrot.[72]

Promoting work at the expense of penalizing idleness, as discussed above, is a goal in Halakhah's social welfare program. But, TANF also promotes work at the expense of penalizing parenting. Encouraging the parental role in the form of child rearing and participation in the educational training of one's children is highly valued in Judaism.[73] If the single parent is fulfilling this role, the parent should be subsidized, not penalized. If a single parent chooses the parenting route rather than the work route, welfare payments should not be cut off unless there are strong indications that the single parent is abrogating his or her role as parent. Alcohol or drug abuse by the single parent and/or truancy by the child provide evidence of this sort. Exemplary performance as a parent and participant in the educational process should be rewarded with additional subsidies in the welfare system.

At the same time, the single parent who opts to seek gainful employment and delegate in a responsible way part of the parental responsibilities to grandparents, caretakers, and/or professionals should not be denied the option to do so. We should not pronounce that it is impossible to be a good parent *and* participate in the workforce as well. Accordingly, the marginal tax rate that the single parent faces should be reduced tremendously and perhaps even made negative up to a certain range of income. Subjecting the initial earnings of an individual to a negative tax rate, or offering subsidies based on need, is already part of the U.S. tax system. This program is called the Earned Income Tax Credit (EITC) and will be dealt with at length later.

Another indication that Halakhah would find disfavor with the stick approach to the work-incentive issue proceeds from an analysis of the source for the self-help requirement. Recall that the job-search requirement for the would-be welfare applicant is derived from the *immo* caveat mentioned in connection with the duty to assist in unloading another's donkey. One can argue for a liberal interpretation of this requirement. Relaxation of the requirement follows from the duty of the passerby to accede to the owner's request to unload the animal without his (the owner's) assistance when the latter is either a *zaken* or a sick person. *Zaken* usually refers to a Talmudic scholar, but in the present context takes on the broader meaning of an individual of standing. Since health reasons prevent the sick person from participating in the work of unloading, and such labor is beneath the dignity of the *zaken*, the passerby must shoulder the task of the unloading operation alone.

Extension of the *zaken* and sick person exemptions of the *immo* caveat to general charity law, in R. Lichtenstein's view, calls for a liberalization of the job-search requirement for the public assistance applicant.

Exemption from the job-search requirement for the handicapped and the female head of a household should also, it seems, fall squarely in the spirit of this indicated relaxation.

Another candidate for relaxation of the job-search requirement is the applicant for public assistance who can secure employment, albeit not in his area of professional training. This *zaken* exemption of the *immo* caveat allows for the public assistance applicant with professional training to draw relief for a limited time even though he can at that time secure employment outside his area of training. The grace period temporarily spares the professionally trained individual the indignity and trauma of being forced to change careers, and at the same time affords him the chance of getting rehired in his area of specialization.

The *zaken* exemption also points to an emphasis on education and job training over a work-first approach.

COMPETING ANTIPOVERTY PROGRAMS

The public sector in the modern welfare state is faced with the choice of competing approaches to pursue its antipoverty program. One option is to promote the welfare of the needy by means of an income tax approach. The negative income tax plan, mentioned earlier, is a program representative of this approach. An alternative option is to promote the welfare of the needy in a price subsidy approach. Within this approach market forces are interfered with to set the price of essential goods lower than market forces would dictate. Accordingly, rent control for housing units and maximum interest rates for credit transactions are set. Rounding out this approach is the setting of a minimum wage in the labor market. By setting the minimum wage, even people who cannot earn subsistence on the basis of the free market price of their labor will be guaranteed a living wage.

Once the state decides on a particular antipoverty strategy, it will have to deal with choosing competing programs within each general approach it chooses. Choosing between AFDC and TANF illustrates this dilemma.

From the standpoint of Halakhah, decision making on both the general approach and specific program levels is a matter of identifying the antipoverty goals and choosing the least-cost method of accomplishing these goals. Pursuing given objectives by means of the least-cost method is what economic efficiency is all about.

Elsewhere,[74] we have developed the thesis that it is a religious duty for the state to pursue all of its given objectives by means of the least-cost method. Efficiency for the state is hence a religious value. To illustrate how the religious mandate to operate at the least-cost method decides on competing programs, let's compare the minimum wage law in Israel against the competing alternative of an EITC approach. We begin by describing these two programs. We will then compare them in terms of meeting Halakhic antipoverty goals.

THE MINIMUM WAGE LAW IN THE STATE OF ISRAEL

Israel's minimum wage law, as amended in April 1997, specifies that anyone working in a full-time position is entitled to a minimum wage equal to 47.5 percent of the average wage that prevailed in the economy over the last three months. Working a minimum of 186 hours a month qualifies as occupying a full-time position.[75]

The specific goal of the minimum wage law is to afford all workers a reasonable standard of living. Toward this end, the minimum wage is geared to the average standard of living and automatically increases as the average standard of living increases. Of all the countries in the Organization for Economic Cooperation and Development (OECD), only France has a minimum wage law similar to Israel's, which provides for partial indexation of the minimum wage to the average wage.[76]

How does Israel's minimum wage law measure up as an antipoverty program for the working poor? In its 1999 Annual Report, the Bank of Israel offered an economic analysis of Israel's minimum wage law. The report points out that the minimum wage law was designed to protect the standard of living of the lowest-paid workers, but operation of the law may very well work against the economic interest of these workers. What bring this about are the negative employment effects an increase in the minimum wage has on low-skilled labor, particularly in the textile and clothing industries. In these industries, employers cannot translate higher costs into higher prices and hence must reduce production and employment in response to higher labor costs. Accordingly, an increase in the average wages of the economy automatically causes the minimum wage to increase, which, in turn, causes employers to reduce production and employment in the low-skilled textile and clothing industries.[77]

Another issue from the perspective of Halakhah is who pays for the cost of financing the minimum wage measure. Consider that it is employers, rather than society at large, who are targeted to be directly responsible to ensure all workers a decent living wage. To be sure, employers will try to pass on their higher labor costs in the form of higher prices. Success in shifting the tax forward to the consumers depends on the elasticity of demand the industry faces.

Addressing this issue, K. Flug, N. Kasir, and Y. Rubinstein maintain that shifting the higher costs of labor in the form of higher prices occurs in the nontradable industries, which make use of skilled labor. In the tradable industries, particularly textiles and clothing, higher labor costs cannot be shifted forward; therefore, higher labor costs lead to lower production and lower employment. Thus, the costs of financing the minimum wage law are borne by employers, by low-skilled workers who lose their jobs as a result of the minimum wage law, or by the general public in the form of higher prices.[78] This distribution of burden does not make for a proportional wealth tax.

Most disturbing of all, however, is the possibility that a significant portion of the minimum wage increase is shifted forward in the form of higher prices. Consider that consumption spending is a decreasing function of income. Financing the cost of the minimum wage law by means of higher prices is hence borne disproportionately by the lower income bracket. There can therefore be no doubt that the minimum wage law violates R. Adret's dictum that antipoverty measures should be financed proportional to wealth.

Yet, there is still a positive side in that the minimum wage law encourages the poor to engage in self-help. Consider that to be eligible a worker must hold down a full-time job. Another advantage of the minimum wage is that it may reduce the dropout rate from the labor force of those with a low level of schooling.

THE EARNED INCOME TAX CREDIT

An alternative to the minimum wage law is the EITC approach. Part of the tax system in the United States for many years, the scope of EITC increased dramatically in 1993. By 1998, the cost of the EITC rose to $22 billion.

The EITC is a subsidy to the earnings of low-income families. Only the working poor are eligible for EITC. As its name implies, the subsidy comes in the form of a tax credit, which is simply a reduction in tax liability. In the phase-in range, the government adds a certain amount of income to a qualifying household for every additional dollar earned. In the phase-out range, the government reduces the additional income the wage earner receives for each additional dollar he earns, until the subsidy disappears entirely. The subsidy also depends on the number of children in the household. Let's illustrate how the EITC worked in recent times for a household with two children.

In 1998, EITC gave the illustrative household a tax credit equal to 40 percent of all wages and salary income up to $9,390. In effect, this was a negative marginal tax rate of 40 percent on earnings. The maximum credit was hence $3,756 (i.e., 0.40 × $9,390). To help guarantee that only the poor benefit from the credit, the credit was phased out at incomes between $12,260 and $30,095. For each dollar of earnings in this phase-out range, the credit was reduced by 21.06 cents. This amounted to an implicit positive marginal tax rate of 21.06 percent.[79]

Given the criterion Halakhah sets for an antipoverty measure, EITC fares better as policy than the minimum wage law. For, in contrast to the minimum wage approach, EITC does not interfere with market forces and artificially raise the wage rate from what it otherwise would be. The direct effect of EITC is hence not to improve the welfare of one group of people at the expense of generating unemployment for others.

Another advantage of EITC is that it puts the burden of antipoverty on society as a whole, rather than on particular groups. To meet R. Adret's proportional-to-wealth criterion, we need only assume that society's tax system is structured as a progressive system and EITC draws on these revenues to finance its subsidy to the working poor.

Finally, EITC works well to promote the value of self-help in the targeted group. EITC does this with its feature of a negative marginal income rate for the phase-in range. EITC's structure lends itself to promote work incentives more effectively than the minimum wage law. Increasing the outer income limit of the phase-in range and/or increasing the marginal negative income rate accomplishes this.

SUMMARY AND CONCLUSION

In extrapolating Jewish public welfare policy for the twenty-first century, our most fundamental task was to identify the concept of poverty.

We proposed that Judaism adopt two different definitions of poverty. From the perspective of the public sector, anyone who cannot manage to achieve subsistence on his own qualifies for assistance. But, subsistence, however broadly we define it, will still be below the commonly enjoyed standard of living. The individual living at the margin of subsistence will assuredly be deprived as far as the commonly enjoyed amenities of life are concerned. It is for the private sector to fill this gap.

Judaism's antipoverty program consists of both public and private components. Deciding on the division of labor between the public and private sectors requires as the first order of business an identification of the goals of an antipoverty program. Once these goals are identified, the division of labor between these sectors will all be a matter of deciding the relative efficiency of each sector in meeting these goals.

The central goal of Judaism's antipoverty program is *dei mahsoro*. What this goal translates into is that the basic needs of the poor must be attended to.

Redistributing income just for the sake of greater equality in the distribution of income is not a goal of Halakhah's antipoverty program.

In meeting *dei mahsoro*, preventing poverty stands higher than poverty relief. While meeting *dei mahsoro* by means of anonymity is virtuous, empathetic involvement with the problems of the poor and practicing social equality with them is also part of society's duty to them. *Dei mahsoro* is a collective, rather than an individual, obligation. Financing antipoverty measures by means of a progressive income tax represents a fair distribution of burden. The recipient and would-be recipient are expected to engage in self-help. Continuing support is tied to the outcome of an investigation against fraud.

In extrapolating the appropriate division of labor in antipoverty measures between the public and the private sectors, we must recognize that there is an inherent tension between the goal of promoting self-help and the value of befriending the poor. By setting up a system wherein a qualified indigent can immediately turn to a government-sponsored program for his basic support, this tension and potential conflict is minimized. Within the framework of the public sector program, the source of any individual's stipend is derived from the entire tax base on a prorated basis, so, from the perspective of the recipient, the source of his stipend is effectively anonymous.

Another advantage of public sector involvement is that it can foster an attitude of self-help. By setting limits on how long it will support a welfare recipient, the government effectively compels these people to find gainful employment. Cutting people off the welfare rolls after a limited time is not insensitive if the government concurrently runs for those on its rolls job training programs and job search services and guarantees a public sector job as a last resort.

Within this framework, the role of the private sector is to befriend the poor and practice social equality with them. Carrying out this role enhances the living standards of the poor both materially and emotionally.

Another area where government must take the initiative is basic research in the health field. The goal of this research would be to discover new drugs to cure and treat devastating diseases. Left to its own devices, the private sector, working on the profit motive, is unlikely to foster basic research in new drugs.

By ensuring a steady and adequate flow of research and development, government taxation effectively shifts the risk associated with the expenditure from private industry to society at large. Under this arrangement, private industry enters the drug-development field only when profit considerations motivate it to do so.

Public funding of basic research carries with it a regulatory responsibility. One aspect of this responsibility relates to the government's role in the area of welfare. It consists of a responsibility to ensure that the poor would be guaranteed free access to the drugs.

Another area where a *dei mahsoro* need falls through the cracks in the private sector is the religious education of poor children. Government taxation in this area can ensure that the religious education of the young would be committed to high quality. In addition, it behooves the public sector to get the most mileage out of the resources it taxes for the religious educational needs of the poor children. We argued that this objective entails the responsibility for government to make its aid available through a voucher system.

Finally, government's role in welfare policy is not limited to taxation. By means of regulation and rule setting, government can optimally promote Halakhah's antipoverty goals. A case in point is the fostering of a humanistic environment. Government can do much to encourage a humane spirit in society. It can, for instance, mandate educational institutions to require students to spend a certain number of hours each week to provide companionship to the aged, shut-ins, and the infirm. Moreover, by dint of both their own personal examples and recruitment efforts, government officials can make voluntarism a status activity in society.

In the Halakhic critique of TANF, we found objection that the legislation does not give the single parent the option of foregoing work outside the home in favor of staying at home to raise a family. Within this option, the single parent who demonstrates superior performance in the role of parent and educator would be positively rewarded. Relatedly, we criticized TANF for encouraging a work-first approach over education and job training.

Finally, in the comparison between minimum wage legislation and the EITC approach, we demonstrated that the EITC approach better promotes Halakhah's antipoverty goals.

NOTES

1. R. Aharon Shapiro, " The Treatment of Poverty in The Talmud," *International Review of Economics and Ethics* 1, 2 (1986): 56.

2. Babylonian Talmud, *Bava Batra* 8b.

3. Karl E. Case and Ray C. Fair, *Principles of Economics*, 6th ed. (Upper Saddle River, NJ: Prentice Hall, 2002), 357.

4. Half of all families have incomes below the median, half above.

5. William J. Baumol and Alan S. Blinder, *Economics*, 8th ed. (New York: Harcourt College Publishers, 2001), 382, 384.

6. Paul A. Samuelson and William D. Nordhaus, *Economics*, 17th ed. (New York: Irwin/McGraw-Hill, 2001), 392.

7. Biblically prescribed charities included *lekket, shikchah,* and *pe'ah* (gleanings, forgotten produce, and the corner of the field), as well as the agricultural tithe. For a description of the operation of these agricultural gifts, see Menachem Elon, ed., *Encyclopedia Judaica* (Jerusalem: Keter Publishing Group, 1972), s.v. "Charity," 343, 344.

8. Mishnah, *Pe'ah* 8:8–9. R. Ephraim of Regensberg and R. Yizhak of Vienna (quoted in R. Yosef Caro, 1488–1575, *Bet Yosef, Tur, Yoreh De'ah* 253) extend the Talmudic 200 *zuz* criterion for eligibility to modern times.

9. R. Ovadia b. Abraham Bartinoro, *Bartenura, Mishnah, Pe'ah* 8:8. R. Shimshon of Sens (ca.1150–ca. 1230, *Rash, Pe'ah* 8:8) understands the 200-*zuz* sum to refer to the subsistence needs of a couple for a year. R. Shelomoh Adani (Yemen, b. 1567, *Melekhet Shelomoh, Pe'ah* ad locum), however, regards the 200-*zuz* figure to refer to an individual's subsistence needs for a year.

10. For a heroic attempt at estimating how the 200 *zuz* translates in purchasing power today, see Shapiro, op. cit., p. 56. In the opinion of this writer, the final step in making this calculation should have taken into account the dispute, cited by R. Shapiro in his work and supra n. 7, whether the 200 *zuz* refers to the subsistence needs of an individual or to a couple.

11. Sidney and Beatrice Webb, *The Prevention of Destitution* (London: Longmans, Green, and Co., 1911), 1.

12. *Baraita, Sanhedrin* 73a; Maimonides *Mishneh Torah, Hilkhot Rozeah Ushmirat Hanefesh* 1:14; *Tur, Hoshen Mishpat* 426:1; *Shulhan Arukh, Hoshen Mishpat* 426:1; R. Jehiel Michel Epstein (Belarus, 1829–1908) *Arukh ha-Shulhan, Hoshen Mishpat* 426:1.

13. R. Nissim b. Reuben Gerondi, *Ran, Sanhedrin* 73a.

14. Fernand Braudel, *The Structures of Everyday Life: The Limits of The Possible,* vol. 1, *Civilization and Capitalism, 15–18th Century* (New York: Harper & Row, 1979).

15. Mishnah *Pe'ah* 8:8; Maimonides (Egypt, 1135–1208), *Mattenot Aniyyim,* 9:14; *Sh. Ar.,* op. cit. 253:1; *Arukh ha-Shulhan, Yoreh De'ah* 253:5.

16. *Sh. Ar.,* op. cit.

17. *Shabbat* 118a; *Mishneh Torah,* op. cit., 9:13; *Sh. Ar.,* op. cit., 253:1; *Ar. ha-Sh.,* op. cit., 253:1.

18. *Shabbat* 118a.

19. R. Solomon b. Isaac (France, 1040–1105), *Rashi, Shabbat* 118a.

20. *Ketubot* 67b.

21. Jerusalem Talmud, *Bava Batra* 1:4; R. Mordecai b. Hillel ha-Kohen (Germany,

1240–1298), *Bava Batra* 1:477; R. Isaac b. Moses of Vienna, *Or Zaru'a, Hilkhot Pesahim, at* 255.

22. *Ar. ha-Sh.*, op. cit. 245:9, 27.

23. *Ketubot* 67b; *Sh. Ar.*, op. cit. 250:1.

24. R. Eliezer Waldenberg, *Ramat Rahel*, no. 24 sec.3.

25. *Sh. Ar.*, op. cit. 253:1.

26. A Roman mile, that is, 2,000 cubits.

27. *Ar. ha-Sh.*, op. cit. 250:2.

28. Gaonim, quoted in *Shittah Mekubbezet Ketubot* 67b.

29. Interview with R. Shalom Zalman Auerbach, quoted in Cyril Domb, ed., *Ma'aser Kesafim* (New York: Association of Orthodox Jewish Scientists, Feldheim, 1980), Hebrew Appendix, 23.

30. R. Yosef Caro, *Sh. Ar.*, op. cit. 253: 2.

31. The grace period for residency is not the same for each of the various charity levies. Before twelve months of residency, one cannot be compelled to participate in the *ma'ot hittin* drive (*Or Zaru'a*, quoted in *Rema, Orah Hayyim,* 429:1). The grace period for the burial and clothing levies is nine and six months, respectively (Babylonian Talmud, *Bava Batra* 8a). The grace period for inclusion in the weekly charity collection and the daily food collection is a matter of dispute. R. Isaac b. Jacob Alfasi (*Rif, Bava Batra* 8a) and Maimonides (*Mishneh Torah*, op. cit., and 9:12) set thirty days for the daily charity collection and three months for the weekly food collection. Inverting these figures, R. Asher b. Jehiel (*Rosh, Bava Batra* 1:27) and R. Jacob b. Asher (*Tur*, op. cit. 256: 5) set thirty days for the weekly food collection and three months for daily charity collection.

32. *Ar. Ha-Sh.*, op. cit. 250:12.

33. R. Samson R. Hirsch, *The Pentateuch, Translation and Commentary* (Gateshead, United Kingdom: Judaica Press, 1982), 5:272.

34. R. Solomon b. Abraham Adret (Spain, 1235–1310), Responsa *Rashba* 3:392, quoted in *Sh. Ar.*, op. cit. 251:4.

35. R. Eliezer b. Samuel (Metz, ca.1175), *Nedarim* 65a, quoted in *Sh. Ar.*, op. cit. 257:8.

36. R. Hayyim Soloveitchik, quoted in the name of R. Joseph B. Soloveitchik by R. Daniel Lander, *"be-Inyan Dei mahsoro,"* in *Kavod ha-Rav* (New York: Student Organization of Yeshiva Rabbi Isaac Elchanan Theological Seminary, 1984), 202–6.

37. R. Mosheh Isserles, *Rema,Yoreh De'ah* 250:1. See *Ar. Ha-Sh.*, op. cit. 250:4–5.

38. R. Solomon b. Abraham Adret, Responsa *Rashba*, 3:381.

39. *Mishneh Torah*, op. cit., 10:8.

40. *Mishneh Torah*, op. cit., 10:14.

41. Babylonian Talmud, *Ketubot* 50a; *Rema*, op. cit. 249:1.

42. R. Ovadia Bartenura, *Mishnah Pe'ah* 1:1.

43. *Mishneh Torah*, op. cit., 10:16.

44. R. Isadore Twersky, "Some Aspects of the Jewish Attitude Toward the Welfare State," *Tradition* 5,2 (1963): 148–49.

45. *Mishneh Torah, Hilkhot Yom Tov*, 6:18.

46. *Sifre*, Deuteronomy 15:7.

47. The Amoraim refers to those scholars who interpreted the Mishnah and other Tannaitic collections. Their discussions constitute the section of the Talmud known as the Gemara.

48. Babylonian Talmud, *Batra* 9a.

49. *Mishneh Torah, Hilkhot Mattenot Aniyyim* 7:6; *Sh. Ar.*, op. cit., 251:10; *Ar. ha-Sh.*, op. cit., 251:12.

50. *Rema, Sh. Ar.*, op. cit., 256:1.

51. R. Shimon, Mishnah *Ketubot* 5:5.

52. *Pesahim* 113a.

53. R. Ephraim Solomon b. Aaron of Lenczycza, *Keli Yakar,* commentary at Exodus 23:5.

54. *Mishneh Torah*, op. cit., 10:19.

55. R. Aharon Lichtenstein, *"Sa'od Tis'od Immo-Hishtatfut ha-mekabbel bi-Gmilot Hasadim,"* in *A Spiegelman Memorial volume* (Israel: Moreshet, 1979), 81–93.

56. *Torat Kohanim* at Leviticus 25:35; *Mishneh Torah,* op. cit. 10:7; *Ar. ha-Sh.,* op. cit. 249:15.

57. See Deuteronomy 14:22.

58. R. Ezra Basri, *Dinei Mamonot* vol.1, p. 405.

59. R. Shabbetai b. Meir ha-Kohen (Poland, 1621–1662), *Siftei Kohen, Sh. Ar., Hoshen Mishpat* 259:5 n. 3; *Ar. ha-Sh., Hoshen Mishpat* 394:11. A minority view in the matter calls for a Jewish court to compel a person to relinquish his legal rights and to act *lifnim meshurat ha-din.* Judicial coercion is, however, only appropriate if the individual is wealthy. Cf. R. Joel Sirkes (Poland, 1561–1650), *Tur, Hoshen Mishpat* 12 n. 4.

60. *Sh. Ar.*, op. cit., 249:16.

61. Mishnah, *Bava Batra* 1:4; *Mishneh Torah, Shekhenim* 6:1; *Sh. Ar., Hoshen Mishpat* 163:1; *Ar. Ha-Sh., Hoshen Mishpat* 163:1.

62. R. Moshe Isserles (Poland, 1525 or 1530–1572) *Rema,* op. cit., 163:1; *Ar. Ha-Sh.,* op. cit., 163:1.

63. For the development of this thesis, see Aaron Levine, *Free Enterprise and Jewish Law: Aspects of Jewish Business Ethics* (New York: KTAV, Yeshiva University Press, 1980), 136–47.

64. See Aaron Levine, "Aspects of The Firm's Responsibility to Its Customers: Pharmaceutical Pricing and Consumer Privacy," in *Jewish Business Ethics: The Firm and Its Stakeholders,* ed. Aaron Levine and Moses Pava (Northvale, NJ: Jason Aronson, 1999), 75–111.

65. R. Ya'akov Yeshayahu Bloi (Israel, contemporary), *Tzedakah ve-Mishpat,* 56–57).

66. Babylonian Talmud, *Kiddushin* 29a.

67. See R. Joseph Stern, "Torah Education Today," *Journal of Halacha and Contemporary Society* No. 7 (Spring 1984): 88-100. The sources the author marshals indicate a negative attitude toward public support of secular education and professional training.

68. Baumol and Blinder, op. cit., 395–96.

69. LaDonna A. Pavetti, "Creating a New Welfare Reality: Early Implementation of the Temporary Assistance for Needy Families Program," *Journal of Social Issues* 56, 4 (2000): 605.

70. Ibid., 609.

71. Ibid., 606–7.

72. Baumol and Blinder, op. cit., 396.

73. Cf. R. Yehoshua Ze'ev Zand, *Nitivot ha-Hinukh* (Jerusalem: Mosdot Einei

Yisrael, 1999), 137–86; R. Joseph David Epstein, *Mizvot ha-Bayit* (New York: Torat ha-Adam, 1972), chapters 5–9; R. Aharon Lichtenstein, "Fundamental Issues in The Religious Training of Women," in *Ha-Peninah,* ed. Dov Rafel (Jerusalem: Benei Hemed, 1989), 205–15.

74. Aaron Levine, "Regulation of Staple Products in The Talmudic Literature: Implications For The Welfare State" (Working Paper, Bar Ilan University, Ramat Gan, Israel, 2001), 21–23.

75. Bank of Israel Annual Report (Jerusalem, March 2000), 136.

76. Loc. cit., 138–39.

77. Loc. cit., 140.

78. Ibid., 140.

79. Harvey S. Rosen, *Public Finance,* 5th ed. (Boston: Irwin/McGraw-Hill, 1999), 172–73.

CHAPTER 8

The Ethics of the Free Market

Meir Tamari

INTRODUCTION

Every society must choose an economic system for the provision and distribution of goods and services. Although this decision is generally described in economic and material terms, neither the results of this decision nor the factors prompting it are ever purely economic in nature. Nor is economics, contrary to the axiom put forward by free market economists, "a value-free discipline akin to the physical sciences." On the contrary, economics as a discipline—and, for that matter, every known economic system and every available method of creating, distributing, and consuming wealth—has deep religious, cultural, and social roots. For economic efficiency, desirable and essential as this is, is only one of many human needs. We are not only economic personalities, important and compelling as this may be, but complex and composite beings with egos, feelings of greed and charity, and we have robust social, political, and cultural needs. Further, economic activity and economic policy often create moral and ethical problems at the same time that they solve other problems.

In the real world, free markets do not always operate as efficiently as they are generally assumed to do. Even though they provide goods and services far more efficiently than any other economic system, nevertheless, when the free market breaks down or needs readjustment, suffering and hardship occur. Furthermore, free markets do not by themselves provide for the weak, inefficient, sick, and elderly members of society. Free markets provide individual liberty but are not always able to provide all-over economic protection or a social safety net. More to the point, the explosion of wealth over the past decades has left more people relatively wealthy than at any other time in human history; this heightens the challenge, since morality and ethics are issues that only those who possess wealth are called on to face.

So, irrespective of the type of economic system chosen, the moral and ethical dimensions of economic activity remain. The public policy challenge, then, is to look and think beyond mere economics in approaching the moral issues associated with the production, consumption, and distribution of goods and services. Although Judaism is not an economic system and our Halakhic sources are not textbooks on economic thought, the Judaic tradition provides a framework for answering these challenges.

ECONOMICS

Very early in history, the rabbis recognized the legitimate and efficient role of the free market in determining prices and in the creation and distribution of goods and services. In the Talmud, roughly fifteen hundred years ago, it was said in the name of Rabbi Akiva, that the stable price is that of the market: "the buyer will pay no more and the seller will not accept less."[1] The sages even differentiated between two types of changes in supply that affect the market mechanism in different ways. "If a seah [measure] of grain costs one sela and the sela is easily obtainable, this is *batzoret* [inflationary conditions]. However if four seah costs only one sela, but the sela is difficult to come by, this is *kafna* [recession]."[2]

These early examples of insights into the workings of the market are not really of great significance, because similar insights can be found in many other societies. What is of great importance, however, is how the forces of supply and demand—determining prices and profits—are allowed to operate freely, within the reality of the moral, social, and ethical issues mentioned above. Judaism, as a value system, provides solutions to questions of equity, mercy, and peace.

In accordance with the unique and specific tenets of justice and mercy that are Judaism's hallmark, a system of checks and balances was introduced into the free market in an attempt to regulate market forces. Because Jews have historically lived under many different economic systems with varying degrees of security and peace, these checks and balances were designed to cope with dynamic economic and social systems. This has meant that, notwithstanding Judaism's consistent, normative conceptual framework, the identity of the economically injured or threatened parties changed along with the nature of the market abuses.

The source material for any discussion of Judaism and economic life cannot be based only on the Jewish legal framework found in the traditional sources, such as the codes or the responsa literature. Any legal system, especially a religious and moralistic one, cannot operate effectively without a philosophical, ethical, and practical framework. So, the discussion must also relate to the biblical commentators, the homiletic literature and the enactments of the various autonomous Jewish communities that have existed for almost two thousand years. Together these sources represent the Jewish ideological and religious framework, the legal decisions, and the operative climate for all economic activity.

Although many of the examples and cases quoted in these sources deal with underdeveloped economies and precapitalist markets, their translation into modern conditions is, in most cases, relatively simple and straightforward. More importantly, since we are dealing with markets that are always rooted in a value structure, we need to remember that human drives, desires, and ethical dilemmas remain unchanged. Market decisions are a function of such human traits, not of corporations, nor of governments, nor of organizations. Judaism's eternal moral and ethical answers for these human problems remain, therefore, relevant and effective.

A CONCEPTUAL FRAMEWORK

It must be borne in mind that Judaism treats economic issues from within a specific religious moral and spiritual framework.

(1) Each individual has the freedom and the right, within his legal jurisdiction, to use his property as he wishes, and others engaged in the same activity cannot prevent him from doing so. At the same time, there has to be some ordering force or mechanism, some cultural or legal framework, to ensure that these activities are not carried out at the expense of or to the detriment of other people's wealth, health, or freedom.

Most familiar on this point is Adam Smith, who, in his *Wealth of Nations*, explains that there is an enlightened self-interest that makes individuals behave in the market in a moral and ethical way. This enlightened self-interest makes the seller and the buyer, the producer and the consumer, the worker and the employee, and all the other market actors behave in a moral and ethical way. It should not be forgotten, however, that Adam Smith had been an Anglican clergyman, so this concept of an enlightened self-interest that keeps the invisible hand of the market moral is a by-product of his Christian theology. This view essentially considers people as being basically moral, except for the distortions of original sin and the temptation of Satan (and other forces); it is the Grace of God that can enlighten the "self-interest" aspect of the human personality. It is pertinent in this regard to note, however, that Amartya Sen has suggested that Adam Smith's enlightened self-interest concept should be understood only in terms of the production side of economic activity. In regard to the distribution of the products of the economic system, there is evidence that Adam Smith's Christian charity would lead him to accept a degree of communal or state intervention.[3]

Now, Judaism understands very well the concept of self-interest, it is the "enlightened" part that is problematic. Human greed means that there are few, if any, limits to what people will do to satisfy their economic needs. By themselves, people will lie, cheat, and defraud in order to increase their share of the economic pie. This is the *yetzer hara*, the inclination to do evil; just like any of our other impulses, it needs to be seen within the framework of our free choice—a fundamental principle in Judaism.

On the one hand, without this economic *yetzer*, people would do nothing. In Talmudic times, we are told, the sages once captured the *yetzer hara*, the evil inclination of man—the source of his greed, his lust, and desire. They locked it in jail and rejoiced, believing that thereby they could now eradicate all evil actions. They discovered, however, that in the whole country they could not find even one single fertilized egg. So they released the evil inclination, understanding that without it there would be no progress, no development, and no human participation in the Divine act of creation.[4]

On the other hand, even though this inclination makes possible the Divine plan for the development of the world, it still retains the ability to do evil. So, Judaism surrounded it with a network of obligatory *mitzvot*, laws and obligations, in order to educate the economic *yetzer* and transform it into an active part of the process of making people holy. The economic inclination is the most powerful human drive. Regarding sex the rabbis taught, "there is a small part of the human body, the more we feed it the more it wants, the less it eats the less it needs."[5] Regarding money however, they taught, "one has a hundred, one wants two hundred."[6] Nobody dies with all his or her material needs satisfied. Therefore, the Torah surrounded economic activity with over 120 obligations, compared to only 3 with regard to the Sabbath and 24 with regard to kosher food. Since there is nothing unlimited in Judaism, an individual's ability to control property is limited to the parameters set by these 120 obligations.

(2) All wealth comes from God. His gifts are given to us for the satisfaction of our human needs. God, the source of all wealth, obligates us to make sure that none of the economic activity that created this financial gain is gotten by immoral or oppressive or corrupt means. Since God is also omniscient and omnipotent and can mete out reward and punishment, the recognition of God as being the source of all wealth is, itself, the major protection against immoral market behavior. At the same time, such knowledge protects people against uncertainty; it is uncertainty that leads people to seek immoral and unethical methods of satisfying their economic needs. If, however, one believes that, "He opens His hand and feeds all living beings"(Psalm 145: 16), then one can take risks in the market without recourse to immoral and unethical methods.

(3) Judaism is a national and communal orientated religion as distinct from Christianity or Islam. Its purpose is not only to create saintly or holy

individuals, but also to create a Holy People and a Nation of Priests. As a consequence, "society," "community," and "state" are all real players in the market and have a legitimate role in the economic affairs of the individual. They have a vital role to play in the realization of the Jewish goals of justice, morality, and the sanctification of all human activities. At the same time, they have obligations to provide for the poor, the weak, the old, and the sick. They are also obligated to maintain a network of social, political, and religious institutions that will realize this vision of creating a holy society. Therefore, they acquire a stake, as it were, in the wealth and economic activities of the individual members of that society. This has meant that alongside the judicial treatment of economic litigation and the protection of private property rights and economic activity, the rabbinic courts and the elected lay leadership have always had a legitimate role in the regulation of prices, profits, and the operations of the market. Despite their knowledge of the market forces and their acceptance of the benefits of its efficiency, the religious authorities throughout the ages took active steps, wherever necessary, to distort the free market out of considerations of justice and charity.[7] All forms of intervention in the free market are undertaken as a correcting mechanism of whatever economic system society has chosen.

(4) Considerations of charity, morality, and kindness are, in Judaism, part of the market structure—a broad-ranging religious educational system has always been provided to make such considerations effective and normative. Furthermore, just as in all other areas—like prayer, ritual, food, or sex—these considerations are not left up to the "agonizing choice" of the individual or to their personal levels of religiosity or to the degree of grace vouchsafed to them. Rather, they are part of a normative and enforceable regulatory code of conduct in the economic sphere. So not only are the Jewish parameters of the market economy enforceable by courts of law and public opinion, but so are the actions these parameters were put in place to ensure.

So, in addition to personal, voluntary acts of charity and philanthropy, there are also coercible acts of charity, funded by taxation. Such taxation creates "holy money," placing an obligation on the individual and the corporation to fulfill their obligations to fund the needs of society, thus placing restraints on tax planning and tax evasion. After all, the Hebrew words for charity, *tzedakah*, and justice, *tzedek*, have the same grammatical root and a common value structure. These concepts are based in the idea of an obligation that has its roots in the belief that the vertical Fatherhood of God entails the horizontal relationships of the Brotherhood of Mankind.

(5) This whole framework applies to men and women equally. This stems from a conception of the *economics of enough*.[8] Although it is difficult to define what is *enough*, it is impossible to envisage the Jewish conceptual framework in a society where more is *always* better than less; sometimes,

like the patriarch Jacob, it is appropriate to say, "I have all I need" (Genesis 33:9, 11).

There are a host of Halakhic injunctions, religious acts, and homiletic writings that are based on this concept of *enough*. The foremost of these is the limit placed on the time spent on economic activity, a result of the obligation to study Torah throughout a person's life, irrespective of their economic status, health, or age.[9] This is in addition to the Sabbath and festivals on which economic activity ceases. The Sabbatical Year [*Shmittah*] and the Jubilee [*Yovel*] are extensions of this limitation, since no work may be done in agriculture.[10] However, these restrictions are not only related to labor and toil but are really an acknowledgment of the denial of the absolutist conception of private property during these periods.

These restrictions apply also to our profits and the fruits of our wealth. Jews in biblical times were not allowed to eat of the new grain harvest, whether from their own fields or from those owned by others, before the offering of the *Omer* was brought to the Temple on the first day of *Chol Ha Moed Pesach*. This applies today to Jews living in the Land of Israel, and according to many authorities, even to those living outside the Holy Land.[11] At the national level, the same concept of having to pay rent—to the real owner of the land, as it were—was introduced by the fact that the meal offerings on behalf of the nation in the Temple could not be brought from the new wheat until after seven weeks from the end of Pesach have been counted.

In addition to such restrictions, there is a concept of the ideal economic role model in Judaism. The chief attribute of this role model is modesty; this includes not only matters of dress and sexual behavior but also standards of living.[12] So, for at least two thousand years, communal enactments were established limiting clothing and other forms of consumption, and a homiletic literature aimed at creating a communal consensus was written making for modesty in economic behavior.[13] It is easy to dismiss such sumptuary laws as simply a means of protecting the Jewish society from the envy and jealousy of the non-Jewish world. However, we may not lose sight of the fact that these enactments existed also in the precapitalist and tolerant world of the Muslim exile.

Furthermore, the books of the prophets show a religious theme wherein such modesty is supposed to be a norm and an understanding that when this modesty is disregarded, corruption, economic oppression, and business immorality will follow.[14] This modesty must not be construed as the notion that Judaism places a religious or spiritual value on poverty; nor should this be construed as an antiprofit or antientrepreneurial bias. Judaism, after all, is the only religion in which all the founders were rich men. Rather, this concept of modesty promotes the ability to share one's wealth, attempts to limit economic activity in order to pursue other religious and spiritual goals, and tries to avoid any semblance of "ends justifying the means" calculations.

FREE ENTRY, PRICES, PROFITS, AND NONPRICE COMPETITION

Free Entry

A free market requires that all the economic players have the right to free entry. This enables people to practice their professions freely, to open new businesses, and, generally, to cater to unexpected or actual changes in demand or to move from one geographic area to another in order to benefit from changed economic conditions. Yet at the same time this free entry, naturally, affects the profits and business prospects of those already established in that area or line of business. In its absence, the veterans can often earn abnormal profits, while its existence may mean unemployment, bankruptcy, or, at the least, a temporary or a permanent loss. Blocking this free entry would deny society at large the benefits of lower prices, innovation, or improved goods and services. The closed shop principle, licensing arrangements, and trade or professional associations and immigration laws are all forms of restriction on economic competition.

In Jewish law the free entry discussion revolves primarily around the property rights of the various players in the market, rather than the theoretical issues of economic behavior. The central issue is whether the existing (or veteran) players in the market have in some fashion acquired a claim to their customers or to the local market for their particular trade or to the use of some natural resource or facilities that are essential to their particular trade. The right, in others words, to block entry and protect them from competition. If such rights exist in Halakhah, then the competitor or the newcomer is, in fact, guilty of stealing something that belongs to somebody else. Of course, even if these rights did exist, they might be modified or even abrogated in those cases where the majority of the members of society would benefit from such a modification or a limitation of these rights. It is in this discussion that we will find what is probably the greatest divergence of opinions in the Jewish approach to economic activity.

The discussion of the right to free entry in the Talmud is part of a prior discussion on the rights of neighbors, or citizens, to limit the establishment of economic institutions that may cause environmental damage.[15] This right is firmly established in Halakhah; it is only the extension of this right to include economic competition that is the center of the Halakhic debate.

However, since the right of a person to pursue his livelihood on his property is firmly established in our sources, the right to free entry is maintained in most cases and by most authorities. "It is permitted for a person to set up shop alongside shop, bathhouse alongside bathhouse, mill alongside mill, etc and the existing firms cannot prevent it. The new firm can argue, 'you conduct your business on your property and I do the same on mine.'"[16] This Talmudic opinion is repeated in the rulings laid down by most of the late authorities. Such decisions provide for marketing arrangements of the most competitive nature in contrast to the shopping centers so common in modern town planning, with their emphasis on one firm for each type of business (i.e., one bookstore, one movie theater, one tobacco shop, etc., per mall).

Now it could be argued that the free entry of competitors or of workers should be permitted only in those cases where all concerned are citizens of the town or country or province under consideration. In our earlier case, all the economic actors are citizens and have equal rights, so the stimulation of competition is to the benefit of the community. If, however, the new workers or entrepreneurs are foreigners or citizens of another town or county, the free entry could be seen as benefiting those towns, rather than the host community; at least it could be argued that such free entry is detrimental to the local population. So, perhaps there is a right to block foreign firms from entry?

This question of whether work and business opportunities can be limited to local or national residents is an age-old, if ever timely, one. Most Jewish biblical commentators, Rabbi Meir Leibush (1809–1879), known as the Malbim, for example, see the primary sin of Sodom and Gomorrah not as homosexuality, nor even as a lack of hospitality, but rather the exclusion of the neighboring workers or traders in order to prevent those workers from sharing in their (the cities') wealth.

The primary source for the treatment of this aspect of free entry is the discussion in the Talmud between Rav Huna and Rav Huna the son of Yehoshua.[17] It is the opinion of the latter sage that became the norm for the Halakhic sources. He argued that a foreigner has full rights of residence, including those of an economic nature provided that they pay the taxes applicable to that community. To allow the freedom of entry without the corresponding tax liability would, however, be considered immoral as well as unfair. A contemporary application of this ruling might be to decide that those earning their livelihood in the city but living in the suburbs are still required to pay city taxes. Interestingly, there is such a ruling in Jewish tax law.[18]

The right of free entry was extended even to outsiders who were not taxpayers, under those situations where the host society benefited from them. So, early in the days of the Second Temple, there was a ruling by Ezra the Scribe (circa 500 B.C.E.) that peddlers may wander from city to city without paying taxes, so that "the daughters of Israel should not lack for jewelry and cosmetics."[19] On the market days, out-of-town merchants could display their goods without becoming liable for municipal taxes, despite the complaints of the local merchants.

In view of the special status accorded to the study of Torah in the Jewish value structure, it is not surprising to find similar free entry for Torah scholars without the constraint of taxation. Tax deductions, monopolistic trading rights, and other such incentives were similarly used to encourage the settlement of Torah scholars. We will find other examples where basic Jewish principles, such as the safety of refugees, set aside restrictive rulings in favor of free enterprise.[20]

However, none of the rights of free entry may be operative where the existing entrepreneurs, merchants, or industrialists have made investment in research and development (R&D), in creating an infrastructure, in establishing public utilities, or in creating a specialized market. Their investments create a property right and therefore other competitors are not allowed to damage these property rights, despite the general acceptance of the free entry principle. The basis for this ruling is the Talmudic dictum that a fisherman can force others to withdraw a distance equal to that which a fish can swim from his nets (fishing was a major occupation in Babylon in those times).

Rabbi Jacob ben Meir Tam (ca. 1100–1171), known as Rabbenu Tam, explained that this does not contradict the free entry rulings mentioned above. The fisherman has already set down his bait, so the fish may be regarded as his; alternatively, the fisherman had acquired, through R&D as it were, knowledge as to the behavior of the fish and the best place to catch them. This R&D is an investment. Customers, however, are free to shop wherever they wish and buy fish from whomever they wish, so nobody can be regarded as belonging to the seller until the sale is made.[21]

On the basis of this concept, that an investment can protect existing businesses from the threat of competition through free entry, the rabbis ruled against such entry. It is interesting to note in this instance that, in keeping with the moral objection to allow even a hint or possibility of legal theft through commerce, the rabbis altered a biblical law. Biblically, a sale is concluded as soon as money changes hands. Regarding movable goods, however, the rabbis made the conclusion of the sale dependent on the transfer of the goods to the possession of the buyer. This meant that until this is done, the seller still has responsibility for the goods.

Historically these rulings regarding investment always took into account the characteristics of the Jewish economy that mirrored those of the surrounding non-Jewish world. Almost all business was conducted on the basis of charters, licensing, and monopolistic arrangements from the secular, or political, overlords or other government authorities. Tax farming, the use of natural resources, banking and money lending, the provisioning of armies and trading in slaves, spices, and luxury goods, all of which were the mainstay of the Jewish economy for many hundreds of years throughout Europe, were all conducted by virtue of these arrangements. Even in more mundane businesses such as textiles and liquor, the right to operate was dependent on permission from the political authorities. Such arrangements were seen as acquired property rights and therefore as deserving of Halakhic protection. These rights became known as *marufiya*, from the Arabic, meaning literally "a constant friend" or "a permanent business associate," and in Eastern Europe, primarily associated with the sale of liquor and natural resources, as *Arunda*. The Halakhic treatment of these monopolistic rights varied in accordance with the degree of their acceptance as norms in the particular period and area.[22]

At the same time that we consider the rights of the investor to protection from competition, we need to examine whether this causes damage to the general public. Society would, therefore, have to weigh the right of the public to cheaper services or goods against the right of the investor to receive a return on his investment. Given the essential nature of books in a society devoted to the study of Torah, the rabbinic treatment of the copyright on such books serves as a good example of Jewish answers to this dilemma.

In the case of the first publication of the printed Talmud, a consensus of rabbinic opinion gave the author and the printers a five-year period of protection. This period of time was arrived at through consideration of a reasonable return on the capital investment. The responsa all show that the rabbis understood that, without such protection, nobody would produce the books needed for Torah study, such that the public would be deprived of them. When the publisher had sold the whole edition in three years, he wished to have the protection continued to the completion of the whole period. Rabbinic opinion was divided. Some held that since the printer had received the return on his capital, anybody should be free to duplicate the publication, whereas others felt that the printer was entitled to the full period. Those in favor of the competition held that Torah study was being hindered by the monopoly; therefore, it should be abrogated.[23]

In much the same way, the communal benefit accruing from rent control of housing in the restricted ghetto was used to prevent competition.[24] Throughout the sources we find a similar balance between the right of restrictive bodies—such as trade associations, unions, or other professional bodies—and the benefits they bring versus the economic and social costs of barring competitive forces in the market. In order to achieve this balance, Halakhah made them dependent on the existence of compulsory arbitration through an *Adam Hasuv,* an important personage or rabbinical specialist.[25] Since widespread government intervention in the economy exists in almost all countries, this concept of obligatory arbitration was seen as the only way of protecting the public.

Since all these monopolistic rights create abnormal profits, there is an incentive for others to approach the source of the right and offer a higher price, thereby forestalling the present owner. This has given rise to a Halakhic treatment that has importance for the concept of free entry in the negotiating process. There is a rabbinic dictum: "a poor man was negotiating for the sale of the cake and one who intervenes is called an 'evil person.'"[26] Opinions among the authorities have been divided as to whether this is just a moral judgment or whether it is one that can be used by the courts to prevent intervention. Furthermore, some have maintained that this is just in the case of a poor person, so that we are dealing with the principle of charity. Indeed, this is an important factor throughout Jewish economic practice and law, often imposing or preventing acts that would otherwise be considered legal and permissible.

So we find numerous cases where the principle of free entry has been denied in favor of the demands of charity:

Reuven maintains a store for selling liquor and now Shimon wishes to open a similar store, even though Reuven has been in business for many years. I have ruled that even though legally justice is with the competitor, nevertheless, since he is rich and has many other businesses, while Reuven is poor and has many children, we may in accordance with the ruling of the majority of the sages, prevent this competition.[27]

Furthermore, all the codes rule that the highest form of charity is to provide somebody with a job or with money and advice so as to enable them to open their own business.[28] It should be clear that there is always the danger of the recipient opening a business similar to that of the donor. An adherence to achieving and maintaining maximum market share does not seem to be always a determining principle of the Jewish free market.

Perhaps the best example of a decision regarding the public benefit derived from restraint on competition is to be found in the institution of the *Herem Hayishuv*. In Franco-Germany of the Middle Ages, the rabbinic decisions were completely in contradiction of the free entry rulings regarding the rights of foreign competitors, noted previously. Here, the competitors, even if they were willing to pay the local taxes, required the permission of the local Jewish authorities or citizens. The veterans had acquired a claim on the right to trade.

This is a right distinctly different from that of the right of the community to protect itself against the settlement in its midst of evil people—those guilty of immorality or any others constituting a danger to its security and morality. Such a right is recognized and accepted by all authorities; what was special to the *Herem Hayishuv* was the use of this right to prevent economic competition.[29] The earliest justification for such protection, which was actually an economic asset that could be sold or inherited, is R. Meir b. Baruch of Rothenberg (1215–1293), the MaHaram, who attributes it to the early authority of Rabbenu Gershom (ca. 960–1028), known as the *MeOr HaGolah,* or Light of the Diaspora.[30] He claimed that such protection was essential to the economic security and well-being of the community at this period of time.

Since Judaism is not an economic system and has no necessary preference for any particular economic system, it constantly reviews the economic system in general, including the issue of free entry, within its moral and religious framework. When it finds that competition is beneficial for society, it protects that competition and encourages it. However, when such competition ruins or lessens not just economic development or profits of individuals but the overall economic basis of a society, then Halakhah will be opposed to such competition.

It is true that free market economists argue that market forces will enable society to find alternative and attractive enterprises without legislative or communal restriction.[31] There is sufficient historical data to show, however, that the period required for such adjustments may be so long that the suffering and deprivation of the community may be unbearable. Furthermore, in the absence of all the conditions needed for a proper free market, the protective nature of such adjustments can be seriously in doubt.

Prices and Profits

Free entry and competitive markets are encrypted in the determining of prices and rates of profits. The competitive markets provide for pricing at the equilibrium of supply and demand while the free entry of new firms would ensure maintaining that same equilibrium. It is this issue that lies at the basis of the responsa regarding the competition by new entrants whether they may be local or foreign. The benchmark decision is that of Rabbi Joseph Ibn Migas (eleventh century, Spain):

that local businessmen can prevent outsiders from operating similar businesses even if the outsiders pay the applicable taxes, provided there is no loss caused to the consumers; for example if the outsiders sell the goods for the same price as the locals. If, however, they offer the same goods more cheaply or provide goods or services of better quality, then they cannot be prevented. The reason for this is that we cannot make the ruling that will benefit part of the population [local businessmen] at the expense of the other part [the consumers].[32]

This consideration of the public welfare is already found in the early days of rabbinic literature as shown in the Mishnah:

Rabbi Yehuda added; "similarly he may not lower his prices." But the Sages said, "the memory of the shopkeeper who lowers his prices shall be blessed" [since he benefits the community in this way].[33]

Rashi adds that the other producers will see that prices are falling and they will sell the goods cheaply, thus adding to the public welfare. Even though Rashi seems to limit the competition to those cases where other merchants also lower prices, we know that, in the reality of the market, this is inevitable. The sages in the Talmud mention that even if the shop-keepers suffer losses, it is the communal welfare that has to dominate. Similarly, the sages in the Mishnah, permitted the decoration of the goods, provided the decoration is declared, and permitted the offering of gifts or similar nonprice incentives to buy, which are forms of price cutting. All the authorities rule like the sages on all these issues; Menachem ben Solomon Meiri (1249–1316) even ruled that the price cutting is valid even where it is only temporary, since there is a temporary benefit to society.[34]

It must be stressed that price cutting, in any form, is permitted only when it is the direct result of low profit margins or lower production costs that can be emulated by other firms. This can be seen from a question concerning competition that flowed from nonpayment of taxes.

It seems to me that Reuven can prevent him if it can be shown that the low prices charged by his competitor, flow from the non-payment of taxes. Even though the *Shulchan Arukh* ruled that one cannot prevent price-cutting since it is for the benefit of the public, this is so because other producers wish to keep the prices high. In our case, however, the sole factor is the nonpayment of taxes which Reuven cannot emulate and therefore no benefit [to the public] occurs from the price cut [presumably since they lose the services paid for with the taxes].[35]

Not only did the rabbis permit such price competition, but they also took steps to promote it because of the public welfare that such competition produced. Sometimes this is done through making temporary changes in matters of ritual.

The local fishermen knowing that the Jews needed fish for Shabbat, raised their prices through a cartel arrangement. The Tzemach Tzedek ruled that the fish were not kosher, so in the absence of demand the price fell out of the market and a cartel was broken.[36]

This seventeenth-century ruling is based on a decision that appears in the Mishnah that deals with the price of doves needed for sacrifice by women after childbirth. When the price was artificially raised by the producers, Rabban Gamaliel ruled that a number of women could fulfill the obligation with only one pair of doves or that one woman could receive purification for a number of cases with only one pair of doves; the market returned to equilibrium.[37]

Throughout the discussion on price competition and the rabbinic acceptance and encouragement thereof, it must be pointed out that often this was related to public benefit or loss. Alternatively, there is a consideration of charity. Two examples:

1. So a modern Israeli responsum prevented a competitor from hiring the blocksman from another butcher, when it was shown that the whole business would fail if he were to leave.[38] There is no restraint on the worker's leaving; Halakhically what has to be adjudicated is only the damage to the employer. Any restraining order would mean that a worker might never be able to take advantage of changes in labor conditions or new technologies. Dayan Weiss limited restrictions on the free movement of employees to the time period required to protect trade secrets or technological knowledge.[39] Such rulings have much relevance to the problem of employee loyalty and the competition for talent, which characterize the high-tech industries.

2. The definition of diminished profits, so often crucial to the Halakhic decisions regarding competition, is a very generous one, not limited to retaining a subsistence level. It seems to relate to the socioeconomic status of the plaintiff. So, for example, Rabbi Moshe Sofer (1762–1838), the Hatam Sofer, ruled to prevent the entry of a new firm if it would reduce the established firm's earnings below the average earnings of its peer group. It must be stressed that such decisions do not flow from economic thought but solely from the implementation of the biblical injunction, "you shall love your neighbor." Wherever society would suffer a loss from such restraints, the competition would be allowed.

The concept of *Ona'ah*, or being wronged, that permitted a return of money or a negation of the sale is a further example of the Jewish insistence on fair and equitable pricing. This concept allowed recourse to rabbinic courts whenever the buyer or seller felt that he had been overcharged or underpaid. In order to allow markets to function efficiently, a cutoff point of one-sixth was determined. Where the market price was underpaid or overpaid to that extent, they considered that people were indifferent; at that figure, the excess could be reclaimed; above that figure, the sale could be cancelled.[40]

Lieberman argues that Halakhah makes a distinction between consumer goods for which the one-sixth cutoff applies and investment goods that require an excessive *Ona'ah* seen sometimes as double the market price.[41] Levine sees the distinction as being between elastic and inelastic demand.[42] Irrespective, *Ona'ah* has to do with price gouging or price fraud relative to the market price, taking into consideration the trader's profit. This is the common definition of *Ona'ah*; it is suggested that what is actually involved is the exploitation of a lack of information of prices and of supply, on the part of one of the parties. Maimonides rules that where full disclosure of the market price is made, there is no *Ona'ah*.[43] This stands in contrast to the Christian medieval concept of the "just price" that denied producers and laborers the right to earn profits—only a trader had that right.[44]

The rabbinic intervention in the market was concerned not only with the fostering of price competition, but also with fair profits and justice in pricing.

It must be remembered throughout the discussion of restrictions on competition in all forms that, not only did the rabbis not see anything wrong with profitable entrepreneurial activity per se, but they even appreciated the difficulties that would befall the whole community should "the bottom fall out of the market." So the sages taught that it is permissible to announce a public fast in the face of impending recession, even on the Sabbath, a day when mourning or expressions of sorrow of any kind are usually forbidden. As the Talmud relates:

Rabbi Yochanan said, "for example in the case of flax in Babylon or wine and oil in Eretz Yisrael." Rabbi Joseph added [the indicator of a serious downturn or recession in these leading industries] "when prices drop by 40 percent."[45]

Despite this understanding, there is nevertheless a Jewish concept of the just price and reasonable profit, a concept that can be enforced by courts and communal institutions. This concept, however, does not seem to flow primarily from analyses of the costs of production, or of the value of labor input, or from utility to the consumer. It flows, rather, from the special character of Jewish concepts of private ownership and economic endeavor, which determines the nature of the concept of these or other forms of price control. Generally speaking, price controls relate only to basic commodities essential for life, *Chayei Nefesh*—investment goods such as land, monetary instruments, and luxury items are excluded.

Although the rabbis understood that the same market forces that operate to price such goods apply to basic commodities and their ingredients as well, nevertheless, they stressed the moral challenge of making the latter available to everybody. Since goods like wine, oil, fruits and vegetables, and bread were essential to existence in those days, they needed to be traded and priced in a manner different from other goods in order to prevent suffering, even though this meant a distortion of the market mechanism. So, we find a number of Talmudic statements expressing disapproval of profits earned from trade in these commodities.

One may not earn a living in the Land of Israel as a middleman in basic commodities; rather, this one brings his produce and sells it, and the other brings his produce for direct sale, in order that they may sell cheaply. In those places, however, where oil [or other produce] is plentiful, it is permissible to earn one's livelihood from trading in it.[46]

Another source taught that one is not permitted to earn twice on the sale of eggs. There is a difference of opinion between the two sages, Rav and

Shmuel, as to whether the word "twice" refers to the marketing chain or to the rate of the profit of the middleman.[47] Most authorities have held the former opinion. Maimonides ruled that this injunction applies specifically to eggs, whereas the majority opinion saw eggs only as an example and, therefore, extended the injunction to all basic goods. It must be noted that where such trade or the existence of marketing chains were to the benefit of society, bringing efficiency, superior choices, or lower prices, the rabbis easily agreed to disrupt the direct sale between producer and buyer.

In most countries and throughout Jewish history, the appointing of inspectors to enforce price controls and reduce profit margins was a common feature of the Jewish communal structure.[48] Naturally, the greater the autonomy enjoyed by the community, the more effective price controls will be. The seller is bound by these fixed prices only as long as they are operative. Should market forces cause prices to rise, the seller is free to charge whatever he wishes until the adjusted price is announced.

Sometimes, the concept of communal price controls was expanded beyond consumer goods to embrace other goods and services seen as vital to society; for example, the wages of marriage brokers and teachers and the fees paid to the judge. Forms of price control, rationing and subsidies often create a black market because some buyers will be willing and able to pay a higher price. It is suggested here that when the general population understands and agrees to the social philosophy and the morality of these measures, recourse to the black market will be diminished, if not eradicated completely.

A MORAL MARKET

Corporations

Over and above questions of competition, efficiency, property rights, and the public good, and the viable Jewish answers presented above, there are moral problems in the marketplace that require solutions. The Jewish solutions usually limit and restrain the activities of the free market. It is perhaps with regard to such issues and solutions that Judaism makes its major contribution to the modern world.

As in all other aspects of life, the solutions in Judaism are not left solely to the discretion or value judgments of the individual or corporation. These solutions are meant to be enforceable by rabbinic courts, guided by religious study, and subject to communal pressure and enactment—and so require the existence of a ramified public sector. These solutions continue irrespective of the comparative morality of the society we find ourselves in, even if they result in loss of profits or marketing opportunities, and these solutions are brought to bear over and above the market's need for an ethical foundation. A major factor encouraging immoral and unethical markets is the development of large corporate and public sector economic entities. The impersonal and distant relationships created by such entities enable those in control of them, and their employees, customers, debtors, and creditors, to act in ways that differ from their personal individual morality.

The separate legal identity of the corporation raises the following ethical problems: (1) Shareholders, directors, and employees view the corporation as a depersonalized economic force, devoid of shared noncontractual rights or obligations. This allows an individual to relax his ethical standards and avoid social obligations to which he would adhere in private life. (2) By separating ownership from control and management, the corporation enables both shareholders and directors to evade responsibility for ethical issues facing its operation.

Directors argue that they cannot determine the ethical beliefs of shareholders or that these may vary widely and contradict one another. Directors say their only task is to operate a company efficiently and within legally imposed limits; to do otherwise would constitute dereliction of duty and make them liable to dismissal. Shareholders argue that they have no control over a corporation's daily operation or often over its general policy. The broader the base of a corporation's stock ownership and the more it relies on hired, nonowner management, the greater will be the effect of these arguments on the corporation's ethical behavior. In this way, the concept of the corporation as a separate legal entity, essential to its existence, has been expanded to create a corporate veil, behind which unethical acts and policies in the market may be pursued.

Judaism can accept the concept of the corporation but this is limited to its limited liability character.[49] Halakhah can certainly recognize a business entity such as a corporation in which creditors' claims are limited to the corporation's share capital, without recourse to private assets of individual stockholders. Such a limitation is public knowledge. Banks, suppliers, and other creditors are aware of it at the time obligations are created. They make their business decisions in light of this knowledge, and claims or counterclaims can be judged accordingly. All the obligations placed on the individual Jew that flow from the ownership of material goods and their use apply to the corporation they own.[50] Jewish law, however, does not seem to accept a separation between corporation and individual when it involves the abrogation of Halakhic responsibilities related to ownership of wealth.

Jewish executive officers of corporations owned or controlled by Jews cannot claim that their sole responsibility is to maximize shareholder profits without regard to Jewish ethical and moral principles. The rabbis reject this claim when made by individual businessmen, and the corporate status of an enterprise provides no exemptions. Halakhah rejects the concept of a *shaliach l'devar aveirah* (an agent for performing forbidden acts), of an agent who "only follows orders" and cannot be held responsible for his actions. Corporate executive officers cannot use the "instructions" of shareholders as an excuse for violating the Torah's ethical laws.

Since the Torah requires gentiles and Jews to observe the same laws regarding monetary matters, the religion of the corporation's shareholders would in many cases be irrelevant. Jewish executive officers of large or multinational corporations in which no individual holds a large block of shares are obligated to follow Halakhic rules in the absence of effective shareholder control or direction. The separation of ownership from control means that such executive officers, in effect, control the wealth of the corporation. The officers are therefore obligated to follow Halakhah in those operations. The shareholders would seem to be required to dismiss their corporate officers if these did not follow Halakhah. If the shareholders did not dismiss corporate officers violating Halakhah, the shareholders would be responsible for the officers' misdeeds.[51]

Principles

This Jewish system of the normative moral market is based on the following Halakhic and spiritual principles, translated over the centuries into legal rulings, communal legislation, and educational perspectives.

Sanctification of God's Name

Each Jew is a standard-bearer of the dignity of the Jewish people and God, so that morality in the marketplace leads to the sanctification of His name, and dishonesty leads to the desecration of His name. The religious status, the degree of Jewish identification, and the communal position of the perpetrator all influence the degree of desecration; the greater the personality, the greater the disgrace.

One must bear in mind that the codification of Maimonides makes the sanctification of His name, in all its forms, a positive commandment incumbent on all Jews, men and women, and applicable in all times. This places a constant obligation to consider each economic act—whether at the corporate or individual role, as buyer or seller, employer or employee—and its implications for sanctifying God's name. It is true that modern authorities relate the degree of responsibility of CEOs and shareholders for non-Halakhic acts to the degree and type of ownership or authority in the corporation.[52] However, there seem to be none who have absolved them from acts of desecrating God's name, irrespective of their economic stake in the corporation or their position in its hierarchy.

THEFT AND ROBBERY

We distinguish between a robber and a thief. A thief is one who steals money from a person in secret and without the other's knowledge. In the marketplace, this would refer to false weights and measures and to fraud in advertising or marketing goods and services. Theft would include the case of a purchasing agent who accepts bribes. Robbery, on the other hand, is the taking of money by force, pressure, coercion, or oppression. Robbery includes also all other misuses of financial, political, or economic power. This would refer to exploitation of workers and withholding their wages or other rights, betraying one's trust as a guardian of someone else's property or trust funds, the denial of loans or other obligations to creditors, and withholding social rights granted by law. Sexual harassment—even with consent, as distinct from rape—is clearly bribery or the abuse of power.

It is easy to argue, as indeed does Maimonides, that the Mosaic rules against dishonest dealings are simply rational and logical sanctions that could be arrived at through human intelligence, sanctions necessary for the functioning of efficient markets. This, however, would place Jewish business morality on a par with that of the teachings of nonmonotheistic religions or, for that matter, with that of any decent secular person. Most other commentators see the injunctions against theft as Revealed Divine Wisdom, which goes far beyond the rational and logical, extending thereby that which could be arrived at through human intelligence alone.

Through this wisdom, dishonesty becomes a transgression against God, incurring retribution even when the damage to others is minimal.[53] This aspect becomes clear when we read the comments of the sages, that the fate of the Generation of the Flood was sealed only because of robbery and theft—even of those things of no intrinsic value. This attitude is at odds with the cost-benefit analysis so prevalent in the present-day teaching of business ethics, which seeks to calculate the cost (imprisonment, shame, etc.) of committing white-collar crime against the benefits (increased profits, status). Basically, this approach argues that crime does not pay and rationally should not be committed. When crime does not pay, however, no moral dilemma exists. In real life, crime is often very profitable, the material benefits far exceeding the cost.

It is true that some studies have shown that those corporations that have the status of being ethical in their practices showed greater profits and better performance, relative to others.[54] The studies, however, are not conclusive, and others have shown little difference between the two types of corporations. More important, however, is the lack of data regarding the personal profits of the CEOs and management of unethical operations. Clearly, this type of cost-benefit analysis does not contribute to an ethical framework. In contrast, the Jewish value structure provides a normative framework of permissible and nonpermissible actions, irrespective of the material gain or loss involved.

All the most developed countries have laws and regulations providing for supervision of weights and measures. However, this is not so in the underdeveloped and economically poor countries. Irrespective of this, laws of the Bible concerning weights and measures have great spiritual and educational value in the creation of a moral market.

The rabbis had difficulty in understanding the linkage between these laws and the exodus from Egypt, which appears in the Bible. Some explained that the purpose of this exodus was to enable Israel to live in a country where it could apply these laws. Others explained that the exodus from Egypt occurred after the death of the firstborn. The status of the firstborn was a most secret and private one, the knowledge of which only God could really have. The same God has knowledge of the most secret and private acts of false weights and measures (white-collar crime).[55] It is this knowledge that Judaism proposes as the major protection against economic immorality.

BEYOND THE LETTER OF THE LAW

Rabbi Moshe Ben Nachman (1194–1270), Nachmanides, commented that it is possible to do evil within the letter of the law (Leviticus 19:1). The rabbis explained that the destruction of the Second Temple was a result of the leaders' and the population's insisting only on their full rights within the confines of the law. It is not surprising therefore, in the light of these and many similar comments, to find ramified teachings about acting beyond the letter of the law, *lifnim meshurat ha-din,* and its application in all the activities of the marketplace.

There are two major concepts in this regard that have a direct bearing on the operative free market: (1) "One has a benefit and the other has no loss," so the second party is obligated to do others favors with its wealth;[56] (2) acting beyond the letter of the law.[57]

The first of these concepts enters Jewish law, for example, in the *dina de bar metzra.* One wishing to sell his legally owned property has to give the neighboring owner the right of first refusal. This applies not only to real estate but also to shares in a nonlisted corporation. When this is not done, the neighbor can have the sale set aside. It should be noticed that this concept is enforced only where the neighbor is willing to pay the market price; the purpose is to do a favor, not to give charity to people who are not poor.[58]

The second concept obligates people to operate in a way that is ethically and morally correct, even when they are not obligated to do so by law. The classic example of this is the ruling in the Talmud that an employer whose workers have damaged some of his property is obligated to pay their wages and may not force them to pay for the damage—provided it was not caused deliberately.[59]

At first glance, such application would seem to be simply a moral imperative, to be used at the discretion or the level of religious development of the people involved. It would be imagined that acts beyond the letter of the law would be left to the individual moral and ethical judgment, yet most Halakhic authorities hold that the courts can force such behavior.[60] Some limited this to persuasion as distinct from legal injunctions; the Rema[61] limited this concept to those cases where the injured party was poor.

PHYSICAL AND SPIRITUAL DAMAGE

Human beings are the pinnacle of creation, everything in the world exists to fulfill their needs.[62] However, even lords of creation have obligations, so all the natural resources are given to us only in a custodian capacity. This is another implementation of the Torah concepts denying absolute private property. Even though the assets are legally and ethically owned, they may not be wasted or wantonly and cruelly destroyed, but must be husbanded and used in a manner that leaves some resources for the needs of future generations as well.[63] In times of war, fruit trees, even those belonging to the enemy, may not be destroyed.[64] Moreover, human beings are always responsible for their actions and are required to face the penalties thereof.

One is forbidden to do harm or damage, either in person or through one's property and assets in the course of economic activity, to another's person, property, or even peace of mind and spiritual well-being—as is demonstrated in all the codes and responsa.[65] This prevents economic activity that causes pollution of water, air, and land, and even activity that destroys aesthetic pleasure. Included in the legal aspects of such prevention are avoidance not only at the individual level, but also at the communal level. Urban planning and zoning can require distancing environmental hazards from other activities or forbidding them completely. Already in the Mishnah we read:

It is necessary to remove from the confines of the village the permanent threshing floors [because of the chaff], burial grounds, tanneries [because of the stench] and kilns because of the smoke.[66]

Not only is a firm engaged in environmentally harmful industries to be removed from residential areas, but it is to be relocated so that natural factors like water or wind will not bring these harmful effects to the area concerned. In Halakhic sources, such pollution is termed "the damages of smoke and bad odors," and it is regarded by the rabbis with special seriousness because it does harm to the body.

So serious is this considered, that the sanctity of contracts—a basic concept in Jewish law—is waived. This can be seen from a case raised in sixteenth-century Italy:

The question you have addressed to me concerning the butchers who have bought from the neighbors the right to build an abattoir, has reached me. At the outset, it would seem that because they have purchased this right from the neighbors, the neighbors had given their consent to its construction, and may not be allowed to retract their consent. [Their silence over time emphasizes this consent.] However, we see that all the authorities agree that with regard to damages of smoke and bad odors, a person is not really able to know if they are able to bear them. Therefore, we may suppose that even if one agreed at the beginning, we may not see this as foregoing their rights in the future.[67]

Such zoning regulations are a feature of rabbinic decisions. These are often extended to account for changes in technology and economic enterprise.

There is also a moral component to causing damage to others. Maimonides ruled that one is not allowed to cause damage even with the intent of paying compensation. There are cases where such compensation is cheaper than the cost of preventing it or of rectifying the cause. This moral component is bolstered by the obligation on the individual to clear dangerous objects or hazards, not only from their private property but even from the public domain.[68] When I raised the question of whistle-blowing regarding environmental damage with one of the authorities in Jerusalem, the answer was related to this obligation. Not only was one obligated to call public attention to it so as to prevent or rectify the situation, but also one was not permitted to work there if the environmental damage was the direct result of the major activity of that firm. As the *Arukh HaShulhan* ruled: "But even more so, is one obligated to prevent damage to the public therefore, if one knows that people [do] or intend to do damage to the public, one has to protest to the best of one's ability."[69]

All the zoning laws and the injunctions against causing damage have to be seen against the background of the conflict between economic growth and environmental and social benefits. The biblical laws concerning the towns of the Levites (Leviticus 25:34; Numbers 36:1–5) form the basis for the Torah's solution to this conflict. These towns included not only the inhabited area, but also the belts of farmland, trees, and open spaces that surrounded the city. The law established that the land, which was set aside for use as urban area, could not be transformed into open fields, nor could the open fields be transformed into either farmland or urban areas.[70] The codes ruled that the same applied to all towns in the Land of Israel.[71]

In other words, the growth of the town was limited to the original plan that left areas for both farming and other activities. The townspeople themselves do not have the right to destroy the greenbelts in order to provide for expansion. Such expansion requires establishment of a new village or town. The Torah would restrict urbanization to small units that have all the communal benefits flowing from a closely knit society that demonstrates concern for the individual; a lack of the estrangement so common to large cities; and preservation of open areas, scenic beauty, pure air, et cetera.[72] Such an urban policy enforced by governmental or local authority legislation places a limitation on economic growth, even though such growth may be a short-term benefit to society. Just as Judaism cannot recognize absolute private property rights, so, too, it cannot accept unlimited economic development in view of the moral and social costs it involves.

While prevention of damage is part of the Halakhic legal system, it is understood that even normal human activity includes some environmental damage and the depletion of natural resources; economic activity being the major factor in such damage. Such damage is the cost of fulfilling human needs in the natural, as distinct from a supernatural, manner. The economic development necessary for human existence, nevertheless, has a legitimate role in Judaism. The responsum of Rabbi Shlomo Cohen in sixteenth-century Turkey makes this quite clear:

The damage caused to the people by the vats used by the dyeing industry is extremely great and has to be considered as similar to that of smoke and bad odors. However, since the textile industry is the main basis for the livelihood of the people of this town, it is incumbent on the neighbors to suffer the damage. This is an enlargement of the principle that where a person is doing work that is essential to his livelihood and that is not possible to do elsewhere, the neighbors cannot have the right to prevent it.[73]

Rabbi Shimon Morpurgo, writing a hundred years later, saw this bias in favor of economic welfare as a temporary phenomenon, necessitated by the distortions introduced by Jewish history in exile. "It is forbidden," he ruled,

to erect industries that are harmful and necessary to remove those that already exist, so as to protect the people of the city. However, in this country since we are closed in and separated into a special Jewish quarter, which is narrow and insufficient for our needs, this injunction to move the offending obstacles is one that the community cannot stand up to.[74]

In the more normal conditions of an independent Jewish state, it should be possible to plan things in such a way that sources of ecological harm will be removed. The community being independent would now be able to allocate land and other resources in such a way as to provide for the common good—the yardstick according to which ecological obstacles are considered in Halakhic sources.

Despite these mitigating circumstances, when questions of health- or life-endangering situations develop, the economic considerations and the need for development are outweighed by the sanctity of life and body; such activities are not to be permitted, even at the expense of preventing economic development. It may well be that, in those cases where technological protection of life is not possible, an industry may not be allowed to exist within a Halakhic system. For example, if coal mining could not be conducted without a definite high risk of black lung disease, a Jewish economy might have to get along with an alternative source of fuel, even if such fuel is more costly.

Now, in the real world, dangers to life and limb exist even in normal activities, so one could argue that no economic activities would be possible. This carrying of the idea *ad absurdum* is not acceptable. Rather, the idea of reasonable risk—*keivan dedasu bo bnei rabim*—is used to permit the pursuit of a livelihood without transgressing the commandment of "Thou shall surely watch yourselves carefully," which is the injunction against risk of physical danger. In medieval times, when men traveled in caravans to trade despite a heavy risk of robbery or capture, this was considered to be a normal risk because not all caravans were captured or robbed.[75]

This concept of reasonable risk would seem to have implications for the obligation of society to spend money to protect the physical welfare of its citizens. In Jewish law, the community is obligated to provide through taxation a sewage system to prevent the spread of disease and plagues, to provide roads and pavements, street lighting, and police forces to prevent physical injury.[76] This is complicated, however, by the question of the cost of such provisions, since there is no society in the world that is able to fund everything without limits.

The issue is whether to limit the community's participation in this protection to the normal, everyday activities of its citizens, or to say that since the safety of human life is so vital, no cost is too great to pay. The latter would mean that unlimited sums of public money would have to be spent on guaranteeing the individual against even the slightest possible injury or danger, irrespective of the cost. Within the Jewish treatment of this issue through the concept of limited risk, society does not have to prevent danger where this exceeds the everyday chances of a person being damaged in the pursuit of normal activities. So, while Halakhah obligates one to take all reasonable steps to prevent one's property or that of others from causing damage, it uses terms like "to withstand reasonable wind" to exempt a person from liability caused in the normal course of travel or work.

Furthermore, the Torah teaches that one has to put up a fence around the roof to prevent innocent blood from being spilt; modern authorities include verandas and raised porches. Falling from these is considered a normal danger, so the owner can be forced to prevent it. However, this fence does not have to be built of reinforced concrete or layered steel, or at great expense; it need only be an ordinary fence, sufficient to withstand the pressure caused by a person leaning against it.[77]

Damage or abuse through assets is not confined to environmental issues alone. The Jewish ethical market forbids the sale of goods and services that are detrimental to the physical or moral health of the consumer. Not only is this the case where the consumer is ignorant of the damage but even where he is cognizant and yet still agrees to purchase the harmful goods or services. The former case requires full disclosure so that the purchaser is fully aware of the risks involved, whereas the latter is a moral injunction on the seller not to make these goods or services available.

Where the seller persists in the transactions with the cooperation of the buyer, the seller is guilty of *putting a stumbling block in the path of the blind*. The buyers are considered to be willfully blind to the consequences of their actions. It seems there is no legal action to be taken against the seller; his activity is merely understood as an infringement of a Torah commandment—with all that this entails. Nevertheless, the moral injunction is part of an educational process that should not be ignored.

This would mean not selling cigarettes in view of the health damage, or pornography in view of the moral damage. This would also mean not selling weapons to those liable to use them for aggressive warfare or against their own citizens, even if these are permitted in the general, non-Jewish society. So, too, one may not buy stolen goods or goods about which one knows taxes or duties have not been paid.[78] By all these actions people are being encouraged and enabled to do things that are forbidden to them by the Torah.

Where a corporation gives bribes to government officials, purchasing agents, or other parties able to promote its business, the recipients are either guilty of theft from their principal or of fraud. However, the corporation is guilty of placing a stumbling block in the path of the blind. The rabbis taught, "It is not the mouse that steals, but the hole."[79]

The concept of a stumbling block in the path of the blind has an aspect beyond that of strengthening through our commercial activities the hands of people who perform immoral or harmful acts. This aspect concerns the conflict of interest arising out of information or consultancy services. As such, it has great importance for those such as accountants, financial advisers, banks, and consultants to businesses and entrepreneurs, for whom this is a major economic role. Commentating on the biblical verse, "You shall not place a stumbling block in the part of the blind" (Leviticus 25:36), Rashi states, "you shall not tell a person to buy a field and sell a donkey, when you wish to buy a donkey and sell a field." All the authorities codify this concept. The rabbis forbade giving information or giving advice that is harmful to other parties—this is to be distinguished from giving bad or incorrect advice—and obligate the consultant to make full disclosure concerning the conflict of interest. It is suggested that this concept has great importance not only in the advertising of goods or services, which might be harmful to people physically, but also to people who might encourage a person to act irresponsibly in his or her financial or economic matters.

Besides mitzvot preventing certain acts, Judaism also has for economic activity—as it has for all areas of life—some positive commandments to perform certain acts. So, the *Shulhan Arukh* places the onus for saving other people's property or wealth from a wide range of dangers, clearly on the shoulders of every Jewish person.[80] In the marketplace, this means not withholding evidence or knowledge that may prevent a loss of other people's money, informing others of shoddy workmanship or of losses through business deals so others may be saved similar losses, or informing the public of hostile takeovers that are the result of coercion, et cetera. None of these are considered tale bearing, *lashon harah,* which is forbidden.[81]

TRUTH IN TRADING

The efficiency of the free market, indeed its very existence, is dependent on the free flow of information regarding the quality, price, and quantity of the particular goods or services being bought and sold. Furthermore, all the parties need to be able to rely on a fraud-free market environment; this necessity to constantly verify the facts would impose a cost that the market would not be able to absorb. All the players are expected to verify that there are no flaws, discrepancies, or illegal aspects to the goods or services involved. Indeed, in the free market, the maxim of "let the buyer beware" is an established and basic principle. Judaism, however, rejects this maxim and presents a system for the market, operative at all levels and in all its varied and sophisticated activities, that places full onus regarding full disclosure of defects on all the players in the market.

It is necessary to divide this aspect of the market morality into two sections: the first relating to defects in the goods or services offered; the second relating to creating a false impression.

DEFECTS IN GOODS OR SERVICES

Not only is it forbidden to cover up or hide defects in the goods or services being offered, but one is also obligated to make a full disclosure of these defects to the other party. This obligation applies even in the absence of a guarantee, such absence considered by the sages to be an error of omission, or in those cases where there is no market legislation. If this is not done, then the other party may cancel the sale upon discovering the flaws or the defects, irrespective of the time that has elapsed, provided use has not been made of the goods—that would constitute acceptance of the flaw.

Such disclosure exists over and above the injunction forbidding the sale of harmful goods or services, and disclosure of conflicts of interest; it relates only to defects and flaws.[82] Here, we do not rely on the knowledge or expertise of the buyer so that goods and services may not be offered "as is." This would preclude the sale of real estate that has physical or illegal defects, a motor car that has been involved in an accident even though the damage has been repaired, or goods for export to a country that forbids the import or subjects it to abnormal tariffs—all of these require a full disclosure.

CREATING A FALSE IMPRESSION

It may well be that the goods or services offered have no flaws and that they fully correspond to the invoices, advertisements, or verbal agreements. Nevertheless, they can be presented in such a way as to create a false impression. In addition to any other rabbinic injunction or religious teaching, this involves transgressing the biblical injunction against telling lies and the obligation to distance oneself from falsehoods. The Talmud presents an interesting example. A scholar was owed money and had recourse to the rabbinic court. Having only one witness—Halakhah requires two—he asked a student to accompany him to court. The student was not expected to make any false statements. He was required only to appear, thus causing the false impression of two valid witnesses.

This falls under the category of *geneivat da'at*, literally "stealing another person's mind." This prohibition would include advertising properties of goods that the goods do not really possess, false statements regarding the comparative efficiency of the article sold, and even decorating the packaging or wrapping it to create a false impression. When a corporation does not make full disclosure, in its financial reporting, of an item that is relevant to its creditors, shareholders, or governmental agencies, it could quite easily be guilty of this. In fact, "window dressing" in corporate financial statements is another example of painting old baskets so that they should look new, which is the Talmud's example of *geneivat da'at*.

When profits are shown to be above or below their real value, by either postponing expenses or bringing forward past ones, or by variations in methods of evaluating inventory and the like, the firm is painting its financial situation. Such obligations for full disclosure are extended to prevent even the creation of false impressions, so, too, they apply to the writing of curricula vitae, or résumés; prospectuses; share offerings; et cetera.

Geneivat da'at is considered a form of theft; together with any product or service defects discovered, it creates a *mekach ta'ut*, literally, "a fraudulent sale." However, this translation is a bit off the mark, if not misleading, for *mekach ta'ut* applies even in those cases where the seller makes no false claims, nor is there any false advertising; it even applies in those cases where the seller was ignorant of the flaw. Furthermore, there does not need to be any intention to defraud, nor can the buyer be coerced into accepting a rebate to compensate for the flaw.

Where this full disclosure does not exist, the sales, contracts, and transactions can be set aside. Those injured by transactions based on *geneivat da'at* have recourse to a rabbinic court. This is recognized by all the codes.[83] It is interesting to note that *geneivat da'at* occurs even when the buyer suffers neither loss nor harm. This may be seen in the example used in the *Shulhan Arukh* forbidding the act of selling to a gentile non-kosher meat that is packaged as if it were kosher, even though a non-Jew may eat such meat.

This concept of *geneivat da'at* is a recognition of the reality of the marketplace. In almost all cases it is simply not true that the buyer always has access to full information and all relevant data; any assumption of equality with the seller is naive and false, even though it is touted as the basis for free market economics. *Geneivat da'at* applies not only to consumers, employees, and debtors, but also to relations between developed and undeveloped countries. It is a moral imperative that buyers are protected from damages stemming from their lack of knowledge; they need to be able to claim redress.

PUBLIC SECTOR RESPONSIBILITY

The right of society to intervene in the marketplace in order to promote economic justice and equity is an accepted fact in Jewish legal and economic thought. This shows itself not only in the prevention of environmental damage and the introduction of zoning laws, but also in the supervision of weights and measures and prices and in the promotion or limiting of competition (as discussed earlier in this chapter). Furthermore, in addition to the philanthropy mandated in the gifts to the poor by the Bible (Leviticus 19:9–10) at the individual level, Judaism obligates society to enforce charity just as any other mitzvah. Already in the Mishnah, the citizens of a city could force each other to pay for the defense of the city, and this was understood in the Talmud to apply to all the needs of the town and community.[84] So, in various places, the codes recognize the right of the state, community, or society to enforce taxation in order to meet needs—as determined by the majority. At times, however, even the minority could enforce taxes required to meet the obligations imposed by the Torah, such as provision for the welfare of the poor, the sick, the aged, and even the lazy.[85] The sections of the codes and the responsa that deal with these matters also state categorically that the individual—or in the modern marketplace, the corporation—has an obligation to abide by these laws.

Macroeconomic policies regarding employment is an area full of pitfalls, which might lead to a distortion of Torah values in order to satisfy some market ideology. Since macroeconomics—beyond taxation, price control, environmental policies, and other areas specifically dealt with in the sources—is a modern creation, it presents problems because of a lack of sources to provide guidance. That said, there do seem to be two Halakhic precedents that could provide guidance even in this area.

UNEMPLOYMENT THROUGH BANKRUPTCY OR DOWNSIZING

Individual firms have a right to fire workers because the firm cannot continue to function, as in cases of business failure; because of a need to improve the firm's financial position; or simply because of downsizing to increase earnings. However, the Jewish outlook requires that we ask: "Who is to take responsibility for the welfare of the unemployed workers or any dispossessed owners?" It would be both immoral and impractical to place this obligation on employers. There would be, at most, only a charitable, and therefore delimited, obligation. The community, however, has an obligation to care for the unemployed person who is now poor. This requires not only financial support, but also provision against the moral, social, and psychological suffering caused by being made "redundant." As Maimonides ruled:

[Of] one who became poor, it is obligatory to provide for them. This even to the extent of providing a horse to ride upon and one to run before [as a sign of honor], if they were accustomed to this.[86]

JOB CREATION AND VOCATIONAL TRAINING

When an unidentified corpse is discovered and the cause of death, or those responsible for the death, is unknown, the Bible requires a public testimonial of innocence from the leaders of the society—the local councilors, the priests from Jerusalem, and the high court (Deuteronomy 21:1–9). These leaders were required to state, "our hands did not shed this blood." The rabbis explained that even though there is no suspicion of their guilt, they share in the murder because they did not provide a livelihood, either for the dead person or for the murderer.[87] This, in addition to the charitable obligation to provide a person with a job, might provide a basis for a public policy against unemployment, over and above the charity to the poor.

SUMMARY

Individuals operating in the free market, responsible for all the effects and implications of their actions, should pattern themselves on the following words of Maimonides:

The commerce of the *Talmid Hakham* [the Jewish role model] has to be in truth and in faith. His yes is to be yes and his no, no; he forces himself to be exact in calculations when he is paying, but is willing to be lenient when others are his debtors. He should keep his obligations in commerce, even where the law allows him to withdraw or retract, so that his word is his bond, but if others have obligations to him, he should deal mercifully, forgiving and extending credit. One should be careful not to deprive one's neighbor of his livelihood [even where this is legal] or cause hardship and anguish to others [bodily or financially—perhaps when firing workers or competing with others]. He who does all these things is the one referred to by the prophet Isaiah. When he said, "You, Israel, are My [God's] servant, with whom I am exalted."[88]

NOTES

1. Jerusalem Talmud, *Bava Metsia* 5:1.

2. Babylonian Talmud, *Ta'anit* 19b.

3. Amartya Sen, "Is Morality in Economics Worthwhile?" in *The Ethics of Business in a Global Economy*, ed. Paul M. Minus (Boston: Kluver Academic Publishers, 1993).

4. Babylonian Talmud, *Yoma* 69b.

5. Babylonian Talmud, *Yoma* 69b.

6. *Avot De' Rabbi Natan* 4:8.

7. Meir Tamari, *The Challenge of Wealth; A Jewish Perspective on Earning and Spending Money* (Northvale, NJ: Jason Aronson, 1995), 150–56.

8. Ibid., 127–46.

9. *Shulhan Arukh, Yoreh De'ah* 246.

10. *Torah Temimah*, Leviticus 25:13.

11. *Shulhan Arukh, Yoreh De'ah* 293.

12. *Mishneh Torah, Hilkhot De'ot* 5:2, 4–13.

13. Louis Finkelstein, *Jewish Self Government in the Middle Ages* (New York: Feldheim, 1964), for examples, 261, 292.

14. Isaiah 3:18–23; Amos 3–4.

15. Mishnah, *Bava Batra* 2:1–3.

16. Babylonian Talmud, *Bava Batra* 21b.

17. *Mishneh Torah, Hilkhot Shekheinim* 6:8; *Tur* and *Shulhan Arukh, Choshen Mishpat* 156:5: based on the above source in the Talmud.

18. *Teshuvot HaRashba* 5:182, 3:196. See, however, *Rema, Hoshen Mishpat* 167, who provides another opinion.

19. Babylonian Talmud, *Bava Batra*, ibid.

20. Babylonian Talmud, *Bava Batra* 25a, re. scholars. *Rema, Hoshen Mishpat, Nizkei Shecheinim* 156:5, removing the restraints on free entry of the Herem HaYishuv, for refugees.

21. Rabbenu Tam in *Tosafot* on *Kiddushin* 59a.

22. Mordechai, *Bava Batra* 514; also *Bet Yosef–Tur Hoshen Mishpat* 156:3; *Rema-Shulhan Arukh* 5.

23. *Pithei Teshuvah, Shulhan Arukh, Yoreh De'ah* 236:1, for two conflicting opinions.

24. *Vaad Kehilah Kedosha Padua,* ed. D. Karfi. (Jerusalem: Hakademia Haleumit, 1973). Enactment dated 1580; also *Avnei Nezer* (nineteenth-century Poland) *Hoshen Mishpat* 28.

25. *Shulhan Arukh, Hoshen Mishpat* 231.

26. Babylonian Talmud, *Kiddushin* 28a; See *Teshuvot Hamaharik* 132.

27. *Teshuvot HaTzemach Tzedek, Hoshen Mishpat* 23.

28. *Mishneh Torah, Hilkhot Mattenot Ahiyyim* 13:7.

29. Louis Isaac Rabinowitz, *Herem Hayishuv* (London: Goldston, 1945).

30. *Teshuvot Maharam of Rothenburg* 883.

31. Dennis W. Carlton and Avi Weiss, "Lessons from *Halakhah* about Competition and Teaching," Center for Business Ethics online library: http://www.besr.org/library/competition.html.

32. *Ibn Migas, Hidushin Bava Batra* 21b.

33. Mishnah, *Bava Metsia* 4:12.

34. *Meiri, Beit ha-Behirah, Bava Metsia,* on the above Mishnah.

35. *Sho'el u Meishiv* 1:20.

36. *Teshuvot HaTsemach Tzedek* 28.

37. Mishnah, *Keritut* 1:7.

38. *Minhat Tzvi, S'chirut Poalim* 8.

39. *Minhat Yitzhak* 2:94.

40. *Responsum of R. Meshullam,* Genizah Fragments, Oxford University Library.

41. Yehoshua Lieberman, *Economic Thought in the Talmud* (Ranat Gan, Israel: Bar Illan University, 1973).

42. Aaron Levine, "The Just Price Doctrine in Judaic Law," *Dine Israel* 8 (1978).

43. *Mishneh Torah, Hilkhot Mechirah* 13:4.

44. *Gratian Decretum* 1.

45. Babylonian Talmud, *Bava Batra* 91a.

46. *Mishneh Torah, Hilkhot Mechirah* 14:4.

47. *Bet Yosef, Hoshen Mishpat* 231:23.

48. Babylonian Talmud, *Bava Batra* 89a.

49. *Mishneh Halakhot* 4:113.

50. *Elef Le Shlomo* 238; *Iggrot Moshe, Orah Hayyim* 1:62:3.

51. Meir Tamari, *The Challenge of Wealth,* 96–97.

52. *Iggrot Moshe,Yoreh De'ah* 3:40–41; *Minhat Yitzhak* 3:1.

53. Abarbanel, Exodus 21:1.

54. Moses L. Pava and Joshua Krausz, *Corporate Responsibilty and Financial Performance: The Paradox of Social Cost* (Westport, CT: Quorum Books, 1995).

55. Babylonian Talmud, *Bava Metsia* 61b.

56. Babylonian Talmud, *Bava Kama* 20a. Also, *Mishneh Torah, Hilkhot Nizkei Mamon* 5:3.

57. Babylonian Talmud, *Bava Metsia* 30b.

58. *Mishneh Torah, Hilkhot Shekhenim* 12:5, 13, 14.

59. *Tur Hoshen Mishpat* 304:1. Another example is brought in *Shulhan Arukh HaRav, Hilkhot Mechirah* 5.

60. Bach, *Tur Hoshen Mishpat* 12, n. 4.

61. Rema, *Hoshen Mishpat* 259:5.

62. Rema, *Even ha-Ezer* 5.

63. *Midrash Rabbah, Kohelet* 713; also *Midrash Tanchuma, Kedoshim.*

64. Babylonian Talmud, *Shabbat* 105b; *bal tashkh* based on this rule in Deuteronomy 20:19.

65. *Shulhan Arukh, Hoshen Mishpat* 155.

66. *Bava Batra* 2:9.

67. *Magen Gibborim, Hoshen Mishpat* 38.

68. *Mishneh Torah, Nizkei Mamon* 13:22.

69. *Arukh Ha-Shulhan, Hoshen Mishpat* 388:15.

70. *Hidushei HaRashba, Bava Batra* 24b.

71. *Sefer HaHinukh*, mitzvah 66, based on *Bava Batra* 10a.

72. Meir Tamari, *The Challenge of Wealth*, 142–45.

73. *Teshuvot Maharshach* 2:98.

74. *Shemesh Tzedakah, Hoshen Mishpat* 34:1.

75. *Noda Biyehuda, Yoreh De'ah* 10. Also *Iggrot Moshe, Hoshen Mishpat* 1:104.

76. *Shulhan Arukh, Hoshen Mishpat* 227; *Rema* 7. *Teshuvot HaBach* 65.

77. *Mishneh Torah, Hilkhot Rotzeah u'Shmirat Hanefesh* 11:3.

78. Meir Tamari, *Sins in the Marketplace* (Northvale, NJ: J. Aronson, 1996), 148–50.

79. Babylonian Talmud, *Gittin* 45a

80. *Shulhan Arukh, Hoshen Mishpat* 426:1.

81. *Chafetz Chayim, Shmirat Halashon*, Shaar 10.

82. *Shulhan Arukh, Hoshen Mishpat* 228:6–9; 232:1–3.

83. *Shulhan Arukh, Yoreh De'ah* 248:2.

84. *Shulhan Arukh, Hoshen Mishpat* 163:1–3. Also *Rema* there.

85. "Takkanot of Kehilat Sugenheim," in Jacob Rader Marcus, *The Jew in the Medieval World* (New York: Harper and Row, 1938).

86. *Mishneh Torah, Hilkhot Mattenot Aniyyim* 7:3–7.

87. Jerusalem Talmud, 9:1; also Babylonian Talmud, *Sotah* 45b; see Rashi.

88. *Mishneh Torah, Hilkhot De'ot* 5:13.

CHAPTER 9

Genetic Engineering in Jewish Law and Ethics

Byron L. Sherwin

So over that art
Which you say adds to Nature,
Is an art That Nature makes. . . .
This is an art
Which does mend Nature,
Change it rather; but
The art itself is Nature.[1]

—Shakespeare

Genetic engineering refers to the artificial manipulation of genetic material to gain a desired result. Often used synonymously with terms like "recombinant DNA" or "biotechnology," genetic engineering can be done in plants, animals, and humans, as well as across species. For example, human genes can be placed in plants, animal genes can be implanted in humans, and so forth. Genetic engineering can be used for benevolent reasons such as curing and treating disease, for malevolent reasons such as biological warfare, as well as for reasons that might be considered frivolous, like the creation of a "geep" (i.e., part goat, part sheep).[2]

Barely a week goes by without reports of new developments in biotechnology. Barely a month goes by without heated debate on the ethical and public policy implications of some aspect of genetic engineering, for example, human cloning, the use of fetal tissue for stem cell research, federal regulation of bioengineered food, the patenting of human tissue and genes.

As the twenty-first century unfolds, developments in biotechnology will occur faster than ethicists and jurists will be able to deal with their implications. Indeed, whereas twentieth-century science and technology had been characterized as the "age of physics," the twenty-first century already has been depicted as the "biotech century."[3]

Currently available and projected future developments in bioengineering will increasingly impact upon many aspects of our daily lives. They will influence the nature of the foods we eat, the pharmaceuticals we ingest, the medical care we receive, the manner in which we reproduce, priorities for national defense spending, the future development of the economy, and more. For example, already most of the food produced in the United States currently contains genetically modified ingredients. Increasing numbers of pharmaceuticals are being produced by recombinant DNA technologies. The use of genetic screening is accelerating in the workplace. Genetic-based therapies are becoming more extensively used in the attempt to treat and to cure a wide variety of diseases and disabilities.

That public policy debate over features of bioengineering evokes raw emotions should not be surprising. Not only will biotechnology irreversibly alter our environment and the way in which we live, but even more, developments in bioengineering promise to alter features of nature itself, including human nature. Consequently, the ethical and public policy implications of biotechnology confront us at a more visceral level than many other public policy and ethical issues. Unlike other issues, bioengineering challenges us to rethink many fundamental philosophical and theological concepts such as the nature of life, human nature and identity, our relationship with nature, and human moral volition.

Biotechnology compels us to reconsider who we are, who we want to become, and what kind of society we want for the future. For example, in a future in which altered genes, infused animal genes and organs, as well as computerized biochips, become "normal" features of each of our bodies, where will we set the boundaries for what and who is a human being?

Biotechnology represents the ability to reengineer and to re-create aspects of nature. It allows us to create new organisms not provided by nature. It offers the means for altering the existing genetic structure of organisms, including the human organism. It claims to be able to predict our individual futures. As scientist James Watson has put it, "We used to think our fate was in the stars. Now, we know in large measure, our future is in our genes."[4]

THE ETHICS OF JUDAISM

Judaism is a religious faith, and as such, it is shaped by certain theological claims and presuppositions about God, human beings, and the place of human beings in the world. Jewish ethics and law may be considered forms of "applied" Jewish theology, in that Jewish law and ethics must articulate the claims of Jewish theology in concrete and specific ways, as they relate to particular issues and situations. Jewish religious literature, from the Bible to contemporary legal responsa (case law), provides a treasure trove of accumulated wisdom and precedent for dealing with the ethical and public policy challenges of the present and future. Applying these resources to contemporary issues is the challenge that confronts today's Jewish theologians, ethicists, and Halakhists.[5] How these resources can be applied to some of the questions elicited by developments in biotechnology is the subject of what follows.

By definition, "genetic engineering" refers to the alteration of existing entities in nature and to the "creation" of new types of biological entities. Whereas the Anglo-American legal tradition would ask whether we have the "right" to engage in such activities, Jewish law would pose the question differently. Jewish law would ask whether such activities are permissible (*hetair, reshut*), forbidden (*assur*), or obligatory (*hovah, mitzvah*). How this question would be answered also depends on the perspective taken with regard to the relationship between human beings and the natural world.

Many objections have been adduced by both religious and secular bioethicists to the very concept of bioengineering, especially where human beings are concerned. Among these is the claim that bioengineering is "unnatural," that it is "playing God" and "tampering" with nature. Would Jewish law and ethics agree or disagree?[6]

PLAYING GOD?

Medieval Jewish texts distinguish between two types of creativity: creation from nothing (*yesh me-ayin*) and creation from something (*yesh mi-yesh*). Creation from nothing is unique to divine creativity. Only God can create something from nothing. Human creativity, however, is restricted to the creation, reformulation, or recombination of something already in existence. Indeed, such human creativity is not considered as "playing God," but rather as articulating the biblical claim that human beings have been created in the divine image (Genesis 1:26–27), and the Talmudic description of human beings as "God's partner in the work of creation."[7] In the words of the sixteenth-century rabbi Judah Loew of Prague, "When we contemplate the works of God [we realize] that everything God created requires [human] repair [*tikkun*] and completion [*hashlamah*]."[8]

Rabbi Judah Loew of Prague is best known not for his voluminous writings, but for a legend ascribed to him over a century after his death. According to this legend, Judah Loew created an "artificial man," a Golem. However, the origin of the Golem legend is already found in the Talmud. In the Talmudic text, two creatures—one humanlike and one

animal-like—are described as having been created through artificial
means.[9] This is akin to genetic engineering in that such creation occurs
"artificially," without usual procreative activity.

From the huge corpus of commentary and discussion on this ancient
text, a number of observations are relevant to our discussion. First, the
creation of life—in this case the anthropoid and the animal, that is, a calf—
are reported in this text in a very matter-of-fact way. The propriety of such
human creativity is not considered a usurpation of God's role as the creator. It is not considered to be a rejection, but rather to be an affirmation
of the biblical description of the human being as having been created in
the divine image and likeness. Here the issue is not seen as one of "playing
God" or of human hubris, but as a desirable fulfillment of *imitatio Dei*.[10]

In his commentary on this Talmudic text, Menahem Meiri discusses
whether such activities should be prohibited as being evil (i.e., witchcraft)
and unnatural. Meiri concludes that they are not evil, prohibited, or unnatural. He writes, "[since] all natural actions cannot be considered witchcraft, even the knowledge to create new beautiful creatures that are not
engendered through sexual reproduction, as noted in books about natural
science, cannot be proscribed."[11] In other words, the "artificial" creation
of organisms, as Judah Loew noted, is not unnatural because it extends
the parameters of nature. New creatures brought into existence through
such means are not unnatural, but are rather a natural extension of what
already has been created in nature by God.

Both Meiri and Loew reflect the attitude toward nature of the thirteenth-
century Spanish scholar Nachmanides, who, in his commentary on the
biblical verse giving human beings dominion over nature (Genesis 1:28),
writes, "[God] gave them [i.e., human beings] power and dominion over
nature to do with it what they wish. This includes animals, plants, etc."[12]
Indeed, as if in anticipation of contemporary developments in bioengineering, Judah Loew writes, "When God created the laws of nature in the
six days of creation, the simple and the complex, and finished creating
the world, there remained additional power to create anew, just like people create new animal species through interspecies breeding. . . . Human
beings can bring to fruition things that were not previously found in nature; nevertheless, since these are not activities that occur through nature,
it is as if they entered the world to be created."[13]

This statement by Loew is a commentary to a Talmudic text that reads,
"After the close of the first Sabbath, God inspired Adam with knowledge
of a kind similar to God's [knowledge]. Adam then took two stones and
rubbed them together and fire came forth. Adam then took two animals
and crossed them, and from them came forth the mule."[14] Here, unlike in
Greek mythology, fire is not stolen from the divine, but "discovered"
through the sanctioned employment of God-given wisdom. In "creating"
the first mule, Adam—the first human being—is already involved in

bringing the first genetically engineered animal into existence. In other words, for Loew, human beings have a divine mandate to repair and to improve on the natural world that God has created.

Unlike classical Catholic tradition that tied moral law to natural law, classical Jewish tradition has little notion of natural law. For Judaism, not that which some may consider "natural," but rather that which Jewish tradition considered mandated by revelation and interpretative tradition, is the central determinant for moral behavior. Whether an action is deemed "natural" or not is not usually a determining factor in Jewish law and ethics.[15] Consequently, religious or secular views that proscribe or discourage various forms of genetic engineering on the grounds that they are unnatural, are not relevant to Jewish legal or ethical discourse on such matters. Furthermore, as medieval Jewish moral teachers have observed, ethical vices such as avarice, cruelty, and greed are natural but not moral.

Equating the natural with the ethical and the will of God can have disastrous implications, as we see in the case of Nazi "racial science" and eugenics. For instance, explicating the principles of "racial science" for the Reich Ministry of Interior, Dr. Achin Gerke wrote, "Let us not bother with the old and false humanitarian ideas. There is in truth only one humane idea, that is: furthering the good and eliminating the bad. The will of nature is the will of God. . . . [Nature] sides with the strong, good, victorious. . . . We simply fulfill the commandments, no more, no less."[16]

Further support for the position that various forms of bioengineering are permitted by Jewish law may be adduced from a Jewish legal principle that states, "Whatever has not been specifically forbidden is presumed to be permitted."[17] Since various types of bioengineering have not been specifically forbidden by any precedent in Jewish law, and since they appear to be explicitly permitted by the Talmud, they cannot be categorically proscribed. Certainly, bioengineering and gene therapies aimed at improving human life, at treating disease and disability, would be sanctioned, encouraged, and even considered mandatory under certain circumstances. Nonetheless, that an activity is deemed permissible does not mean that it may be practiced indiscriminately. There must be a valid purpose behind it. There must be boundaries restricting its implementation. The legal category of "the permitted" does not offer a carte blanche. The morally determining factor here is the purpose and use for which such bioengineered entities are created. As Rabbi Immanuel Jakobovits has insightfully pointed out, God knew that there is both a time to create as well as a time to stop creating. Humans who have harnessed the divine power to create should also know when and where to stop.[18]

THE MANDATE TO HEAL

Jewish law considers each moment of human life to be precious. It therefore mandates the preservation and extension of life and health whenever possible.[19] Indeed, Jewish law not only permits, but obliges a person to violate other Jewish legal strictures (e.g., Sabbath observance) in order to extend the life of a dying person, even if only for a short time. The mandate to heal, to preserve health and life, is almost a categorical imperative in Judaism. Consequently, forms of bioengineering that aim at the preservation of life would not only be permissible, but might be obligatory (*mitzvah, hovah*) as well. Furthermore, the failure to utilize available medical treatments and technologies—including those that have been developed through biotechnology—might be considered a violation of the biblical requirement to preserve life and health.[20] For example, a diabetic would be prohibited from refusing insulin.

In the past, insulin was obtained from the pancreases of thousands of slaughtered animals. Today it can be cheaply and efficiently manufactured by using recombinant DNA. In this method, the DNA of insulin is inserted into the DNA of a bacterium, which then reproduces or clones itself, yielding the desired hormone in substantial quantities. Drugs for a wide variety of other diseases can be similarly produced.

Human hormones and genes are being implanted in milk-producing animals such as goats and cows. Quantities of those hormones are harvested from the animal's milk to treat a variety of diseases. Hence, because of the therapeutic benefits of these drugs, even the transfer of human genes to animals, that is, certain forms of transgenics, would be permitted. As noted above, it is the purpose and not the process that determines the ethical propriety of various methods of bioengineering.

GENETIC SCREENING

In January 1997, in his second inaugural address, President Clinton said, "Scientists are now decoding the blueprint of human life. Cures for our most feared illnesses seem close at hand." This was a naïve and misleading statement. Certainly, we know more than we once did. We can do more than we once could, but much remains obscure.

We now have most of the text of the human genome, but the process of understanding and interpreting it is still in its infancy. We have yet to learn what genes do, how they work, what proteins they make, how they interact. Though increasing numbers of genetic screening tests are available, there is a wide gap between the diagnostic and the therapeutic. We can identify certain genetic predispositions toward a variety of diseases, but we cannot yet treat most of those diseases. In other words, we can gather genetic information, but we are often unsure of what it means and of what to do with it once we have it. Even when available, we are not sure of its consequences.[21] Since most of us have eight to twelve genetic defects, the more we screen, the more problematic treating the information we acquire becomes.

Though a genetic predisposition toward a disease does not necessarily mean that we will fall victim to that disease, the information collected by genetic screening compels us to rethink our self-image and to reassess our future. Certainly, such information would have an influence on our life-style, on our future planning, on how others would relate to us. Should such genetic information cause us to feel condemned to a certain future by our genes? As legal scholar Lori Andrews puts it, "People's most intimate sense of themselves and feelings of security can be shaken by the use of genetic services."[22] For example, should a young girl who has not yet developed breasts be advised to undergo a removal of her uterus and breasts, when she develops them, if she has a gene that indicates a predisposition to breast cancer (e.g., BRAC1)? That defective gene may not give her breast cancer. And, even if she tries to avoid cancer by preventative radical mastectomies, there is still a possibility that breast or ovarian cancer might still occur. She could, upon reaching puberty, begin a regular regimen of breast X-rays, but the radiation exposure could also trigger breast cancer.

Genetic screening may discover a genetic mutation such as sickle-cell anemia. However, carrying that mutation, which may or may not express itself in disease, also has another side. People with a predisposition to sickle-cell anemia often have a higher-than-normal immunity to malaria. Like various other genetic mutations, this one has an enhancing, as well as a diminishing, aspect.

The growing availability of genetic information has dangerous social and economic implications.[23] Genetic screening is now required by many employers as a condition of employment. Initiated in the 1970s, genetic screening was a response to legislation making businesses responsible for health in the workplace. At first voluntary with no threat of job loss, the goal initially (by chemical companies) was to reduce employee risk in hazardous jobs. More recently, however, genetic screening has been used to deny jobs to workers, to prevent workers from obtaining promotions, to exclude individuals from life and health insurance, and to discourage marriages—even when the genetic evidence is hardly conclusive.[24] Though efforts have been made to eliminate discrimination based on genetic screening, such efforts are difficult to enforce. As one legal scholar has put it, "We risk increasing the number of people who are defined as unemployable, uneducable or unsuitable. We risk, in other words, creating a genetic underclass."[25]

Because certain cohesive groups, like Ashkenazic Jews, have proven to be a fruitful population on which to do genetic research and testing, more data is currently available on members of such groups than on others. This exposes members of such groups to a higher possibility of genetic discrimination than members of other groups.[26]

Both legal scholars and physicians are apprehensive to hear some of

their colleagues advocating "compassionate eugenics," meaning that giving birth to a child with genetic disorders that could have been discovered
through prenatal genetic screening should be considered a crime, a form
of child abuse.[27]

Already, legal categories that echo twentieth-century politically driven
eugenic policies, such as "wrongful life," are entering our legal lexicon.
Should parents who did not have children screened for certain genetic
disorders be liable for child abuse if such disorders surface later in life?
Should children with genetic disorders or children who do not believe
their parents gave them adequate "enhancement therapies" such as
growth hormones be able to sue their parents for neglect or abuse? Should
parents who paid for donated sperm or eggs have a basis for a product
liability suit if the child did not turn out as handsome or as intelligent as
expected?

In itself, eugenics is not evil. However, when it is coupled with coercion,
it can easily become dangerous, whether that coercion is politically or
socially generated. Ironically, Jews have been both the victims as well as
the beneficiaries of eugenics. Nazi racial theories of eugenics were employed against Jews in the Holocaust. However, one of the success stories
of contemporary genetic screening and eugenics relates to the virtual elimination of Tay-Sachs and cystic fibrosis among Ashkenazic Jews in Israel
and America. The offering of free or cheap genetic testing and counseling
has led to the virtual elimination of such diseases in many segments of
the Jewish community. However, had the Tay-Sachs gene or the test for
its presence been patented, the patent holder could have shut down genetic testing altogether or made it prohibitively expensive.

In its code of ethics, the American Medical Association prohibits its
members from patenting procedures, because it found that such patents
compromised the quality of medical care. The medical organization of
genetic specialists—The American College of Medical Genetics—opposes
gene patenting.[28] Meanwhile, biotech companies patent genes, genetic
tests, and genetic therapies, compromising medical care and driving up
medical costs, and thereby excluding many from access to care, even when
some of the research they use was financed by public funds. In contrast,
when Jonas Salk developed the polio vaccine, he said, "There is no patent.
Could you patent the sun?"[29]

Genetic screening is now being encouraged by direct-to-consumer advertising. Sometimes, such advertising utilizes "scare tactics." Sometimes,
it offers misleading and incorrect information. Especially because of the
issues discussed above regarding genetic screening, "truth in advertising,"
rather than exploitative commercial greed, should govern the emotionally
volatile area of advertising for genetic screening.[30] While Jewish law and
ethics affirm the legitimacy of the profit motive, Jewish business ethics
would not consider exploitative or false advertising to be justifiable. Nor

would Jewish ethics condone price gouging of the naïve or the poor based on what has been termed the "biopiracy" of greed characteristic of some segments of the biotech industry.

GENE THERAPY

Various forms of genetic therapy hold forth great promise for the treatment of many diseases. At the time of this writing, genetic therapies have had an uneven record of success. Here it is important to distinguish between the use of gene therapies—especially experimental gene therapies—as a last resort (with the patient's informed consent) to treat a fatal disease in its last stages, and the use of such therapies in less than life-threatening situations. [31] Precedents in Jewish law allow such therapies in cases where life could potentially be saved and, in certain circumstances, even in cases in which the patient is not suffering from a terminal disease.

The attitude of Jewish tradition toward genetic therapy on human beings has been succinctly summarized by physician and bioethicist Fred Rosner. He writes, "Genetic screening, gene therapy and other applications of genetic engineering are permissible in Judaism when used for the treatment, cure, and prevention of disease. Such genetic manipulation is not considered to be a violation of God's natural law but a legitimate implementation of the biblical mandate to heal. According to Jewish law, if Tay-Sachs disease, diabetes, hemophilia, cystic fibrosis, Huntington's disease or other genetic diseases could be cured or prevented by gene surgery, it is certainly permitted. . . . The main purposes of gene therapy are to cure disease, restore health, and prolong life, all goals within the physician's Divine license to heal. Gene grafting is no different than an organ graft such as a kidney or corneal transplant, which nearly all rabbis consider permissible." [32]

Rosner is, of course, speaking of gene therapies that are mostly currently unavailable or, if available, are not yet considered adequately developed for public application. Rosner also considers most genetic "enhancement" therapies—since they have no clear physical (as opposed to psychological) therapeutic purpose, and because some may be considered "frivolous" or merely cosmetic—to be discouraged by Jewish law. However, the line between therapeutic treatment and enhancement therapies is not always crisp.

Such enhancement therapies serve to "raise the bar" for what is "normal" and desirable, setting a standard that will remain out of the reach of many who may find it desirable. Many examples might be given. For instance, once bioengineered growth hormones became available, they were widely used to help ensure that short children would be able to attain an "acceptable" height. Parents did not want their children to be stigmatized or discriminated against for being "short." Consequently, growth hormones that were once restricted to combating dwarfism were given to thousands of children who were not threatened with dwarfism. The widespread use of these hormones is troubling, especially in view of possible side effects.

That parents would want enhancement for their children is understandable; however, how far do we go? Many parents want more intelligent children, but heightened intelligence has been linked to aggressive and even antisocial behavior. Do we want to extend genetic enhancement to culturally imposed views of beauty, like hair or eye color, sex selection? Prenatal sex selection has been used to prevent the passing down of certain harmful genes, for example, Huntington's disease. However, how extensively do we use prenatal sex selection and other criteria of selection, and for what reasons? Will genetic screening of fetuses lead to "frivolous" elective abortions, as the "right to life" advocates correctly fear? Consider, for example, that 12 percent of potential parents said they would abort a fetus with a genetic predisposition to obesity.[33] What of a predisposition to certain diseases like diabetes? Clearly, parents want children with particular traits and enhancements, but where should we draw the line?

STEM CELLS

For centuries, the primary cause of disease was considered to be entities outside the body (e.g., viruses, bacteria) that invade the body. With recent developments in genetics, we are becoming increasingly aware of diseases that are either completely or partially caused by the genetic composition of the body itself. This awareness challenges us to reconceptualize our views of medical science, to refocus the nature of how medical care is delivered, and to consider reallocating funding in medical research.

Therapies utilizing stem cells promise to alter the very nature of medical care and cure. A wide variety of diseases and disabilities may be treated with stem cell–related therapies, including Alzheimer's, Parkinson's, and diabetes. Stem cells might be transplanted into diseased tissue where they would turn into the desired cell type. For example, stem cells transformed into islet cells could restore function to a diabetic's pancreas. Stem cells that change into nerves could replace tissue damaged by strokes, spinal cord injuries, Lou Gehrig's disease (ALS), Alzheimer's, and Parkinson's. Stem cells (as well as discarded foreskins) could be used to generate bio-engineered skin tissue to treat victims of severe burns. Lab-grown heart tissue could improve the functioning of damaged hearts and arteries. Injecting stem cells into a liver might rejuvenate a liver damaged by cirrhosis or hepatitis, or stem cells might be used to repair cartilage ravaged by arthritis. Furthermore, if adult stem cells can be "reprogrammed," it raises the possibility that each of us carries within us the seeds of our own self-renewal. It is currently estimated that if successful, stem cell therapies could treat diseases and disabilities that currently afflict over half of the American population.

Despite the enormous potential of stem cell research and therapy to address the treatment of myriad diseases, many oppose it on ethical grounds. Because fetal tissue is currently considered the most desirable source of stem cells, those who claim that human life begins with conception oppose the destruction of embryos to capture their stem cells. Opponents of abortion maintain that the use of fetal stem cells for therapeutic reasons will inevitably lead to an increase in the number of abortions done, and that abortion is nothing less than the murder of a human person.[34]

For Jewish law and ethics, these objections are not adequately compelling for a number of reasons. First, fertility clinics already possess tens of thousands of frozen embryos (the products of in vitro fertilization—IVF) that are slated to be discarded. To sacrifice people whose lives might be saved and whose health might be restored because of a reticence to use existing embryos that would otherwise be destroyed would be morally problematic. Furthermore, should adult stem cells become usable, or should cells from umbilical cords be used, there would be no possible moral objection to the use of stem cells for research and therapies.

Jewish law does not consider an embryo to have the legal status of a "person" with the protections that entails. The use of embryos—frozen in IVF clinics, destined for destruction, with no implantation in a womb contemplated—would be permissible because the purpose for their use would be aimed at the preservation of life and the restoration of health. Indeed, in certain instances, even aborting an embryo might be permissible, as it is a principle in Jewish law that the life of an existing "person" takes precedent over than of a "potential person."

Some bioethicists distinguish between embryos and "preembryos." Preembryos that consist of only a few cells that have no distinguishing human characteristics found in more developed fetal tissue and that will not be implanted in a womb would be permissible for stem cell research and therapies, according to Jewish law.[35] Since Jewish law does not grant the status of "personhood" to a fetus, abortion, while not desirable, and in many cases not permitted, would never be considered murder by Jewish law.

Despite the enormous promise that stem cell research holds forth in the treatment of a host of maladies, it is far from clear at the time of this writing that stem cell use is the panacea many consider it to be.[36] Use of stem cells has had limited success. We may find that stem cells' potential has been exaggerated. Yet, this does not mean that they bear no future therapeutic value. Precisely because of their potential, research should proceed, whether with adult stem cells or already available fetal stem cells.

HUMAN CLONING

Cloning of human beings is not prohibited by Jewish law. Since there is no particular stricture for forbidding it, cloning must be considered permissible. However, two criteria must be invoked before it could be attempted. The first is valid purpose. The second is safety.[37]

Cloning would not be defensible for all purposes. However, for certain purposes it might not only be permissible, but obligatory. One example is that of a Holocaust survivor who lost his children during the Holocaust and who is sterile. His only chance to have a child, and to fulfill the biblical commandment to be "fruitful and multiply," would be through cloning. In such a case, cloning might be a mitzvah. In addition, for an infertile couple with no other way of having a child, cloning might be their only option.

Current cloning technology in animals is far too dangerous to be used for human cloning. Cloned mammals demonstrate the disproportionate presence of abnormalities such as premature aging, birth defects that manifest themselves as the animals mature, deformed limbs and organs, et cetera.[38] However, once these dangers are overcome, human cloning could proceed, although with caution and with certain restrictions.

While surveys consistently find that the vast majority of Americans oppose the cloning of human beings, such opposition may diminish over time once the technology of cloning is improved.[39] Newly introduced medical technologies often face public disapproval at the outset, as did heart transplants and IVF. Already in 1966, physicians Kleegman and Kaufman wrote, "Any change in custom or practice in this emotionally charged area [of reproductive biotechnology] has always elicited a response from established custom and law of horrified negation at first; then negation without horror; then slow and gradual curiosity, study, evaluation, and finally a very slow steady acceptance."[40]

As in other cases of bioengineering and reproductive biotechnology, some contemporary theologians have claimed that human cloning is immoral because it is unnatural. However, with regard to cloning, it should be noted that unlike some other forms of bioengineering, it is not a phenomenon invented by human beings in a laboratory. Cloning occurs in nature. Bioengineered clones, therefore, do not subvert nature, but rather are imitative of certain natural phenomenon.

Already in 1973, zoologist George Hudok—though he opposed human cloning—wrote, "except for gametes, a human being is a clone because all its cells are derived from a single fertilized ovum. Moreover, identical twins, those derived from one fertilized ovum, are a clone."[41] Put another way, not only is human cloning a natural phenomenon, but each of us can be considered a clone. Or, in golemic terms, each of us was a Golem who has moved from the status of Golem to the status of a human person. This is precisely the view found in Talmudic and Midrashic sources that describe God as creating the first human being through means other than bisexual reproduction.[42] Adam is derived from inert matter; Eve is then "cloned" from cells of Adam's body. Thus, the asexual creation of human beings by human beings through cloning may be viewed as an act of *imitatio Dei*.

According to Jewish law, a clone would have full human status. While the clone would have the same genetic composition as that of the nucleic donor, the clone would be a unique and discrete human person with his or her own personal history and experiences. Born into a different historical and social environment and shaped by different experiences than the nucleic donor, the clone would live a different life from that of the donor.

Fears like those generated in novels and films like *The Boys from Brazil*, that cloning Hitler would inevitably produce a "new" Hitler, are unfounded. As physicist Michio Kaku has written, "Cloning Hitler may do no more than produce a second rate artist. Similarly, cloning an Einstein does not guarantee that a great physicist will be born since Einstein lived at a time when physics was in deep crisis. . . . Great individuals are probably as much the product of great turmoil and opportunity as the product of favorable genes."[43]

MORAL VOLITION

Human cloning raises a fundamental question about human moral volition. This is a question that echoes throughout the contemporary preoccupation with the implications of genetic research. Is the case—as James Watson put it—that our fate is no longer in the stars, but in our genes? Can human beings still claim to have moral freedom of choice and hence moral responsibility and accountability?

Behavioral genetics claims that certain types of behavior may be genetically determined. Indeed, behavioral genetics has been used to relieve personal guilt about certain types of behavior, such as tardiness; certain lifestyles, for example, homosexuality; certain medical conditions, for example, obesity. However, behavioral genetics also has been used to justify certain types of criminal behavior and, consequently, to defend cutbacks in funding social and economic programs aimed at treating criminal and antisocial behavior. In addition, behavioral genetics has been used to stigmatize certain racial and ethnic groups as being prone to crime, to violence, and therefore immune to efforts at social rehabilitation.[44] All of which is a throwback to eugenic teachings of a century ago, but with the current availability of genetic testing and computerized magnetic resonance machinery.

Despite some of the claims of behavioral geneticists, leading geneticists warn against the dangers of genetic determinism, whether with regard to health or to morality. A genetic mutation may only point to a predisposition toward a certain disease or form of behavior. Indeed, in the past, genetic defects like Klinefelter's syndrome were incorrectly linked to inevitable violent behavior. J. Craig Venter, president of Celera Genomics, and his rival in human genome research, Francis Collins, both caution against drawing the conclusion that choices in life are "hard-wired into our DNA and free will goes out the window."[45]

While Maimonides, the great medieval philosopher, physician, and Halakhist, affirmed that human beings have certain attitudinal and behavioral predispositions, he opposed ethical determinism of any kind. At a time when astrology was considered a predictive science, not unlike today's genetics, Maimonides condemned astrology as a form of idolatry. Had Maimonides lived today, he would deny that our fate is either in the stars or in our genes.

For Maimonides, all of Judaism rests on the presupposition that the human being is a free moral agent. While he recognized that innate physical traits predispose us to certain types of behavior, Maimonides was not willing to concede that undesirable moral behavior is in any way inevitable. Rather, he taught that predispositions toward certain moral vices could be overcome through acts of will and behavior modification techniques.[46]

ETHICS AND SCIENCE

Judaism's affirmation of human moral volition in opposition to theories of genetic behaviorism is an example of how, when, and why faith-based theology and ethics can and should challenge certain alleged scientific theories that it finds morally or theologically objectionable. Another example is the sanctity of existing human life, which is a nonnegotiable claim of Jewish theology and ethics.

Jewish law and ethics deems each human life as being sacred from birth until death. However, certain contemporary scientists, like Francis Crick, who shared the Nobel Prize with James Watson for unraveling the structure of DNA, would not agree. Watson's claim that our fate is in our genes would be rejected by Jewish theology and ethics when applied to moral behavior. Similarly, Crick's suggestion that the sanctity of human life is a now-obsolete idea, a remnant of religious sentimentality, would be rejected by Jewish teachings. So would Crick's further recommendation that children be deemed born—and therefore legally protected—only when it has been established that they will be "acceptable members of society," and that people over eighty years of age ought to be designated as already legally dead to avoid incurring expensive medical treatments. Clearly, as one Jewish scholar has noted, such views "are all too reminiscent of the eugenic policies of Nazi Germany."[47]

As cultural historians and cultural anthropologists have taught us, what is sometimes presented as scientific truth may be culturally, politically, and/or economically driven. Such was the case of Nazi eugenics and "racial hygiene." Such is also the case in certain segments of the exploding biotech industry. Indeed, Americans should not forget that racially and ethnically motivated eugenics were very much a part of American life in the early twentieth century, and that some of the eugenic teachings of Nazi Germany were based on eugenic teachings and policies that derived from American academe and the American political and social policies of those times.[48]

There is currently an attempt being made by the exploding biotech industry to convince us to alter our views of human personhood, human dignity, human freedom, and medical care, and even to relinquish some basic human rights, including property rights over our own bodies, in the name of scientific truth and promised scientific progress. There is now an attempt to convince us to see the future of genetics as an explanation of, and as a panacea for, all of our medical and social ills, and for us to be prepared to pay any price to avail ourselves of its benefits.

For Jewish tradition, our body is a loan from God, a bailment given us by God for our lifetime. However, for some of the biotech industry, our bodies are fast becoming both commodities as well as consumers. While Jewish business ethics considers a fair profit to be legitimate, it would not endorse some current practices in the biotech industry that have been characterized as predatory economically driven opportunism and unbridled greed. For example, biologist Erwin Chargoff has described the current situation "as an Auschwitz in which valuable enzymes, hormones and so on will be extracted instead of gold teeth."[49] A "reasonable price clause"—like the one once imposed by the National Institutes of Health—should be reintroduced with regard to genetic therapies. Furthermore, the courts should reverse the currently legally acceptable practice of patenting human genes.[50]

From the perspective of Jewish law and ethics, the purpose of medical research is to help fulfill the divine mandate to cure—to preserve and extend life, and to restore and preserve health. Reasonable profits from such efforts are justifiable, but unbridled greed is not. Neither is the withholding of available therapies for financial motivations. Indeed, Jewish law requires payment to be made for receiving medical treatment. The Talmud says, "A physician who cures for free is worth the price of his cure." However, Jewish law also obliges the medical caregiver to provide his or her services gratis to an indigent patient.

HONEY AND THE STING

Bioengineering tinkers in the toolbox of nature without being fully aware of the consequences of what it is doing, without full cognizance of the possible and unanticipated dangers of its activities. Developments in biotechnology may become like the Golem, which was created for benevolent purposes, but which—according to legend—turned violent and destructive. Indeed, recent sociological studies of science and technology have compared contemporary science and technology to a Golem, where unexpected consequences have led to both malevolent and benevolent results.[51]

The potential dangers of twenty-first century biotechnology eclipse those of the twentieth century. For example, the biological and chemical weapons used in World War I seem as primitive to us today as the other weapons used in that war. Virulent biotech weapons now threaten large civilian populations, especially those in the hands of "rogue states" and terrorist organizations. A strain of a bioengineered bacteria or virus could decimate a major city, or even an entire continent. It is therefore in the American national interest to increase vigilance and defense spending against a bioterrorist attack.[52]

Bioengineering need not degenerate into social or political engineering, but it can, as history has all too tragically shown us. Some scientists are already predicting a future with two distinct biological classes that one scientist calls "the naturals" and the "Genrich."[53] The chilling moral, legal, and social realities of such a future are poignantly portrayed in the 1997 film *Gattaca*, which takes its name from the abbreviations of the four base proteins in the human genome: GATC.

In conclusion, bioengineering holds forth the promise of preserving and extending human life and health in ways that even science fiction has not yet imagined. Yet, developments in bioengineering also pose a variety of dangers to life itself. Biotechnology both threatens and challenges our conceptions of human identity, human freedom, and human dignity. The task of our religious traditions is to marshal and to apply the cumulative wisdom of the past to offer us guidance both through the garden and the jungle of contemporary biotechnology. In sum, the problems we confront may be accurately described by a Talmudic adage that reminds us that the bee has both honey and a sting. The Talmud asks us to consider this question: Should we forgo the benefits of the honey because of the danger of the sting?

NOTES

1. William Shakespeare, *A Winter's Tale*, Act IV, Scene 4.
2. A sheep-goat chimera dubbed a "geep" was first created in 1984.

3. See, for example, Jeremy Rifkin, *The Biotech Century* (New York: Putnam, 1988).

4. Quoted in Rifkin, 154.

5. On the nature of Jewish ethics as a form of theological ethics and for a method of "doing" Jewish ethics, see, for example, Byron L. Sherwin, *Jewish Ethics for the Twenty-First Century* (Syracuse, NY: Syracuse University Press, 2000), 1–12.

6. Already in 1977, Professor Seymour Siegel of The Jewish Theological Seminary advocated the cause of bioengineering. See his "Genetic Engineering," *Proceedings of the Rabbinical Assembly* 40 (1978):164–67. Physician and bioethicist Fred Rosner has also been an advocate. See, for example, Fred Rosner, "The Case for Genetic Engineering," *Torah u-Maddah Journal* 9 (2000): 211–15. This issue of this Orthodox Jewish journal contains a number of articles on cloning and other forms of bioengineering. None of the scholars writing there considers any form of genetic engineering to be a violation of the biblical prohibition of *kilayim* or mixing species.

7. *Shabbat* 10b. According to Soloveitchik, the divine image implanted in human beings is not a gratuitous gift but a challenge to be met. See Joseph B. Soloveitchik, *Halakhic Man* (Philadelphia: Jewish Publication Society, 1983), 101.

8. Judah Loew, *Tiferet Yisrael* (New York: Judaica Press, 1969), chap. 69, 216.

9. Babylonian Talmud, *Sanhedrin* 65b.

10. See, for example, Gershom Scholem, "The Idea of the Golem," in *Kabbalah and Its Symbolism* (New York: Schocken, 1965), and Moshe Idel, *Golem* (Albany: State University of New York Press, 1990).

11. Menahem Meiri, *Beit ha-Behirah-Sanhedrin* (Jerusalem: Tehiya, 1965), 248.

12. Moses Nachmanides, *Peirush al ha-Torah* (Jerusalem: Mosad ha-Rav Kook, 1959), 28, on Genesis 1:28.

13. Judah Loew, *Be'er ha-Golah* (New York: Judaica Press, 1969), chap. 2, 38.

14. Babylonian Talmud, *Pesahim* 54a.

15. A vocal opponent of most forms of bioengineering and genetic therapies who bases his views on a secular version of natural law theory, is the eminent bioethicist Leon Kass. See his *Toward a More Natural Science* (New York: Free Press, 1985). Kass even opposes unduly lengthening life, speaking about a normal or "proper" life span for humans, 305–17.

16. Quoted in Max Weinreich, *Hitler's Professors* (New York: YIVO, 1946), 30. For further information on the view that "the unfit is doomed to extinction," see 27–36.

17. Solomon ibn Adret, *Sheilot u-Teshuvot* (Pietrikov: Belkhatavsky, 1883), no. 364. See also Israel Lifshutz of Danzig, *Tiferet Yisrael* on "*Yadayim*," 4:3.

18. Cited in Lori Andrews, *The Clone Age* (New York: Henry Holt, 1999), 221.

19. See, for example, Babylonian Talmud, *Bava Kama* 85a; Maimonides, *Peirush al-ha-Mishnah, Nedarim* 4:4, and sources noted in Sherwin, 24–29.

20. See, for example, Deuteronomy 4:9 as interpreted by Talmudic and medieval commentaries. Note the discussion and sources cited in Sherwin, 29–34.

21. See, for example, Jennifer Couzin, "Quandaries in the Genes," *US News & World Report* (November 1, 1999): 64–66. See also, Lori Andrews, *Future Perfect* (New York: Columbia University Press, 2001).

22. Andrews, *Future Perfect*, 43.

23. On discrimination against the disabled based on genetic screening, see, for example, Erik Parens and Adrienne Asch, "The Disabilities Rights Critique of

Prenatal Genetic Screening," *Hastings Center Report* 29, 5 (September/October 1999): S1–S22.

24. See, for example, Joseph Kupfer, "The Ethics of Genetic Screening in the Workplace," *Business Ethics Quarterly* 3, 1 (January 1993): 17–26.

25. Lori Andrews and Dorothy Nelkin, *Body Bazaar* (New York: Crown, 2001), 101.

26. See, for example, Matt Ridley, *Genome* (New York: HarperCollins, 1999), 191: "Jewish people retained their genetic integrity. . . . As a result the Ashkenazim in particular are a favourite people for genetic studies."

27. Andrews, *The Clone Age*, 161.

28. See Andrews and Nelkin, 54.

29. Cited in Andrews, *The Clone Age*, 186. For further discussion of why human genes should not be patented, see Kass, 128–53.

30. See Sara Hull and Kiran Prasad, "Direct-to-Consumer Advertising of Genetic Testing," *Hastings Center Report* 31, 3 (May/June 2001): 33–35.

31. There is precedent in Jewish law for using new experimental techniques that may be life threatening to address non–life threatening conditions. When surgery to remove kidney stones was new and considered to be life threatening, a Halakhic authority permitted the surgery even though having kidney stones was not a life-threatening or terminal condition. See sources noted in Sherwin, 57.

32. Fred Rosner, "Judaism, Genetic Screening and Genetic Therapy," *Mt. Sinai Journal of Medicine* 65, 5, 6 (October/November 1998): 411.

33. See Andrews, *The Clone Age*, 154.

34. On stem cell research, therapies, and related public policy issues, see, for example, Sharon Begley, "Cellular Divide," *Newsweek* (July 9, 2001): 22–27.

35. On the whole issue of the status and disposition of "preembryos" and embryos in Jewish law, see, for example, Yitzchak Breitowitz, "A Halachic Approach to the Resolution of Disputes Concerning the Disposition of Preembryos," in *Jewish Law and The New Reproductive Technologies*, ed. Emmanuel Feldman and Joel B. Wolowelsky (Hoboken, NJ: KTAV, 1997), 155–86.

36. See, for example, the failure of the use of stem cells in treating Parkinson's disease as reported by Arthur Caplan, "Fetal Cell Implants: What We Learned," *Hastings Center Report* 31, 3 (May/June 2001): 6.

37. On cloning in Jewish law and ethics, see Sherwin, 110–26, and sources noted there. Also see the informative study by Michael J. Broyde, "Cloning People and Jewish Law," *Journal of Halacha and Contemporary Society* 24 (1997): 27–65. On cloning from a variety of perspectives, see, for example, Gregory E. Pence, ed., *Flesh of My Flesh: The Ethics of Cloning Human Beings* (Lanham, MD: Rowman and Littlefield, 1998). A leading Reform Jewish bioethicist, Rabbi Richard Address has opposed human cloning. He said, "Cloning is an area where we cannot go. It violates the mystery of what it means to be human." This sounds very much like something a Catholic bioethicist might say. Address was quoted in Herbert Wray, "The World After Cloning," *U.S. News & World Report* (March 10, 1997).

38. See, for example, Gina Kolata, "Researchers Find Big Risk of Defect in Cloning Animals," *New York Times* (March 25, 2001): sec. 1, 1, 12. Also see Kolata's book, *Clone* (New York: William Morrow, 1998).

39. For example, a Time/CNN poll taken in February 2001 reported that "90 percent of the respondents thought it was a bad idea to clone human beings." Nancy Gibbs, "Baby, It's You! And You, and You," *Time* (February 19, 2001): 50.

40. Quoted in Lee Silver, *Remaking Eden* (New York: Avon, 1997), 75.

41. George Hudock, "Gene Therapy and Genetic Engineering," *Indiana Law Journal* 48 (Summer 1973): 533–58.

42. See discussion and sources in Sherwin, 62–63.

43. Michio Kaku, *Visions* (New York: Anchor Books, 1997), 254.

44. On some of the moral and legal implications of "behavioral genetics," see, for example, Andrews and Nelkin, 93–96.

45. Quoted in Nicholas Wade, "The Other Secrets of the Genome," *New York Times* (February 18, 2001): sec. 4, 3.

46. On moral volition as being essential to Judaism, see Maimonides, *Mishneh Torah, Hilkhot Teshuvah,* chap. 5, paras. 3, 4. On moral predispositions see *Mishneh Torah, Hilkhot De'ot.*

47. See the citations of Crick and the comparison to Nazi eugenic policies in Ben Zion Bokser, "Problems in Bio-Medical Ethics," *Judaism* 24 (Spring 1975): 140.

48. On eugenics in early twentieth-century America and its influence on Nazi eugenics, see, for example, Rifkin, 117–27.

49. Quoted in Andrews and Nelkin, 8.

50. On the patenting of human genes, see the thoughtful analysis in Gregory Pence, *Re-Creating Medicine* (Lanham, MD: Rowman and Littlefield, 2000), 137–61. On the strange case in California of the patenting of a person's body tissue without his permission, see the case of John Moore discussed by Andrews, *The Clone Age,* 191–94.

51. See Harry Collins and Trevor Pinch, *The Golem: What You Should Know About Science* (New York: Cambridge University Press, 1993), and their *The Golem At Large: What You Should Know About Technology* (Cambridge: Cambridge University Press, 1998).

52. See, for example, Jeremy Manier, "Genetics May Prove Fast Test for Biological Attack," *Chicago Tribune* (February 18, 2001): sec. 1, 8. See also the 2001 made-for-television movie, *World War III.*

53. See Silver, 4–7.

CHAPTER 10

Jewish Family Values

Joshua E. London

The "family values" debate is one area of political life in which the traditional Jewish sources have much to contribute. To speak of "family values" in Judaism is to speak to the heart of Jewish society and the foundation of Jewish life. Indeed, there is a direct correlation between the physical and spiritual well-being of the Jewish family and the spiritual and physical well-being of the Jewish community. Only when the home is strong, stable, and healthy will the other institutions and aspects of Jewish life—religious, educational, social, political, et cetera—have the ability to continue and thrive. Concomitantly, when the Jewish family weakens—emotionally, morally, or spiritually—the Jewish community becomes enfeebled.

Although the "Culture Wars" seem to have dropped out of much of the public debate, the smaller cultural battles continue robustly. The popular culture still sneers at normative family life and the values that maintain it. Our legal institutions often treat marriage as very little more than a lifestyle choice, and divorce and abortion advance apace, without any signs of moral stigma or sober restraint. Any attempt to reintroduce traditional morality or its language into the debate is considered untoward, even insulting, by the cultural and media elite. Thus, the family suffers.

More depressing, however, is the rising proportion of women who bear and raise children out of wedlock—devastating the social and cultural institution of the *family* and, by extension, society as a whole. At one time, as social scientist James Q. Wilson recently pointed out, this phenomenon was thought to exist only within the African-American community. Now, however, it affects all Americans, so much so that the rate of broken-home births in the white community is now as high as it was in the black community in the mid-1960s. At present, the rate for whites is one-fifth; for blacks it is over one-half.[1] Most reputable studies indicate that children of broken homes are more likely to demonstrate behavioral problems in school, become socially delinquent, have emotional problems, take drugs, and suffer from abuse than are children born to and raised in two-parent families. While it is difficult to pinpoint scientifically exactly which factors cause or most contribute to these social problems, it is easy to recognize why broken homes might handicap a child's socialization.[2]

The family, most people would agree, is the institution through which children learn the most basic moral and ethical values. Yet, these values have become less secure; this is partly because the strength of the family as an institution has been lessened and partly because the other primary sources of cultural influence—movies, television, music, video games, et cetera—have grown stronger. There are various factors behind the weakening of the family, one of which is the "no-fault divorce" sort of legal mindset, which makes marriage an easy thing to exit and treats the institution as little more than a lifestyle preference. Another factor is that huge numbers of children are being raised in one-parent families and often the single parent is a teenager living in poverty. Further, parents are spending increasingly less time with their children, are providing increasingly poorer discipline for them, and often reinforce or reward bad behavior. However, the most pervasive problem to beset the family is the moral relativism of our culture—whether high, low, or pop—which serves to erode the best efforts of those parents who do still embrace traditional values of one sort or another.[3]

The course set for a child by its parents during infancy and adolescence is crucial to the child, and to the community that child is born into. At birth, the individual is pure, free of all sin. This is most succinctly put in the daily morning prayer (as taken from the Talmud): "O my God, the soul which you gave me is pure, you created it, you fashioned it, you breathed it into me."[4] It is only in the course of life that one can act against God's will and accumulate sins. In the Jewish tradition, however, a child's ability to act for himself, whether in accordance with or in defiance of God's will, does not begin until religious maturity.[5] Family life, consequently, is crucial to all moral and spiritual development, both for the individual and the community.[6]

In the Jewish tradition, the family is established and constituted only through heterosexual marriage between two Jews; no other domestic arrangement is recognized, and all other sexual relationships are strongly condemned.[7] Marriage is a universal ideal and marks the true beginning of every Jew's contribution to life and to the Jewish people. It is for this reason that the Hebrew term designated for marriage is *kiddushin*, or "sanctification."[8] The basis for this sanctified relationship is the creation of an atmosphere in which the precepts of God will be fulfilled and where children will be raised in an environment of religious faith. Virtually all aspects of Jewish religious practice are intimately bound to or hinge on family life. Thus, "family values" as such are crucial to the very fiber of Jewish existence.

MARRIAGE

In the traditional Jewish sources, the primary reason for marriage is, classically, procreation. As the Bible records, God instructed Adam to "Be fruitful and multiply and fill the earth" (Genesis 1:28). Indeed, the Talmud even relates the view that this verse should be understood to be the first commandment in the Torah.[9] Thus, Rabbi Yosef Caro, the author of the *Shulhan Arukh*, the authoritative code of Jewish law written in the sixteenth century, begins his legal volume on laws pertaining to family life with the explicit declaration, "Every man is required to marry a wife in order to procreate."[10] Maimonides (hereafter, the Rambam), in the twelfth century, instructed that a man becomes obligated in this commandment at age seventeen and stipulated that, "If he reaches twenty and has not married, he is considered to have transgressed and negated this positive commandment."[11] Although this particular approach has long since been abandoned,[12] the *Shulhan Arukh* states that the Jewish court of each community ought to compel a Jewish male to marry by the age of twenty, unless he is devoting his time to the study of Torah.[13]

Despite the fact that procreation is stressed in the legal literature, marriage is considered to have legitimacy, significance, and sanctity apart from procreation.[14] Before God commanded Adam to be fruitful and multiply, He first created Eve, saying, "It is not good for man to be alone. I will make a help-mate for him" (Genesis 2:18). Thus, companionship is presented as the first and primary purpose of marriage. So, the love and goodwill needed to make this relationship succeed should be predicated on the bond between husband and wife independent of the obligation to have and raise children. The Talmud offers substantial ground to this emotional basis for marriage, and the rabbinic literature contains many stories that celebrate the love between husband and wife (the famous story of Rabbi Akiva's wife, who waited for him while he went off to study, can be understood in this light).[15] Thus, we find that Rabbi Moshe Isserles, writing in sixteenth-century Poland, records in his commentary to the *Shulhan Arukh* that, "for several generations" rabbinic courts had not protested when a man married a woman who was incapable of bearing children "because he desired her. . . ."[16]

Throughout the Talmud, the virtues of marriage are celebrated; the following example is typical:

R. Tanchum stated in the name of R. Chanilai: Any man who has no wife lives without joy, without blessing, without goodness. *Without Joy,* for it is written, "And rejoice—you and your household" (Deuteronomy 14:26). *Without blessing,* for it is written, "To cause a blessing to rest on your house" (Ezekiel 44:30). *Without Goodness,* for it is written, "It is not good that man should be alone" (Genesis 2:18).

In the west [i.e., in Palestine] it was stated [of an unmarried man]: That he lives without Torah and without a protecting wall. *Without Torah,* for it is written "Is it that my own help [i.e., a wife] is not with me, and that sound wisdom [i.e., Torah] is driven quite from me?" (Job 6:13). *Without a protecting wall,* for it is written, "A woman shall encompass a man" (Jeremiah 31:22).

Raba b. Ulla said [of an unmarried man]: That he is without peace, for it is written, "And you will know that your tent [i.e., wife] is at peace, and you will visit your home and find nothing amiss" (Job 5:24).

. . . Eleazar said: Any man who has no wife is no proper man; for it is said, "Male and female created He them and called their name Adam" (Genesis 5:2).[17]

Indeed, the union of marriage as an independently worthwhile and necessary relationship is treated at great length. As the Talmud relates, "God waits impatiently for man to marry,"[18] "One who does not marry is in constant sin and God forsakes him,"[19] et cetera. Marriage is considered absolutely vital to the human condition, and no man is considered whole without a wife: "No man without a wife, neither a woman without a husband, nor both of them without God."[20]

No more powerful testimony to the significance of marital love and faithfulness in Judaism is required than the fact that the prophets of Israel use the love of husband and wife as a metaphor for the relationship between God and Israel. Best known is the exquisite description in Hosea: "And I will betroth you unto Me forever; Yes, I will betroth you unto Me in righteousness and in justice, and in loving-kindness and in compassion. And I will betroth you unto Me in faithfulness. And you shall know the Lord" (Hosea 21:22).

Or consider the Song of Songs, a song of uncommon passion for the biblical canon. Rabbi Akiva, one of the greatest sages of the Talmud, said, ". . . . All the songs of Scripture are holy, but the Song of Songs is the Holy of Holies."[21] The major sections of the Song deal with courtship (1:2–3:5), a wedding (3:6–5:1), and maturation in marriage (5:2–8:4). The Song concludes with a climactic statement about the nature of love (8:5–7) and an epilogue explaining how the love of the couple in the Song began (8:8–14). The rabbinic sources interpret Song of Songs as an allegory; the love between a man and his wife in Song of Songs is thus viewed as symbolic of the covenant of God and Israel.[22] The Midrash goes further in creating an expansive text that understands Song of Songs as a complete record of Israel's sacred history in biblical times: the Exodus from Egypt, the crossing of the Red Sea, the revelation at Mt. Sinai, the entrance into Canaan, the subjugation to the kingdoms, and the coming redemption by reason of Israel's faithfulness to the covenant.[23] The use of the model of a man and a woman to explain the love between God and the Jewish people demonstrates the high regard that the traditional sources have for love and sexuality in the male-female relationship.[24]

Of course, the traditional sources are more practical than poetical, so this emphasis on love and companionship should also be understood to encompass the realities of the couple's physical and emotional needs. The Jew is forbidden from denying his wife the satisfaction of her sexual wants, apart from any consideration of procreation: "Her food, her clothing and her conjugal rights, shall he not withhold" (Exodus 21:10).[25] As the Talmud instructs, "It is a man's obligation to make his wife happy."[26] Indeed, the Jewish notion of marital sex is, strictly, that of conjugal rights or *onah* in Hebrew; marital intimacy is not for the husband's sake, but rather for the wife's:

Rabbi Judah said: "He should [endeavor] to make her happy at the time when he is engaged in fulfilling the commandment [of marital intercourse] as it is stated: 'He who obeys the commandment will know no evil'" (Ecclesiastes 8:5).[27]

The word *onah* also means "respond." A man should be responding to his wife's desires and satisfying her wishes for closeness.

The Rambam codifies this obligation more fully:

A wife has the right to prevent her husband from making business trips except to close places, so that he will not be prevented from fulfilling his conjugal duties. He may make such journeys only with her permission.

Similarly, she has the prerogative of preventing him from changing from a profession that grants her more frequent conjugal rights to one that grants her less frequent rights. . . . [i.e., switching from a profession that is less physically demanding to one that is more so].[28]

FAMILY PURITY

The Jewish laws governing the conjugal relationship are generally referred to as *taharat ha'mishpachah* or "family purity," though this description captures more the theme than the substance of the laws involved. The major responsibility for keeping these laws rests on the woman. Yet, the process involved in keeping these laws of family purity serve to enhance and uplift the entire family, husband and child alike. As the Talmud relates, ". . . blessing is found in a man's home only by virtue of one's wife."[29]

The laws, in brief, proscribe conjugal relations for not less than five days from the onset of menstruation, and, following the cessation of the menstrual flow, for another seven consecutive days when no menstrual presence is detected. Following that, the wife immerses in a specially constructed and filled pool of water called a *mikveh*. After immersion, conjugal relations are resumed.

The husband is required to be intimately involved in the obligations of his wife, for the spiritual core and purity of the family depends on following such guidelines and fulfilling such requirements. Emotional support, encouragement, understanding, and appreciation of her dedication are just some of the ways he is required to demonstrate to his wife that she is not alone. By doing this, the husband confirms that the rules and their benefits are for the family and, by extension, the spiritual well-being of the community.

The translation of the Hebrew word *tahara* as "purity" is actually inexact in a misleading way.[30] A woman in a menstrual state is not impure; she is *tameah*. There is no exact English word to convey what *tamei* (the masculine form of *tameah*) means. *Tameh* is a condition that arises from the loss of potential life, as in the case of menstruation, or from being in the immediate proximity of death.[31] Suffice it to say that, when one is *tamei*, one is in limbo, not yet ready to assume or resume certain social and interactive relationships. This is a contemplative state, when one focuses on the inner causes and implications of the *tamei* condition. This is why the person who is *tamei* separates himself or, in this case, herself from social intimacy. Thus, the technical term for a woman in this state is *niddah*, which literally means, "to be separated."

Immersion in a *mikveh* at the culmination of the *tamei* condition signifies reentry into human interaction, presumably energized by the contemplation that took place during the period of separation. This ready eagerness to resume spiritually creative social intimacy is called *tahora*.

The purpose for this biblically mandated separation during the menstrual period and the week following is clearly enunciated in the Talmud. It is to re-create the excitement and thrill of the wedding night for the husband and wife.

It was taught: R. Meir used to say, Why did the Torah ordain that the *tameah* of menstruation should continue for seven days? Because being in constant contact with his wife [a husband might] develop a loathing towards her. The Torah, therefore, ordained: Let her be *tameah* for seven days in order that she shall be beloved by her husband as at the time of her first entry into the bridal chamber.[32]

The law actually effects a renewal, a monthly emotional reunion. This helps prevent the relationship from falling into a dull routine.[33] The separation also teaches the couple that while sex is a special part of marriage, it is not the only part; they are put in a situation that requires them to develop other modes of emotional communication and recognize other means of spiritual connection.

According to the Talmud, the separation during the menstrual period is an affirmation, not a denial, of the marital bond. Neither spouse is taken for granted sexually; both learn to appreciate each other as they spend almost half of each month refraining from physical relations. The purpose of the enforced separation is to enhance togetherness. The purpose of the menstrual laws is to enable a more intense intimacy.

Indeed, the community is deemed to be much better off with happy and healthy families. This is so much the case that building a *mikveh* is a communal obligation—one that takes precedence over building a synagogue or writing a Torah scroll for a community. Indeed, both a synagogue and a Torah scroll may be sold to raise funds for the building of a *mikveh*.[34]

In fact, in the eyes of Jewish law, a group of Jewish families living together do not attain the status of a community if they do not have a communal *mikveh*.[35] The reason for this is simple and straightforward: private and communal prayer and assembly can be held in virtually any location, but Jewish married life—and therefore the birth of future generations in accordance with Halakhah—is possible only where there is accessibility to a *mikveh*.

MARRIAGE AS A SOCIAL GOOD

Note the seriousness and the sanctity with which marriage and marital obligations are taken in the traditional sources.[36] Marriage is not treated as merely a lifestyle choice but, rather, marriage is a social and public institution that is central to Judaism in both theory and practice. It is backed by God and given specific and enforceable delimitation. More significantly, because the strength of the Jewish community rests in the strength of marriage as an institution, marriage is recognized and actively encouraged as a social good, and is also subject to communal protection.

The community not only has an interest in supporting and protecting marriage as an institution, and families generally, but is also obligated to do so in a variety of concrete ways that requires social action. It is for this reason that the rabbis allowed, endorsed, and encouraged all sorts of community interference in the inception of the marital union. Sometimes, as mentioned before, they went so far as to force men to marry before they reached the age of twenty.[37] This is also why the rabbis retained the authority to refuse or annul marriages deemed unacceptable, for example, forbidden relationships or unions that did not have proper social sanction, and to actively punish and condemn illicit relationships.

So, for example, the Talmud discusses the case of a man who "snatched" a woman who was already betrothed to another man and compelled her to marry him. The rabbis responded by annulling her marriage with the man.[38] Similarly, in a case from eighteenth-century Germany, a young man was married in secret to the family servant girl—she was said to have "seduced" the son. Again, the Jewish court annulled the marriage.[39] The Talmud even specifies at length the punishments for unceremonious forms of betrothal and other related unorthodox practices.[40]

Often, such communal involvement took the form of positive encouragement and subsidy. Consider, for example, the practice of Jewish communal institutions taking on the responsibility of providing *Hakhnasat Kallah* or dowries for poor brides. For many Jewish communities in the Diaspora, this *kupah,* or fund, was an important component of their welfare system.[41] This is also the context for the communal obligation to build and maintain a *mikveh.*

More expansively, and more substantively, it was concern for the preservation of marriage and to facilitate a woman's right to remarry, that led to the famous tenth-century edict of Rabbenu Gershom of Mayence (960–1028) that ended the practice of polygamy. Rabbenu Gershom's edict also established that any man who divorced his wife without her consent—that is, he did not give her a bill of divorce, freeing her to remarry—was subject to excommunication.[42]

Another example of the breadth of communal authority in marriage is the following ruling, issued in the sixteenth and seventeenth centuries by the Council of Lithuania:

Anyone who deliberately and brazenly violates the customs of Israel by marrying . . . without a minyan and a chupah shall, together with the witnesses who assisted . . . in this foul deed, be excommunicated and ostracized in this world and in the world to come. Their sin shall not be forgiven and the court shall punish them severely by hanging them from a post and administering forty lashes without any possibility of ransom [bail]. They shall be punished . . . as a means of preventing the promiscuity of the generation.[43]

It was also a common practice for Jewish communities to specify the age until which a young man required parental consent to get married. Consider, for example, the following stipulation from the Council of the Four Lands (the governing body of the Polish Jews from the sixteenth to the eighteenth centuries):

. . . young men who have not reached the age of twenty and who contract to marry a woman without the knowledge or consent of their relatives and parents shall have their engagement contracts declared void. . . .[44]

DIVORCE

Although marriage is a sacred, universal norm in Jewish life, is considered a social good, and is an institution the community is obligated to promote and protect, the tradition recognizes that there are times when marriages fail. As the contemporary author and educator Rabbi Hayim Donin (died 1982) eloquently put it:

Where, despite every effort to preserve the peace of the home and the harmony of the husband-wife relationship, bitterness, continuous strife, and the flames of dissension nevertheless prevail, it is better that the couple should be parted and not continue to live together. In such instances, the Torah provides for the bonds of marriage to be dissolved by a divorce.[45]

Although it is not encouraged, divorce is regarded as a legitimate solution to marital disharmony, and is justified for a wide variety of reasons, including basic incompatibility. Indeed, the Torah gives an explicit procedure for divorce;[46] just as marriage can be instituted only within the community of the faithful, so, too, divorce can be executed only through the Jewish communal authority. Even though divorce is sanctioned, there is an element of human tragedy inherent in any dissolution of marriage. This is especially true when there are children in the family. This is poignantly expressed by the Talmudic adage that whenever couples get divorced, "even the Altar sheds tears."[47]

In principle, only the husband can initiate a divorce; in practice, however, the rabbis established certain criteria that allow the wife to ask the Jewish court to compel her husband to divorce her.[48] The divorce itself must be supervised by a Jewish court and must be attested to by two Jewish witnesses. The husband hires a scribe to write a *get*, a Jewish bill of divorce; the *get* serves as public documentation that the marriage has been dissolved. As a procedural matter, the husband must give his wife this *get*, and she must receive it. It is a simple ceremonial procedure that generally takes less than two hours to complete.

As a practical matter, however, the rabbis went to great lengths to guard against hasty divorces. Rabbenu Gershom's tenth-century edict prohibiting divorce without a wife's consent, for example, also functioned as an enabling device that the wife might use to force better terms in the divorce. Thus, divorce became, in practice, a mutual affair—there are a few explicitly stated exceptions, such as adultery.

The *ketubah*, the marriage contract, itself served as a substantial deterrent to easy divorce. The *ketubah* guarantees the wife a sum of money—provided she was divorced without cause—and so acts as a form of alimony or divorce insurance enforceable through the Jewish court. Since most men could not afford to pay the *ketubah* and most women could not afford to live without it if divorced, the marriage had to reach real crises before divorce was even conceivable.

Another practice to guard against hasty divorces was for the court to set aside the *ketubah* should they deem it inadequate, and award the wife *mezonot* or "sustenance" payments. Further, if the wife brought property into the marriage, whether through dowry or through her own business dealings, she had the right to retrieve it in the divorce settlement—though this excluded any profits or the interest the husband might have earned from the property.

The Jewish tradition is very specific with regard to child custody, and in this context children have rights with respect to their parents, but parents have only obligations with respect to their children.[49] Children's interests are held paramount in such proceedings, so unless circumstances warranted changing the general rule, each child would be placed in the custody of the parent most naturally suited to provide moral and cultural socialization into the Jewish faith given the respective age and gender of the child. Until the age of six, all children remain with the mother, and after six, the boys go with the father and the girls go with the mother. However, even if the father does not have custody over his children, he is obligated to continue to support them. The court may force him to do so.

CHILDREN

In the Jewish tradition, there is no greater or more important role in life than raising a child to responsible adulthood.[50] Bringing children into this world entails some fundamental parental obligations: to feed and care for them, to love and protect them, and to educate them for religious life in the real world.[51] These obligations apply regardless of whether the parents have custody of their children.

The father is obliged to support his children until they are deemed religiously, and legally, mature (thirteen for a boy, twelve for a girl).[52] The Talmud succinctly states that the father is also "obligated to circumcise his son, to redeem him [if he is the firstborn of his mother], to teach him Torah, to find him a wife and to teach him a trade. Some say that he must also teach him to swim."[53] The mother is required to support her children if the father is too poor, and she is obliged to nourish her children and to raise both son and daughter until age six, and only her daughter after age six—unless the father cannot provide for the boy's instruction and guidance.

The father's obligations to both circumcise his son[54] and to redeem his son (if the son is the firstborn of his mother)[55] are religious requirements that bring the son into the faith and into the community. Circumcision introduces the child into the covenant with God, and the redemption of the firstborn—whereby the father frees the firstborn son from consecration into service of the priestly class—introduces the child into his family's domain. The obligation to find a wife for one's son was meant to be taken literally in the original context in that parents at the time arranged their children's marriages; however, today this is understood as the obligation merely to enable a relationship.

The duty to educate, or provide for the education of, one's children is crucial to the development of the child and to the continuity and cohesion of the community.[56] This entails providing both a religious and a secular education. The Hebrew term for this formal schooling, *chinuch*, literally means "consecration" and refers to training a child for living, not only for a livelihood. The primary obligation, however, is to provide religious instruction. As the *Shulhan Arukh* states:

There is an obligation upon each person to teach his son Jewish law. . . . When does one begin to teach a child? When he begins to speak one teaches him that God commanded Moses on the Mount with the Torah and the principle of the unity of God. Afterwards one teaches him a little bit until he is six or seven at which point one sends him to elementary school.[57]

Indeed, this duty to educate children is considered so crucial that the rabbis established it as a communal obligation. Every Jewish community must provide an elementary school for religious instruction, and one that fails to do so is shunned until the school is built. For, as the Talmud says, "the world only exists out of the merit of the discourse found when small children study."[58] In fact, the rabbis took particular care in this mandate, even going so far as to address issues of classroom management: twenty-five children per teacher; if there are more than twenty-five children but less than forty, a teacher's aide is required; when there are more than forty students, a second teacher must be provided.[59] They even explicitly endorsed competition in the provision of education:

One landowner in a courtyard who wants to establish a school in his residence cannot be stopped [through zoning ordinances] from doing so. So too, when one teacher opens a school next to another school, so as to encourage the students to go to this institution [and not the first one], one cannot stop this conduct.[60]

Furthermore, the religious education that the parent is obligated to provide has two components. The first is to raise the child with an understanding of the traditional values and moral imperatives of a just and virtuous life; the other is to provide the child with a formal education in the technical aspects of Jewish law and observances, in preparation for his or her becoming a functioning adult on becoming a Bar or Bat Mitzvah.[61] The primary aims of this approach are to instill the moral and ethical values of the Jewish heritage; encourage active observance of the Torah's commandments; transmit knowledge of the Torah, the Talmud, and the primary Jewish sources; and cultivate a strong sense of identification with and concern for all Jewish people. Through this approach, the child is thought to be well prepared for moral and legal independence.

As the ultimate goal is to provide the child with the "survival skills" needed for everyday life, the Talmud makes a point of saying that parents are obligated to teach their children to swim (this was deemed necessary for survival).[62] The Talmud's phrase, "to swim," is generally understood, however, as an idiom directing parents to instruct their children in the material skills needed for their survival. The tradition recognizes, of course, that moral and legal independence do not go very far if the child cannot achieve financial independence, and so it obligates the father to teach his children a profession. The Talmud recounts:

Rabbi Judah states: "Anyone who does not teach his children a profession, it is as if he has taught them robbery."[63]

The Talmudic commentator Rabbi Joshua Boaz (Spain and Italy, ca. 1470–1557) notes that a parent does not fulfill this obligation merely by providing a child with an ongoing source of income, such as a trust fund, or even with an income-producing business that the child does not run but derives an income from. Rather, the law mandates that the child be taught a profession or some skill-set through which the child might *work* for a living.[64] Thus, a parent is obligated to provide the child with the skills that prepare the child for a righteous and upstanding life. Providing only a secular education, however, is considered incomplete fulfillment of the father's obligation. The religious education is paramount and takes precedence.

The obligations of children toward their parents find expression in the Decalogue, as the fifth commandment states, "Honor your father and your mother."[65] As a practical matter, the rabbinic tradition understands this to require obedience, reverence, and material support—which is generally understood to mean personal service, not financial contribution.[66]

The general principle underlying all these obligations between parents and children is that parents support their children when the children are young and the children support their parents when the parents become old. Families are always meant to support themselves—even across generations—as well as they can before considering charity or public assistance. Although the first impulse is self-sufficiency within families, communal involvement is an established resource in Jewish familial affairs.[67]

CONCLUSIONS AND PUBLIC POLICY DIRECTIONS

The Jewish tradition is unequivocally pro–family and the traditional values that anchor and maintain family life. The communal public policy that emerges from the traditional sources is designed primarily around support and preservation of family life, the purpose being to promote a stable, healthy, happy, morally good, and spiritually uplifted family and to establish a family-friendly community.

In terms of contemporary policy, it is the more conservative policy approaches to family, child welfare, divorce, and education that seem to be most similar to the ethos of the traditional Jewish sources. The notion that government should, for example, be engaged with the effects of marriage and marriage breakdown is not discordant with the Jewish tradition, particularly if that same government is already involved in spending money through welfare and other means to manage the fallout from the breakdown of the family. As with issues like abortion and homosexual marriage—both of which have been considered elsewhere in this volume—Jewish sources offer comparatively unequivocal guidance on many, if not most, family-related issues as compared to contemporary understandings and approaches.

Consider divorce. The Jewish tradition tries to guard against hasty divorce, yet strives to protect an individual's ability and position to dissolve an unbearable marriage. Indeed, the *ketubah* as a form of divorce insurance, the *mezonot* as a form of alimony, and the *hakhnasat kallah* as an inducement to marriage may have contemporary relevance to improve on the current trend of no-fault divorce, which leaves divorced women to fend for themselves and discourages long-term marriage commitments. Further, the Jewish child custody laws represent very clear child welfare–centered consequences to marriage dissolution. It both protects children and promotes marital commitment and fidelity—a clear improvement over the current system. The Jewish tradition is also very clear about the obligations of "deadbeat" or delinquent fathers: Unless the father is suffering privation, he is obligated to support his children—even if he has not been granted custody following the divorce.

Besides these measures guarding against easy divorce, the Jewish tradition takes great pains to protect the family and to maintain a family-friendly environment. Clearly then, in terms of contemporary public policy, the Jewish tradition would encourage policies that promote marriage stability. Louisiana, Arizona, and Arkansas have, for example, passed "covenant marriage" laws in which parties voluntarily agree before they get married to receive marriage education or counseling, and convene that, should it not work out, they will undergo an onerous divorce process and again receive counseling before the divorce can proceed; Oklahoma has spent $100 million in marriage promotion workshops and videos; Florida cut the marriage license fee in half for couples who have taken a marriage preparation course, et cetera. All such policy efforts would find tremendous support from Jewish sources, as would similar measures at the federal level. Support in the traditional sources for efforts to protect the heterosexual nature of the institution of marriage, as discussed elsewhere in this volume, is abundant and unequivocal.

In terms of education, the Jewish sources seem even more prescient. In the traditional sources, private and public education providers are allowed to compete with each other on an equal playing field because educating children is not just the primary goal, but the only goal—the sources give little support for the use of children's educational programs to protect jobs or engage in social engineering schemes. Indeed, the Jewish sources would never allow competition in educational provision to be discouraged through acts of legislation or other public policy measures. The Jewish tradition would not long tolerate failing schools, overcrowding, or poor teachers. Although the primary obligation to teach children rests with the parents rather than the public, the public is expected to provide education should the parents choose a public school over a private school.

There are two fundamental aspects of public morality: personal commitment and social expectation. Not only should people pledge themselves to the right and proper path in life, but others should also act as if they expect people to behave rightly and properly. The first component is mostly a matter of individual conscience, but the latter is a social obligation, and one that public policy by its very nature ought to be concerned with. All public policy expenditure directly or indirectly sends a message about what society expects of others. We subsidize that which we wish more of, and penalize that which we wish less of. In this respect, Judaism clearly supports the traditional morality side in the culture wars. The source literature is unabashedly promarriage, profamily, pro–traditional values, and it very clearly supports public policy approaches that promote right and proper, traditionally defined activity on the part of the citizenry—as fathers and mothers, as husbands and wives, and as individuals.

NOTES

1. James Q. Wilson, "Why We Don't Marry," *City Journal* 12, 1 (Winter 2002): 46.

2. Ibid., 46–55; see also James Q. Wilson, *The Marriage Problem: How Our Culture Has Weakened Families* (New York: HarperCollins, 2002), 1–22, 197–222.

3. James Q. Wilson, "The Family-Values Debate," *Commentary* 95, 4 (April 1993): 24–28.

4. Babylonian Talmud, *Berakhot* 60b.

5. A boy reaches his religious maturity and becomes a Bar Mitzvah when he reaches thirteen years of age (according to the Hebrew calendar), and a girl reaches her maturity and becomes a Bat Mitzvah at age twelve. These two Hebrew terms mean "subject to the commandments" and imply that a person is no longer treated

as a minor by Jewish law, and that the person has assumed full responsibility for the observance of all precepts and commandments.

6. Hayim Halevy Donin, *To Be A Jew: A Guide to Jewish Observance in Contemporary Life* (New York: Basic Books, 2001), 271.

7. See, for example, *Mishneh Torah, Hilkhot Ishut*.

8. The thirteenth-century Kabbalists considered God to have both male and female dimensions. When human beings marry and join sexually, they mystically unite these aspects of God and cause harmony in the universe. See Gershom Scholem, *Major Trends in Jewish Mysticism,* 3rd ed. (New York: Schocken Publishing House, 1961), 226–27.

9. See Babylonian Talmud, *Yevamot* 63b: "He who does not engage in propagation of the race is as though he sheds blood" and "as though he has diminished the Divine image."

10. *Shulhan Arukh, Even ha-Ezer* 1:1.

11. *Mishneh Torah, Hilkhot Ishut* 15:2.

12. See the Rema's commentary on *Even ha-Ezer* 1:3.

13. *Shulhan Arukh, Even ha-Ezer* 1:3.

14. See David Biale's "Classical Teachings and Historical Experience," in *The Jewish Family and Jewish Continuity,* ed. Steven Bayme and Gladys Rosen (Hoboken, NJ: KTAV, 1994), 136–39.

15. Babylonian Talmud, *Ketubot* 62b–63a. The Talmud recounts how Rabbi Akiva's wife sacrificed to enable him to learn Torah and how he honored and appreciated her. Rabbi Akiva, one of the greatest sages of the Talmud, grew up knowing no Torah. He was an uneducated shepherd. His employer's daughter recognized that he was modest and of superlative character. She said that if he would learn Torah she would marry him and he agreed. He married her and went away to yeshiva. Her wealthy father, infuriated that his daughter would marry the shepherd, disowned her. She lived in abject poverty and by herself for twelve years. When he returned, he had advanced to the point at which he had twelve thousand disciples. When he was arriving home, he heard an old man say to his wife, "How long will you live as a widow?" She replied, "I would have him learn another twelve years." Rabbi Akiva said, "This is her will," and he immediately about-faced and returned to yeshiva for another twelve years. When he returned home, he had twenty-four thousand disciples. When she heard that Rabbi Akiva was finally returning, she ran to meet him. Her clothes were those of a poor beggar and she fell on her face to kiss his feet. His students, thinking that this strange woman was publicly dishonoring their rabbi with immodest behavior, were about to push her aside. He told them to leave her alone and said to them, "All of my Torah and all of your Torah is hers!"

16. *Shulhan Arukh, Even ha-Ezer* 1:4.

17. Babylonian Talmud, *Yevamot* 62b–63a.

18. Babylonian Talmud, *Kiddushin* 29b.

19. Babylonian Talmud, *Kiddushin* 29b, see also Babylonian Talmud, *Pesahim* 113a.

20. *Genesis Rabbah* 8:9.

21. *Mishnah Yadayim* 3:5

22. See Rashi's commentary to Song of Songs 1:1.

23. *Midrash Rabbah, Shir HaShirim.*

24. See Rabbi Joseph Telushkin, *Jewish Wisdom: Ethical, Spiritual, and Historical Lessons from the Great Works and Thinkers* (New York: William Morrow and Company, 1994), 128–30.

25. See also *Mishneh Torah, Hilkhot Ishut* 14:7, also 12:1–6. Further, both *Sefer HaMitzvot* (Negative Commandment 262) and *Sefer HaChinuch* (Mitzvah 46) consider this to be one of the 613 mitzvot of the Torah.

26. Babylonian Talmud, *Kiddushin* 34b

27. Babylonian Talmud, *Kallah* 51a.

28. *Mishneh Torah, Hilkhot Ishut* 14:2. The Gemara in *Ketubot* 62b states that, even if the other profession is more profitable, the prerogative is granted to the woman, for a woman values intimacy with her husband more than financial advancement.

29. Babylonian Talmud, *Bava Metsia* 59a.

30. See *Shulhan Arukh, Yoreh De'ah* 201:3; Maimonides, *Mishneh Torah, Hilkhot Mikvaot* 4:12. See further, Norman Lamm, *A Hedge of Roses: Jewish Insights into Marriage and Married Life* (New York: Feldheim, 1966), 84–89. See also Aryeh Kaplan, *Waters of Eden: The Mystery of the Mikveh* (New York: National Conference of Synagogue Youth, Union of Orthodox Jewish Congregations of America, 1976), 45–46.

31. See Maimonides, *Mishneh Torah, Hilkhot Mikvaot* 11:12; also Rabbi Barukh Yashar, *Le'Bat Yisrael B'Gil Ha'Nisuin* (Jerusalem: Weinfeld Press, 1972), 9–10. See also the incisive piece by Norman Lamm, "Jewish Mothers" in *The Royal Reach: Discourses on the Jewish Tradition and the World Today* (New York: Feldheim, 1970), 291–302.

32. Babylonian Talmud, *Niddah* 31b. R. Meir is assertive and precise in his language in stating that the reason for the separation is to re-create the wedding night excitement. There is no need to mitigate the impact or lessen the significance of his words. See also Leo (Yehudah) Levi, *Man and Woman: The Torah Perspective* (Jerusalem: Ezer La'Yeled, 1979), 10.

33. See Lamm, *Hedge of Roses* (1966)55. Also, Jane Appleton and William Appleton, *How Not to Split Up* (New York: Berkeley Books, 1979), 13. One of the leading causes of marital boredom is clinging to rigid routine.

34. This is the ruling of the Chafetz Chayim in *Sefer Bet Yisrael*. See Rabbi Menahem Zaks, ed., *Kol Kitvey Chafetz Chayim Ha'Shalem* (New York: Friedman, 1952), 1:25–26.

35. Ibid.

36. Of particular value here is David Biale's "Classical Teachings and Historical Experience," in *The Jewish Family and Jewish Continuity*, ed. Steven Bayme and Gladys Rosen (Hoboken, NJ: KTAV, 1994), 133–71; see also Eliot Gertel's "Jewish Views on Divorce," in *The Jewish Family and Jewish Continuity*, ed. Steven Bayme and Gladys Rosen (Hoboken, NJ: KTAV, 1994), 201–30.

37. *Shulhan Arukh, Even ha-Ezer* 1:3.

38. Babylonian Talmud, *Yevamot* 110a.

39. See the responsa of Rabbi Yaakov Reisher of Prague (1710–1789), *Shvut Ya'akov* 2:112.

40. Babylonian Talmud, *Kiddushin* 12b.

41. See, for example, *Pinkas Medinat Lita*, no. 128.

42. See, for example, Louis M. Epstein, *Marriage Laws in the Bible and the Talmud* (Cambridge, MA: Harvard University Press, 1942), 25–33.

43. *Minute Book of the Council of Lithuania*, no.43.

44. *Pinkas Va'ad Arba ha-Aratzot*, no. 165.

45. Donin, *To Be A Jew*, 135.

46. Deuteronomy 24:1–4.

47. Babylonian Talmud, *Gittin* 90b.

48. These included lack of support, the husband's failure to meet his sexual obligations, and various occupations and medical conditions that would make it obnoxious for his wife to live with him.

49. For a good general discussion of child custody in Halakhah, see Rabbi Basil Herring's *Jewish Ethics and Halakhah For Our Time*, vol. 2 (New York: KTAV, 1989).

50. See Hayim Halevy Donin's *To Raise a Jewish Child: A Guide for Parents* (New York: Basic Books, 1977).

51. For a general survey, see Shoshana Matzner-Bekerman, *The Jewish Child: Halakhic Perspectives* (New York: KTAV, 1984); see also David J. Schnall, "Caring For the Incapacitated Parent: Filial Obligation in Classic Jewish Sources," in *Crisis and Continuity: The Jewish Family in the 21st Century*, ed. Norman Linzer, Irving N. Levitz, and David J. Schnall (Hoboken, NJ: KTAV, 1995), 165–83.

52. Babylonian Talmud, *Ketubot* 49b, 65b.

53. Babylonian Talmud, *Kiddushin* 29a.

54. Genesis 17:10–14.

55. Numbers 8:14–18; It was originally intended that the firstborn sons constitute the priesthood and be consecrated to the service of the Lord, since the first of everything belongs to God. After the sin of the Golden Calf, however, the priesthood was given to the tribe of Levi, so the firstborn son now has to be formally redeemed from that role.

56. Of particular interest and value here is Rabbi Michael J. Broyde's "The Duty to Educate in Jewish Law: A Right With A Purpose," in *Religious Human Rights in Global Perspective: Religious Perspectives*, ed. John Witte, Jr., and Johan D. van der Vyver (The Netherlands: Kluwer Law International, 1996), 323–35. Much of our discussion here follows Rabbi Broyde's general analysis.

57. *Shulhan Arukh, Yoreh De'ah* 245:1, 5.

58. Babylonian Talmud, *Shabbat* 119b; see also *Shulhan Arukh, Yoreh De'ah* 245:7.

59. *Shulhan Arukh, Yoreh De'ah* 245:15.

60. *Shulhan Arukh, Yoreh De'ah* 245:22.

61. See, for example, Rabbi Naphtali Tzvi Yehuda Berlin, *Meshech Chochma*, or Rabbenu Manoach, *Shevit Haessor* 2:10.

62. Babylonian Talmud, *Kiddushin* 29b.

63. Babylonian Talmud, *Kiddushin* 29a, 30b.

64. *Shiltai Gibborim*, commenting on *Kiddushin* 12a(1) (Rif pages); see also *Magen Avraham, Orah Hayyim* 156.

65. Exodus 20:12.

66. *Mekhilta, Yitro, Bahodesh* 8; for a general discussion, see Gerald Blidstein, *Honor Thy Father and Mother: Filial Responsibility in Jewish Law and Ethics* (New York: KTAV, 1975).

67. See Schnall, "Caring For the Incapacitated Parent," 165–83.

CHAPTER 11

Judaism, International Relations, and American Foreign Policy

Harvey Sicherman

The Muslims who struck the World Trade Center and the Pentagon on September 11, 2001, invoked religion to justify their suicidal assault. Their propaganda announced a war against "the Jews and the Crusaders"; this sounded like an attack on the Judeo-Christian heritage, the oft-invoked source of most American beliefs. Americans have therefore rallied not only to military action against the enemy, but also to a renewed affirmation of the American creed; not only the civic culture symbolized by the flag, but also the underlying religious convictions that make references to God second nature in American public life. In short, we would fight for both our physical security and our beliefs.

The war on terrorism, however, also raises crucial issues that involve both immediate military tactics and our longer-term objectives. Is our purpose to eliminate a particular type of violence—terrorism—or to work a more far-reaching change in the international order? Is it moral to wage a war that could lead to loss of civilian lives? Is it just to attack states like Iraq because they seek weapons of mass destruction? The debate over these issues has already engaged many religious leaders and political philosophers. Concepts such as the "just war" developed by various Christian theologians over a thousand years are being reexamined for their possible guidance through the thicket of events.[1]

There is no danger then that the Christian side of the Judeo-Christian heritage on international relations will be overlooked. The Jewish side, however, remains largely a closed book. Biblical (and sometimes Talmudic) texts provided a basis for many of the early propounders of international law. But there exists in addition a vast corpus of biblical,

Talmudic, medieval, and early modern discussion of international relations that is worth exploring for what it may teach us as we confront
current dilemmas.

This essay will examine a more than three-thousand-year-old religious
tradition for ideas and attitudes on international relations and state conduct that provide a background for contemporary debates. Given the vast-
ness and range of such sources and the argumentative, if not combative,
nature of rabbinical interpretation, no single work can be regarded as
either comprehensive or authoritative. What follows therefore is a tentative "sounding" of selective aspects of Judaism and international relations.
I conclude with some observations about American foreign policy in light
of this research.[2]

THE BIBLE AND JEWISH LAW ON
INTERNATIONAL RELATIONS

Judaism, as found in the Hebrew Bible and Jewish law (halacha), offers
at least two approaches to international relations, one concerning the here
and now, the other concerning a world yet to come.[3] The first may be
symbolized by the figure of the king, the second by the highly charged
idea of the Messiah. The Bible, although often written in a narrative style,
is not chiefly concerned with history but rather the relationship between
God and the Jewish people. It thus contains selections bearing on other
events but only as they relate to the main theme, and refers to other peoples and politics only in passing. The international system described in
these passages contains all the main features we would recognize today:
peoples identified with areas or states (Canaanites, Egyptians, Babylonians, Assyrians); a variety of political forms, ranging from city-state to
empire; war-making coalitions (e.g., the four kings versus the five in Genesis 14); alliances; treaties; covenants (commercial and political); boundaries; and sovereignty. The dominant form of rule is that of a monarch,
sometimes absolute (pharaoh), often limited (most kings of Judah and
Israel), especially by judicial code. Conflict is found in all of its forms:
limited and unlimited, wars commanded by God or waged for reasons of
state. War is conducted with a variety of weapons ranging from the simplest (the stone) to the super weapons of the day, whether they be giant
men (Goliath) or strange panic-inducing animals (the battle elephant). Biblical annals are also well populated by generals, diplomats, and spies—
some wellborn but disastrous (Moses' spies), others in the best traditions
of the silent service (Joshua's spies), and still others who seduce their
victims.

Alongside these descriptions of international politics stands another tradition: the transformation brought about by the redemption of Israel and
mankind, which relates the practice of international relations to morality.

Thus, the very origins of national differences are to be found in the re-bellion against God symbolized by the Tower of Babel and followed by the disunity of mankind, divided by language and interests. The sins of the Canaanites in worshiping idols caused their expulsion in favor of the Jews (Deuteronomy 18:9–13). The Jews later also suffer harm and even-tually exile for the sins of either idol worship or civil strife. The prophets foresee an era of redemption, the signs of which are Israel's repentance and return to God, the defeat of its oppressors, the revival of Jewish sov-ereignty in the Land of Israel, and the recognition of God's sovereignty by all nations. At that blessed time, "nation shall not lift up sword against nation, neither shall men learn war any more," and "swords will be beaten into plowshares" (Isaiah 2:4; Micah 4:3). Thus, moral rearmament will lead to military disarmament. This transformation is associated with the final redemption of the messianic era.

In short, the Bible describes two international systems, the one of brutal realism, the other of noble aspiration. As we shall see, it contains rules that govern the conduct of the Jewish ruler or state in the context of the world as it is. The prophets, however, foresee a radical reordering of this context. Disastrous experience—the loss of sovereignty and eventually the Land of Israel itself—led both the prophets and later Jewish commentators to closely link the revival of a Jewish state with the messianic era, a prob-lematic idea that still influences Jewish (and not only Jewish) political thought.

THE JEWISH STATE AND ITS INTERNATIONAL CONDUCT

International relations play a major role in Judaism because of the as-sociation of religion, people, and land. Judaism is organized around the covenant between God and the people of Israel, whereby Israel is "cho-sen" to be the bearer of divine guidance (the literal meaning of "Torah"), expressed in 613 commandments (*mitzvot*). In return for a faithful fulfilling of the *mitzvot*, the "kingdom of priests and holy people" (Numbers 19:6) are promised a secure and prosperous tenure in their territory.

As is clear from the Bible, the Jews were in great need of such divine protection. The land chosen for them was rich and vulnerable; it possessed considerable resources ("a land of milk and honey" in Deuteronomy 9:9) and was located on the best route for the armies of clashing empires work-ing their way north from Egypt, south from Anatolia, or west from Mes-opotamia. Moreover, the land was not empty when the Israelites arrived from Egypt. The local peoples worshiped a crowded pantheon of deities, patrons of places, dynasties, and forces of nature. In short, the union of God, people, and land plunged Israel into the maelstrom of international politics from the outset.

The Five Books of Moses, known to Judaism as the Torah, recognize a world of peoples, states, borders, and sovereignty. The Jews have a special right to the land of Canaan, but they are not the only nation with rights to territory. In Deuteronomy 2:3, as the Jews are about to enter the land, God warned them against taking any of the area belonging to the "descendants of Esau" because "I will not give to you from this land." A similar warning is issued for the land of Moab, given to the "descendants of Lot." The holdings of Esau, the son of Isaac, and Lot, nephew of Abraham, apparently fall under the covenant made between God and Abraham that promises a broad area—from the "River of Egypt to the Euphrates"—to the patriarch's descendants (Genesis 15:18).

Several implications can be drawn from this and other references scattered throughout the Bible. First, territory, sovereignty, and borders can be fixed or altered by agreement and are not determined only by geography, demography, or force. "In the world of the Hebrew Bible . . . artificial separations and boundaries integrate the distinct territorial entities into a single system of relations."[4] There are no "free" or "common areas," an argument John Selden was to use in the sixteenth century to oppose Hugo Grotius's proposition that the high seas were naturally open to free concourse by all nations.[5]

Moreover, the covenant that entitles the Jews to the Land of Israel is special in that it comes from God, however much other people might contest Jewish claims. Judges 11:12–29 records the argument between Yiftach, a local Israelite strongman, and the king of Ammon. The king accuses Israel of seizing his land, but Yiftach rebuts the king by reminding him that Israel avoided the Edomites and Moabites when refused safe passage on the way to Canaan, and concludes "that which your god Chemosh has caused you to inherit, that is what you will inherit, as that which the Lord our God has caused us to inherit (now), that we will inherit" (v. 24). This theme of Israel's contested title and Jewish insistence that it derives from God sounds through the ages.[6]

A second implication is that the specific area of the Land of Israel can be precisely delineated. Indeed, Moses points out the areas in some detail when he takes leave of the twelve tribes just before his death. This conception, however, was not rigid around the edges. Two and one-half of the tribes decided to take their inheritance to the other side of the Jordan River because of its pasturage, an area clearly not of the Promised Land of Israel. Thus, the Promised Land is not necessarily the same as Israel's political jurisdiction.

Several "maps" of the Promised Land are given in the Bible. The most extensive territory (Numbers 34:2–13) ranges from the Mediterranean to the Jordan River in the east; some miles beyond Sidon in the north to encompass the Syrian plateau before swinging back around the Sea of Galilee and back over to the Jordan; and in the south to Kadesh and on to the "River of Egypt." This area, however, was only briefly under Israelite control during the kingdoms of David and Solomon. There is also the concept of the "Holy Land" for which borders had to be set for the collection of the tithe.[7] The rabbinical authorities in the early Talmudic period distinguished between the original area conquered by Joshua and the restoration by Ezra after the Babylonian Exile; only the "holiness" of Ezra, a much smaller area, was considered permanent because acquired peacefully.[8] They excluded such towns as Caesaria (between modern Tel Aviv and Mt. Carmel) and Bet Shean (the lower Galilee), apparently because they were not part of the area sanctified by Ezra or the Jewish population was too small. In another example, the city of Acre is divided in half for the purpose of giving evidence in divorce cases.[9] Thus, the Torah and Halakhah recognize different religious, political, and legal borders, allowing for the expansion and contraction of states in the normal course of history without necessarily losing their essential identities in the broader scheme of things.

A third implication is that peoples may lose their titles to land because of immoral behavior. This theme echoes throughout the Bible: the generations of the flood are destroyed, as are Sodom and Gomorrah; mankind forfeits its unity because the Tower of Babel challenges God; and the Canaanites pollute the Holy Land with idolatry and lose their right to settlement (Leviticus 18:2–28). Put another way, domestic behavior has international consequences. The Jews are subjected to similar rules but never lose the Covenant entirely. If they repent, they will be restored or redemption will occur according to a hidden divine plan (cf. Isaiah 40, 49). Thus, as noted earlier, the holiness of both people and land endure because they are both inseparably linked to the divine.

PEACE, WAR, AND OTHER NATIONS

Judaism emphasizes the importance of peace. The high priest concludes his three-fold blessing with peace (Numbers 6:22–27). Hillel, a prominent Talmudic sage of the first century B.C.E., advises, "Be of the disciples of Aaron [the first high priest], loving peace and pursuing peace" (Mishnah Avot 1:12), echoing the Psalmist (34:15), "Seek ye peace and pursue it." Rabbi Simon ben Gamaliel, father of Rabbi Judah, the redactor of the Mishnah, the digest of Talmudic laws derived from the Bible, observed, "By three things is the world preserved: by justice, by truth, and by peace" (Mishnah Avot 1:18). And the ancient kaddish prayer, still recited today, closes with an appeal to "He who makes peace" to "make peace upon us and on all Israel."

The emphasis on peace is reinforced by regard for the value of human life. "Whosoever preserves a single soul (of Israel), scripture ascribes merit to him as though he had preserved an entire world," reads one Talmudic injunction (Babylonian Talmud, *Sanhedrin* 37a; some texts omit the reference "of Israel"). According to Halakhah, the saving of life, including one's own, takes precedence over all other *mitzvot*. Self-sacrifice is justified only when the alternative is to commit murder, idol worship, or sexual transgressions such as rape (Babylonian Talmud, *Sanhedrin* 74a). While the Torah contains a large number of crimes punishable by death, the court cannot enforce the death penalty in the absence of prior warning and two witnesses (Deuteronomy 17:6; Mishnah *Makkot* 1.9). Even the common tribal custom of allowing families to avenge accidental homicide is abridged by setting aside cities of refuge for the perpetrator (Deuteronomy 19:4–10).

Judaism, however, does not prescribe pacifism. The Talmud advises, "If one seeks to kill you, kill him first" (Babylonian Talmud, *Sanhedrin* 72a). The Torah also instructs the Jews about two types of war, obligatory and permitted or optional. The obligatory war is to be directed at the people of Canaan (the seven nations), because they are idolaters, and Amalek, singled out for special treatment because of its attack on the Jews in the desert prior to their entry into the land. The strictures are severe: utter destruction and no mercy (Deuteronomy 20:16–18). Moses condemns the raid against Midian when the war party returns with cattle and slaves. Samuel withdraws divine sanction on the first Israelite king, Saul, when he fails to destroy all of Amalek, bringing the bounty back instead (1 Samuel 15).

This war of obligation, however, was clearly not as complete or extensive as suggested by the text. A large, non-Jewish population evidently remained, to judge by the prophetic condemnation of the Jews for adopting their idolatrous ways.

These facts suggested to the rabbis either that Joshua and his righteous successors had failed in their duty (unthinkable), or that the Torah's instructions should be understood differently. Combining the injunction to destroy the Canaanites with other instructions to offer peace before making war, the commentators softened the impact of the plain verse. For example, the Jerusalem Talmud (*Shevi'it* 6), records the view that Joshua offered the Canaanites three choices: (1) to flee, (2) to make peace, or (3) to make war. A condition of peace was to abandon idolatry for the universal moral code, the so-called Seven Laws of Noah, that applies to all nations except Israel.[10]

THE OPTIONAL WAR

The obligatory war was, in any event, a matter of history and had become moot by the end of the First Temple (586 B.C.E.) with the exception of the struggle against Amalek, which was eternal, if, of course, Amalek could still be identified. The biblical rules for the second type of war, the permitted or optional, are therefore of more lasting interest. Found primarily in Deuteronomy 20, they include the following:

1. Peace must be offered first, the conditions being acknowledgment of Israel's sovereignty and a tax.
2. If peace is refused, males of military age are to be killed, the women, children, animals, and possessions are to be confiscated.
3. In siege warfare, fruit-bearing trees are not to be uprooted (vv. 19–20).
4. A captured woman cannot be taken into the household until a month elapses and a religious conversion of free will takes place.

Before making "war on your enemies," the priest must make a speech to the soldiers (vv. 1–10) and tell the army that God is on their side, hence they should not be fearful or lack courage. Officers appointed by the judiciary then prune the ranks, exempting from battle:

1. Men recently engaged to be married;
2. Those who had just built new homes but who had not "dedicated" them;
3. Those who planted new vineyards;
4. Those fearful and faint of heart.

The connecting principle seems to be that such soldiers will be too distracted or anxious about what is being left behind, leading to an infectious loss of morale. (In Judges 49, Gideon, at God's instruction, goes beyond this, compelling each of his soldiers to drink water, kneeling before a pool before he accepts them, apparently judging from the man's posture whether he had been accustomed to worship idols.)

Maimonides, the great twelfth-century rabbi, philosopher, and physician, adds a few more strictures to these rules (*Mishneh Torah, Hilkhot Melakhim* 5–8). Once in enemy territory, soldiers are to be exempt from the dietary laws because armies of old had to live off the land. A rear guard is to be appointed, with authority to prevent desertion. Exemptions do not apply to an obligatory war, which includes a war of self-defense. Exemptions apply only if the excusing event occurred within the same year. Those exempt on account of fear are to serve in the logistics. In a siege, an escape route should be left so that the enemy can flee rather than fight. War is also permitted on the Sabbath. The dead are to be buried on-site. Those who allow themselves to be distracted from their military duties by thoughts of family or friends and those who fail to do their utmost "have blood on their hands." There should be no forced conversions of the captives.

The Torah also contains some instructions about relations with other nations. As noted earlier, Israel is to regard the seven nations and Amalek with permanent enmity; Ammon and Moab are also singled out. The latter three behaved badly toward the Israelites on their way into the Holy Land, either by refusing hospitality or by attacking weak points of their camp. Otherwise, Jews are instructed to respect the rights of other peoples and, above all, not to oppress the foreigner or "stranger," "because ye were slaves in the Land of Egypt" (Numbers 24:17–22). The temple service on the Jewish Festival of Tabernacles provides for seventy sacrifices on behalf of the traditional seventy nations that comprise the world.

Treaties, compacts, and agreements are very important and are not to be violated. Keeping one's obligation, both as an individual and nation, is of the highest order. Even where that treaty may violate another law of the Torah—as some commentators say about the case of the Gibeonites (Joshua 9; 2 Samuel 21:1–6)—failure to abide by one's word amounts to the crime of "profaning God's name" and thus violates the Torah's injunction for Israelites to be a holy people (Babylonian Talmud, *Gittin* 46a).

THE MESSIAH (ANOINTED) KING

The constitutional arrangements in any state offer an important commentary on its approach to foreign policy. In 1787, for example, the makers of the American Constitution assigned the role of commander in chief to the president, but withheld from him the dictatorial powers they feared by giving Congress alone the right to declare war, ratify treaties, and raise money. By contrast, most European kings of that era made treaties and wars on their own prerogative, although prudence counseled them to consult with some of their subjects, especially those needed to finance the enterprise.

The Bible recognizes three main branches of government: a king or executive, judges, and priests. In addition, the prophet plays a role independent of the others. These separate authorities have their own obvious function—judges to run courts, priests to run the temple—and some analysts see a kind of federalism in this structure, especially when placed atop what was originally a confederation of tribes.[11] Deuteronomy 16 contains the major instructions about kings: "When you enter the land that the Lord your God is giving to you, and you inherit it and dwell therein and you will say, I will put upon me a king like all the nations that are around me. You shall put upon yourself a king that God your Lord will choose." Subsequent verses specify that the monarch be Jewish and male, and, among other things, that he not multiply his horses, wives, or treasure. He must also write a Torah, which he must keep beside him and observe its laws. The king is enjoined not to be arrogant or vain or despotic. Indeed, the Bible records the judge Samuel's warnings about these very vices when the people do demand a king like all the nations to judge them and conduct their wars (1 Samuel 8:4–22).

The Israelite king was also given a special legitimacy through his anointment with pure olive oil as God's ruler. The Hebrew word for the anointed one, *Mashiah*, or "Messiah," thus designated the special status of the king and gave him religious sanction for the mundane activities of war and judgment. Indeed, as explained by later commentators in the Talmud and codes, the king has powers that exceed even those of the highest court, especially on capital punishment: He can execute rebels without warning or witnesses, and he can punish for offenses to his dignity, which he cannot compromise. The king has special rules for his household (e.g., his widow cannot remarry, and his utensils must be burned after his death), and all but the high priest must bow before him.[12]

Limits on the king's power, however, reflect some of the skepticism shown by Samuel's reaction and indeed the rules in Deuteronomy. These relate to important restrictions not only on his personal morality, but also on his ability to carry on foreign relations. For example, according to Maimonides, he is limited in toto to eighteen wives, including concubines— about the number of King David's harem rather than Solomon's reported one thousand wives. Marriages for reason of state were the common coin of alliances in ancient (and even modern) times, and the Bible evidently feared that the Judaism of the royal household would be compromised by too many foreign women (some of Solomon's wives did indeed introduce idolatry). The wives must profess Judaism, and even the concubines are to enjoy the protection of a marriage contract. The king is also not to accumulate personal wealth and should own no horses beyond his chariot. He must pay for personal services. Most importantly, he cannot declare an optional war unless approved by the largest Jewish court, a Sanhedrin of seventy-one members.[13] To be sure, the king may tax, draft, seize the property of those he executes, and claim half of the booty and all of the lands seized in war. But as Maimonides concluded, "One does not appoint a king at all except to do justice and make wars" (*Mishneh Torah, Hilkhot Melakhim* 4).

Compared to his peers, therefore, the Jewish king emerges as a surprisingly limited figure in the conduct of international relations. He is not considered a divinity, as were most ancient rulers, but an anointed agent ruling over a people who owe their allegiance to God and a superseding legal code, the Torah.[14] In theory, he cannot go to war without the consent of a legal body, the rules of war limit both the size of his army and some of his tactics (as noted earlier), and he is apparently prohibited from obtaining either the personal fortune or the large standing cavalry common to kings. His ability to forge alliances is also constrained by rules (number of wives, etc.) intended to reinforce both the practice of Judaism and the king's modesty before his subjects. As the king goes about the mundane, if not profane, business of politics, he carries a heavy sacred yoke, right down to the presence of a Torah at his side.

After Saul's false start, David and Solomon raised the kingdom of Israel to its apogee of power, wealth, and influence. Solomon's Temple also represented the fulfillment of Judaism. But this golden age did not outlast Solomon, and the rest of the biblical narrative recounts the moral and political failings of various rulers that lead to a split of the kingdom into a northern state of Israel (ten tribes) and a southern state of Judah (two tribes), still centered in Jerusalem. Both were destroyed; the ten tribes were exiled and lost to history, if not to myth, while the others (Judah and the Levites) survived their brief stay in Babylon to return to Jerusalem by permission of Cyrus the Great. Thereforth, with the brief exception of the early Hasmoneans (ca. 165 B.C.E.) and the occasional ruler such as Herod the Great (37–4 B.C.E.), Israel's independence lapsed. The rebuilt Temple itself, greatly enlarged under Herod, lasted until the war of 66–70 C.E. Following the Bar Kochba revolt of 15–38 C.E., the Romans renamed the country Palestina (Land of the Philistines), hoping to efface the Jewish political identity.

This cursory history reveals that by the end of the Second Commonwealth, Judaism had experienced a loss of sovereignty, religious freedom, or both. The unity of people, land, and Torah broke down: both the later Talmudic commentators and such figures as Josephus attributed this to Israel's own sins, manifested by the blunders of the various kings and deadly quarrels among the people themselves.[15] The connection between Israel's repentance and the recovery of independent political existence becomes a main theme of the later prophets as they foresee a redemption led by a messianic king.

THE PROPHETS AND INTERNATIONAL RELATIONS: EXILE AND HOPE

Prophecy played an essential role in ancient Judaism. As the recipients of a divine message, prophets counseled kings and commoners, and while they occasionally served up political advice, their main message was about sin, repentance, and redemption. The future they foresaw was conditional on Israel's action: Repentance could stay the punishment decreed for sins. The prophets' primary purpose, therefore, was to bring about a moral renewal before it was too late.

Most failed, as the Bible records. For violating the covenant by which Israel took title to its land, the fitting punishment was a loss of sovereignty followed by exile. Thus, the disasters that befell the kingdoms of Judah and Israel at the hands of foreign nations were related by the prophets to the iniquities of both domestic policy (idol worship, murder, theft, fratricide) and foreign policy (relying on foreign princes, futile revolts against superior force, excessive pride in one's own strength, hypocrisy).[16] Israel was not alone in bearing the prophetic wrath: Egypt, Assyria, Edom, Babylon, and others were all consigned to a bad end (Jeremiah 46).

While the prophets have plenty to say about international relations, "this fascination with international political activity is in reality only a commentary upon the acts of God for his people, Israel, and for the salvation of the world."[17] In the absence of repentance, the future holds exile and suffering. But there is another message: Eventually there will be redemption, either through repentance or as the culmination of human history according to a hidden divine timetable.

This prophetic vision foresees a two-stage redemption. The main characteristic of the first stage is the restoration of Israel to its land and sovereignty, often the outcome of some stupendous battle accompanied by earthquakes (Ezekiel 38–39). Judah and Israel will be reunited and reconciled, the exiles will return, and the nations of the world will either recognize God's kingdom or suffer accordingly.

The second stage is the miraculous redemption itself, characterized by resurrection of the dead, the unity of mankind, acknowledgment by all of the one, true God, and his overlordship of the universe (Ezekiel 37). This is the moment of universal peace and, in a sense, the end of history as we know it; the Messiah-king of the house of David ushers in the "messianic age," preceded by the prophet Elijah or, in some views, by a Messiah-king of the house of Joseph, representing the ten lost tribes. In these prophetic visions one encounters the notion that Israel, reborn as ruler of its own land, is a sign of the messianic era. This powerful theme gathered force in Judaism as the uplifting answer to the depressing question of Israel's destiny once its political sovereignty had been lost. Not long after the Temple's destruction, for example, the miraculous military victories of Simeon Bar Koziba in 32 C.E. led no less a figure than the great Rabbi Akiva to declare him Bar Kochba ("Son of the Star of Redemption"), but this new Messiah was rejected by other scholars and dealt a crushing defeat by Emperor Hadrian.[18]

As the Jewish community eventually dispersed to Mesopotamia, the Mediterranean littoral and thence north and east in Europe, the prophetic legacy that linked the recovery of Jewish sovereignty with the messianic era naturally became the subject of intense speculation. The Talmud and associated biblical commentaries known as Midrash contain numerous references to the messianic era, including the suffering that precedes it.[19] One of the most intriguing is the saying of the sage Samuel: "The only difference between this world and the time of the Messiah will be Israel's servitude to the nations."[20] When, in the twelfth century, the great Maimonides composed his code of Jewish law, he used this source for his own conclusion that the messianic era would be "part of history" rather than the end of it and would be inaugurated by the resumption of Jewish sovereignty in the Promised Land. The agency of Jewish leadership would be a king, required by the Torah, who, in his messianic form, will usher in the redemption.[21]

This association of the messianic era with the resumption of Israel's place among the nations under the supremacy of the king was much contested by subsequent commentators.[22] Among them, the fifteenth-century diplomat, financier, and scholar Don Isaac Abravanel (1437–1509) had the most political experience. He had been counselor to the kings of Portugal and Spain, debated divine right theory before Ferdinand and Isabella, and led the Jews expelled from Spain in 1492—the Holocaust of that time. Abravanel thought and hoped the Messiah was near because of Jewish suffering; he also identified the wars between Christians and Turks with Gog and Magog of Ezekiel. He admired the republican constitution of Venice and argued that Maimonides' idea of kingship ignored both the biblical antipathy to kingly vices and the historical record, inasmuch as kings meant war and oppression. Most of all, he attacked the notion that the messianic era would resemble the known world (except insofar as Israel would regain its independence), because this implied a mere repetition of human history rather than the transformation of history, as was envisioned by the prophets.[23]

This medieval argument over the Jewish state and the messianic era would echo in later debates over the meaning of modern Zionism for Judaism. To Maimonides, the rationalist, statehood and the messianic era appear almost as "normal" phenomena: history continues, only the society of nations, a closed club during the exile, must now admit a triumphant Jewish state led by the Messiah-king. For Abravanel, the supremely experienced statesman, history and international politics are a profane arena; the king, an undesirable leader; and the messianic era, to be holy, must effect a transformation of humanity.[24]

Jewish history held several subsequent examples of messianic expectation and profane reality, the most notorious being the career of Sabbatai Sevi, whose pretensions ended in 1666 when he converted to Islam under the sultan's tutelage.[25] But the messianic idea remained alive through the longing for the restoration of Zion, an integral part of Judaism—in prayer, poetry, philosophy, and jurisprudence. It could not be otherwise, so long as Halakhah emphasized the commandments as the key measure of Jewish practice and the covenant that linked God, Israel, and the Promised Land as the ultimate source of Jewish destiny.

From the mid-nineteenth century onward, the association between the Jewish state and the messianic era became entangled with the various streams of Zionism, both religious and secular, that were transformed by the brief but sensational career of Theodore Herzl. This fascinating chapter, which returns Judaism to international relations in the form of a renewed Jewish state, belongs to another essay.

JUDAISM AND AMERICAN FOREIGN POLICY

What, then, does this review tell us about Judaism's approach to international relations? We find a spectrum ranging from holy to profane, from ideal to real.

First, Judaism associates a particular people, a territory, and God to an extraordinary degree. A perfect world for Judaism is one in which the Jews, living in a Jewish state encompassing the Land of Israel, fulfill the Torah in divine obedience. This combination of circumstances existed for only a short time, and by the end of the Second Temple, a revived Jewish state had become associated with the messianic idea of redemption. But this ideal of the holy has its profane counterpart: Israel's right to take its place among the nations with its own land and government. And profane though it might be, the Jewish state cannot be entirely like other states. It has a unique destiny, whether to be a "light unto the nations," a model society, or the onset of the messianic era.

Second, Judaism prescribes an international "order." The ideal, in the prophetic vision, includes the elimination of war and division through the unity of mankind under the sovereignty of God. Such a transformation is to occur in the course of restoring Israel to its rightful place through the Messiah-king of the house of David. This holy order, in turn, has as its profane counterpart an international system bound by rules and limits. The so-called optional war, the role of the king, treaties, covenants, and the like are all regulated with an eye to minimizing the loss of life and physical damage and to control the ruler's ego. Intended originally only for the Jews, some of these biblical injunctions have made their impact on history largely through Christian and Islamic jurisprudence.

Third, Judaism connects domestic behavior with international consequences. Ideally, by following the Torah, the Jews achieve the ultimate security in that God is enlisted on their side. Being holy, the state is protected by divine power. In contrast, a sinful social order—whether stained by idol worship, injustice to the weak, or excessive pride in one's own strength—leads to a downfall. The state has violated God's law, and it suffers the consequences of defeat, including the exile of its people. Again, these strictures apply primarily to the Jewish state, although both the Five Books of Moses and the prophets illustrate the same principle at work in other nations such as Canaan and the Babylonian monarchy (e.g., the "handwriting on the wall").

Lastly, Judaism prescribes a higher allegiance beyond the state. The ideal Jewish polity, like its ruler, is measured by its subservience to the Torah and the commandments. It exists to carry these out. The king's command (or the state's laws) do not supersede or negate the law of God. While the personal oath to a monarch carries great importance—as do all others in the Bible—it cannot override the covenant with God. The profane counterpart to this ideal is that authority is very important and anarchy must be avoided. Thus, the saying "Yiftach in his generation is like Samuel in his generation" (Babylonian Talmud, *Rosh Hashanah* p. 105b) means that while today's leaders may be quite inferior when measured against their predecessors, allegiance to them is necessary for society to function. The state, though imperfect and rough, must be sustained. "Pray for the government," advises Rabbi Hanina (first century c.e.), "for without fear of it men would swallow each other alive" (*Mishnah Avot* 3.2). Thus, the state, while not the ultimate allegiance of the citizens, offers an important instrument whereby society can be preserved if not perfected.

It is remarkable to note the extent to which these ideas found their way into American statecraft, whether its practitioners knew it or not. The first is the American identity. Walter McDougall, reviewing the history of U.S. foreign policy, chose the telling title, *Promised Land, Crusader State*, with doctrinal variations assigned to each.[26] The Promised Land was the essence of America's first century: a unique people in a special land working out a special destiny, an experiment that could be protected primarily by staying clear of foreign entanglements. The Crusader State set as its mission the redemption of mankind's international order as the justification and ultimate purpose of America's international relations. But the American identity is not in permanent balance between these two dichotomies. Instead, we swing through a bewildering variety of doctrines and inclinations. As McDougall wrote: ". . . confusion and discord have been the norm in American foreign relations not because we lack principles to guide us, but because we have canonized so many diplomatic principles since 1776 that we are pulled every which way at once. . . . A democracy of many religious and secular faiths . . . is constantly at war with itself over matters of right and wrong, prudence and folly."[27] No less than in ancient Israel, these quarrels, if they persist, can be fatal to the success of the enterprise.

A second similarity lies in the conviction that the world needs some sort of international order with rules and limits in order to secure the minimum of justice both at home and abroad. Like the ancient Jews, Americans recognize the need for an international order; we also recognize the need for duly constituted authority to deal with this foreign policy, the equivalent of an anointed king with special powers. The president, however, is a limited monarch and must consult with a latter-day Sanhedrin—the Congress—whose members, though not necessarily professional judges, surely regard themselves as gifted advisors, a fact obvious to any official who has experienced a committee hearing.

The executive and the lawmakers are also the authorities who decide on war. As noted earlier, the Jewish idea of a just war can be either an obligatory war commanded by God (including self-defense), or an optional war undertaken according to human judgment. Both are subject to rules that resemble those of the Christians' just war tradition, which they preceded: the cause must transcend the king's or people's naked desire for wealth or glory; warriors must distinguish between combatants and noncombatants; and the violence itself must not be indiscriminate but rather subject to authority. A war against terrorists who target civilians, hide among them, and openly threaten Americans everywhere surely fits the Bible's description of a just, obligatory war.

What Judaism has to say here beyond support for the just war tradition is its tendency to side with authority, especially the executive, in the conduct of war. The Talmudic sages recognized no less than modern critics that institutions are defective because they are human. The Sanhedrin, wise as they were, still erred; so does the Congress. Nonetheless, the Talmud and, earlier, the Bible are replete with incidents in which American-style individualism is not tolerated lest it destroy institutional authority. The ultimate corrective on authority is not individual dissent but the Torah itself. A king who violates the Torah loses his legitimacy no less than a prophet who repudiates the Law. Americans have also acquired a reverence for the U.S. Constitution that makes the reference point for the behavior of our chief executive during war and peace.

With respect to war powers, the Constitution assigns different roles to the president and Congress that approximate the difference between an executive commander in chief and an authoritative advisory body. The Torah, like the Constitution, offers little support for the view that wars can be waged by committee, and less support for the idea that a king can plunge the nation into war on his sole authority.

Americans also have a strong streak of homegrown morality, the lack thereof they associate with foreign policy disasters. Thus, critics of the Vietnam War soon connected the evils they condemned abroad with the failings of American society at home. Only when America ceased to do wrong abroad, might it begin to do right at home.[28] All these critics—and their opponents—were quick to cite immutable moral principles beyond the Constitution or any body of law or diplomacy to justify their positions. Without judging the rights or wrongs of Vietnam, Americans' tendency to insist that their own society's righteousness be the bedrock of their approach to other nations is a valuable source of introspection that reflects the prophetic portions of the Bible. In those texts, too, one finds a rebuke to a smug assertion of superiority over others or a sanctimonious complacency that often irritates foreigners subject to American preachments.

PREEMPTION

Does Judaism offer any support for preemptive attack? Perhaps surprisingly, the idea is less foreign to Jewish law than it is to American experience. The idea of preemptive attack, now being discussed with respect to Iraq, is one entirely foreign to American international practice. All of America's wars have begun with an enemy attack on U.S. territory, citizens, or military forces. Even the infamous Tonkin Gulf Resolution was passed in reaction to a supposed North Vietnamese assault on American warships.

The Gulf War of 1990–1991, however, was the first of a new pattern. In that case, Kuwait, not a U.S. ally, was invaded, and the United States relied heavily on the threat to the international order as described by the U.N. Security Council. Subsequent "humanitarian interventions" in the Balkans, Somalia, and Haiti all relied on similar grounds, although President Clinton was careful to describe both the Bosnian and Kosovo military actions in classic terms of American and NATO obligations to keep regional peace.

Jewish jurisprudence does recognize what might be called "humanitarian interventions," at least on the individual level. There are numerous provisions that bid the Jew to help rescue his neighbor's property. These rules are obligatory, not optional, but one may question whether an entire society is required to put itself at risk to save another. Jewish law has no precedents from history to serve as a guide in this case. Yet, there is a special instance that combines regard for one's fellow man and preemption: the "pursuer." Under this concept, just as one should kill a would-be assailant before he kills you (self-defense), so one should intercept a killer "in pursuit" of another. (See Babylonian Talmud, *Sanhedrin* 77a based on Leviticus 19:16). The king, too, has the power to kill plotters without going through the warning-witnesses requirement of ordinary criminal procedure. These cases require great certainty; as Abravanel points out in his commentary on the rules of war in Deuteronomy, the law of the pursuer does not apply to the typical quarrel where there is right on both sides. A "man armed with a sword or spear" chasing another man, however, is a different case: the intent is obvious. One could make a reasonable case that Saddam Hussein's record marks him as a "pursuer"; disarming him of weapons that might kill his neighbors (or Americans) could easily be justified. Prudence rather than morality is therefore the issue in a war against Iraq.

Action against Iraq, however, should not necessarily be described as preemption. By the terms of the cease-fire of 1991, Saddam was compelled to accept inspections. He abrogated that part of the terms in 1998. Thus, any attack on Saddam would seem to be a consequence of his failure to abide by cease-fire terms rather than a fresh war.

THE MESSIANIC TRADITION: A FINAL NOTE

As for America's overall purposes in foreign policy, the Jewish approach to international relations offers a cautionary note. When the United States, after World War I, tried to remake the world order along Wilsonian lines, it did so in response to messianic rhetoric. "The war to end all wars"; the creation of a permanent coalition against aggression through the League of Nations; the Kellogg-Briand Pact outlawing war: these were all actions promising a radically different international system. Wilson's own concept of national self-determination, as opposed to the imperial habits of statecraft prevalent since ancient times, was a case in point.

Wilson's flirtation with messianism in foreign policy ended badly. Arguably the subsequent American retreat into isolationism in the 1930s replicated Wilson's own flight from reality. Since then, Americans have experimented fitfully with these two tendencies and even a third, the realpolitik often associated with advocates of the pure national interest school. We have been satisfied with none of them: Messianism offends our sense of reality, while realpolitik and isolationism alike offend our sense of right.

Today, the same battle has emerged over the war on terrorism. Some advocate a limited campaign against clearly identified enemies with a minimum of experimentation in rehabilitating failed states, such as Afghanistan, or rearranging others, such as Iraq, into new democracies. Others claim that unless we drastically alter circumstances overseas, the war on terrorism cannot be won and greater terrors will afflict us.

Perhaps Maimonides and Abravanel can shed some light on this debate. Maimonides sought to give the messianic promise a practical footing that did not rely on miracles to get started; this could be done only through the state and state action. Abravanel doubted that the state alone, that clanking, inefficient, and dangerous device subject to all of man's imperfections, could realize any such promise in the absence of miraculous change. The history of the messianic idea suggests that Abravanel was right about the state and that Maimonides was right about the hope. They might advise us today: Set not the messianic transformation as the test of success in foreign policy even as one takes steps in that direction.

NOTES

1. See, for example, "Just War: An Exchange," the debate between George Weigel and Paul Griffiths in *First Things* (April 2002).

2. This essay is adapted from my article, "Judaism and the World: The Holy and the Profane," *Orbis* (Spring 1998), and The Sixth Templeton Lecture on Religion and World Affairs, February 21, 2001.

3. For the purpose of this article, these texts include the Five Books of Moses and the Prophets and Writings, what the Christians call the Old Testament. Halakhah, the legal code explaining the Mosaic Law, consists of the so-called Oral Law; the Mishnah (redacted ca. 200 C.E.), or digest of laws; and the Gemara (or Talmud), the discussions of these laws (Jerusalem [Palestinian] version, 400 C.E.,-

and Babylonian version, redacted ca. 500 C.E.). These were supplemented by responsa to questions over succeeding centuries from rabbinical courts and widely accepted Halakhic authorities that stretch to our time. Among modern Jews, it should be noted that the Orthodox consider Halakhah as binding on their behavior, Reform Jews do not, and Conservative Jews accept Halakhah but have made changes in the ritual and rabbinate (such as ordination of women) that the Orthodox do not accept.

4. See Abraham Berkowitz, "John Selden and the Biblical Origins of the Modern International System," *Jewish Political Studies Review* 6 (Spring 1994): 1–2.

5. Ibid.

6. Two notable examples are Josephus *Contra Apion* and Rashi (acronym of Rabbi Solomon Itzchaki of Troyes). See Peter Schaefer, *Judeophobia: Attitudes Toward the Jews in the Ancient World* (Cambridge, MA: Harvard University Press, 1997), and Harvey Sicherman and Gilad Gevaryahu, "Rashi and The First Crusade," *Judaism* 48, 150 (Spring 1999): 183–84.

7. "The Land of Israel is the holiest of all lands and what is its holiness? That they bring out of it the Omer, the first fruits and the breads (for the temple). . . ." Mishnah *Kelim* 1.6.

8. See Maimonides, chap. 1 of "Laws of Offerings," in *Mishneh Torah, Hilkhot Terumot* 1. Maimonides (1135–1204) composed a digest of Jewish law in a concise style; his brevity and lack of citations gave birth to a vast industry of commentators that still continues to this day. Chapter 8 in Rabbi J. David Bleich, *Contemporary Halachic Problems*, vol. 2 (New York: Yeshiva University Press, 1983) has an excellent summary of this controversy as it applies to modern problems.

9. See Babylonian Talmud, *Hullin* 6b; and Babylonian Talmud, *Gittin* 2a. See also Gedaliah Alon, *The Jews and their Land in the Talmudic Age* (Jerusalem: Magnes Press, 1984), 2:731.

10. This is the view of Maimonides in his authoritative twelfth-century code *Mishneh Torah*. Rabad of Posquieres severely criticizes Maimonides on this point and even suggests that the text is defective because it seems to contradict the Torah's instructions to destroy the seven nations, but most other commentators reject the criticism. Modern commentaries such as Gerhard von Rad's *Holy War in Ancient Israel* (Grand Rapids, MI: W.B. Eerdman's, 1991) make the obligatory war a central part of ancient Judaism, following Schwzlly Wellhausan and Weber, concluding that an essential feature of the war was Israel's (almost pacifistic) dependence on Divine Interventions. Hitherto von Rad's critics' new debate over *Holy War* can be reviewed here. Suffice it to say that this author views von Rad's interpretation as erroneous both as a statement of war's place in Judaism and of the role of the Israelites in the obligatory war, which was certainly waged often without benefit of miracles.

11. See Daniel J. Elazar, "Israel as a Jewish State," *Jewish Political Studies Review* 2 (Fall 1990): 3–4, for a good review of the classical Jewish political structure.

12. Maimonides, *Mishneh Torah, Hilkhot Melakhim* 1–5.

13. Ibid.

14. Rabbi Nissim of Gerondi (1290–1380?), an authoritative Spanish Halakhist, reduces the king to a kind of glorified civil servant who backstops the judicial system, especially to deal with those who murder or commit other crimes without warning or witnesses and may therefore escape court punishment. See R. Nissim

(b. Reuben Gerondi [Ran]) *Derashot,* ed. Leon A. Feldman (Jerusalem: [Hebrew] Institute Shalom, 1973), 189–94.

15. See Josephus, *The Jewish War,* trans. G.A. Williamson (Baltimore: Penguin Books, 1970), 276–325, and Babylonian Talmud, *Yoma* 9b and *Gittin* 66b.

16. See, for example, Hosea 7, 8; and Isaiah 9.

17. Norman K. Gottwald, *All the Kingdoms of the Earth* (New York: Harper & Row, 1964), 348.

18. "Grass will grow through your eye sockets, Akiva, and the Messiah will still not have come." Midrash on Lamentations called *Eicha Rabbati* 4.

19. See Babylonian Talmud, *Sanhedrin* 97, for a collection of those views, many of which portray anarchic and decadent conditions before the messianic arrival, for example, Rabbi Judah's description of a "generation with a dog's face [shamelessly] bereft of truth."

20. Babylonian Talmud, *Shabbat* 151.

21. *Mishneh Torah.*

22. See David Polish, "Rabbinic Views on Kingship: A Study in Jewish Sovereignty," in *Jewish Political Studies Review* 3 (Spring 1991): 1–2.

23. For a statement of his view, see Don Isaac Abravanel, *Sefer Yeshuot M'Shiko: Concerning Questions of Redemption and the Messiah,* 2nd ed. (Jerusalem: Library of Jewish Philosophy, 1967), 30–33. Abravanel analyzes over 150 references to the Messiah in the Talmud and Midrash. See also Benzion Netanyahu, *Don Isaac Abravanel: Statesman and Philosopher* (Philadelphia, PA: Jewish Publication Society of America, 1968), 150–250.

24. See Abravanel, *Sefer Yeshuot M'Shiko.* Abravanel describes the later Hasmonean period as the first stage of the exile, a daring concept that Israel could, in effect, be in "exile" even when in the Holy Land if its society was corrupt. He also uses this as polemic against Christianity by contrasting the prophetic premises of the messianic era against the conflict and oppression in the Christian world.

25. See Gershom Scholem, *Sabbatai Sevi: The Mystical Messiah,* Bollingen Series XCIII, trans. R.J. Zwi Werblowsky (Princeton, NJ: Princeton University Press, 1973). See also Scholem, *The Messianic Idea in Judaism and Other Essays in Jewish Spirituality* (New York: Schocken Press, 1971).

26. Walter A. McDougall, *Promised Land, Crusader State* (New York: Houghton Mifflin, 1997).

27. Ibid., 4.

28. See Adam Garfinkle, *Telltale Hearts: Origins and Impact of the Vietnam Anti-War Movement* (New York: St. Martin's, 1995).

Index

Abel, 24, 39, 116, 123
Ability-to-pay principle, 142
Abortion, 30n20, 65–75, 206, 207, 229
Abraham, 36–37, 38, 39, 40, 41, 62, 123, 238
Abram. *See* Abraham
Abravanel, Don Isaac, 246, 250, 251, 253n24
Accountability, 153, 209
Ada bar Ahava, 102n80
Adam: environment and, 123, 124–25; family values, 219, 220; genetic engineering, 200–201, 209; personal responsibility, 22–24; sexual responsibility, 52; *Tikkun Olam*, 39
Adret, Solomon b. Abraham, 142, 157, 158
Adultery, 52, 53, 225
Advertising, 191, 204
AFDC. *See* Aid to Families with Dependent Children
Afghanistan, 251
African Americans, 217–18
Afterlife, 82, 83–84, 86–87, 88–89
Aggadah, 9–10, 36, 109
Agreements. *See* Contracts; Treaties
Agriculture, 23, 40, 134, 136, 140, 170

Agudath Israel, 7
Ahad Ha'am, 17
Aher. *See* Elisha b. Abuya
Aid to Families with Dependent Children (AFDC), 153, 156
Air pollution, 121
Akiva: environment, 117; family values, 220, 231n15; free markets, 166; international relations, 245; personal responsibility, 18, 19–20; physician-assisted dying, 86–87; sexual responsibility, 52; welfare programs, 136
Alaska, 80
Albo, Joseph, 83
Alcohol, Prohibition of, 54
Aleichem, Shalom, 5
Aleinu prayer, 39, 42
Alimony, 229
Alliances, 243
Alter, Robert, 26, 32n55, 32n66
Amalek, 240, 241–42
American College of Medical Genetics, 204
American identity, 248
American Jewish politics, 7–9, 14nn24, 25

American Medical Association, 204
Ammon, 242
Amoraic dispute, 143–44
Amoraim, 162n47
Anarchy, 5, 248
Anatolia, 237
Andrews, Lori, 203
Animal experimentation, 115–16
Animal protection, 114
Animals, 122, 241
Animism, 127
Annulment, 223–24
Anonymity, 149–50
Anti-Defamation League, 127
Antipoverty programs, 133, 140–42,
    146–47, 153–56, 159, 160. *See also*
    Welfare programs
Antisocial behavior, 209
Arba'ah Turim (Tur), 14–15n27
Ares, 127
Aristocratic pauper, 139
Arizona, 229
Ark, 125
Arkansas, 229
Armies, 241, 243
Arranged marriages, 226
Artificial creation, 199–200
Arukh HaShulhan, 186
Arunda, 174
Ashcroft, John, 81
Asher, Rabbenu, 101n65
Ashkenazic Jews, 203, 204
Assimilation, 38, 44
Assyria, 245
Assyrians, 236
Atonement, 87, 89
Auerbach, Shlomo Zalman, 95–96,
    106n126, 107n134, 139–40
Augustine, Saint, 31n43
Auschwitz, 33n87, 34n98
Australia, 81
Authority, 9, 248, 249. *See also* Kings
Autonomy, 29, 83, 85–86, 99n31
Azzai, Ben, 18

Babel, tower of, 39, 40, 41, 123, 237,
    239
Babylon, 244, 245, 247

Babylonian Exile, 239
Babylonians, 236
Balkans, 250
Bal tashkhit. See Wanton destruction
Bank of Israel, 157
Bankruptcy, 193
Banks, 181
Bar Kochba, 245
Bar Kochba revolt, 38, 244
Bar Mitzvah, 227, 230–31n5
Bartinoro, Ovadia b. Avraham, 135
Baruch, Meir b. *See* MaHaram
Basri, Ezra, 147
Bat Mitzvah, 227, 230–31n5
Battery, 82
Baum, David, 43
Behavior: environment, 123; family
    values, 218, 230; genetic
    engineering, 201; international
    relations, 239, 247; personal
    responsibility, 18, 21, 28, 32n52. *See
    also* Homoerotic acts
Behavioral genetics, 209–10
Belgium, 82, 91
Ben Azzai. *See* Azzai, Ben
Benjamin, 26, 33n79
Ben Peturah. *See* Peturah, Ben
Bereishit, 38, 39
Besamin Rosh, 101n65, 102–3n83
Bestiality, 52, 53
Bet Shean, 239
Bet Yosef (Caro), 15n28, 103n89, 161n8
Bible, 2; abortion, 69, 71; American
    foreign policy, 247, 249; animal
    protection, 114, 115; environmental
    studies, 109; family values, 219;
    free markets, 184, 193; geochemical
    cycling, 125; international relations,
    235, 236–37; Jewish state, 238, 239;
    kings, 242, 243; paganism, 127;
    peace, 239; personal responsibility,
    18, 23; physician-assisted dying, 91;
    precautionary principle, 119;
    prophets, 244; sustainability, 123,
    124; sustenance, 122; wanton
    destruction, 111, 112. *See also
    specific books*
Biodiversity, 124–25

Bioengineering. *See* Genetic
    engineering
Bioethicists, 207
Biological weapons, 212
Biosphere, 124
Biotech industry, 204–5, 211
Biotechnology, 197–98, 202, 208, 212.
    See also Genetic engineering
Bioterrorist attacks, 212
Birthrate, 62
Black market, 180
Bleich, J. David, 96, 106n117, 107n134
Block grants, 153
Boaz, David, 6
Boaz, Joshua, 228
Body (human), 187, 211
Borders, 238, 239
Bosnia, 250
Brain-stem death, 97n1
Breast cancer, 203
Breastplate of Judgment, 14–15n27
Breger, Marshall J., 1–15
Bribes, 189
Britain, 97n2
Broken homes, 217–18
Brundtland, Gro Harlem, 131n81
Brundtland Commission, 122, 124
B'tzelem elohim, 19
Bullfights, 115–16
Burial, 102–3n83, 118
Burke, Edmund, 3–5
Burns, Sue, 44
Business ethics, 204, 211. *See also*
    Ethics; Free market
Business immorality, 170
Buyers. *See* Consumers

Caesaria, 239
Cain, 24, 39, 116, 123
Canaan, 238, 240, 247
Canaanites, 236, 237, 239, 240
Canada, 49, 50, 56, 60, 81
Cancer, 203
Capital, 139, 140, 174
Caro, Yosef, 10, 15n28, 140, 219
Catholicism, 201
CATO Institute, 6
Cavalry, 243

Celera Genomics, 210
Cemeteries, 118
Chajes, Zvi Hirsch, 36
Chanilai, 220
Chanina, 248
Chargoff, Erwin, 211
Charity, 4; antipoverty programs, 140,
    141, 142; fraud, 144; free markets,
    167, 169, 175, 178, 192, 193;
    humanistic climate, 149; medical
    research, 150; personal
    responsibility, 19; poverty, 133,
    142–43, 145–46, 147, 148, 162n31;
    private assistance, 138–39; public
    assistance, 136; religious education,
    152; self-help, 144–45
Chauvinism, 31n43
Chayei Nefesh, 179
Chayei olam, 35
Chayei sha'ah, 35
Checks and balances, 166
Chemical weapons, 212
Childbirth, 23
Child custody, 226, 229
Children: family values, 217–18, 225,
    226–28, 229, 230–31n5; genetic
    engineering, 204, 205–6, 210;
    international relations, 241;
    personal responsibility, 31–32n48;
    physician-assisted dying, 103n88;
    religious education for, 147, 152–53,
    160; same-sex marriage, 53, 56, 57,
    59, 63–64n12; *Tikkun Olam*, 36–37,
    38; welfare programs, 138, 154, 158.
    See also Family; Parents;
    Procreation
Chinuch, 227
Choice: abortion, 74; free markets,
    168; personal responsibility, 22, 24,
    28, 29–30, 32n52; physician-assisted
    dying, 83, 85, 86. *See also* Freedom
Chol Ha Moed Pesach, 170
Christianity: abortion, 66, 67;
    environment, 126–27, 128; genetic
    engineering, 201; international
    relations, 235, 247, 249; personal
    responsibility, 23; same-sex

marriage, 54, 55, 62–63; *Tikkun Olam,* 42
Circumcision, 226
Citizens, 57, 172, 175
Civilians, in war, 235
Civil law, 55
Civil marriage, 59, 61
Clinton, William Jefferson, 202, 250
Cloning, human, 197, 208–9, 213n6, 214n37, 214–15n39
Closed shop principle, 171
Clothing, 137, 170
Clothing industry, 157
Coercion, 6; free markets, 169; genetic engineering, 204; physician-assisted dying, 92, 104n98; welfare programs, 133, 141, 142, 146, 151–52, 163n59
Cohen, Hermann, 17
Cohen, Shlomo, 187
Collective conscious, 41–42
Collins, Francis, 210
Colombia, 81–82
Commandments, 246, 247. *See also* Jewish law
Commercial relationships, 59
Communism, 34n103
Community, 2; American Jewish politics, 8; conservatism versus liberalism, 4, 5, 6, 7; family values and, 217, 218, 223, 224–25, 227, 228–29; free markets, 169, 172, 175, 176, 177, 180, 187, 188, 193; international relations, 245; same-sex marriage, 59; textual Judaic sources and, 11; welfare programs, 133, 138, 140, 141, 142, 147
Compacts, 242
Companionship, with poor, 143, 148–49, 150, 159–60
Compassion, 88
Compensation, 76–77n25, 186
Competition: economic, 171–72, 174–75, 176, 177–79, 192; price, 177–79
Concentration camps, 33n87, 34n98
Conception, 72
Concubines, 243

Conduct, 85. *See also* Behavior
Conflict, 236
Conjugal relations, 221–22
Conscientious objectors, 61
Consent, 54
Conservatism, 1, 3–7, 55, 60, 61
Conservative Jews, 251–52n3
Constitution. *See* U.S. Constitution
Consumer goods, 178, 180
Consumers, 189, 192
Consumption, 117, 125, 134, 170
Contraction, divine theory of. *See* *Tzimtzum*
Contracts, 58–59, 185–86, 242
Controlled Substances Act (1970), 81
Conversion: forced, 90, 103n88, 126, 241; free, 241
Corporations, 180–82, 189, 191, 192
Corruption, 6, 170
Cost-benefit analysis, 183
Costs, 157, 177, 188
Council of Lithuania, 224
Council of the Four Lands, 224
Courts, 60–61, 80, 180, 225, 226, 242, 243, 251–52n3
Covenants, 58–59, 239, 244
Crane, Edward H., 6
Creation, 39, 199–201
Creativity, 199–201
Creditors, 181
Crescas, Hasdai, 83
Crick, Francis, 210
Crimes, 183, 240
Criminal behavior, 209
Crucifixion, 23
Cruelty, to animals, 115–16
Cruzan v. Director, Missouri Department of Health, 99n28
Cultural pluralism, 50
Culture, 58, 217, 218, 230, 235
Customers, 173
Cyrus the Great, 244
Cystic fibrosis, 204

Damage, physical and spiritual, 185–90
Daughters, 226, 230–31n5. *See also* Children; Family; Family values

David, 239, 243, 244, 245
Death, 23
Death camps, 34n98. *See also*
   Auschwitz
Death with Dignity Act, 80–81, 91
Decalogue, 114, 228
Deception, 145. *See also* Fraud; Theft
Declaration of Independence, 75n3
Defects, in goods or services, 190–91
Defense of Marriage Act, 60
Degradation, 138, 139
Dei mahsoro, 138, 139, 142, 144–45,
   146, 148, 150, 152, 159
Demand, 147, 157, 166, 176
Dematerialization, 126
Democratic Party, 8
Dependence, 23, 31n43, 66
Depression (economic), 147
Depression (psychological), 89
Desecration, 90, 182, 183
Destitution, 135
Destruction. *See* Wanton destruction
Determinism, genetic, 210
Deuteronomy: animal protection, 114;
   family values, 220; free markets,
   193; international relations, 237,
   238, 240, 241, 242, 243, 250;
   personal responsibility, 19, 32n52;
   Tikkun Olam, 36; welfare programs,
   135, 137, 141, 143
Developed nations, 192. *See also*
   specific nations
Development, 122, 124, 131n81
Diaspora, the, 1–2, 37
Dietary laws, 115, 126
Difference, dignity of, 41, 46
Dignity: of difference, 41, 46; free
   markets, 182; personal
   responsibility, 17, 25; welfare
   programs, 142–143, 145, 148–49,
   150
Dina de bar metzra, 184
Dinah, 27
Directors, 181
Disabilities, 206
Disadvantaged, 122. *See also* Poverty;
   Welfare programs
Discipline, 218

Disclosure, 189, 190–92
Discrimination, 7, 203
Diseases, 203, 204, 205, 206
Dishonesty, 182. *See also* Fraud; Theft
Displacement, 42
Distribution, 166
Diversity of species. *See* Biodiversity
Divorce, 57, 59, 218, 224–26, 229
DNA, recombinant, 198, 202
Domestic policy, 244. *See also* Public
   policy
Donin, Hayim, 225
Double effect doctrine, 89
Downsizing, 193
Dowry, 226
Drugs. *See* Pharmaceuticals
Dualism, 126
Durability, 125
Duran, Simon Ben Zemach, 83
Duty, 3; family values, 227;
   international relations, 240, 241;
   physician-assisted dying, 83, 87,
   91–92, 94, 96, 107n134; private
   assistance, 138–39; public
   assistance, 135; religious education,
   153; welfare/antipoverty programs,
   133, 144, 145, 148, 149, 155, 156
Dwarfism, 206

Earned Income Tax Credit (EITC),
   155, 156, 158, 160
Ecclesiastes, 125, 221
Ecologism, 127
Economic competition, 171–72,
   174–75, 176, 177–79, 192
Economic discrimination, 7
Economic growth and development,
   186–88
Economic justice, 192
Economic malaise, 147–148
Economic oppression, 170
Economics, 4, 14n15, 119–20, 166–67.
   See also Free market
Economics of enough, 169–70
Economy, 148
Ecosystem, 110, 123, 124
Edom, 245
Edomites, 238

Education: family values, 227, 228, 230; welfare programs, 147, 148, 150, 152–53, 154, 155, 160
Egotism, 21
Egypt, 184, 220–21, 237, 245
Egyptians, 236
Einstein, Albert, 209
EITC. *See* Earned Income Tax Credit
Elasticity of demand, 157
Eleazar, 21, 32n52
Elijah, 245
Elisha b. Abuya, 84
Elon, Menachem, 10–11, 105–6n115
Emancipation, American Jewish politics and, 7, 14n24
Embryos, 207
Emden, Jacob, 70–71
Emergence (childbirth), 71
Emotional problems, 51
Emotional support, 222–23
Empathetic involvement, with poor, 143, 148–49, 150, 159–60
Employees, 178, 181
Employers, 157, 203
Employment: free markets, 192–93; genetic engineering, 203; welfare programs, 144, 149, 154, 155, 157, 158
Employment Division v. Smith, 67
Emunah, 46
End-of-life decisions. *See* Physician-assisted dying
England, 80
Enlightened self-interest, 167–68
Ensoulment, 72
Environment, 109, 128–32; Adam and Eve, 123; animal protection, 114; approaches to, 110–11; biodiversity, 124–25; consumption, excessive, 125; dematerialization, 126; development, 124; economic interests versus, 119–20; emergency policies, 116–17; externalities, internalizing, 121–22; free markets, 171, 185–86, 192; fur coats, animal experimentation, and bullfights, 115–16; genetic engineering, 198; geochemical cycling, 125; Greens,

128; Jerusalem, 118–19; Jewish law, 113–14; Jewish studies, 109–10; land policies, 119; legal aspects, 122; Maimonides approach, 112–13; Nazism, 128; neopaganism, 127–28; nuisance, 117–18, 120–21; paganism, classical, 127; pollution, 117–18; religious sustainability, 123–24; resource policies, 116; spoliation of nature debate, 126–27; stench, 120–21; sustainability policies, 122, 125; Talmud, 114–15; wanton destruction, 111–14
Environmentalism: 110–11, 127, 128
Ephraim Solomon b. Aaron of Lenczycza, 144, 145
Equality, 41, 42, 146, 172
Equal protection clause, 97n5
Equity, 20, 125, 166, 192
Er, 25
Esau, 115, 238
Ethics: Adam and Eve, 22–24; business, 204, 211; free markets, 180–82, 183, 184; genetic engineering and, 198–99, 201, 204–5, 210–11; honor, 20–22; Joseph, 26–28; love, 18–20; personal responsibility, 32n52; physician-assisted dying, 79, 85; same-sex marriage, 50–52; Tamar and Judah, 24–26; theological implications, 28–30; *Tikkun Olam*, 43. *See also* Family values; Free market; Immorality; Morality
Ethnic pluralism, 8
Eugenics, 204, 209, 211
European Court of Human Rights, 97n2
Euthanasia, 79, 90–92; afterlife, 83–84; independence or interdependence, 84–85; Jewish law perspective, 82–83; life-preserving medical treatment, refusal of, 92–97; personal autonomy and objective moral values, 85–86; secular legal developments, 80–82; suicide and, 86–90
Eve, 22–24, 39, 52, 123, 209, 219

Even ha-Ezer, 14–15n27
Evil: free markets, 168, 175; genetic
    engineering, 200; human nature,
    4–5; personal responsibility, 24, 28,
    29, 32n52, 33n87; physician-assisted
    dying, 85
Evil impulse. *See Yetzer harah*
Excrement, burial of, 117
Executive officers, 181, 182
Exile, 37, 42, 123, 187, 239, 244–46,
    247, 253n24
Exodus (from Egypt), 184, 220–21
Exodus (literature), 37, 69, 114, 144
Externalities, internalizing, 121–22
Ezekiel, 220, 245
Ezra the Scribe, 172, 239

Faith, 46
False impressions, 190, 191–92. *See
    also* Dishonesty; Fraud
Family, 2; same-sex marriage, 53–54,
    59, 60, 61, 62, 63–64n12; single-
    parent, 217–18; Temporary Aid to
    Needy Families and, 153–55; *Tikkun
    Olam*, 38; welfare programs, 138,
    141, 149, 152, 158, 160. *See also*
    Marriage; Parents
Family values, 217–19; children,
    226–28; divorce, 224–26; family
    purity, 219–23; marriage, 219–21,
    223–24; public policy directions,
    228–30
Fascism, 128
Fathers, 57, 141, 153, 226, 228, 229. *See
    also* Family; Family values; Parents
Federalism, 242
Fees, 180
Feinstein, Moshe: abortion, 72–73;
    physician-assisted dying, 92, 95–96,
    102n80, 104n97, 105n113, 105–6n115,
    106–7n128, 107nn131–134
Female subjugation, 31n43
Feminism, 31n43
Fertility clinics, 207
Festivals, 143, 170, 242
Feticide, 69, 73
Fetuses: abortion, 66, 67–70, 71, 72–74,
    75; genetic engineering, 206, 207

Fidelity, 229
Financial statements, 191
Fire, 200
First Temple, 240
Fiscal policies, 142, 148
Five Books of Moses, 105n110. *See also*
    Torah
Flood, 39, 124, 125
Florida, 229
Florida Supreme Court, 80
Flug, K., 157
Food, 112–13, 134, 137, 144, 197
Foreign policy, American, 247–50. *See
    also* International relations
Forests, 117
Four Lands, Council of the, 224
France, 140, 156
Fratricide, 24, 91
Fraud, 143–44, 145, 148–49, 178, 189
Free choice, 168
Freedom: abortion, 67; economic, 4;
    family values, 209; genetic
    engineering, 210; international
    relations, 244; personal
    responsibility, 29, 34n103; *Tikkun
    Olam*, 41
Free entry, 171–76
Free market, 165–66, 193–94;
    conceptual framework, 167–71;
    defects in goods or services,
    190–91; economics, 166–67; false
    impressions, 191–92; free entry,
    171–76; full disclosure, 190–92;
    Jewish law and, 184–85; job
    creation and vocational trading,
    193; moral problems, 180–82;
    physical and spiritual damage,
    185–90; prices and profits, 176–80;
    public sector responsibility, 192–93;
    theft and robbery, 182–84;
    unemployment through
    bankruptcy or downsizing, 193
Free will. *See* Choice
Freundel, Barry, 12, 65–77
Friendships, 57–58, 141, 149
Full disclosure, 189, 190–92
Fur coats, 115–16

Galilee, Sea of, 238
Gamaliel, 177
Gaonim, 139
Gattaca (film), 212
Gay movement, 55. *See also*
    Homoerotic acts; Homosexuality;
    Same-sex marriage
Gemara, 9; abortion, 68, 69–70, 71–72;
    family values, 232n28; international
    relations, 251–52n3; welfare
    programs, 162n47
Gemilat hasadim, 150
Gene grafting, 205
Geneivat da'at, 191–92
Genes, 197, 202, 204, 215n50
Genesis: abortion, 70; environment,
    124–25, 126; family values, 219,
    220; free markets, 170; genetic
    engineering, 199, 200; international
    relations, 238; personal
    responsibility, 18, 22–28, 31n43,
    32n67, 33n79; same-sex marriage,
    53; *Tikkun Olam*, 36–37, 38, 39
Gene therapy, 201, 204, 205–6
Genetic behaviorism, 209–10
Genetic determinism, 210
Genetic discrimination, 203
Genetic disorders, 204
Genetic engineering, 197–98, 212–15;
    creativity and creation, 199–201;
    ethics, 198–99, 210–11; gene
    therapy, 205–6; genetic screening,
    202–5; healing and health, 201–2;
    human cloning, 208–9; moral
    volition, 209–10; stem cells, 206–7
Genetic mutations, 203, 210
Genetic predispositions, 202–3
Genetic research, 203
Genetic screening, 198, 202–5
Genome, 202
Gentiles, 68
Geochemical cycling, 125
Gerke, Achin, 201
Germany, 128, 224
Gershom, Rabbenu, 175–76, 224, 225
Gerstenfeld, Manfred, 12, 109–32
Gestation, 71–72. *See also* Abortion
Get, 225

Gibeonites, 242
Gideon, 241
Gifts, anonymous, 142–43. *See also*
    Charity
Gillis, Michael, 127
Gillui arayot, 53
Ginsburg, Allen, 31n47
Globalization, 62
God: environment, 116, 123, 124, 125,
    126; family values, 218, 219,
    220–21, 223, 231n8; free markets,
    168, 182; genetic engineering,
    200–201, 211; international
    relations, 236, 237, 238, 241, 242,
    243, 245, 246, 247; personal
    responsibility, 22, 24, 28, 29, 32n52,
    33n87; physician-assisted dying, 85,
    86, 87–88, 89–90, 93, 97; same-sex
    marriage, 52; sanctification of, 182;
    Tikkun Olam, 36–37, 39, 39–40, 41
Golden calf, 126, 233n55
Golem, 199, 208–9, 212
Gombiner, Avraham Abeli, 104n98
Gomorrah, 123, 172, 239
Goodness, 5, 29, 32n52, 85
Goods, 166, 178, 179, 180, 189, 190–91
Goses, 92–94, 95, 105nn107, 113,
    105–6n115
Government, 148, 174, 192–93, 229,
    242. *See also* Public assistance;
    Welfare programs
Grafting, gene, 205
Grants, 153
Graves, 118
Grazing, 123
Greed, 55, 168, 204, 205, 211
Greens, 128
Grotius, Hugo, 238
Growth hormones, 204, 205–6
Gulf War (1990–91), 250

Hadrian, 245
Haggai, Rab, 32n52
Haiti, 250
Hakhnasat Kallah, 224, 229
Halakhah, 9–10; abortion, 66, 70, 72;
    antipoverty measures, 140–42, 143,
    144, 146–47, 156, 158, 160;

corporations, 181; Earned Income
Tax Credit, 157; environment, 109,
114, 116, 119, 121, 128; free entry,
171, 174–75, 176; free markets, 170,
185, 187–88; full disclosure, 191;
international relations, 236, 239,
246, 251–52n3; medical research,
150, 152; poverty, 133; prices and
profits, 178; private assistance,
137–39; public assistance, 134, 135,
136, 193; same-sex marriage, 50;
Temporary Assistance to Needy
Families, 155; *Tikkun Olam*, 42, 43,
45. *See also* Judaism; Normative
Judaism
Halevi, Chayim David, 115
Halivni, David Weiss, 28–29, 33n86
Ha-mishpat ha-'ivri (Elon), 10–11
Hananya ben Gamaliel, 114, 177
HaNasi, Yehuda, 83, 94–95
Hanina b. Teradion, 88, 101n65
Harm, physical and spiritual, 185–90
Hasmoneans, 244
Hatam Sofer. *See* Sofer, Moshe
Hazardous materials, 121
Healing, 201–2, 205
Health: abortion and, 72;
   environment, 120; genetic
   engineering, 201–2, 205; welfare
   programs, 137, 150–52, 160
Health care, 138, 147, 202
Health insurance, 203
Health-related research, 150–52, 160
Herem Hayishuv, 175
Herod the Great, 244
Herring, Basil F., 101n65, 102–3n83,
   103n88
Herzl, Theodor, 37, 246
Heschel, Abraham Joshua, 9–10
Heterosexual culture, 58
Hezekiah, 33n87, 87–88
Hidka, 114
Hierarchy, 40
Hillel, 18, 239
Hillul Ha-shem, 90
Hirsch, Samson Raphael, 113, 140
Hisda, 72, 112
Historical facts, 11

Hitler, Adolf, 209
Holocaust, 29, 33nn86, 87, 37, 204. *See
   also* Shoah
Holy Land, 239, 242, 253n24
Holy War in Ancient Israel (von Rad),
   252n10
Homicide, 69, 91
Homiletic literature, 170
Homoerotic acts, 51–52, 53, 54, 55, 56
Homosexual culture, 58
Homosexuality, 51, 52, 53, 55, 56, 57,
   60, 229. *See also* Same-sex marriage
Honesty, 182, 183. *See also* Fraud; Full
   disclosure
Honi the Circle-Drawer, 102n80
Honor, 18, 20–22, 27, 30
Hope, 244–46, 251
Hormones, 202, 204, 205–6
Hoshen Mishpat, 14–15n27
Hospitality, 242
Housing, 134, 135–36, 137, 138, 147,
   174
Howe, Irving, 8
Hubris, 40
Hudok, George, 208
Human cloning, 197, 208–9, 213n6,
   214n37, 214–15n39, 215n41
Human genome, 202
Humanistic climate, 149–50
Humanitarian interventions, 250
Human nature, 4–5, 198
Human rights, 211
Human tissue, patenting, 197
Humiliation, 138
Huna, 112–13, 172
Huna the son of Yehosha, 172
Hunger, 30n11
Hunting, 115
Husbands, 64n23, 219, 220, 221, 222,
   226, 232n28. *See also* Family;
   Marriage
Hussein, Saddam, 250

Identity: American, 248; family, 61;
   Jewish, 35, 244
Idleness, 144
Idolatry, 90, 126, 237, 239, 240, 241,
   243

Ilani, Zvi, 121
Imitatio Dei, 209
Immigration laws, 171
Immo caveat, 155
Immorality, 24, 123, 144, 170, 175, 239.
    See also Ethics; Morality; Personal
    responsibility; Responsibility;
    Sexual responsibility
Immortality, 83. *See also* Afterlife
Impediments, 93–94
Imperialism, 251
Incest, 52, 53
Income, 144, 145, 146
Income inadequacy, 139–40
Income redistribution, 133, 146–47,
    159
Income tax, 142, 146, 156, 158. *See also*
    Taxation
Independence, 83, 84–85, 227, 244
Indignities, 149
Individuals/individualism, 7, 169, 218,
    249
Inflation, 147
Information, 190
Innocence, 23, 193
Insulin, 202
Insurance, 203
Interdependence, 84–85
Interest groups, Jewish, 7
International relations, 235–36;
    American foreign policy and
    Judaism, 247–49; Jewish law and
    Bible, 236–37; Jewish state, 237–39;
    messiah king, 242–44; messianic
    tradition, 250–51; optional war,
    240–42; peace and war, 239–40;
    preemption, 249–50; prophets,
    244–46
Intimacy, marital, 221–23, 232n28
Investment, 151, 173–74
Investment goods, 178
In vitro fertilization (IVF), 207
Iraq, 235, 250, 251
Isaac, 36, 143, 238
Isaac, Solomon b. *See* Solomon b.
    Isaac
Isaiah, 33n87, 41, 124, 125, 194, 237,
    239

Islam, 42, 62, 247
Isolationism, 251
Israel: family values, 220–21; genetic
    engineering, 204; international
    relations, 236, 237–39, 241, 244, 245,
    246, 247, 252n10; minimum wage
    laws, 156–57, 160; personal
    responsibility, 29; *Tikkun Olam,* 37,
    38–39, 43. *See also* Land of Israel
Isserles, Moshe (Rema), 15n28, 93, 94,
    95, 144, 185, 219
Italy, 185–86

Jacob: environment, 113; free markets,
    170; personal responsibility, 24, 26,
    27, 28, 33n79; *Tikkun Olam,* 36
Jakobovits, Immanuel, 201
Japan, 82
Jeremiah, 28, 33n87, 220, 245
Jerusalem, 37, 118–19, 244
Jesus, 23
Jewish environmental studies, 109–10
Jewish family values. *See* Family
    values
Jewish identity, 35, 244
Jewish law, 2; environment, 113–14;
    family values, 219; free markets,
    184–85; income redistribution,
    146–47; international relations,
    236–37, 245; physician-assisted
    dying, 82–83, 92–97, 102n79,
    105n110; preemption, 249–50;
    textual Judaic sources, 9, 10. *See
    also* Abortion; Aggadah;
    Environment; Ethics; Family
    values; Free market; Gemara;
    Genetic engineering; Halakhah;
    International relations; Mishnah;
    Personal responsibility; Physician-
    assisted dying; Responsa literature;
    Responsibility; Sexual
    responsibility; Talmud; Textual
    Judaic sources; Torah; Welfare
    programs
Jewish politics: American, 7–9,
    14nn24, 25; sexual responsibility
    and, 50, 54–58, 59, 60–62; *Tikkun*

Olam, 45–46. *See also* International relations
Jewish Population Survey (1990), 37
Jewish public policy, 1, 11–13; American Jewish politics and, 7–9; liberalism versus conservatism, 3–7; political thought and action, 3; sexual responsibility and, 49–50. *See also* Abortion; Environment; Ethics; Family values; Free market; Genetic engineering; International relations; Personal responsibility; Physician-assisted dying; Responsibility; Sexual responsibility; Welfare programs
Jewish self-interest, 62–63
Jewish state. *See* Israel
Jewish tradition. *See* Normative Judaism
Jews for Jesus, 126
Job, 220
Job creation, 4, 193. *See also* Employment
Job search services, 149
Job training, 148, 149, 155
Johnson, Paul, 41–42, 44–45
Jordan River, 238
Joseph, 24, 26–28, 32n67, 179
Josephus, 244
Joshua, 117, 239, 240, 242
Jubilee year, 116, 119, 170
Judah: biblical, 24–26, 27–28, 33n79; Talmudic, 19, 125, 144, 228
Judah (state), 244
Judaism, 2; American foreign policy and, 247–49; environment, 128; family values, 223, 230; free markets, 168–69, 180, 181, 187, 190, 192; genetic engineering and, 198–99; genetic engineering, 205; international relations, 236, 237, 239, 240, 244, 247–49, 249; same-sex marriage, 45–46; *Tikkun Olam*, 40, 41. *See also* Abortion; Environment; Ethics; Family values; Free market; Genetic engineering; Halakhah; International relations; Normative Judaism; Personal responsibility;

Physician-assisted dying; Responsibility; Sexual responsibility; Welfare programs
Judeo-Christian heritage, 235
Judges, 238, 241
Judiciary, 60–61, 241, 242. *See also* Courts; U.S. Supreme Court
Justice, 26, 166, 169, 192
Just price, 178–79
Just war, 235, 248–49

Kabbalists, 231n8
Kadesh, 238
Kahana, 144
Kaminetsky, Yaacov, 38
Kant, Immanuel, 17
Kasir, N., 157
Kass, Leon, 213n15
Kavod, 18, 20
Kedushah, 35
Keivan dedasu bo bnei rabim, 188
Kellogg-Briand Pact, 251
Ketubah, 225, 229
Kevorkian, Jack, 81
Kiddush Ha-Shem, 43–44, 90, 126
Kiddushin (sacred covenant), 52
Kilns, prohibition against, 118
Kings, 242–44, 246, 247, 249, 250, 252–53n14
Kirk, Russell, 5
Kosher laws, 115
Kosovo, 250
Kotler, Aaron, 38
Kovno Ghetto, 90
Koziba, Simeon Bar. *See* Simeon Bar Koziba
Kratz, Peter, 128
Kuppah, 136, 140, 224
Kuwait, 250

Labor (childbirth), 67, 70, 71
Labor costs, 157
Lakish, Reish, 102n80
Lamentations, 32n52, 34n98
Lamm, Maurice, 83
Land, 36, 37, 38. *See also* Property
Land of Israel, 116, 120, 170, 186, 237, 238, 247. *See also* Israel

Land policies, 119

Landau, Yehezkel (Noda Biyehuda),
    76n13, 115, 130n32

Laqueur, Walter, 128

Lashon harah, 190

Lavan, 27

Law. *See* Civil law; Jewish law

Laws of the Neighbors, 109

Laziness, 144

League of Nations, 251

Leah, 26, 27

Learning, 2

Least-cost method, 156

Least interest, principle of, 23

Left-wing politics. *See* Liberalism

Legal codes. *See* Aggadah; Gemara;
    Halakhah; Jewish law; Mishnah;
    Responsa literature; Talmud;
    Textual Judaic sources; Torah

Legislation: abortion, 67, 74;
    environment, 122; family values,
    230; free markets, 187; physician-
    assisted dying, 79, 80–82, 92; same-
    sex marriage, 60; welfare, 133

Leib, Aryeh, 104n98

Leibush, Meir (Malbin), 172

Lesbianism, 55. *See also* Homoerotic
    acts; Homosexuality; Same-sex
    marriage

Letter of the law, 184–85

Levi, 27

Levies. *See* Taxation

Levine, Aaron, 12, 133–64, 178

Levites, 119, 186, 244

Leviticus: abortion, 71; free markets,
    184, 186, 189, 192; international
    relations, 239, 250; personal
    responsibility, 18, 20, 28, 33–34n90;
    welfare programs, 135, 141

Liberalism, 3–7, 8, 14nn24, 25

Libertarianism, 4, 6, 14n15

Librach, Clifford E., 12, 17–34

Licensing, 171

Lichtenstein, Aaron, 41, 145, 155

Lieberman, Yehoshua, 178

Life insurance, 203

Life-preserving medical treatment,

    refusal of, 79, 82, 92–97, 99n28,
    106–7n128

Lifestyles, 218

Lifnim mishurat ha-din, 147, 184

Limited liability, 181

Liquidity, 136, 138, 139

Literature. *See* Textual Judaic sources

Living wage, 156, 157

Loafing, 144

Loans, 148

Loew, Judah, 199, 200–201

London, Joshua E., 12–13, 217–33

Lot, 123–24, 238

Louisiana, 229

Love, 18–20, 21, 22, 26, 30, 42

Luria, Isaac, 29

Lust, 55

Luxuries, 139

Macroeconomics, 192–93

MaHaram (Meir b. Baruch), 83–84,
    175–76

Maharit. *See* Trani, Joseph

Maidanek, 34n98

Maimonides (Rambam), 10; abortion,
    67–68, 69, 70, 73, 74, 76–77n25;
    environment, 109, 112–13, 118;
    family values, 219, 221; free
    markets, 178, 180, 182, 183, 193–94;
    genetic engineering, 210;
    international relations, 241, 243,
    245, 246, 251, 252nn8, 10;
    physician-assisted dying, 83,
    101n65; *Tikkun Olam,* 45; welfare
    programs, 142, 145

Male domination, 25, 31n43. *See also*
    Men

Malnutrition, 122

Management, 181, 183

Manners, 17

Manslaughter, 97–98n6

Maot hittin, 138

Marginal tax rate, 153, 155, 158

Marital intimacy, 221–23, 232n28

Marital sex, 221–22

Market price, 178

Market share, 175

Market. *See* Free market

Marketing, 172
Marketing chain, 180
Marriage: arranged, 226; family
    purity, 221–23; family values, 217,
    218, 219–23, 226, 229–30, 231nn8,
    15; international relations, 241, 243;
    personal responsibility, 31–32n48;
    sexual responsibility, 53, 55, 56–57,
    58–59, 60, 61, 62, 63–64n12; as
    social good, 223–24. *See also*
    Divorce; Family; Parents; Same-sex
    marriage
Mars, 127
Marufiya, 174
Marx, Karl, 40
Marxism, 4
Masorah, 5
Matching grants, 153
McDougall, Walter, 248
Mecklenburg, Jacob Zevi, 91, 104n91
Medical research, 150–52, 160, 206
Medical treatment, 89, 202. *See also*
    Healing; Health care; Life-
    preserving medical treatment
Mediterranean Sea, 238
Meir, 22, 83–84
Meir b. Baruch. *See* MaHaram
Meiri, Menachem ben Solomon, 118,
    145, 177, 200
Mekach ta'ut, 191
Men, 23–24, 52–53, 169–70, 241. *See
    also* Family; Family values; Fathers;
    Husbands; Male domination;
    Marriage; Parents; Sexual
    responsibility
Menstruation, 222–23
MeOr HaGolah. See Gershon, Rabbenu
Mercy, 166
Mesopotamia, 40, 237, 245
Messiah, 236, 242–44, 245–46
Messianic era, 237, 245, 246, 247,
    253n24
Messianic tradition, 250–51
Mezonot, 226, 229
Micah, 237
Middlemen, 179–80
Midian, 240

Midrash, 99n37, 116, 125, 209, 220,
    245
Migas, Joseph Ibn, 176
Mikveh, 222, 223, 224
Military tactics, 235, 243
Minimum wage laws, 156–57, 160
Mining, 117
Miracles, 245, 251, 252n10
Miscarriage, 69, 71
Mishnah, 9; abortion, 66, 67, 68,
    69–70, 71–72; environment, 109,
    118, 120, 121; free markets, 176,
    177, 185, 192; international
    relations, 239, 251–52n3; personal
    responsibility, 19, 21; physician-
    assisted dying, 83, 84, 94; welfare
    programs, 134, 162n47
Mishneh le-Melekh, 72
Misogyny, 22, 25
Mitzvah (mitzvot), 42, 137, 168, 208,
    237, 240
Moab, 238, 242
Modesty, 170–71
Monarchs. *See* Kings
Monetary compensation, 69, 76–77n25
Monetary policies, 148
Money, 168
Monopoly, 174
Monotheism, 85, 126
Moral behavior, 201, 210
Moral freedom, 34n103
Moral law, 201
Moral relativism, 218
Moral values, objective, 85–86
Moral volition, 209–10
Morality: abortion, 74–75;
    environment, 123; family values,
    230; free markets, 175, 179, 180–82,
    183, 184, 186; genetic engineering,
    201, 209–10; international relations,
    236, 249; physician-assisted dying,
    85; same-sex marriages, 56; social,
    5. *See also* Ethics; Family values;
    Personal responsibility;
    Responsibility; Sexual
    responsibility
Morpurgo, Shimon, 187
Mosaic Law, 9, 183, 251–52n3

Moses, 36, 37, 38–39, 227, 238, 240
Moses ben Maimon. *See* Maimonides
Mothers: abortion, 66, 69, 70, 72, 73,
    74; family values, 226, 228; sexual
    responsibility, 57. *See also* Family;
    Family values; Parents
Mutuality, 17, 21

Nachman bar Isaac, Rab, 21
Nachmanides (Moshe Ben Nachman),
    184, 200
Names, 31–32n48
National Academy of Sciences, 134
National Institute of Health, 211
National interest, 251
Nationalism, 127–28
National Jewish Population Survey
    (1990), 37
NATO, 250
Natural law, 201, 205
Natural resources, 116, 131n81, 185,
    187
Nature, divinity of, 127. *See also*
    Environment
Nazism, 28, 34n103, 128, 201, 204, 211
Negative income tax, 156
Negligent homicide, 69
Negotiation, 175
Nehemiah, 29
Neighbors, personal responsibility
    and, 18–20
Neo-Nazism, 127–28
Neopaganism, 127–28
Net worth, 135, 137, 138
Netherlands, 82, 91
New Age paganism, 128
Newman, Eugene, 103n88
Niddah, 222
Nietzsche, Friedrich, 128
Nimrod, 115
Nissim of Gerondi, 252–53n14
Noah, 39–40, 41, 123, 124, 125
Noahide laws, 53, 54, 114, 240
Noda Biyehuda. *See* Landau,
    Yehezkel
No-fault divorce, 218, 229
Noise, 120–21
Normative Judaism, 1, 3–7, 11–13. *See*

also Abortion; Aggadah;
    Environment; Ethics; Family
    values; Free market; Gemara;
    Genetic engineering; Halakhah;
    International relations; Jewish law;
    Judaism; Mishnah; Personal
    responsibility; Physician-assisted
    dying; Responsa literature;
    Responsibility; Sexual
    responsibility; Talmud; Textual
    Judaic sources; Torah; Welfare
    programs
Novak, David, 12, 49–64
Nozick, Robert, 6
Nuisance, 117–18, 120–21
Numbers, 69, 186, 233n55, 237, 238,
    239, 242
Nurturing, 59

Obesity, 206
Obligation. *See* Duty
Obligatory war, 240, 241, 248–49,
    252n10
Odinism, 127
Oklahoma, 229
Ona'ah, 178
Onah, 221
Onan, 25
Oppression, 170, 242, 246
Optional war, 240–42, 243, 247,
    248–49
Orah Hayyim, 14–15n27
Oral Law, 9, 91, 105n110, 109,
    251–52n3
Oregon Death with Dignity Act,
    80–81, 91
Organization for Economic
    Cooperation and Development
    (OECD), 156
Original Sin, 23
Orthodox Jews, 251–52n3
Oshry, Ephraim, 90, 102–3n83
Ownership, 179, 181, 182

Paganism, 126, 127
Pain Relief Promotion Act, 81
Pain/suffering: abortion, 70, 73;
    animal protection, 114, 115; free

markets, 179; international
relations, 245, 246; life-preserving
medical treatment, refusal of,
94–95; personal responsibility, 19,
30n11, 33n86; physician-assisted
dying, 81, 99n37, 101n65, 102nn76,
79, 80, 103n86, 104n91, 106n117;
suicide, 88–90; welfare programs,
150
Palaggi, Haim, 95
Palliation, 96, 102n79
Palliative medications, 89
Papa, 112
Paradise narrative, 123, 124–25
Parents: abortion, 72–73; family
values, 218, 226, 228, 230; genetic
engineering, 204, 205–6; physician-
assisted dying, 99n28, 103n88;
same-sex marriage, 53, 56, 57, 59,
63–64n12; single, 154–55, 160;
welfare programs, 153, 154–55, 160.
See also Family; Family values;
Fathers; Mothers; Marriage
Partial birth abortions, 71
Particularism, 40, 44–45
Passover, 138, 147
Patents, 197, 204, 215n50
Pazzi. See Simon ben Pazzi
Peace, 42, 166, 239–40, 241, 245
Pentagon attack (9/11/2001), 235
Pentateuch, 141
Personal autonomy, 83, 85–86, 99n31
Personal commitment, 230. See also
Marriage
Personal involvement, with poor, 143,
148–49, 150, 159–60
Personal responsibility, 17–18, 31n43,
31–32n48, 32n52; Adam and Eve,
22–24; honor, 20–22; Joseph, 26–28;
love, 18–20; Tamar and Judah,
24–26; theological implications,
28–30
Peturah, Ben, 19–20, 117
Pharmaceutical research, 152, 160
Pharmaceuticals, 198, 202
Philanthropy. See Charity
Philosophy, 17, 50, 52–54. See also
Ethics; Morality

Physical damage, 185–90
Physical treatment, 89
Physician-assisted suicide, 79, 90–92;
afterlife, 83–84; independence or
interdependence, 84–85; Jewish law
perspective, 82–83; life-preserving
medical treatment, refusal of,
92–97; personal autonomy and
objective moral values, 85–86;
secular legal developments, 80–82;
suicide, 86–90
Pittsburgh Platform (1885), 44
Plato, 40
Poison, 121
Polio vaccine, 204
Political freedom, 34n103
Politics, 50, 54–58, 59, 60–62. See also
International relations; Jewish
politics
Pollution, 117–18, 120, 121, 185
Polytheism, 85, 127
Popular culture, 217
Poverty, 4, 135, 158; defining, 133–34;
dignity of, 142–143, 148–49;
environment, 122; family values,
218; personal responsibility, 19;
social equality, 143, 148–49, 150,
159–60; support for, 143–44. See also
Antipoverty programs; Charity;
Welfare programs
Poverty prevention, 145–46, 148
Poverty relief, 145–46
Prayer, 95–96, 102n80, 218, 239
Prayer liturgy, 2
Precapitalist markets, 167
Preembryos, 207
Preemption, 249–50
Pregnancy, 71–72. See also Abortion
President (U.S.), 248–49
Pretty v. The United Kingdom, 97n2
Price competition, 177–79
Price controls, 179, 180
Price fraud, 178
Price gouging, 178
Prices, 157, 166, 175, 176–80, 192
Price subsidies, 156
Priests, 36, 41, 233n55, 241, 242
Primal Fall, 23

Priority, 19
Privacy: environment, 118; physician-assisted dying, 80, 82; same-sex marriage, 54–55, 57–58, 61, 64n15
Private assistance, antipoverty measures, 140–42; Earned Income Tax Credit, 158; economic malaise, 147; eligibility for, 134, 137–40; poverty prevention, 145, 146; self-help, 148, 149; social equality, 159–60
Private contracts. *See* Contracts
Private education, 230
Private industry: biotech industry, 204–5, 211; medical research, 151, 152, 160
Private ownership. *See* Ownership
Private property. *See* Property
Pro-choice, 65, 66, 74
Procreation, 23, 31n47, 53, 59, 63–64n12, 87, 219
Production, 157, 167, 177
Profane, 246, 247–48
Professional associations, 171
Professional education, 148
Profits, 166, 170, 174–75, 176–80, 183, 211
Profit motive, 151, 152, 160, 204
Progressive income tax, 142, 146, 158
Prohibition (alcohol), 54
Pro-life, 65, 66, 74
Promised Land, 36, 37, 238, 246, 248
Promised Land, Crusader State (McDougall), 248
Property, 4; family values, 226; free entry, 171, 173; free markets, 167, 168, 170, 184, 185, 186, 188, 190; genetic engineering, 211; international relations, 241, 250; same-sex marriage, 58, 59; welfare programs, 147
Prophetic sensibility, 45
Prophets: family values, 220; international relations, 237, 242, 244–46, 247, 249, 251–52n3; personal responsibility, 28; *Tikkun Olam*, 36
Proportionality, 146

Prostitution, 54
Proteins, 202
Prudence, 250
Psychological treatment, 89
Psychotherapy, 51
Public assistance, 158, 159, 160; antipoverty programs, 140–42, 155–56; eligibility for, 134–37; fraud, 143; humanistic climate, 149–50; income redistribution, 147; poverty prevention, 145–46, 148; religious education, 152–53; self-help, 144; Temporary Aid to Needy Families, 153–55
Public education, 230
Public morality, 230
Public policy, 198, 228–30. *See also* Jewish public policy
Public sector, market responsibility and, 181, 192–93. *See also* Government
Public welfare, 176–77
Punishment, 28–29, 86, 87, 224, 243, 244
Pure public good phenomenon, 151–52
Purity, family, 219–23
Pursuer principle, 67–68, 73, 250

Rabad of Posquieres, 252n10
Rabbah, 20
Rabbenu Tam. *See* Tam, Jacob ben Meir
Rabbinic Judaism. *See* Normative Judaism
Rabina, 120
Rachel, 24, 26, 27, 37
Racial hygiene, 211
Racial science, 201, 204
"Radical Chic" (Wolfe), 45
Rambam. *See* Maimonides
Rashi: abortion, 69, 73, 74; environment, 113; free markets, 177, 189; personal responsibility, 19; *Tikkun Olam*, 37–38, 39
Rationing, 180
Rav, 179
Realpolitik, 251

Reason, 54
Rebbe, Lubavitcher, 38
Rebecca, 37
Rebels, 243
Recession, 148
Recombinant DNA, 198, 202
Recycling, 125
Redemption, 2, 41, 237, 245, 247, 248
Refael, Shilo, 104n98
Reform Jews, 251–52n3
Reform movement, 126
Regulation, 4; environment, 111, 112,
    118, 122; free markets, 166, 169,
    174, 183, 185–86; genetic
    engineering, 197; welfare
    programs, 152, 160
Relatives, 141, 145–46, 149. *See also*
    Family
Religions, 110
Religious education, 147, 152–53, 160,
    227, 228, 230
Religious Freedom Restoration Act
    (RFRA), 67
Religious sustainability, 123–24
Rema. *See* Isserles, Moshe
Rent, 170, 174
Repentance, 87, 101n58, 237, 239, 244,
    245
Republic, The (Plato), 40
Republican Party, 8
Research: economic, 173; genetic, 203;
    medical, 150–52, 160; stem cell,
    206–7
Residency, 162n31
Resnicoff, Steven H., 12, 79–107
Resource policies, 116
Responsa literature, 10–11;
    environment, 120; free markets,
    174, 176, 178, 187, 192;
    international relations, 251–52n3;
    Tikkun Olam, 35
Responsibility: abortion, 65; family
    values, 221, 226, 230–31n5; free
    markets, 181–82, 185; genetic
    engineering, 209; liberalism versus
    conservatism, 4, 5, 7; parental, 59;
    Tikkun Olam, 42; welfare programs,
    140, 142, 146, 148, 150, 152, 160. *See*

also Personal responsibility; Sexual
    responsibility
Resurrection, 83, 245
Revealed Divine Wisdom, 183
Revenge, 27
Rights, 3; abortion, 65, 75n3;
    American Jewish politics, 7; free
    markets, 172; genetic engineering,
    211; international relations, 242;
    marital, 58; physician-assisted
    suicide, 83, 85, 92. *See also* Privacy;
    Same-sex marriage
Right-wing politics. *See* Conservatism
Robbery, 182–84
Romans, 244
Rosanes, Yehuda, 72
Rosner, Fred, 205, 213n6
Rothbard, Murray, 6
Rubinstein, Y., 157

Sabbath laws, 2; abortion, 68, 70, 71;
    free markets, 168, 170; genetic
    engineering, 202; international
    relations, 241; physician-assisted
    dying, 86, 93, 96, 106n126; welfare
    programs, 136–37
Sabbatical year, 116, 119, 170
Sacks, Jonathan, 4, 5–6, 12, 35–48
Sacrifices, 242
Salary, 158
Salk, Jonas, 204
Same-sex marriage, 50; contracts and
    covenants, 58–59; ethical criteria,
    50–52; family values, 229; Jewish
    self-interest and, 62–63;
    philosophical criteria, 52–54;
    political criteria, 54–58; political
    strategies, 60–62
Samuel, 240, 242–43, 245, 248
Sanctity/sanctification, 35, 41, 90, 182,
    187, 210, 218–19,
Sanhedrin, 243, 249
Sarah, 36, 37, 38, 62
Saul, 90, 240, 244
Schools, 38
Scholem, Gershom, 48n27, 253n25
Science, 198, 210–11, 212. *See also*
    Genetic engineering

Scruton, Robert, 14n15
Sea of Galilee, 238
Second Commonwealth, 244
Second Temple, 172, 184, 247
Secularism: environment, 124, 127;
    physician-assisted dying, 80–83, 84,
    88; same-sex marriage, 49, 50, 56,
    62, 63
Security, 175, 176, 235
Sefer HaHinukh, 112
Segregation, 44, 46
Selden, John, 238
Self-absorption, 21
Self-defense, 241, 248, 250
Self-denial, 19
Self-determination, 251
Self-help, 144–45, 148–49, 157, 159
Self-interest, 19, 62–63, 167–68
Self-love, 18, 19, 20
Self-sacrifice, 240
Sellers, 189
Sen, Amartya, 167
Seven Laws of Noah. *See* Noachide
    laws
Sevi, Sabbatai, 246
Sex selection, 206
Sexism, 31n43
Sexual drives, 53
Sexual harassment, 183
Sexuality, 23, 52, 53
Sexual prohibitions, 52, 54, 63n10
Sexual relations, 221–22
Sexual responsibility: contracts and
    covenants, 58–59; ethical criteria,
    50–52; Jewish public policy and,
    49–50; Jewish self-interest, 62–63;
    philosophical criteria, 52–54;
    political criteria, 54–58; political
    strategies, 60–62
Shabbat laws, 126
Shame, 25, 71
Shapiro, David, 127
Shareholders, 181, 182
Sharing, 143. *See also* Welfare
    programs
Shelah, 25
Shelter. *See* Housing
Shemita, 116

Sherwin, Byron L., 12, 197–215
Shiluah haken, 116
Shimon, 27
Shmuel, 180
Shmuelevitz, Haim, 87–88, 103n88
Shoah, 28–29, 33n87. *See also*
    Holocaust
Shtadlan, 7
Shtadlanut, 7, 45
Shua, 25
Shulhan Arukh (Caro), 10, 15n28, 35,
    190, 192, 219, 227
Siblings, 53
Sicherman, Harvey, 13, 235–53
Sickle-cell anemia, 203
Sidon, 238
Siegel, Seymour, 213n6
Siege warfare, 241
Sifre, 111
Silberstein, Yitschak, 113
Simeon Bar Koziba, 245
Simon ben Gamaliel, 239
Simon ben Pazzi, 130n38
Sin: family values, 218, 220;
    international relations, 237, 244,
    247; Original Sin, 23; personal
    responsibility, 23, 24, 28, 31n43,
    33nn86, 87; physician-assisted
    dying, 87, 88–89, 99n37
Sinai, 2, 9, 41
Single parents, 154–55, 160, 217–18
Slaughter laws, 115, 116
Smith, Adam, 4, 167
Social conservatism, 55, 60, 61
Social discrimination, 7
Social equality, 143, 148–49, 150,
    159–60
Social expectations, 230
Social intimacy, 222
Socialism, 4
Social morality, 5
Social order, 5
Social problems, 218
Social rehabilitation, 209
Social responsibility, 42
Social stratification, 150
Social welfare. *See* Welfare programs

Society, 6, 169, 174. *See also*
    Community
Sodom, 123, 172, 239
Sofer, Moshe, 101n65, 120, 178
Soldiers, 241
Solomon, 239, 243, 244
Solomon b. Isaac, 136
Soloveitchik, Hayyim, 141
Soloveitchik, Joseph, 38
Solow, Robert M., 122
Somalia, 250
Song of Songs, 220
Sons, 226, 230–31n5, 233n55. *See also*
    Children; Family; Family values
Soteh, 89, 102n76
South Africa, 81
Sovereignty, 2; international relations,
    237, 238, 241, 244, 245–46, 247;
    liberalism versus conservatism, 7;
    physician-assisted dying, 90; *Tikkun
    Olam*, 38, 39
Species, diversity of. *See* Biodiversity
Spiritual damage, 185–90
Spiritual impurity, 71, 72
Spirituality, 86, 222–23
Spoliation of nature debate, 126–27
Stagflation, 147
Standard of living: antipoverty
    programs, 142; free markets, 170;
    minimum wage laws, 156–57;
    poverty, 133, 134; poverty
    prevention, 145–46; private
    assistance, 138, 139; public
    assistance, 135, 136, 137; social
    equality, 149, 160
State: free markets, 169; international
    relations, 236, 239, 242, 243, 247,
    248, 251; liberalism versus
    socialism, 6, 7; same-sex marriage,
    56, 57, 61; welfare programs, 156
State constitutions (United States), 80
State courts, 99n28
States (U.S.), 154
State supreme courts (United States),
    80
Status, 139, 150
Stem cells, 197, 206–7
Strangers, 149

Subjugation, female, 31n43
Subsidies, 180
Subsistence: antipoverty programs,
    142; fraud, 144; poverty, 134;
    poverty prevention, 145; private
    assistance, 137, 138; public
    assistance, 135, 136, 159; self-help,
    144
Suffering. *See* Pain/suffering
Suicide, 79, 86–90, 100n48, 102–3n83,
    103n86. *See also* Physician-assisted
    suicide
Suppliers, 181
Supply, 166, 176, 178
Supreme Court. *See* U.S. Supreme
    Court
Sustainability, 122, 123–24, 125, 126
Sustainable development, 122
Sustenance, 122, 123
Syrian plateau, 238

Tahara, 222
Talmid Hakham, 194
Talmud, 5, 9–10; abortion, 66, 68,
    69–70, 71–72, 76–77n25; animal
    protection, 114; environment and,
    114–15; environment, 112–13,
    116–17, 118, 119–20, 121, 125;
    family values, 218, 219–20, 221,
    223, 224, 226, 227, 228, 231n15; free
    markets, 168, 171–72, 174, 179, 179,
    184, 191; genetic engineering, 199,
    201, 209, 211, 212; international
    relations, 235, 242, 244, 245, 248,
    249, 250; peace, 239–40; physician-
    assisted dying, 84, 87, 88–89, 90, 94,
    95; same-sex marriage, 52, 55, 63n10;
    Tikkun Olam, 42; welfare programs,
    136, 140, 143, 145, 146, 147
Tam, Jacob ben Meir, 90, 103nn85, 86,
    173
Tamar, 24–26, 27
Tamari, Meir, 12, 165–96
Tameah, 222
Tamei, 222
Tamhui, 140
Tanchum, 220

TANF. *See* Temporary Aid to Needy Families
Tanna, 21
Tarfon, 46
Taxation, 4; antipoverty programs, 140, 156; charity, 162n31; *dei mahsoro*, 142; Earned Income Tax Credit, 158; free markets, 169, 172–73, 177, 188, 192; international relations, 241; medical research, 151–52; minimum wage laws, 157; poverty prevention, 148; religious education, 160; Temporary Aid to Needy Families, 153, 155. *See also* Progressive income tax
Tax credits, 158
Tax evasion, 169
Tax planning, 169
Tay-Sachs disease, 72, 73, 77n41, 204
Technology, 186, 198, 202. *See also* Biotechnology; Genetic engineering
Temporary Aid to Needy Families (TANF), 153–55, 156, 160
Temptation, 24
Terminal illnesses, 94–95, 96
Territory, 19, 238, 239, 247
Terrorism, 212, 235, 249, 251
Textile industry, 157
Textual Judaic sources, 2–3, 5, 9–11. *See also* Aggadah; Gemara; Halakhah; Mishnah; Responsa literature; Talmud; Torah
Teyve, 5
Theft, 145, 182–84, 189, 191
Tikkun Olam, 35–48
Tonkin Gulf Resolution, 250
Torah, 2, 6, 9; abortion, 65, 69; American foreign policy, 247, 249; bullfights, 115–16; family values, 219, 220, 222, 223, 225, 226, 231n15; free markets, 170, 173, 174, 182, 185, 186, 188, 189, 192–93; hunting, 115; Jewish state, 237, 238, 239; peace, 240; personal responsibility, 18, 22, 24, 28, 30n24; physician-assisted dying, 84, 91, 93, 94, 96, 99n37, 105n110; prophets, 246; same-sex marriage, 51, 52; *Tikkun*

Olam, 35–36, 38, 39, 40, 43; war, 241, 242, 252n10; welfare programs, 152
Torat Kohanim, 35
Torat Nevi'im, 36, 43
Torat Yisrael, 38
Tosafot, 103n86
Tosefta, 117
Trade associations, 171
Training programs, 154, 155, 160
Trani, Joseph, 70
Transformation, 246, 247, 251
Transgenics, 202
Treachery, 25
Treaties, 242
Tree of knowledge, 123
Tumah, 71
Tur, 14–15n27
Turkey, 187
Twersky, Isadore, 143
Tzedakah, 133; antipoverty programs, 141–42; free markets, 169; humanistic climate, 149; poverty, 135; poverty prevention, 145, 148; private assistance, 138, 139; social equality, 143
Tzedek, 169
Tzimtzum, 29
Tzitz Eliezer. *See* Waldenberg, Eliezer

U.S. Congress, 81, 242, 248
U.S. Constitution, 60, 75n3, 80, 81, 97n5, 99n28, 242, 249
U.S. Department of Agriculture, 134
U.S. Supreme Court, 60, 67, 80, 81, 82, 89, 99n28
Ulla, 55
Umbilical cords, stem cells from, 207
Uncertainty, 46
Underdeveloped economies, 167, 183, 192
Unemployment, 139, 158, 193
United Nations, 110
United Nations Security Council, 250
United States: foreign policy, 247–50; genetic engineering, 198, 204, 211; international relations, 235, 247–50; Jewish politics in, 7–9, 14nn24, 25;

physician-assisted dying, 80, 91, 92;
  same-sex marriage, 49, 50, 54, 56,
  60; welfare programs, 133–34, 135
Unity, 8, 18, 21, 244, 245, 247
Universalism, 39, 40, 44–45
Universities, 60
Unterman, Isser Yehuda, 68
Urbanization, 186
Urban planning and zoning, 185
Urban policy, 186–87
Uziel, Ben Zion Meir, 70–71, 116

Values, moral, 85–86. *See also* Family
  values
Vegetarianism, 125
Vengeance, 27
Venter, J. Craig, 210
Venus, 127
Viability (fetus), 66, 71
Vietnam War, 249, 250
Violence, 209, 210
Vocational training, 148, 193
Voegelin, Eric, 40
Voluntarism: antipoverty programs,
  142; economic malaise, 147;
  humanistic climate, 150; medical
  research, 151; poverty, 133; private
  assistance, 149; religious education,
  152; self-help, 148; status, 160
Voluntary physician euthanasia, 79.
  See also Euthanasia
Von Rad, Gerhard, 252n10
Voucher system, 153, 160
Vulnerability, 23

Wages, 156, 157, 158, 180
Waldenberg, Eliezer, 72–73, 76n17,
  76n23, 77n41, 77n44, 77nn48–49,
  115
Walzer, Michael, 11, 14n24
Wandering Jew, 42
Wanton destruction, 111–14, 115,
  116–17, 119–20
War: environment, 117; international
  relations, 235, 236, 243, 246, 251;
  just, 235, 248–49; obligatory, 240,
  241, 248–49, 252n10; optional,

240–42, 243, 247, 248–49; peace
  and, 239–40
Washington v. Glucksberg, 97nn3, 5,
  99n28
Water use, 117, 118
Waterways, 111
Watson, James, 198, 209, 210
Wealth: free markets, 166, 168, 170,
  190; international relations, 243;
  physician-assisted dying, 96,
  106n117, 107n134; redistribution of,
  4, 146–47; welfare programs, 139,
  142, 145, 146
Wealth of Nations (Smith), 167
Weapons of mass destruction, 235
Webb, Beatrice, 135
Webb, Sidney, 135
Weber, Max, 42
Weights and measures, 183–84, 192
Weinberg, Yechiel Ya'akov, 72, 115
Weiss, Dayan, 178
Welfare fraud, 143–44, 145, 148–49
Welfare programs, 133, 158–60;
  antipoverty programs, 140–42,
  155–56; *dei mahsoro*, 142, 144–45;
  dignity of poor, 142–143, 148–49;
  Earned Income Tax Credit, 158;
  economic malaise, 147–148;
  empathetic and personal
  involvement, 143, 148–49; fraud
  investigations and support for
  poor, 143–44, 148–49; Halakhah
  antipoverty measures, 140–42;
  humanistic climate, 149–50; income
  redistribution and Jewish law,
  146–47; medical research, 150–52;
  minimum wage laws in Israel,
  156–57; poverty, 133–34; poverty
  prevention, 145–46, 148; poverty
  relief, 145–46; private assistance,
  eligibility for, 137–40; public
  assistance, eligibility for, 134–37;
  religious education of children,
  152–53; self-help, 144–45, 148–49;
  Temporary Aid to Needy Families,
  153–55
White, Lynn, Jr., 126, 127
White-collar crime, 183

Whole-brain death, 97n1
Wilson, James Q., 217
Wilson, Woodrow, 251
Wind, 118
Winston, Lord Robert, 43–44
Wives, 64n23, 219, 220, 221–22,
   225–26, 231n15, 232n28, 243. *See
   also* Family; Marriage
Wolfe, Tom, 45
Women: family values, 217, 221, 224,
   232n28; free markets, 169–70;
   international relations, 241,
   251–52n3; personal responsibility,
   23–24, 31n43; sexual responsibility,
   52–53. *See also* Abortion; Family
   values; Marriage; Mothers; Parents;
   Sexual responsibility; Wives
Work, 144, 154, 158, 160. *See also*
   Employment
Working poor, 157. *See also* Poverty;
   Welfare programs
World Commission on Environment
   and Development, 131n81
World of Our Fathers (Howe), 8
World to Come. *See* Afterlife
World Trade Center attack (9/11/
   2001), 235

World War I, 212, 251
Written Law, 9, 105n110, 109,
   251–52n3
Wurzburger, Walter, 85
Wyschogrod, Michael, 4, 43, 127, 128

Yaakov ben Asher. *See* Tur
Yavneh, Rabbis of, 21
Yesh me-ayin, 199
Yesh mi-yesh, 199
Yeshivas, 7
Yetzer harah, 21, 168
Yiftach, 248
Yishmael, 68
Yitzhak of Corbeil, 139, 140
Yochanan ben Zakkai, 21–22, 102n80,
   179
Yoreh De'ah, 14–15n27
Yosef, Ovadia, 33n86, 113–14, 115
Yossi, 117

Zaken, 155
Zakkai, Yochanan ben. *See* Yochanan
   ben Zakkai
Zionism, 38, 246
Zionist Congress, 37
Zohar, 67
Zoning, 185–86, 192

About the Editor and Contributors

MARSHALL J. BREGER is a professor of law at the Columbus School of Law, The Catholic University of America. From 1993–1995, he was Senior Fellow at the Heritage Foundation specializing in regulatory and trade policy (including NAFTA) as well as Middle East issues. During the Bush administration, he served as Solicitor of Labor, the chief lawyer of the Labor Department with a staff of over 800 attorneys. During 1992, he concurrently served by presidential designation as Assistant Secretary for Labor Management Standards. From 1985–1991, Breger was Chairman of the Administrative Conference of the United States, an independent federal agency. During 1987–1989, he also served as Alternate Delegate of the United States to the U.N. Human Rights Commission in Geneva. From 1982–1984, he served as special assistant to President Reagan and was his liaison to the Jewish community. He writes and speaks regularly on both legal issues and issues of Jewish public policy and has published in numerous law reviews as well as in periodicals such as the *Commentary*, *Middle East Quarterly*, the *Los Angeles Times*, the *Washington Post*, the *Wall Street Journal*, and the *New York Times*. He has testified over thirty times before the United States Congress. He is the editor (with Ora Ahimeir) of *Jerusalem: A City and Its Future* (2002) and the author (with Tom Idinopolis) of the monograph, *Jerusalem's Holy Places and the Peace Process* (1998). Together with David M. Gordis, he coedited *Vouchers for School Choice: Challenge or Opportunity? An American Jewish Reappraisal* (1998). His collection of articles on Vatican-Israel relations, *The Vatican-Israel Accords: Political, Legal, and Theological Contexts*, will be published in 2003. Breger serves as vice president of the Jewish Policy Center, a public policy think tank in Washington, D.C. In fall 2002, Breger was a Lady Davis Visiting Professor of Law at the Hebrew University in Jerusalem. He is a regular contributor to *Moment* magazine.

BARRY FREUNDEL has been the rabbi at Kesher Israel Congregation, at the Georgetown Synagogue, in Washington, D.C., since 1989. Previously he was the rabbi at Congregation Rosh Pinah in Riverdale, New York, and Beth Israel Synagogue of Norwalk, Connecticut. He has been an adjunct professor at Baltimore Hebrew University, the University of Maryland, Georgetown University, and Yeshiva University. He served as a consultant to the Presidential Commission on Cloning and has served as scholar-in-residence for the Association of Orthodox Jewish Scientists. He is vice president and ethics committee chairman of the Rabbinical Council of America.

MANFRED GERSTENFELD is chairman of the steering committee of the Jerusalem Center for Public Affairs, and is an international consultant specializing in business and environmental strategy to the senior ranks of multinational corporations. He was a board member of the Israel Corporation. His books include the bestseller *Revaluing Italy* (with Lorenzo Necci, Sperling and Kupfer, 1992; Italian), *The State as a Business* (1994; Italian), and *Israel's New Future: Interviews* (1994). His newest book, *The Jewish Environmental Tradition: A Sustainable World*, will be published later this year. He is both cochair of the Judaism Task Force on the Environment and one of the associate editors of the *Encyclopaedia of Religion and Nature*.

AARON LEVINE is the Samson and Halina Bitensky Professor of Economics and chairman of the Economics Department at Yeshiva University. A noted authority on Jewish commercial law, Professor Levine's research specialty is the interface between economics and Halakhah, especially as it relates to public policy and modern business practices. He has published widely on these issues, including four books and numerous monographs. His books include *Free Enterprise and Jewish Law* (1980); *Economics and Jewish Law* (1987); *Economic Public Policy and Jewish Law* (1993); and *Case Studies in Jewish Business Ethics* (2000).

CLIFFORD E. LIBRACH has been the rabbi at Temple Sinai in Sharon, Massachusetts, since 1993. His rabbinic training took place at Hebrew Union College Jewish Institute of Religion in Cincinnati, Ohio, and he holds a Juris Doctorate degree from New York University. Librach served as law clerk to Chief Justice Robert Seiler of the Supreme Court of Missouri, was a litigator in St. Louis, and reviews in the fields of Judaism, prayer, and rabbinics.

JOSHUA E. LONDON, formerly a senior editor with *The American Spectator* magazine, is a Washington, D.C.–based writer on Jewish political affairs. He has written on American Jewish politics, literature, history, and culture for a variety of periodicals and media outlets, including *The American Spectator, Details: Promoting Jewish, Conservative Values, National Review Online, Spintech,* and *Human Events.* Mr. London has taught Talmud, Jewish philosophy, and Jewish law classes at the Kenesset Israel Torah Center in Sacramento, California, and was involved in curriculum development for the center's adult education program. Mr. London holds an MA in social science from the University of Chicago and a BA in political science from the University of California, Davis. He is currently writing a book on the Barbary pirates.

DAVID NOVAK holds the J. Richard and Dorothy Shiff Chair of Jewish Studies at the University of Toronto. He is also the director of the University's Jewish Studies program. Previously, he was a professor at the University of Virginia, Oklahoma City University, Old Dominion University, the New School for Social Research, Jewish Theological Seminary, and Baruch College. He served as a pulpit rabbi in several American cities from 1966 to 1989. Novak is the author of ten books, including *Natural Law in Judaism* and *Covenental Rights* (1999).

STEVEN H. RESNICOFF is a professor of law at the DePaul University College of Law in Chicago, where, in 2000–2001, he held the prestigious Wicklander Chair in Professional Ethics. He has written and lectured extensively on a variety of subjects, including alternate dispute resolution, bankruptcy, commercial paper, legal ethics, and medical ethics. Drawing on his formal Talmudic training (he was ordained by the late Rabbi Moshe Feinstein) and his law firm experience, he analyzes issues from both secular and religious perspectives, often exploring how these disparate systems interact. His relatively recent works can be found in the *Notre Dame L.R.* 77, 937 (2002); *Jewish Law Association Studies XIII* (2002); *Current Legal Developments* (2001); *Notre Dame J.L. Ethics & Pub. Pol'y* 14, 349 (2000); *Jewish Law Association Studies* (2000); *J. Halacha & Cont. Soc.* 37, 47 (1999); and *Touro L. Rev.* 15, 73 (1998).

JONATHAN SACKS has been chief rabbi of the United Hebrew Congregations of the Commonwealth since September 1, 1991, the sixth incumbent since 1845.

At the time of his appointment, he was principal of Jews' College, London, where he also held the Chair in Modern Jewish Thought. He gained his rabbinic ordination from Jews' College as well as from London's Yeshiva Etz Chaim. He has been rabbi of the Golders Green and Marble Arch Synagogues in London. In September 2001, the Archbishop of Canterbury, the Rt. Hon. Rev. George Carey, conferred on the chief rabbi a Doctorate of Divinity in recognition of the chief rabbi's ten years in the Chief Rabbinate. Professor Sacks holds honorary doctorates from the universities of Cambridge, Glasgow, Haifa, Middlesex, Yeshiva University, New York, Liverpool, and St. Andrews. He is also an honorary fellow of Gonville and Caius College, Cambridge, and King's College, London, where he is currently visiting professor of theology and religious studies. Professor Sacks is a frequent contributor to radio, television, and the national press. He is the author of twelve books: *Tradition in an Untraditional Age* (1990), *Persistence of Faith* (1991), *Arguments for the Sake of Heaven* (1991), *Crisis and Covenant* (1992), *One People?* (1993), *Will We have Jewish Grandchildren* (1994), *Community of Faith* (1995), *The Politics of Hope* (1997), *Morals and Markets* (1999), *New Revised Edition: The Politics of Hope* (2000), and *Celebrating Life* (2000). His most recent book, *The Dignity of Difference*, was published in September 2002.

BYRON L. SHERWIN is the Distinguished Service Professor of Jewish Philosophy and Mysticism at the Spertus Institute of Jewish Studies in Chicago. An ordained rabbi and a recipient of the Presidential Medal from the Republic of Poland in 1995, he is the author of twenty-two books, including *No Religion Is an Island* and *Sparks Amidst the Ashes: The Spiritual Legacy of Polish Jewry* (1997).

HARVEY SICHERMAN is president and director of the Foreign Policy Research Institute in Philadelphia, Pennsylvania. He has extensive experience in writing, research, and analysis of U.S. foreign and national security policy, both in government and out.

He served as special assistant to Secretary of State Alexander M. Haig, Jr. (1981–82), and he was a member of the policy planning staff of Secretary of State James A. Baker, III. Dr. Sicherman was also a consultant to Secretary of the Navy John F. Lehman, Jr. (1982–1987), and Secretary of State George Shultz (1988).

He is author or editor of numerous articles and books, including *America the Vulnerable: Our Military Problems and How to Fix Them*, coedited with John Lehman (2002); *The Chinese Economy: A New Scenario*, coedited with Murray Weidenbaum (1999); *Palestinian Autonomy, Self-Government and Peace* (1993).

MEIR TAMARI is director of the Centre for Business Ethics at the Jerusalem College of Technology, consultant to the Jewish Association for Business Ethics in the United Kingdom, and dean of the American Association for Jewish Business Ethics. After making *aliyah* from South Africa to a religious kibbutz in 1950, he served in the Bank of Israel in corporate research from 1960 to 1990, achieving the position of chief economist, office of the governor. Dr. Tamari is the author of numerous books and articles—academic and rabbinic—on business ethics, small firms, risk evaluation, and entrepreneurship, and is publisher of the *Business Ethics Newsletter* in Jerusalem. Dr. Tamari authored the articles on Jewish Business Ethics in the *Encyclopedia Judaica* and the *Encyclopedic Dictionary of Business Ethics*. The pioneer of a special course on Jewish ethics and economics at Bar-Ilan University, Dr. Tamari has lectured internationally and has served as consultant to various governmental bodies in the United Kingdom, France, and the United States.